Mariners on the Margins:

Plundering Seals in Colonial Australasia

David Prior

Acknowledgements

The writing of this history would not have been possible without the significant support and encouragement I received from many people since my school days. In particular, I would firstly like to thank the teacher who fostered in me a love of all things history, namely Brother Stanley Cusack, unfortunately now deceased. Secondly, my university lecturers and tutors such as Professors Iain McCalman, Dirk Moses and Kirsten McKenzie and Professor Emerita Penny Russell who all taught me how to think more widely and differently about the way history might be written. Then I would like to acknowledge and thank my editorial 'team.' Irina Dunn of the Australian Writers Network took on the challenge of working with me to initially mold my manuscript into a much more accessible and readable form. I was then introduced to Dr David Reiter of Interactive Publications Pty Ltd. Dr David has been a tower of strength and support for me and has engaged with me tirelessly to assist me in editing and rewriting parts of *Mariners*. While always adopting a critical and objective approach to the task at hand, he has encouraged me in my pursuit of a task to make *Mariners on the Margins* a much more attractive and interesting book for my reading public. I would also like to thank his associate James Devitt for his valuable comments and insights while delving into the history so written. In addition, the First Nations writer and historian Emeritus Professor John Maynard of the University of Newcastle has given me every encouragement to pursue this work. Finally, I would like to thank my closest supporters. These are my partner Ali, our children Orlena, Chimene, Bianca, Liam and Isla, my granddaughter Zuleika and, for special mention, for the calm and comfort he brings, our Kelpie Arlo.

Glass House Books
an imprint of IP (Interactive Publications Pty Ltd)
Treetop Studio • 9 Kuhler Court
Carindale, Queensland, Australia 4152
sales@ipoz.biz
http://ipoz.biz/shop

© 2025, David Prior (text) and IP (design)
eBook versions © 2025

All rights reserved. Without limiting the rights under copyright reserved above, no part of this publication may be reproduced, stored in or introduced into a retrieval system, or transmitted, in any form or by any means (electronic, mechanical, photocopying, recording or otherwise), without the prior written permission of the copyright owner and the publisher of this book.

Printed in 12 pt Adobe Caslon Pro on 14 pt Avenir Book

ISBN: 978192830852 (PB); 978192830869 (eBk)

A catalogue record for this book is available from the National Library of Australia

Glass House Books
Mariners on the Margins

David Prior (B.A. M.A., L.L.B.) has always been interested in history. He studied ancient history at school before matriculating to study arts and law at Sydney University. His thesis, completed in 2011, was Pirates Slave Traders Savages or simply misunderstood? Colonial Imagination of the Sealers and the Frustration of Authority.

Since then, David's research has led to the publication of *Stone Carver: The Life and Times of Franco Vallario*, as well as *Mariners on the Margins*. David is now working on a third manuscript, Beyond Dystopia: The Enduring legacy of the Chief and Missionary.

David has reviewed three books on maritime subjects, published in *The Great Circle*, a journal of the Australian Association for Maritime History. He was recently granted a residency at the Lighthouse Arts Centre at Nobbys in Newcastle.

Apart from his interest in Australian colonial history, David is an avid photographer, gardener and plays field hockey at a reasonably high level. He practices part-time as a business family and commercial lawyer.

Glass House Books
Brisbane

Contents

Chapter 1: Navigating the World of the Mariners on the Margins — 1

Chapter 2: Entrepreneurs, Adventurers and Opportunists of all Nations and Natures — 20

Chapter 3: Diving into the Deep Past — 61

Chapter 4: A Polyglot Cluster of Maritime Peoples — 81

Chapter 5: Australia's First Enterprise — 107

Chapter 6: Foreigners at the Tipping Edge — 135

Chapter 7: Opportunity and Adversity in the Eastern Fishery — 158

Chapter 8: Rogues, Rapscallions and Survivors Haunt the Antipodes — 193

Chapter 9: Preying on the Environment — 211

Chapter 10: Fact and Fantasy in the Lives of the Independent Sealers — 225

Chapter 11: How Do We Remove the Banditti? — 254

Chapter 12: Perpetrators and Partners — 269

Chapter 13: Resistance, Survival and Cultural Change in the Straits — 309

Chapter 14: Barely a Ripple—the End of Colonial Sealing — 330

Chapter 15: Lessons from the Colonial Sealing Epoch — 341

Bibliography — 345

  Primary sources — 345

  Newspapers — 349

  Court Cases — 350

  Legislation — 350

  Secondary Sources — 351

To Ali, Orlena, Chimene, Bianca Liam and Isla
Those enterprising compassionate and resolute humans closest to me

Chapter 1: Navigating the World of the Mariners on the Margins

The English ship's captain was excited. Staring out from the primitive docks of the nascent colony of Port Jackson in October 1798, he had previously encountered two respectable colonial explorers and the survivors of a shipwreck who had given him what was called 'intelligence'. They convinced the captain that he could make his fortune by voyaging to the extreme south of New Holland in pursuit of the abundant seal rookeries they had previously observed there. At that time the fledgling colony of New South Wales was in poor economic circumstances, having gained little success in feeding its small population from any enterprise that may have been attempted. Galvanised by what he had been told, the captain left Sydney Town on 7 October 1798 in a 110-ton brig crewed by a gang of men, called for all time 'sealers'. He was accompanied by another vessel carrying the two explorers and a small crew. In doing so, he was the first of many captains to plunder the mammals in the southern Antipodes. Several months later the brig anchored back in the settlement. It was fully laden with a cargo of seal skins.

In a few short years after this initial foray into the sealing trade, entrepreneurs known as the 'Sydney Traders' engaged captains to sail brigs, schooners, snows, cutters and merchantmen into the icy waters of the southern Antipodes in search of fur and elephant seals. They employed a polyglot of mariners to man their ships to engage in a frenzy of activity in slaughtering these mammals. After a time, many of these employed mariners became tired of their lot. Often left on empty promises in very harsh and difficult remote littoral places, they chose lives of independence from mainstream colonial society and set up their own hybrid and collective communities. In these new "societies", they partnered voluntarily or often by force with First Nations peoples, primarily women, to eke out a living. This is a history of Australia's first real industry and the marginal characters who plied their trade in it.

The English captain's hunt for seals was nothing new to human endeavour. Well before the time Lieutenant Governor Arthur Phillip arrived with the First Fleet in Sydney Harbour in 1788, First Nations peoples throughout the world had been involved in slaughtering seals for food or trade. Since about the twelfth century, First Nation's peoples in the Arctic Circle had understood that the seal was a multi-functional resource. They made use of the oil for providing light, and the skins and fur for clothing and shelters. In the maritime environments of the Great Southern Continent, the Aboriginal nations had been seeking seals for generations. In more modern times, Europeans had begun procuring these mammals as a resource by the sixteenth century. The Spaniard Juan De Solfo sailed to South America in 1515, and his crew returned to Seville with a vessel filled to the brim with a plethora of seal skins. This was despite the death of their captain following a skirmish with the American local First Nations people.

The well-known adventurer, privateer and maritime knight, Francis Drake, and his 164 'gentlemen and sailors', feasted on what they described as 'sea wolves' to supplement their diet when sailing around the Cape of Joy near Brazil in 1577.[1] On his second global voyage in 1580, Drake, embarked, officially, on a journey of exploration. But, like many an explorer, he had other intentions: to exploit the natural and man-made resources he encountered. His ships entered a harbour with 'a wonderful great store of seals' which were 'of a wonderful great bigness, huge and monstrous of shape.' The crews killed several and hungrily devoured the flensed meat. A short time later Dutch mariners were hunting African seals for their skins and oil as early as 1610. In the late 17th century, another English privateer and explorer, Willian Dampier, anchored off Juan Fernandez Island near Chile and observed that:

---

[1] Richard Hakluyt. *The Principal Navigations, Voyages, Traffiques and Discoveries of the English Nation* (Harmondsworth Middlesex: Penguin Books, 1972), 173.

Chapter 1: Navigating the World of Mariners on the Margins

'Seals swam around... there is not a bay nor rock... but it is full of them. For wherever there be plenty of fysh, there be seals'.[2]

However, despite observations made by many maritime explorers and navigators of the vast colonies of pinnipeds[3] located around the globe, it was not until the 18th century that the first known commercial sealing operation took place. By then, Russian mariners were the first to trade seals of the Aleutian type with the Chinese. While the Russians conducted occasional exchanges with the Oriental merchants, it was English and American mariners who were the first to conduct sealing as a large-scale trading enterprise. This occurred when these maritime men systematically procured seals in South Georgia, the Magellan Straits and the Falklands in the 1770s. After some mariners discovered the vast seal rookeries[4] in the waters of South America and, below that, Antarctica, multitudes of vessels voyaged there to take advantage of the pinnipeds. They set out on a feeding frenzy to procure as many seals as would fill a boat. By 1788, ships were carrying cargoes of as many as 40,000 seal skins from the Falkland Islands to London. That same year, men who became known as sealers, sailed to South Georgia and quickly established a thriving industry. This meant that, by 1800, a New York sealer was able to procure 57,000 seal skins in one expedition. On board that vessel, the skins were given priority in the brig over the crew.

John Nicol, a mariner adventurer, was employed as a cooper on the *Amelia* in 1791-1792. He described in graphic detail to his biographer John Howell in 1822 the practices and methodologies Europeans employed to hunt down seals near Peru. The dangers of such activity were clearly emphasised:

> I pursued my labours with all the ardour of a seaman. After taking a sufficient quantity of spermaceti we stood as far down as latitude 3° to the island of Lopes where we killed 30,000 seals. We had a busy time chasing and killing them. When we had a sufficient number, we began to kill Sea Lions to get their skins

---
[2] See Henry Wood Elliot, *The Fur Seal Islands of Alaska*. Washington: Government Printing Office, 1884), 64, quoting William Dampier.

[3] 'Pinnipeds' is a generic word used to describe fin or flipper footed sea mammals, including seals, walruses and sea lions.

[4] Seals live in colonies around rocks.

> for the ship's use. One of their skins was a sufficient load for two men. We used to stand in a gap of the rocks in the morning and knock them down with our clubs as they approach the sea and stabbed them with our long knives.
>
> George Parker our mate made a blow at one end and missed him. He made a snap at George and sent his tusk right through his arm, a little above the wrist, and walked away at his leisure with him into the sea, Parker roaring like a bull from the pain and terror. Robert Wyld, perceiving his danger, rushed into the water to rescue him, was up to the armpits before he succeeded in dispatching the unwieldy monster. He then dragged them both onshore where, with difficulty the tusk was drawn from between the bones, it was so firmly jammed.[5]

Nicol, who described himself to Howell as 'a wanderer and the child of chance all my days', illustrates in this passage that boats used were often employed not only in procuring seals but also other maritime creatures such as whales in a brutal and bloody trade.

Evidence of the opportunity to exploit seals in the new colony occurred when vast quantities of pinnipeds were sighted by maritime explorers around the southern areas of Australia from the time of Cook's expedition.[6] By the early 1790s, colonial men in New Holland were aware that seals grouped in rookeries inhabited coastal regions of the southern continent. For example, M. De Rossei, a "principal" officer, was on board *La Recherche* under Rear-Admiral Bruny D'Entrecasteaux on a mission to locate the missing explorer La Pérouse. The French expedition made landfall on the southwest coast of the country near Cape Leeuwin on 5 December 1791. By 9 December, the vessel had anchored near Termination Island. This island is about 63 kilometres to the south of the present-day town of Esperance. The region has many islands which in general are low lying and surrounded by the beauty of the aqua marine seas.

De Rossei reported in his journal:

---
[5] Tim Flannery (ed.), John Nicole Mariner. *Life and Adventures 1776-1801* (London: William Blackwood and T. Cadell),1822,139.
[6] Sir Joseph Banks. *Endeavour Journal*. (Sydney: Angus & Robertson, 1963), 866-868. For example: 'We saw several seals but much smaller than those which I have seen in Newfoundland and black, they generally appeared in lively action leaping out of the water like porpoises.'.

> Seals, penguins, and some kangaroos were seen; but no fresh water, accessible to shipping, could anywhere be found; the country within their reach being sandy and sterile.[7]

By the time James Cook had voyaged up the east coast of what was called New Holland in 1770, European maritime traders were conscious of the fact that an enterprise could be developed in what became known as "sealing". At that time, the British East India Company[8] had a monopoly on the trade in the fur trade in the Pacific. But after the American War of Independence, this did not stop Yankee mariners from exploiting both whales and seals wherever they might be found. By the late 1790s, markets for the mammals had been flourishing in Canton and later London. For example, in England over 360,000 skins from fur seals were traded during 1793. The American traders dominated this enterprise. Free from the reaches of the Company, they operated with impunity.

Once it became clear to maritime traders and masters that seal rookeries were in abundance around those subantarctic coasts, and were relatively easy to capture and kill, it was open season on them. Indeed, the furious expansion of the sealing trade along these coastal environments led to an astonishing depletion in seal populations. For example, the explorer and seal hunter James Weddell had voyaged towards Antarctica to investigate the region and procure seals on three voyages. Writing about his experiences, he expertly estimated that 1.2 million fur seals had been killed by sealers in that region alone. Maritime traders who were well supported financially by their owners, mainly from America and England, would endeavour to cram their boats with as many seals as they could. Other sealers from all parts of the European world came to that region and competed with some success. One eye was on the profits that could be generated in London and China from their endeavours, and the other was on their competitors. This quickly caused the depletion, and sometimes the exhaustion of, the seal rookeries.

---

[7] See Matthew Flinders. *A Voyage to Terra Australis*. (London: G & W Nicol, 1814), Vol. 1.
[8] Known where mentioned as 'The Company'.

By the late 1790s, the southern Antipodes[9] region was just one of several where English colonists and American mariners had become aware that seals abounded in littoral environments along the coasts of what are now known as Western Australia, Tasmania, Victoria and New Zealand, and also on many islands off these coasts. Despite such early observations of these mammals made by explorers and navigators, it would be some years before the seals became a target as a resource to exploit for reward by the colonisers. Following the arrival of the First Fleet with its maritime and military crew and their prisoners, not much thought had been given to how they were all going to survive once provisions had been exhausted. Several years of drought meant that the early attempts to grow crops and establish an agrarian industry had largely failed. Effectively, it was no accident that it forced the authorities and maritime traders to look to the sea as a resource to exploit. Several naval and military men in charge of the convicts came from a maritime background and looked to develop ship building and marine-based enterprises when opportunities arose.[10]

Meanwhile, others were more adventurous. Some, such as Robert Campbell, were already trading in commodities over in the Asian English colonies, such as Bengal. Others grabbed opportunities given to them by those in positions of power to establish their own enterprises. Men like former convicts Thomas Palmer and Simeon Lord were quick off the mark and took measured risks to establish themselves. These colonists became heavily involved in the sealing industry for a time. Then there were respectable mariners who arranged with the governor of the colony to explore the coastal regions of New Holland mainly for political and geographic purposes but also to seek opportunities for commercial exploitation. One of those was Lieutenant Matthew Flinders.

In 1798, the great navigator Finders was accompanied by the surgeon George Bass in the *Norfolk*, a converted whaleboat. The

---

[9] The 'Antipodes' normally means 'Australia' or 'Australasia' in the context of being the Antipodes of Britain (literally the points diametrically opposed to each other on the globe). *Macquarie Dictionary,* Revised Third Edition, 1977, 79.

[10] The first four governors were naval captains in charge of sailors who would have looked naturally to the sea as a familiar environment.

Norfolk left Port Jackson on a mission to establish whether there was a body of water separating Van Diemen's Land (known as Lutruwita to the First Nations people of that island) from New Holand. These men encountered a barren island near Sealers Cove in Bass Strait. There, Flinders observed the seals were basking on rocks everywhere, leading the surgeon to assert that there was an opportunity where 'a commercial speculation on a *small scale* might be made with advantage'. What is not well publicized is the fact that they were joined on their voyage south by the master mariner Bishop in the *Nautilus*.

On that now famous journey, the adventurers discovered thousands of seals lying on rocks in Kent Bay in the Straits.[11] From that time until the mid-1830s or so, the sealing industry intermittently flourished, predominantly from 1798 until about 1810, around the southern waters of Australia and New Zealand, and again from 1820 for several years. In the latter period, the hunt for the pinnipeds occurred mainly on the subantarctic islands south of New Zealand and the Recherche Archipelago. By then, the seal populations in the Straits had almost been wiped out by the enthusiasm and zeal by which mariners had operated. Ultimately, it was Bass' prophecy that won the day. The industry became only a small enterprise for a few independent sealers.

Arguably the discovery of these numerous seal rookeries in Bass Strait led initially to the rise of a successful industry controlled by aggressive and opportunistic colonial entrepreneurs known in this work as 'traders'. In fostering this industry, these traders built ships and employed captains known as "masters" to sail these vessels with crews of mariners[12] capable of procuring the aquatic mammals. The sealers were an international and colourful cohort. Some of these mariners were colonial seamen who had jumped ship, enticed by the possibilities of a greater 'lay'.[13] Others had been pressganged

---

[11] Although prior to that we know Captain William Raven's gang in 1792 had slaughtered 4,500 seals off the coast of New Zealand and reaped the economic rewards.

[12] Wherever the term "mariners" is used in this work, it refers mainly to the men known in colonial circles as sealers but also includes the masters of the sealing vessels.

[13] A 'lay' was normally a part of the overall catch of fish or seals that a ship

into service by the English Navy or commercial traders. Several were emancipists keen to seek a living from the sea. Many were from a multinational background including New Zealand, India, the Americas, Europe and the Polynesian Islands. Collectively, these mariners became engaged in what became known as the 'sealing trade'.

After news came back to Port Jackson about the plethora of seals living around the Bass Strait islands, traders organised their masters to urgently fit out vessels and employ mariners to voyage to those islands on missions to engage in the mass-scale slaughter of the fur and elephant varieties of these mammals. From the early 1800s, they were joined by American, English and French whaling and sealing vessels. Mariners began plundering the Fishery mainly in the Straits, but, after those littoral regions were exhausted, their attention turned to rookeries found further afield as far west as the French Islands of St Paul and Amsterdam and as far east as the Chatham Islands, 800 nautical miles from New Zealand. In between those parameters, mariners, by design or accident, voyaged to other coasts in pursuit of the mammals. The First Nations peoples of the Antipodes were already familiar with the locations of the rookeries with few exceptions. But the colonial mariners 'discovered' the pinnipeds inhabited islands and coasts previously unknown to the Western world.

Abundant seal rookeries were found over a vast watery southern expanse. We can hardly imagine this expansive spectacle. But colonial mariners plied their trade over such enormous distances. Picture yourself being in a small 100-foot schooner, or worse a 15-foot whaleboat, anchoring at Amsterdam and St. Paul's Islands in the middle of the Indian Ocean some 4,230 kilometres from Perth. Now, imagine sailing it down to Albany and Esperance in the south-west of Australia. Then voyage another 2,385 kilometres across to Kangaroo Island in the Great Australian Bight. Then sail across the Bight to Portland and Westernport in what is now

---

brought back to the trading ports, although it could be in other kind or in cash. See Estelle May Stewart and Jesse Chester Bowman, "History of Wages in the United States from Colonial Times to 1928," *Bulletin of the United States Bureau of Labor Statistics* No. 499 (October,1929), 101-102.

known as Victoria over another 885 kilometres. After navigating the treacheries of Bass Strait, you then voyage across the Tasman and anchor near Stewart Island to the extreme south of New Zealand. The next journey you'd take if you were trying to follow the path taken by sealers would be south to sail some 2,000 kilometres to the icy sub-Antarctic islands such as Campbell and Macquarie. In the second decade of the 19th century, there was a constant sea highway traversed by men in boats who zealously plundered the sea elephant seals almost to extinction there. Meanwhile, you could choose an alternative destination to find seals. Over 800 kilometres to the east of Aotearoa you reach the Chatham Islands which was populated by sealers seeking new killing fields in the early colonial decades. Finally, closer to the main settlement, some seals were found in colonies from Twofold Bay to Port Stephens on the mid north coast of New South Wales. In these littoral spaces, the pinnipeds dwelling around beaches, outcrops and rocks close to seashores became easy targets for zealous mariners.

These mammals had been and continued to be consumed as a portion of the diet of the First Nations people that inhabited these littoral fringes prior to the arrival of any white men. To access this marine mammal, the First Nations people adopted a variety of techniques, some of which involved the use of watercraft. As observed by George Briggs and James Kelly on their voyage around Tasmania, Australian women were the main protagonists in procuring the seals, and by using methods that were quite ingenious.[14] These included the close mimicking of the mammals, which camouflaged the hunters' ultimate intent. The mimicry lulled the seals into a false sense of security, which facilitated a rapid response from the hunters. But this did not deplete or exhaust the rookeries as primarily the First Nations peoples preyed on the seals to feed clothe and protect themselves. Apart from some trading between nations, the Australasians did not possess a capitalist mentality. The extensive pre-colonial history of the relationship between the First Nations inhabitants of the Southern Fishery and the pinnipeds has not previously been explored to any great extent

---

[14] James Kelly and James Hobbs. *Van Diemen's Land in 1815 and 1824*. (Hobart: Sullivan's Cove), 1984.

and will be in this work. Furthermore, in all the histories written about the sealers, not much attention has been devoted to the local fauna that was subject to the devastating adverse impact of sealing.

Once "intelligence" about the seal rookeries found its way back to Port Jackson, the commercial opportunities to exploit the seals became a reality. The early industry became dominated by commercial traders operating out of Sydney and Hobart together with other overseas maritime entrepreneurs, particularly the Americans. In what became some historians have designated Australia's first export industry,[15] maritime men of various social, ethnic and racial backgrounds were employed from mobile whale boats to hunt and slaughter seals across the full extent of the Fishery. Even during this first era, there were concerns expressed by Governor King about the effect the slaughtering of seals was having on their chances of survival.[16] Between 1800 and 1806, over 133,000 seal skins were traded through Sydney alone, according to Bolton.[17] Their populations became so depleted that the capitalist traders forsook the killing fields of Bass Straits by 1810. After this time, they turned their attention to other maritime spaces.[18] Some, such as James Murrell and Daniel Cooper, were already aware of the potential that existed at Kangaroo Island. They voyaged with crews there to create permanent settlements.

Due to the abundance of seal rookeries there, Kangaroo Island became one of the destinations populated by mariners in search of seals. That island was known as *Karta*, or the Island of the Dead, by New Holland First Nations peoples. There is a dreamtime story involving the ancestral spirit called Ngurunderi, who came to the island in pursuit of his errant wives, forcing them to drown. He then flew up into the sky disposing of his weapons. According to Aboriginal myth, the spirits of the ancestors thrive on the island.

---

[15] James Boyce. *Van Diemen's Land*. (Melbourne: Black Inc., 2008),15-16 Rebe Taylor *Unearthed: The Aboriginal Tasmanians of Kangaroo Island* (Adelaide: Wakefield Press, 2002), 14.
[16] Report of Governor King to Lord Hobart, 14 August 1804.
[17] Geoffrey Bolton. *Spoils and Spoilers*. (St Leonards: Allen & Unwin,1981), 51.
[18] An extensive attempt to set out chronologically the exploitation of the seals at Macquarie Island is contained within John Stanley. Cumpston's work *Macquarie Island*. Canberra: Government Printing Office, 1968.

After observing islets 'frequented by seals' off Esperance, he anchored at Karta, finding no evidence of any human habitations on the island but merely docile kangaroos and seals. However, it has subsequently been verified that the island had once joined the mainland more than 10,000 years ago. Here there was a First Nations culture present for thousands of years prior to the split. Even after water separated the island from the mainland, it has been established that there was a relic population still present for some years. Apparently, the survivors may have continued to live there under very difficult circumstances until they died out, perhaps some 4300 years ago. By the early 19th century, sealers began to establish themselves in small collectives across the island but without a First Nations cultural foundation to support their practice. As they found it impossible to trade with passing vessels sufficient to sustain themselves, they quickly realised the importance of establishing camps on the island's eastern side and partnering by exchange or by force with Aboriginal women. The island's eastern landscape offered greater elemental protection, a more fertile soil, and an abundance of salt and other natural resources. The southern side, though situated ideally for trade with other mariners, was subject to the fierce icy winds blowing from the Antarctic.

The commercial exploitation enterprises conducted by the maritime traders was not exclusive to the colonial entrepreneurs and independent sealing communities like those on Kangaroo Island. There were other international maritime stakeholders who had already discovered the opportunities available to them by the late 1790s. French and American sealing and whaling ships sought to cash in on the discovery of seal rookeries. Source documents refer to international crews visiting King Georges Sound, Kangaroo Island, Wilsons Promontory and Bass Strait. The hunt for the pinnipeds led to intense rivalry between American and colonial crews, particularly in and around the islands in the Strait, culminating in disputes and violent confrontations between the sealer Joseph Murrell and assertive Captain Amasa Delano over the procurement of seals in that region. Other relationships were more harmonious, like those that existed between Captain Pendleton and the sealers on Kangaroo Island in 1803. Here, the American successfully enlisted the support of local sealers to assist him. In addition, the French, with few exceptions. appeared to enjoy good relationships with the colonial mariners, both sealer and master. The Americans, in particular, also sought to exploit another marine mammal, namely the whale, both on shore and on the high seas.

In their enterprises across the southern Antipodes, enterprising traders employed mariners under articles of agreement whereby they received "the lay" in return for their services and were generally paid in kind on their return to Sydney Town. That is, if they returned. Often, the mariners were left at various places in and around the islands to procure seals over many months and sometimes years on a shaky promise by a master to collect them at an uncertain future time.[19] Relying on such a promise, the mariners would faithfully separate out skins kept under shelters from oil poured into and stored in barrels in anticipation of the captains' return. These men were often left in harsh and oppressive conditions, which led to them expressing a significant degree of hostility about their treatment on arrival at the settlements. Many a mariner was marooned on coast and islands away for colonial civilisation living in makeshift huts made of timber and covered in the skins of animals butchered for food. They survived on whatever they could procure from the sea and occasionally native edible flora. Being surrounded by the smell of rotting seal carcasses and rancid oil pots was never going to fit the picture of an idle idyllic existence. Several starved to death or were drowned due to accident or misadventure. Many sealers took their employers to Court to seek redress, with mixed outcomes. The potential for and actual abandonment of these mariners was the subject of major concern in the press and, sometimes, from the colony's officials.

Disgruntled men who were left to fend for themselves abandoned their mainstream employment. These mariners chose to settle in the vicinity of rocks where seals were found and conducted their own independent small-scale enterprises. Some sealers were seeking independence, others, an alternative lifestyle and, those fleeing

---
[19] For example, Joseph Murrell and his gang of sealers, who were left for years on islands where seals but not much else abounded.

sanction, an escape from the gaze of colonial authority. However, other seamen chose to remain indentured to the traders who tasked men such as Bishop, James Kelly and Frederick Hasselborough to lead expeditions seeking other opportunities to exploit resources in the many islands, bays and estuaries throughout the Fishery. In doing so, they also were in the forefront of the "discovery" of new remote islands and locations untouched by Europeans previously.

At the time, colonial society was thirsty for tales of adventure on the high seas, particularly after the publication of Daniel Defoe's *Robinson Crusoe* and other such stories. Mariners such as the sealers represented total freedom from the constraints of Georgian, and later Victorian, colonial society. They enjoyed a relatively carefree existence unfettered by any controls imposed by colonial authorities. From about 1815 until the demise of the sealing communities in the late 1830s, a consistent theme runs through the discourse emanating from colonial circles. It was almost a fetish, if not more certainly a fascination, circulating among colonial populations anxious for maritime tales involving pirates and adventurers on the high seas.

The print media were keen to further public interest in this type of adventure and found a ready source for their avid readers in the unusual experiences of the masters and sealers in the Antipodes. While endeavouring to entertain colonial readers with tales designed to titillate them, the press and others were hell bent on portraying sealers as the scum of society – vagabonds, pirates, slave traders and worse. The sealers were regularly described in pejorative terms. Polite society's concept of these men (and women) reached its nadir when, in a frenzy of diatribe, a Major Lockyer described them as 'a complete set of pirates'.[20] Lockyer wrote this among his observations in Albany during the late 1820s, while on a mission to reconnoitre the continent's southwest coast. This mainstream maritime colonial discourse about the Bass Strait sealers came from three main sources: the colonial press, the correspondence, and the collective dialogue from mainstream traders, officials, and the journals of George Augustus Robinson, all of which had axes to

---

[20] Major Edmund Lockyer. *HRA Series III,* Vol. 6, 471.

grind and do not necessarily accurately represent the reality of these sealer's histories, characters, or cultures. The only humans portrayed as lower on the rung of humanity were the First Nations peoples.

While operating on the margins of the British colony the sealers who chose an independent divergent lifestyle were the first to encounter First Nations peoples. They sought relationships with them, trading seals, dogs and Western goods in exchange for women, food, and local knowledge. Most of these early encounters were friendly, and sometimes First Nations women, with the authority of the tribal elders, willingly accepted an invitation to join the mariners as sexual partners and to assist in the trade. However, after a time, several men abducted women from Tasmania and the mainland to satisfy various needs. Abductions became popular primarily as an outcome of the almost complete lack of any white females inhabiting the Fishery along with hostility arising between European crews and Aboriginal Nations over aberrant conduct and behaviour.[21] This caused significant discord between whites and blacks. Several of the women were exploited unmercifully and suffered both physical and other abuse at the hands of unscrupulous mariners. The practice tarnished the reputation of sealers for time immemorial. After a while, more complex relationships developed.

After the decline of the inaugural sealing phase after 1810, some crews of the Sydney trader vessels remaining on the islands set up more permanent camps and settlements. Many mariners formed intimate relationships with the First Nations women procured by abduction, exchange or both with whom they lived in the small collective communities. They developed their own hybrid sub-cultures and communities from 1810 to 1820. Some of these relationships were short-lived. Others were traditional, monogamous and exclusive,[22] while several were polygamous. In

---

[21] According to Murray Smith, only one colonial couple, namely John and Bridget Lee, lived on islands in the Straits from about 1826. . Stephen Murray-Smith, 'Beyond the Pale; The Islander Community of Bass Strait in the Nineteenth Century," *Tasmanian Historical Research Association* 20, No. 4, 1973, 2.

[22] Examples include James Allen, who arrived at Kangaroo Island in about 1820 and had one partner, namely Dranetunnerminnener; Thomas Beedon, who came to Van Diemen's Land in 1818 and by 1831 had a monogamous relationship with Bet Smith; and Samuel Chase, who married the First Nations

such cases, many children were born to the common-law wives, but some of these relationships were longstanding. For example, George Robertson, an older sealer, lived with at least two First Nations women on King and Woody Islands, while James Munro may have lived for many years with up to five females, including one from New Zealand.[23]

At the same time, frustration arose from the inability of capitalist traders and governors to sanction the activities of these mariners who seemed to operate with impunity. Sealers lived and worked in communities on the edges of the Empire, often in parts of the Fishery where the sealers themselves were effectively the first European explorers, and where there were no legal or societal constraints, such as in King Georges Sound, the coast of South Australia and Kangaroo Island. In these places, these mariners enjoyed a free reign, only interrupted by Aboriginal men seeking revenge against mariners who had acted in a manner they considered transgressed their beliefs and values.

By around 1830, a mixed contingent of European Islander and First Nations men and women had established themselves in sealing communities across the Fishery. They were located principally in Bass Strait, Kangaroo Island, Wilsons Promontory, King Georges Sound and other places near coastlines.[24] The industry had changed significantly from one controlled and managed by the traders previously, when seals were in abundant supply, to one dominated by what were termed 'the Islanders'.

Due to the inability of colonial authority to fetter their activities, and a lack of effort by Governor Macquarie to harness the resources necessary to do so, the sealers were largely left alone. However, with the visit by Commissioner Bigge to New Holland and Van Diemen's Land between 1819 and 1821, that all changed. The content of Bigge's reports on the colony to his masters in England included a scathing attack on Governor Macquarie's management

---

daughter of David Collins in 1806.
[23] Brian Plomley and Kristen Anne Henley. *The Sealers of Bass Strait*. (Hobart: Blubber Head Press,1990), 56 and 60.
[24] For example, along the coast of South Australia and much later at Heard Island.

of the colony. In particular, Bigge perceived there was a lack discipline exercised by the Governor over the colony's convicts which led to a general lack of control and lawless behaviour among the colony's population. After the reports were handed down, colonial authorities started to impose stringent control over those they perceived were living outside accepted colonial boundaries. These included the sealers.

From about 1820, concerns arose in colonial circles, the press and elsewhere about both the activities and living arrangements of the sealers and the perceived hostility of the First Nations peoples of Van Diemen's Land towards the colonisers. In March 1829, the Lieutenant Governor advertised in the *Hobart Town Gazette* calling for 'a steady person of good character' to be paid £50 per annum plus rations 'to take an interest in this unfortunate race' and to reside at Bruny Island. An evangelistic devout Christian and former builder, George Arthur Robinson was one of nine men who applied. In his letter, he begged 'to offer [him]self for the situation' but was troubled by the poor salary. The concern about salary was overcome and George was appointed conciliator to the remaining First Nations people of Van Diemen's Land. Impressions of this man portray him as a clean-shaven, stocky, middle-aged Englishman who nearly always wore a tall peaked blue hat, a kerchief around his neck, white breeches and a dark coat to keep out the chills. Robinson was given an extraordinarily liberal mandate to gather together all First Nations people that remained in Van Diemen's Land and coerce or persuade them to follow him like a "pied piper" to a destination where they could be confined in missionary-like conditions. This would be in an isolated community away from their Country to essentially "protect" them from further demise and aggression perpetrated by certain sections of colonial society, including many sealers. It also had as its primary function a mission to civilize and convert those peoples to Christianity. In undertaking his role Robinson was handsomely rewarded for his services. It is not certain whether his original good intentions were influenced by the prospect of additional monetary and property remuneration.

Robinson kept a very detailed, but sometimes, almost

indecipherable journal of his conciliatory efforts from the time he first met with First Nations inhabitants at Bruny Island. He not only made observations and personal comments about those people, but also about the sealers who he felt were mainly responsible for the demise of them.[25] Throughout his journals, he describes the sealers in very negative terms, and makes clear his intentions to have all the women removed from these mariners and their island establishments destroyed. However, he was only partly successful.

Many First Nations women living with sealers in Bass Strait resisted attempts by Robinson to herd them into 'The Aboriginal Establishment' known as Wybalenna on Flinders Island. The settlement itself was located about halfway up the western side of the island in a reasonably well protected area, some hundreds of metres from the coast where it would have otherwise been exposed to adverse weather conditions all year round. It became effectively a prison for its inhabitants with 107 of its 150 First Nations occupants dying from disease and illness. As will be demonstrated, it became an overwhelming tragedy. Meanwhile, a leader among the mariners, James Munro, in the company of another sealer and a half-caste boy, obtained an audience with Lieutenant Governor George Arthur to seek his assistance in allowing the sealers to maintain some of their relationships. Arthur was supportive of this to the great frustration of Robinson.

As the sealing stocks decreased due to over-exploitation, making a living from sealing became uneconomical. Maritime colonisers and Australian women became partners in a more diverse trade. These enterprises involved not only sealing but also mutton birding,[26] agriculture, farming, herding and exchanging other goods with maritime masters, their employers and the colonial commercial markets. They also realised the value of education; it was not unusual for some of these island community members to send their children to the mainland for their schooling. The forming

---

[25] Brian Plomley was one of the first to attempt to decipher Robinson's notes and comments.
[26] The mutton bird is the most abundant native seabird in Australia from the genus *Puffinus tenuirostris*. It is commonly called the Short-Tailed Shearwater and inhabits Bass Strait and Tasmania.

of these Islander communities and their development of a hybrid culture has arguably been primarily responsible for the survival of First Nations Tasmanians, despite attempts by mainstream colonial commentators of the late 19th century to portray the First Nations woman, Truganini, as the last of her people.

By the time Robinson had ceased to occupy the role as pied piper to what remained of the Tasmanian First Nations population, there were scarce returns for masters, traders and sealers. The independent mariners were no longer beyond the control of their colonial authorities and had become dependent upon regular trade with upstanding colonial society. Furthermore, with the suspicious circumstances that surrounded the pillaging of the *Britomart* following its sinking off Preservation Island,[27] they were under increasing pressure to live within the law. Although most continued to co-exist in their island communities with their First Nations partners and children, the Islanders developed a hybrid and collective means of subsistence, for, by the 1830s, the sealing industry was no longer viable.

When Truganini died in 1876, it was represented incorrectly in the press of the day and by colonial authority that the Tasmanian First Nations people had then become 'extinct'. However, that was not the case as these peoples continued to subsist albeit through the progeny of the Islander relationships.

Most early colonial maritime history of Australasia focuses on the world of mainstream exploration around the coasts of Australia and New Zealand and the exploitation of what became known as the 'Fishery'[28] by those who controlled the politics, economics and recorded history of colonial society. The dominant theme in this record portrays a respectable maritime community that earned its great successes through the employment of both capital and labour

---

[27] The infamous narrative surrounding the loss of the Britomart and all on board is contained within Chapter 14.
[28] The 'Fishery' or 'Southern Fishery' was initially the coastal marine environment inhabited by seals off the islands in Bass Strait but later expanded to include the whole southern seacoast of Australia, New Zealand and other several islands. *The Sydney Gazette and New South Wales Advertiser* (31 August 1805) mentions the term in a government regulation prohibiting married men from engaging in the 'Fishery' because of conflicts with Americans.

in trying circumstances. It does not speak to the over exploitation of the mammals that were prey to the mariners nor to the difficulties experienced by the sealers whilst in the employ of the traders let alone the First Nations occupants of that world, and only works to further marginalise these people. With few exceptions, these marginal characters do not have a voice in the written history of the time and ever since.

The purpose of this work is firstly to give those sealers who I call 'mariners on the margins' and their First Nations partners a voice in this history and to provide a more balanced and objective analysis of sealing around the Fishery. Secondly, it is to demonstrate the environmental impact on the fauna that was the subject of exploitation not only by the mariners but also by the mainstream capitalist traders and to demonstrate the minimal impact Tasmanian First Nations people had on them. to a much lesser extent. But this work does not overlook the important role played by the entrepreneurs who stepped up to take the risks in building boats and employing men to lead the charge to develop a somewhat partly successful industry for the benefit of a nascent colony. It also does not forget these masters who "discovered" and exploited seal colonies while also providing essential "intelligence" to their employers and the authorities. The world occupied by the sealers and their interaction with the other stakeholders in this world, including colonial authorities, traders and the First Nations people, was a much more complex, divergent and interesting world than has been portrayed previously. It was a time when these mariners were pivotal in developing relationships which crisscrossed colonial boundaries in exploring and exploiting that world. The sealing industry and the development of an alternative for some mariners only came about almost by chance and involved various maritime men and women who populated that world and interacted with one another in a frenzy of activity on the fringes of the colony.

Chapter 2: Entrepreneurs, Adventurers and Opportunists of all Nations and Natures

There is no better way to illustrate the colour, complexity and cross- cultural nature of the marginal existence of those traders, commanders and sealers who collectively I term mariners inhabiting the fringes of Empire than by focussing on the lives of some of these men who populated this colonial world. Capitalist free traders like Robert Campbell, and the emancipist entrepreneurs like James Underwood, Henry Kable, J.T. Palmer and Simeon Lord all had a substantial hand in founding the ship building and sealing industries in the Antipodes.

Leaving aside the scarcity of resources that were available in the colony for the first 10 years of its existence for one minute, there were opportunities that presented themselves to men who were prepared to take their chances. With few exceptions, these entrepreneurs would rarely, if ever, involve themselves in the day-to-day organisation and preparation required to fit out vessels destined for the remote islands to the south of New Holland. That task was left for their trusted commanders, then called "masters." These men were normally seasoned mariners such as Charles Bishop, James Kelly and Joseph Murrell and, to a lesser extent, Thomas Chaseling.

They had prior knowledge and experience that was required to equip the brigs, sloops, cutters and other boats owned by the traders for sealing missions. Meanwhile advertisements would appear in the colonial press designed to attract seafarers to join gangs needed to man the vessels and plunder the rookeries once the boats had reached their destination. On inquiry at the Port Jackson docks, the sealers who answered the call would be "interviewed" unless already known to the master and then required to sign what were termed 'articles of agreement'.[1] The crews who signed up were a diverse racial and ethnic multinational mix of men. Some were emancipists, others were experienced mariners and adventurers, while a third sector were seeking to escape from creditors or colonial authorities. A few had "jumped ship". The sealing gangs included men such as William Tucker, George Briggs, and James Munro.

After some years, the lure and enticement offered to the crews by traders and masters did not satisfy some mariners. Disgruntled by months or years of hard backbreaking toil on windswept, cold and icy coasts and islands where they had been marooned on false promises, several sought to establish their own micro enterprises away from colonial settlements. The whaler Black-Jack Anderson and his accomplice John Bathurst were two of the more infamous mariners to "achieve" a nefarious but successful independent sealing operation in the Western part of the Fishery. Separately, Briggs, Munro and Murrell early on worked the Bass Strait and Kangaroo Islands while others, like Tucker, went further afield to the east. However, to survive and, in some cases prosper, mariners realised the opportunities that could be gained by seeking out the First Nations peoples of the Antipodes. While on sealing missions they organised for First Nations people to accompany them on their voyages in procuring the seals. They encountered both men and women who were either willing or could be forced to "assist" in the hunt for the mammals. Their lives, interactions and encounters with others and the seascape tell the tale of the marginal nature of the industry and the cross-cultural sub-cultures that developed within it. However, it was their former employers who first took the risk to establish enterprises on the edge of the southern Antipodes.

The Sydney Traders

On 8th February 1797, a leaky, battered and damaged Indian merchantman, *The Sydney Cove*, carrying a valuable cargo of provisions destined for Port Jackson, limped into Bass Strait and

---

[1] The 'articles' were a written contract handed to each mariner by their employer before they ventured on a sealing mission setting out the terms of their engagement which had to be signed or crossed and were commonly used throughout the colonial period.

started to sink in treacherous waters near what later became known as Preservation Island. Crew members under the command of Captain Guy Hamilton frantically retrieved some ammunition, rice and firearms just as the merchantman was about to sink. They jumped into a longboat before the vessel capsized. Reaching the island, the captain ordered 15 of his best sailors, including some called 'lascars',[2] under the chief mate Hugh Thompson, to set out for Sydney in a small boat to call for help. Meanwhile the captain and the rest of the desperate crew were left to their fate, grappling with a salvage operation of the valuable cargo. In that regard, the most important provisions consisted of alcohol of 7000 gallons including several casks of Bengal rum, four pipes of Madeira wine, brandy and beer. Some of the grog washed up on the shore of a small outcrop soon named Rum Island. Eventually, Hamilton and a few of his gang were rescued by a Mr Armstrong in the 41-ton Government schooner *Francis*. Unfortunately, only three of the men who had been sent ahead to raise the alarm, survived the arduous ordeal. Fortunately for the owner of the wrecked *Sydney Cove* most of the cargo that had gone down with the ship was retrieved and later sold by public auction.[3]

That owner operated a small commercial firm out of Bengal. It was known as Campbell Clark & Co. Two of its directors were the Campbell brothers. The younger, Robert, would become known as the first major trader in the colony. Robert had come to India to join his brother John in the enterprise. The younger Campbell was a clean shaven rather portly man who dressed in the manner of a Scottish gentleman and was keen to seek his fortune. His company traded mainly in the supply of commodities and had a licence to operate granted by the Company. In those days, the latter entity basically had a monopoly on any trade conducted in the Pacific and exercised its rights prodigiously. By 1797, several English entrepreneurs with businesses located in India had already voyaged

---

[2] Lascars was the colonial term applied to crew originating from India and surrounding nations.

[3] An interesting report and description of the whole circumstances surrounding the wreck of the *Sydney Cove* appeared in the *Asiatic Mirror*, Calcutta, in 1797 and also see *Historical Records of NSW*, Vol. III, 757-769.

to Sydney to trade goods. Opportunities to make a killing there were known to Robert and his brother. Meanwhile, the Campbells had also established a rum distillery near the populous and busy city of Calcutta. This would become a source of significant earnings once Robert established himself in the new colony.

After receiving the news of the loss of the *Sydney Cove*, Robert was devastated. It took him a while to contemplate what he would do next. He would have gleaned from the masters who docked in the Bengal harbour that the infant settlement at Port Jackson was in much need of provisions Being aware of the scarcity of much sought after commodities in the colony, he decided to try his luck. Fitting out another vessel to the brim with a huge cargo in 1798, he sailed for Sydney Town. Finding a suitable plot of land on the harbour at Dawes Point, he acquired a grant before returning to Calcutta to resume the trade with his brother. There is reference to Campbell supplying the colony with the largest value of trading commodities even in September 1798 when his vessel *The Hunter* anchored in Sydney Harbour with provisions worth over £7000, a small fortune in those days.

Two years later, he was back. He established an outpost of the firm shortened to Campbell & Co and arranged for a wharf to be built directly into the harbour, opening for business in warehouses established on the waterfront. These became known as the 'Campbell House'. Early on, Robert mainly imported Indian commodities into the colony rather than focussing on the sea. The loss of the *Sydney Cove* may have caused him to baulk at entering the maritime trade. But, like many a merchant who owned boats anchored in Sydney Harbour, this was not the only loss Robert was to suffer. Sailing vessels across the seas and in and around the Antipodes was a dangerous and at times perilous occupation for all involved in the trade. One such vessel was the Campbell brig *Fly*. In 1802, that boat, laden with spirits and other commodities, went missing in action while on a return voyage from Sydney to Calcutta. All hands were presumed deceased, including the master John Black, who the editor of the *Sydney Gazette* referred to as a 'young man most esteemed by all who knew him'. Over the years several other vessels Robert had built or used in the trade were either wrecked or went missing in action, at great financial cost to him. The loss of ships and their sealing crews who perished in icy and dangerous seas, was a regular occurrence and adversely impacted on many a trader, apart from Campbell.

Notwithstanding his initial hesitation, by 1800, Robert had become the dominant maritime trader in the colony. An indication of how he dominated that trade is reflected in what was called the *Ship News*, a regular section contained in the only colonial newspaper of the time. Its editor reported in 1804 that three vessels, namely the *Mersey*, *Hunter* and *Lady Barlow*, all in port at the same time were owned and had cargoes consigned to Mr. Campbell.[4]

In the meantime, Robert involved himself heavily in the colony and became quite wealthy. In 1804 alone, the merchant had goods to the value of £50,000 stored in his warehouses. This represented an absolute fortune at the time. Eventually, Campbell, who was not risk averse, decided to take his chances in the fishing trade. He initially fitted out the 'country ship' the *Lady Barlow* with skins and oil and sent her to London with instructions to the master to sell the cargo on arrival. Falling foul of the notoriously protective Company on anchoring at the docks, he suffered losses of over £7000. Despite this major setback, he enlisted the support of the influential Sir Joseph Banks, who lobbied the government to relax restrictions to encourage free enterprise emanating from the colony. His efforts succeeded. The former Lieutenant Governor of New South Wales David Collins demonstrated the success of Bank's endeavours when he wrote to the Board of Trade of the Company by letter in June 1806 about the next Campbell vessel to arrive:

> I am commanded by the Lords of the Committee of P.C. for Trade to acquaint you, for the information of the Court of Directors, that their Lordships have received advice of the sailing ship Sydney from His Majesty's colony of New South Wales, laden with elephant oil, sealskins... entirely the produce of the collected industry of the colonists, resident there; and that, in consideration the increasing activity of this distant colo-

---

[4] *Sydney Gazette*, 15 April ,1804, 4.

ny, and of the ship having actually sailed from thence before the news of the Lady [sic Barlow) their Lordships are inclined to admit the cargo to entry, in case the Court of Directors see no objection to this measure of indulgence towards an important and an improving colony.[5]

After hearing this news, Campbell realised the money that could be made from the trade. To further his interests in it, he began building boats from his wharf from about 1807. Known as 'Merchant Campbell' in Australasia, he then employed a manager to oversee his operations in the Antipodes. In the meantime, he also established business relationships with other entrepreneurs namely his brother-in-law John T. Palmer, a former convict penalised for his political beliefs, and the emancipist traders including Simeon Lord, James Underwood and Henry Kable, who feature later in this chapter. Robert's connections extended to having an agent by the name of William Wilson based in London who interceded on his behalf as and when required as well as intermediaries in Canton. Always looking to pursue profit, he arranged for some of the emancipist entrepreneurs in the colony to develop trading relationships with his various agents and no doubt reaped commissions from such arrangements.

Despite his success in trading goods supplied from Europe, China and India to the fledgling colony, it was the sealing trade that occupied his major endeavours during the period from about 1804 to 1811. In particular, he had employed a man called Charles Hook to look after and manage his vessels and the procurement of seals during that time. Hook it was who employed the masters of Campbell's fleet and sought out by advertisement and word of mouth the seasoned sealing gangs who would crew the vessels on missions to the Fishery. The most prominent of these missions was a voyage fraught with risk and uncertainty, after the Bass Strait islands had been fished out almost to oblivion in 1810. There were rumours circulating around the maritime fraternity that there were sub-Antarctic islands yet to be visited by Europeans in the southern oceans.

---

[5] Lieutenant Governor David Collins, Letter to Board of Trade, June 30, 1806; *Banks Papers*.

Campbell was prepared to take the risk on a hunch that rookeries existed in that region and organised through Hook to equip a 136-ton brig known as the *Perseverance*, manned by an experienced crew, to voyage into maritime territory unknown to Europeans in search of seals. In doing so, the crew by chance "discovered" two separate islands where seals proliferated. The abundance of fur and elephant seals slumbering on rocks surrounding those islands led to a "feeding frenzy" of boats procuring seal skins and oil for some years until those colonies of the mammals were also exhausted. By the 1820s, Campbell was no longer actively involved in the trade and turned his attention to other pursuits including politics and banking. Some would call him the 'founding father' of maritime trade in the colony. He was a major employer of the gangs who occupied boats visiting remote outcrops in the southern Fishery. His path crossed with other entrepreneurs seeking their fortune in seal skins and oil. One was Simeon Lord.

In June 1806, a Spanish merchantman called the *Honduras Packet* arrived in the Thames laden down with 'more than 35,000 seal skins' worth over £10,000'. The ship was under the control of or on consignment to a former convict called Simeon Lord. One of the few colonial portraits of him reveals a short stocky clean-shaven grey-haired man with piercing hazel eyes and tight lips dressed in a black suit and wearing a colonial decorated white shirt and kerchief. Lord was important enough for Dr. Henry Waterhouse of the Royal Navy, stationed in the colony, to write to Banks about this man as the merchantman anchored in the Thames. The naval surgeon described Lord as being "emancipated", having been transported for theft arriving in Port Jackson with the Third Fleet in 1791. But that was no impediment to Lord at all. He was quick to seize any initiative offered. Due to good conduct, by 1795 he had been "assisted" by a New South Wales Corps captain to commence trade as a supplier of bread and liquor to the residents of Sydney town. But he was destined for greater fame and notoriety. A chameleon-like character, he soon took advantage of the changing nature of business in Port Jackson and became an auctioneer selling goods at inflated prices to gullible dealers on the docks. His earnings enabled him to construct a warehouse to store cargo adjacent to his house near the wharves. This residence was set up in such a way that masters and crew of vessels anchoring in the harbour were his regular guests paying for board and lodgings. This enabled him other opportunities to have these men deposit their supplies with him for sale at inflated prices. He earned a small fortune that enabled him to buy two 'Spanish prizes'[6] in 1799 and 1800, and, by these acquisitions, enter the commodities trade between Sydney and Bengal. By 1800, Lord and Campbell's ventures basically destroyed any chance for the military men who previously enjoyed a monopoly on trade in the colony to prosper on their own account. Some former officers became Lord's junior assistants, helping to promote his commercial interests mainly in the Antipodes.

By at least 1803, Lord began the sealing trade in Bass Strait. He was no fool and realised early on that he needed to take steps to make it worth his while. Aware of the success that Campell had enjoyed by trading through London agents, he formed a limited alliance with Robert and tested the waters. He approached the Governor who he knew would be amenable and obtained the financial benefit of free freight for a ship to voyage to London laden with 2000 seal skins and 8 tonnes of elephant seal oil. In addition, due to the restrictions imposed by the Company, he thought outside the square by acquiring the Spanish prizes which were allowed to trade on certain strict conditions and by contracting with American vessel owners and masters to get around the harsh restrictions imposed from London. Unfortunately, for at least one American captain and his estate, this led to disaster. Lord, by ruse or trick, acquired the proceeds of the sale of several thousand skins owned by the Yankee for his own use and benefit. They were meant to be primarily to make profits going back to Boston. Meanwhile, Lord, increasingly prosperous, built ships of up to 80 tonnes, which he used to trade goods in and around the colony including coal from Newcastle.

---

[6] These were Spanish boats seized or confiscated by British naval personnel.

When the Americans either ceased to procure seals in the Fishery or were prevented from doing so following the introduction of punitive sanctions imposed by Governor King, Lord found another way to outwit the Company and British government. He approached a London agent namely Plummers to purchase ships on his behalf and effectively hold them on trust for him. One such vessel was the new *Sydney Cove* which was acquired by the agent for and on behalf of Lord and two other emancipist entrepreneurs for more than £7000. The agent consigned the vessel to the partners, and, like others, it was used extensively in the sealing trade to the annoyance of Governor Bligh, who was entirely suspicious of Simeon's intentions but was foiled by Lord and could do nothing.

Between 1803 and 1807, Lord, either on his own account, with his business partners or using agents circumvented the restrictive laws and rules in place which had thwarted many a colonist. By fair means or foul, he organised boats for procuring seals and selling cargoes in London, Canton and Calcutta. One of the main benefits of establishing contacts with influential people in London, including Plummers, was that it gave him access to lines of credit to enable him to prosper without having to fork out monies continuously. During the relevant period Lord and his partners dominated the sealing industry. They either built or had consigned to them no less than 11 vessels of between 20 and 282 tonnes many of which were wrecked on voyages or sold off by 1810. His arrangements with the other trading partners and his agents were often complicated and fraught with difficulty. Take, for example, his agreement with an American master Nathaniel Cogswell in 1807 where the parties had a convoluted agreement in place about how profits were to be shared:

> Cogswell is to receive the nett amount of the sandalwood and seal skins which is the property of the said Lord's shipped and which may be shipped at the Feejee Islands on board the brig Hannah and Sally and disposed of in China for the following purposes viz: Should a vessel be chartered or purchased on the joint account of Messrs Simeon Lord Henry Kable or James Underwood to proceed to this place…[7]

---
[7] See David Roger Hainsworth. *Builders and Adventurers*, 82-84.

Chapter 2: Entrepreneurs, Adventurers and Opportunists

Although initially successful in his sealing ventures, they were not to become long-term prospects for Lord. Apart from his losses of vessels, cargo and crews, he was a notorious litigant who fell out with all and sundry and sued on a whim. This tied him up at great cost over several years. After a while, he abandoned sealing for manufacturing. His business partners, including Kable and Underwood were happy to see him go.

In 1798, well prior to Lord's entry into the fishing trade, 12 men, including two emancipists, met at a shipyard on the docks at Port Jackson. They were there, encouraged by Governor Hunter, to see what could be done to establish a shipbuilding enterprise. All were initially enthusiastic and agreed to the construction of a vessel, but, after their gangs started building the boat, their early enthusiasm waned. In the end, only the two emancipists, Henry Kable and James Underwood, were prepared to continue with the construction. The former had arrived as a convict on the First Fleet. He had established a degree of trust and, due to good behaviour, had been freed and appointed Chief Constable of Sydney Town by the Governor. The latter had arrived on the *Admiral Barrington* in 1791. He had been convicted and sentenced initially to death for theft but had his sentence commuted to transportation from Portsmouth. For a while, the two men formed a strong partnership trading as such from about 1800 out of Underwood's shipping yards on the Tank Stream. It was at that time that they entered into agreements with their first sealing crew. They would have known Campbell and encountered the assertive and deceptive Lord early on and from time to time carried out joint ventures with both entrepreneurs. Over about a year, three of their vessels anchored back at the docks in Sydney laden with over 28,000 seal skins and 183 tonnes of elephant seal oil, procured form the Straits. They tried to sell into the China market using Campbell's agents but without great success as by then prices were dropping substantially. This forced them to consider approaching Lord to get access through his connections to the London market, which had some success.

In company with the confident Lord, they sought out the very best of the masters who were available in the colony to captain their vessels. These included the American Samuel Chace who had already had a track record as a trustworthy and experienced sealer in the Straits. Other prominent chief mariners included Murrell, Rook and Moody – all sealers who had manned boats on multiple voyages to the south. They became the largest employers of crews in the colony. At one stage the partners had 200 mariners on their books who they could call on if they were not at sea. Kable looked after the employment of the men they needed to man the ships, while Underwood focussed on their business dealings.

How successful they were is illustrated by the fact that, in 1804, they entered into all 15 articles signed by crews and approved by the judge advocate in the colony. Cognisant of the adverse restrictions imposed by the Company, they also signed contracts with English merchants to avoid sanctions where they could and to achieve the best prices. At the time, skins sold in London for 25 shillings, and they could get £25-£40 for oil in Europe; whereas the market in Sydney and, later in China, only allowed them to achieve about five shillings for skins and 10 shillings to one pound for oil.

Although they reaped the benefits of early procurement of seals in Bass Strait for about three years, they constantly faced difficulties during and after that time. Apart from restrictions imposed by the Company and the depressed Asian markets, several of their boats were wrecked at significant financial loss. Of the five vessels built by the firm, four foundered and the fifth, the *King George*, was used for sealing until 1822, when it became a hulk rotting away in Sydney Harbour. Furthermore, there was always the prospect that skins would become spoilt or damaged and subject to worm rot. To top that off, after the Americans entered the trade in the Straits, they suffered losses sustained due to the outright hostility that existed between colonial and Yankee crews. Rubbing salt into their wounds, some of their crews "jumped ship" in favour of the more lucrative rewards being offered by American owners and masters. Some of these mariners absconded with gear owned by the firm. The latter practice led ultimately to Kable and Underwood placing a notice in *The Sydney Gazette* entitled 'Felony'. In that article they offered a reward for the detention of the offending sealers who they named and who had deserted their employment taking with them:

> One Suit of Sails and Rigging belonging to a Boat and A Quantity of Tackling and other Implements Furnished and provided by the said Employers for the use and convenience of a Gang or Gangs of men stationed at and about the aforesaid Islands, for the purposes of procuring skins and Oil.[8]

The stolen sealing equipment probably had come from the 24-tonne Underwood sloop the *Surprise*, under the command of Joseph Murrell. Whether they succeeded in having anyone apprehend the perpetrators was unlikely, given the former crewmen were now employed by the Americans who abandoned the Straits shortly after this occurred and moved further east with their new colonial employees.

By 1807, the partnership between Kable and Underwood was becoming fractured. Disputes arose, not only between the partners but also with Lord separately. After Simeon had a falling out with his London agent, he commenced legal actions not only against that firm but also his colonial "partners" hell bent on recovering what he thought were his damages for which he blamed everyone else but himself. Henry and James became tangled up in litigation. This led to claims being made that were not settled until almost the end of the next decade.

While Underwood continued in the sealing trade until about 1814, he was only as a minor player. Two particular events between 1810 and 1814 are noteworthy, one demonstrating the rewards that Underwood achieved albeit by dishonesty, and the other showing the worst of the difficulties faced not only by the trader but also the crews who manned his vessels. Like Lord, James was not above resorting to trickery to further his mercantile aims. As an outcome of a ruse in 1810 where he tricked a sealer called James O'Burne in disclosing the coordinates of a newly discovered island where seals abounded, he directed his master sealer Daniel Cooper to proceed to the island in the vessel *Unity*. His gang easily located the sub-

---

[8] *Sydney Gazette,* 11 November, 1804.

Antarctic island and were pleasantly surprised to observe seals lying on every rock. With alacrity, the crew slaughtered as many of the mammals as they could and loaded the vessel to the brim with skins and elephant seal oil. This cargo he sold off in London at a huge profit.

Four years later he purchased the *Betsey* for £3000. He then employed a master by the name of Captain Goodenough to organise a gang of sealers to crew the vessel to the same island to procure skins and oil. At that time, there was still money to be made from seeking good-quality fur seals and elephant seal oil. The crew, which consisted of 27 Europeans and 6 lascars, set out on the voyage in late 1814, hoping to repeat the success enjoyed by the gang of the *Unity*. No such luck. In one of the worst sealing debacles of all time, many of the sealers on this vessel died from scurvy, drowned or perished from starvation. The *Betsey* was eventually wrecked off New Zealand, and the survivors were captured by a Māori clan. Only a few would live to tell the tale. Nothing further was heard of either Kable or Underwood as far as their involvement in the sealing trade is concerned.

Although the four Sydney Traders referred to above are not the principal focus of this work, they were instrumental in setting up enterprises on which the sealing industry was founded and, for a time, flourished. They also were in the forefront of providing employment for many of the masters and sealers who were otherwise unable to earn a living in the colony. Early on, they made huge profits out of the sealing trade, which enabled them to build ostentatious Georgian style mansions around Sydney Harbour where they could proudly display their wealth as the nouveaux riche of the colony. They were no longer on the lowest rung of Western colonial society but now middle-class merchants. Their financial gain was made on the back of the masters and crews who manned their vessels on the fringes of Empire in harsh and oppressive conditions. Campbell Lord Kable and Underwood were some of the traders who jointly and severally gave the colony its first real staple industry. They played key roles for a few years before ceasing their involvement as an outcome of the downturn in the sealing economy. By then, it was at best a marginal concern. That left a vacuum which was filled partly by new traders who sought to investigate other littoral regions where their ships could anchor in pursuit of the pinnipeds but mostly by the characters that competed for scarce resources on the fringes of the Fishery. I now turn to these men and women.

The Masters

Master mariners were usually the most experienced and responsible sailors whom a trader would employ to captain his vessels. Their roles were extensive and fraught with risk. Not only did they have to plan a voyage but also outfit the ships with provisions and organise the crews to man the boats and have them sign articles of agreement. Once this was arranged, they dealt with port authorities and ensured that they complied with maritime regulations. If this was satisfactory, they had to sail the boat out of the harbour safely and navigate their way often by dead reckoning or compass, to remote outcrops. Then they had to manage a gang and earn their respect to prevent unruly behaviour or even worse. Across the entire voyage they were in a position of complete power over the crew, even meting out punishments for misbehaviour. Sometimes, they also conducted a divine service on Sundays, compelling all the crew to attend. They could make life for a sealer very difficult or pleasant depending on their demeanour.

A handful of masters came from similar backgrounds as the sealers, and many established themselves as experienced and capable mariners by operating across the difficult and dangerous expanses of the Fishery. Accompanied by the sealers, they were in the forefront of establishing the sealing operations for their employers. While some unscrupulous masters were, unfortunately, instrumentally involved in the abandonment of sealing crews from time to time, these men also sought and found new coastal places and spaces where seal rookeries thrived. In doing so, they passed on valuable geographic and nautical intelligence to mainstream traders and officials. This often meant that later, other explorers, settlers and governors had a much better knowledge of the maritime edges of the southern parts of Australia. Such information was then used to establish settlements and strategic outposts. Like many men who experienced success in their maritime endeavours, most had to adapt to a changing maritime and economic environment and did so with mixed results. Many ultimately suffered declines in their fortunes and health due to circumstances beyond their control. Four of the more prominent of these mariners on the margins were Charles Bishop, James Kelly, Joseph Murrell and Thomas Chaseland. Their histories are examples of those that led the charge into the deep waters of the southern Antipodes in pursuit of marine mammals.

In March 1798, the *Nautilus* anchored at Matavi Bay in Otaheiti in a dilapidated state while on its way to procure sea otters off the coast of North America. The captain of this vessel had been less than fortunate in his previous fishing endeavours on behalf of the owner of the boat. Firstly, his trader had provided him with an unseaworthy ship prior to the current vessel which had to be sold off for scrap. Secondly, he had been almost a total failure in his attempts to procure fish and otters for his employer, who was unimpressed. The master was a man called Charles Bishop. He would never again reach North America. Initially, it was the need for repairs to the leaky brig that delayed his departure to the east. But then, quite by chance, five missionaries from the London Missionary Society approached him in a frightened and agitated state. They informed him that their lives were endangered by hostile 'natives'. Pleading with him to take them on board immediately and paying him in advance, they convinced Bishop to sail for Port Jackson. It was to be a fortuitous decision.

When Bishop's boat limped into Sydney Harbour in May 1798 with the grateful missionaries on board, he encountered some of the survivors of the wrecked *Sydney Cove* around the docks. They provided him with "intelligence" about the bountiful seal rookeries inhabiting Bass Strait. He also met Matthew Flinders and the surgeon George Bass. They were keen to sail on a voyage of exploration to the southern waters to find out, with the encouragement of Governor Hunter, if there were a channel between the mainland and Van Diemen's Land. Once the *Nautilus* was ready to sail again, Bishop cobbled together a multinational crew who had all signed and were bound by articles to accept 'lays' instead of wages. On 7 October 1798, they set out on a voyage of discovery and exploitation to the south, excited by a potential fishing foray. Bishop was able to use the services of the volunteer missionaries he had collected from Tahiti. Bass and Flinders accompanied him in the *Norfolk*. Sailing around Bass Strait, with ample provisions provided partly by the government, and with the support of the knowledgeable Flinders and the influential Bass, meant Bishop was free to move around the islands unimpeded. To his delight, he observed hundreds of fur seals inhabiting the islands.

Unlike in his previous attempts at sealing, this time he was entirely successful, returning to Sydney with 5,000 skins and 350 gallons of oil. This was effectively the first successful sealing venture in the colony. On his arrival there, he wrote to his employer, anxious to please him with reports of his bounty. By then, intelligence about the discoveries of the seal colonies had been passed on to the mainstream maritime operators, which galvanised them into what can only be described as a "gold rush" of maritime activity. Fortunes were made almost overnight for a relatively short period of time by many traders who relied on their maritime employees to seek out pinnipeds.

Bishop left Port Jackson soon afterwards and delivered his profits to his long-suffering employer, and the missionaries he had rescued from Otaheiti, to their final place of safety in China. While on his now famous voyage, he had formed a friendship of sorts with George Bass that led to a maritime partnership being established in 1799. They agreed to seek their fortunes by procuring sandalwood, pork and other commodities in the Pacific. Although both may have had very good intentions, the relationship quickly descended into acrimony, with the partnership ultimately being dissolved. Bishop relocated all his operations to Sydney, where he terminated his interest in the maritime trade in favour of farming out at Prospect. Unfortunately for him, his mental health was declining rapidly. Just like other mariners, he ended his days in an impecunious position. Notwithstanding, he will be remembered as the founding master of the sealing industry in Australia. He was the first in a line of mariners who would captain boats destined for the southern Antipodes.

Well after Bishop departed the Fishery in late 1815, a 24-year-old seasoned mariner set about organising a motley crew of four in the satellite settlement at Hobart to accompany him on a maiden voyage to circumnavigate Van Diemen's Land. He had been engaged for that purpose by the one-time surgeon and now sealer and whaler T.W. Birch. The mariner had previously been employed by Birch on several expeditions on his vessels in the sealing trade. Given the danger that maritime men had experienced before in sailing along the west coast of the island, one would have thought that a sound and sturdy brig or schooner would have been required. But the mariner had other ideas. He chose a 28-foot lightly coloured wooden whaleboat, the *Elizabeth*,[9] as his choice. It was fitted out with a mast that could hold two sails and had five oars for use as the need arose. It was light weight and easy to steer. With Birch's encouragement, five men set off on what turned out to be an important voyage of exploration, discovery and cross-cultural awakening.

The mariner was James Kelly who was a "currency lad", having been born at Parramatta in 1791. He had gone to sea early having involved himself in sealing at the young age of 13 years. Initially apprenticed by a firm to a vessel under a Captain Siddons, he mainly worked for Birch. Kelly would come to earn his fame and fortune in the industry before turning his attention to other maritime pursuits. Portraits of him later in life depict him as a stocky reasonably short man, who wore a dark cap and warm coat whenever he went sealing. Around his neck, he wore a scarf above which were long side levers, as was the custom amongst sailors. His hair was kept short. He was powerfully built, which was to be of

---

[9] There is a replica of the *Elizabeth* in the Bass and Flinders Centre, Georgetown, Tasmania on display.

great benefit to him in difficult circumstances later in life.

So far as can be ascertained from reliable sources, the first we hear of him is when he was employed on voyages to Fiji to seek sandalwood in 1807 before being directed into the local sealing trade. He regularly voyaged between Sydney and Hobart Town procuring seals in the Straits, with an occasional diversion to places such as India and New Zealand. By 1812, his maritime abilities were officially recognised. He was appointed chief officer of the 148-ton Underwood-owned *Campbell Macquarie* to venture to the recently discovered Macquarie Island and procure skins and oil. While there, the vessel was wrecked. Kelly was fortunate as only one of a handful of men who survived and was able to return to Sydney in the *Perseverance*, which was in the vicinity at the time. But this terrible early experience did not daunt him. He returned to the island in September 1813, having been promoted to captain now on the small brig, the *Mary and Sally*, owned by Wiliam Collins. When the vessel almost capsized, Kelly still managed to procure 80 tonnes of elephant seal oil, returning via Hobart in early 1814. Before the age of 26, James had successfully completed several sealing ventures and was by 1815 well recognised as one of the better dependable and experienced masters a trader like Birch could utilise.

And so it was in December 1815 that Kelly, the sealer George Briggs, John Griffiths, described as a 'native of the colony', Thomas Toombs, who was apparently a noted English bushranger[10] and one other Englishman, William Jones, departed from Constitution dock in Hobart in the whaleboat. Kelly's intention was to be the first to circumnavigate Van Diemen's Land and explore the unknown west coast. The journey was to take about a month.

One has to wonder at Kelly's audacity in choosing such a craft, although whaleboats were commonly used as a means of transportation by sealers during the early 19th century. No doubt Birch wanted Kelly to undertake the voyage both as explorer and to

---

[10] Why Kelly, who was by then a respected citizen of Hobart Town, would choose someone like Toombs to accompany him is odd. See James Calder (ed.) *Van Diemen's Land in 1815*.

seek out opportunities for further exploitation of maritime creatures and other natural resources such as the Huon pine. The treacherous mountainous seas along the west coast of the island awaited the crew. But the choice of Briggs and Griffiths as crew members would have been informed by the former's relationship with the First Nations peoples to the north, and of the latter's general maritime experience in those waters. Kelly was most probably concerned about possible hostility from the northern tribes and perhaps wanted to use Briggs as some kind of emissary. On the voyage, the master made some useful observations of the abilities of the Tasmanian First Nations people known as the Palawa[11] to procure seals, but he also undertook significant explorations around Macquarie Harbour. After entering through the notoriously difficult Hell's Gates, he observed vast tracts of Huon pine and other natural resources which would later be commercially exploited mainly by Birch. The entrepreneur was later rewarded with a licence for that purpose by the Governor.

It is hard to find anything in the records to indicate that, while in Van Diemen's Land, Kelly was other than a man of exemplary character. But his reputation changed after he reached the southern part of New Zealand in 1817. He became involved in a significant "skirmish" with the Māori peoples who occupied the lands around Otago, known as Port Daniel. Kelly and crew voyaged there in the Birch ship *Sophia* and their relationship with the locals, although harmonious to begin with, quickly descended into outright hostility. After anchoring in the port area, Kelly and three others, including his brother-in-law Griffiths, left the vessel on a smaller craft and paddled towards the beach. Here, they were suddenly met by several local inhabitants. The Māoris surprised them with a violent attack, killing all but Kelly. Such aggression was a common experience early in the encounters between Māori and Pakeha[12]

---

[11] The word 'Palawa' appears to be a derivation of the word 'Parlevar' meaning 'first man', derived from a spiritual ancestor associated with the kangaroo, and now is identified as the term for all the First Nations Tasmanian . See "The Palawa Voice," *Companion to Tasmanian History*. Also see Maykutenner (Vicki Matson-Green) "Tasmania 2," *Contested Ground: Australian Aborigines under the British Crown,* 339.

[12] The term used by Māori to describe white men.

mariners. The clashes often arose where mariners had attempted to abscond with local females, misunderstandings or from past poor experiences on first contact. Later, the surviving ship's crew were confronted by an estimated 150 Māori men who had 'swarmed' on board Kelly's vessel. With assistance from the remaining men, he managed to repel the attackers, largely by use of the musketry they discharged, killing several local men in reprisal.

We next hear about Kelly when he is in charge of a vessel employed by the local officials with 'an armed detachment' to bring to justice what the editor of *The Sydney Gazette* described as "sanguinary pirates." These desperate men had been accused of taking by force vessels belonging to traders operating in Van Diemen's Land and absconding to places along the east coast of the island. The master Kelly was successful in his task and received a "handsome piece of plate" inscribed with details of his meritorious conduct.[13] By 1819, Kelly had left the sealing game and had been appointed jointly as the harbour master and pilot for the southern settlement, a position he held for 12 years. During that time, he amassed a considerable fortune and was involved in various profitable pursuits including interests in whaling, land and agriculture. By then, he had earned sufficient income to send his sons to England to further their education.

Unfortunately for Kelly, his skill as a maritime man on the fringes of the Fishery, and his previous good fortune, deserted him. During the 1830s, he suffered several significant losses which ultimately lead to his demise both personally and financially. The death of his wife in 1831, and the loss of his vessel the *Australian* in 1834, with a significant quantity of whale oil on board, caused him great hardship. However, these incidences paled into insignificance against the dire consequences he faced when unsuccessfully defending a court action, with damages and costs awarded against

---

[13] The Editor wrote: "We hold to public view and admiration the bold spirited faithful conduct of Captain Kelly which cannot be too highly commended or appreciated and the masters and crews of the Colonial Shipping are called on by every principle of duty to show an equal zeal in defence of the persons and property entrusted to their charge."

him.¹⁴ The downturn in the global economy in the early 1840s resulted in Kelly being left destitute. Due to his "connections", he managed to secure employment as a wharfinger¹⁵ but later died a pauper. Many Hobart edifices and public amenities were named after him, the most famous being the Kelly Steps down to the harbour. In a career that spanned more than 38 years, Kelly would experience almost the entire gamut of activities and events that came to define what it meant to be a mariner in the colony. He had enormous success and abject failure towards the end of his days.

Above all else he was a great survivor of adversity in the Fishery. Another who faced similar adversity was Joseph Murrell. Murrell was never backward in coming forward. He was in charge of a gang of sealers employed by Kable and Underwood who anchored in Kent Bay in Bass Strait in the brig known as the *Surprise* in October 1804. While there he and some of his crew were set upon by a team of disgruntled American sealers led by the Delano brothers. By this time, sealing was recognised as a profitable enterprise across the entire Western world.¹⁶ American traders, mainly from Boston and Nantucket, had learned of the marine "bonanza" that awaited eager mariners in the Straits. It seems that the local mariners perceived the Americans as a significant threat to their trade. The Yankees retaliated. The colonial men did whatever they could to frustrate the Americans, as reported in Delano's journal.¹⁷ The Yankees were active and belligerent in seeking to procure seals and also did not tolerate any competition. The animosity that developed was a "powder keg" about to explode.

The dispute arose after Amasa Delano came to the rescue of a colonial vessel, the *Integrity*, under the command of Lieutenant Bowen, which had lost its rudder pin. He ordered the boat be towed into Kent's Bay, where he encountered Murrell's sealing camp. The arrival of the Americans surprised the colonials who

---

[14] See Tolman v. Kelly [1839] *TAS Superior Cases*, 40.

[15] A wharfinger is an old maritime term for a man who in charge of the goods coming to and from the docks.

[16] Letter from Governor King to Lord Hobart, 9 May, 1803.

[17] Amasa Delano. *Narrative of Voyages and Travels in the Northern and southern hemispheres*, 461-466.

had the sealing grounds all to themselves.

Murrell distrusted the Americans and told Bowen that he would be better off having his vessel tow the *Integrity* to Hobart. Too late as the lieutenant had already entered into a contract with Delano and was bound by its terms. While Amasa was away enjoying the hospitality of the prominent residents of Hobart, several of his crew remained at Kent's Bay. Unfortunately, tensions surfaced between the Murrell gang and the men from Nantucket. The dispute escalated into a melee of fists and clubs whereby the Murrell gang were punished and suffered a humiliating defeat.

Meanwhile, the colonial sealers had been busy either enticing or inducing several of Delano's employees to abandon ship in return for greater rewards on their sealing vessels. Some of the colonial men were even pilfering from the American boats. Delano complained to Governor King about Murrell's behaviour, describing the sealer in these terms:

> I at first thought the man too insignificant to take notice of, but I was mistaken; he made interest with so many of my people to run away from me, that it has distressed me very much. He has carried six of them out of this bay at one time in his vessel notwithstanding I had forbid him receiving or harbouring them, in the presence of several respectable witnesses… He still holds a number of them, and articles have been stolen from me or I am very much deceived'.[18]

The American's attempts to have the Governor act against the colonial sealers proved a failure. Like so much of the "sabre rattling" that occurred in these times, nothing much came of it, and the Delano vessels apparently left the Straits in October 1804. This was reported by Murrell to the *Sydney Gazette* when he returned to the main settlement in January 1805.[19] The master would not be stopped and continued to seal unimpeded despite suffering severe injuries in the skirmish referred to above.

---

[18] Letter from Amasa Delano to Governor King dated 4 August 1804 written on the Perseverance and delivered to the Governor by his brother Samuel Delano, *Narratives of Voyages and Travels*, 461-462.
[19] *The Sydney Gazette,* 27 January, 1805, 3.

His life both before and after the American incidents speaks of determination courage and resilience. In 1784, Murrell[20] and another man were convicted in the English courts of stealing on two counts and sentenced to be transported to America. Many malnourished men such as Joseph would have stolen food or sold pilfered goods to survive. Like most convicts awaiting transport, he would have spent time either in an English prison or on a hulk in the ports of London Woolwich or Plymouth. Life would have been tough, as the living conditions on such vessels were deplorable. He, like many prisoners, would have been working the docks near his 'prison' from daylight to dusk.

After some time in port, Joseph and his fellow convicts were on board a boat voyaging to the Americas. While on route, the opportunistic Murrell escaped lawful custody, but, on his return to the old country, he was found out, prosecuted and sentenced to death in 1786. Later, as so often was the case with those convicted of that penalty, his sentence was commuted to life imprisonment, and he was sent to Port Jackson, arriving in September 1789 aboard the *Scarborough*.[21] Though Murrell's physical appearance is not recorded, we can draw from the sheer difficulty of his accomplishments that he was a man who was physically very strong with a determined demeanour, who was successful in seizing the double-edged opportunities available to him in the maritime trade. He also found he had leadership qualities and, after a time, commanded the respect and loyalty of those mariners who came to make up his crews. Although we know nothing of his exploits until 1803, he was by then appointed master of colonial vessel *Surprise* by the Sydney emancipist traders.

Although Murrell was regularly engaged in leading his crews to and from the Fishery in search of skins and oil, it was probably never without incident. Within about two weeks of his return from the Straits following his skirmishes with the Americans, and despite his injuries, he again set sail, this time in a boat named *Endeavour*

---

[20] Also known in the convict records as 'Robert Murrell' or 'Jos Murrell' or 'Morrill'.
[21] See Gordon Copland, "The Mysteries of Karta (alias Kangaroo Island) Creation Colonizers and Crusoes", in *Counterpoints*, Department of Archaeology (2002),.9.

with a new crew, for Kent's Bay. Once there, the crew purchased an illegal quantity of alcohol. Fuelled by the substance, some crew mutinied, which delayed their departure. Murrell had other ideas and quickly quelled the insurrection, returning to port 'with 13 tons of elephant oil, an article excessively scarce and difficult to procure in small quantities'.[22]

Maintaining control over unruly crews was one thing but the relationship between Murrell and his employer, Kable, was another. As so often occurred, a dispute arose over the payment of wages. When the sealer heatedly confronted Kable and demanded payment of wages outstanding, he was punched and bloodied for his trouble. Murrell would have none of this and commenced legal proceedings against his pugilistic employer, seeking damages for assault. We do not know the outcome of these proceedings but, disenchanted by his treatment at the hands of his employer, Murrell procured a new vessel for his gang of sealers and set sail for the Straits. Voyaging down the east coast, he anchored at Jervis Bay to seek water. There, the crew was allegedly attacked by the local Dharawal people and Murrell was speared and suffered a wound. The First Nations people may have been provoked by the mariners or had previous poor experience of Europeans when the surviving crew of the *Sydney Cove* had ventured across their Country some years before. Managing to escape, Joseph with all hands returned to port. Within two weeks, Murrell was reported to have 'almost perfectly recovered from his spear wound'.[23]

After he was regularly featured in dispatches from 1803 to 1805, nothing was heard of Murrell for three years. The mystery of his whereabouts was solved when an Underwood-owned sloop, the *Eliza*, sailed to Kangaroo Island and found Murrell along with six other sealers, camping in huts and slaughtering seals. They had been living primarily on fish and seal meat for two and a half years.[24] Although there is no direct evidence, it is thought that Murrell and other mariners had been left there by their employer who had

---

[22] J. Selkirk Provost, "Joseph Murrell – Sealer," *Descent Magazine*, 81.
[23] *The Sydney Gazette*, 3 November, 1805.
[24] John Stanley. *Cumpston, Kangaroo Island 1800-1836*, 31.

neglected to return, a common occurrence in colonial Australasia. After his return to Sydney, Murrell did not waste much time seeking further employment. He was placed in charge of the *Endeavour* on a trading trip to Norfolk Island. There he sought supplies of pork and soap, but the ship was in poor shape, and it limped into Port Jackson in July 1809.

This sealer led many other maritime voyages, mainly pursuing the seal trade over the course of the next six years, criss-crossing the oceans that comprised the Fishery and elsewhere. On a voyage to Kangaroo Island from December 1811 to June 1812, he brought back not only between 2,500 to 3,000 seal skins but also near 60 tons of salt, a much-needed commodity in the colony.[25] Murrell provided intelligence to colonial traders about the vast quantities of that product that abounded on the island which was then exploited by all and sundry as it became the main supply of salt.

By February 1815, Murrell was given command of the *Governor Hunter*, owned by Isaac Nicholls, and reportedly set sail for Kangaroo Island. Nothing more was heard about that boat until 1818, when its wreck was discovered in an inlet 45 miles from Port Stephens. How it got there remains a mystery. Both editors of the *Sydney Gazette* and the *Hobart Town Gazette* reported its discovery in October and November of that year. These pressmen surmised that Murrel and his 'ill fated' crew had been 'killed by the natives'. No clear evidence of this was ever produced, but Murrell's apparent demise was 'much to be lamented', according to the press. Clearly, Jos Murrell led a precarious, industrious and somewhat brutal existence at the tipping edge of the sealing trade, but had the good fortune, versatility, ability and leadership skills to play a significant role in the industry. Another with invaluable skills who criss-crossed the entire Eastern Fishery was Thomas Chaseland.

In January 1827, a vessel owned by Robert Campbell voyaged to the Chatham Islands in search of the dwindling numbers of fur seals. By then, the mammals had been decimated across the Fishery. On board was a 30-year-old headsman of mixed First Nations and European descent. Campbell had employed him as he came with

---

[25] Cumpston, 33.

a vast experience in sealing and was a man of exceptional strength and ability who would have been asset to the trader. He was also accompanied by his Māori life partner. On board were several European crew led by the captain, Thomas Swindells. When they reached Pitt Island off the northern coast of Chatham, the boat struck rocks and was wrecked. The headsman and his wife were at least 800 miles from their home on Ruapake near Stewart Island off the southern tip of New Zealand's southern island. There were no trading or other boats in the near vicinity to take them on board and deliver them to a safe port. Swindells and most of his gang commandeered the longboat and set off for the Bay of Islands. The headsman had other plans and set about building a sealing boat from whatever timber he could find. Without adequate tools, it took several weeks to complete the build. According to anecdotal evidence, he and his partner filled the vessel with enough provisions to feed themselves on what would be a difficult journey and set off eventually reaching Moeraki near Dunedin by March of that year. During the journey, to placate the sea gods and, in accordance with First Nations New Zealand culture, the wife plucked a hair from her head throwing it into the sea to calm the waters for a safe passage. The headsman was called *Tame Titirene* by the local people of Stewart Island. This man was Chaseland.

Although it is not certain, Thomas was most likely born to a First Nations mother in about 1797 and brought up by his English convict father in a large family household that included six other children. During his teenage years, he worked in the docks and upper reaches of the Hawkesbury. He probably assisted the boat builder and trader John Grono with his maritime activities there. By 1817, Chaseland was ready to broaden his horizons being indentured on the *Jupiter*. Thomas was part of the crew who undertook a sealing voyage to Bass Strait to procure the very last of the fur seals inhabiting the rookeries there. Over the next five years, he had voyaged on several vessels seeking oil, seal and kangaroo skins, sandalwood, pork and other economically valuable resources in and around Australasia and the Pacific. Here, he would have come into contact with adventurers from many parts of the world.[26] At this time, the sealing industry had diminished around Australia, and Chaseland was looking for a fresh start elsewhere. While voyaging on the Campbell owned *Nereus* in January 1824, he sought a discharge from the captain when he arrived at Stewart Island, a most desirable sealing environment. He wanted his independence. After some time, he became proficient at using the Māori language, because he was later employed as an interpreter. He spent almost all of the rest of his life in the whaling and sealing trades around that region basically operating either independently or under articles as a master or headsman.

Chaseland was physically imposing. He has been described as a strong tall muscular man who had a deep scar down the left side of his face. He was something of an eccentric character, often being called an inveterate drunkard with a mild or happy disposition, unlike many of his colleagues. Known for his excellent eyesight he was often the first mariner to pin-point the location of whales and seals. Admired by many, Thomas became a Southlands legend and was involved in several significant events that were to define a turbulent but fortunate life. In 1844, he was described in the *Nelson Examiner* as having experienced a "life of great adventure, hardship and damage". That is somewhat of an understatement. There were prominent events that were to shape the otherwise orthodox history of Chaseland's life more than any other in New Zealand. Such experiences illustrate his extraordinary survival skills, his occasional aggressive temperament and the intermittent dangers that confronted many a colonial mariner.

The first event occurred in the 1820s, when he was surviving with a gang of sealers at a camp near Arawhata on the south-west coast of New Zealand. Late one night, some local Māori stealthily rowed their canoes over to the beach occupied by Chaseland's sleeping party. While the colonials slept, the unwelcome visitors were rumoured to have stolen some fishing gear stealing away into the darkness. Sometime hours later, the alarm was raised. Chaseland was outraged as the fishing gear was vital to his crew's

---

[26] Lynette Russell, "A New Holland Half Caste. Sealer and Whaler Tommy Chaseland," in *History Australia* Vol. 5, No. 1.

survival. Quickly manning the whaleboat, the mariners went in pursuit. Following an initial altercation with some Māori they believed responsible, Chaseland then led a band of his crew into skirmishes that resulted in many deaths, mainly of the local men, allegedly in a massacre perpetrated by the mariners. The part First Nations sealer felt vindicated.

Ten years later, Chaseland was again in the forefront of action when he performed a rescue following a shipwreck near Codfish Island, (also known as Whenuahou) located three kilometres off the north-west coast of Stewart Island, below Invercargill. Tommy almost single handedly rescued several survivors, including his Māori partner. The third event was the epic journey he navigated across the wide expanse of the South Pacific Ocean in a small boat he built from the Chathams. Finally, when engaged in a sealing venture off the south coast of New Zealand near Cape Saunders, Chaseland was part of a crew who were finding it near impossible to land on an island inhabited by seals in treacherous seas. The waves were mountainous. When Chaseland realised that the vessel was about to founder, he ran as fast as he could and leapt high into the air, just managing to land awkwardly on a rocky ledge. His fellow mariners did not react as quickly. They all drowned as the boat crashed into rocks, capsized and broke up in the dreadful conditions. Chaseland shivered through the night but was fortunate to be rescued the next day by another vessel.[27] Chaseland is a significant maritime sealing figure who not only managed to straddle two entirely different marine industries but also found a leadership role in both, surviving extreme environmental conditions against significant odds.

Bishop, Kelly, Murrell and Chaseland were four of many men who plied their trades as masters or headsmen of traders for most of their careers. Each achieved a fair degree of fame and some fortune. Each commanded vessels in with crews who generally worked for a percentage of the catch, while the masters enjoyed the second largest share after their employers on the completion

---

[27] Edward Shortland. *The Southern Districts of New Zealand; A Journal with passing references to the Customs of the Aborigines*, Chapter VIII,154.

of each voyage. While masters had generally good fortune to make somewhat of a living out of the sealing industry and occasionally could also operate independently, many of the crew could not. As a direct outcome of this and the harsh and oppressive and sometimes restrictive conditions under which they were employed, several sealers ceased their employment for the Sydney Traders and chose an entirely different life independent of the mainstream maritime entrepreneurs away from the main settlements. Some of these men stand out as the more prominent marginal characters.

The Sealers

In January 1820, an article appeared on page 3 of the *Sydney Gazette* signed by a person describing themselves as 'Candor'. The anonymous author was raging against sealers who had occupied the Foveaux Straits across the southern New Zealand channel and had earned significant profits made from selling human heads on their return to Sydney. After complaining about the 'depredations' that the mariners had caused 'the natives', the author singled out a sealer by the name of William Tucker. According to Candor, Tucker had led the charge in triggering this nefarious trade when he had been one of the first in the sealing gangs to visit New Zealand in 1811. By the time of the anonymous article, Tucker had been dead some years, after becoming a victim in what was known as the Sealers War. By then, William had experienced the full gamut of a mischievous and adventurous life as a sealer, trader and wheeler dealer.

By the age of 14, Tucker had already been convicted of theft and sentenced to death. Fortunately, his sentence was commuted to seven years' transportation and, in 1798, he was transported to the colony on the infamous vessel known as the *Hillsborough*. Infamous, because on the voyage, almost one third of the convicts on board died of typhoid, having been confined in very cramped conditions, The vessel earned a reputation as the 'Death Ship' having the worst record for convict losses of any coming from London to the colony. William arrived in a bedraggled and pallid state. He was representative of the prisoners who Governor Hunter in a letter to the Under Secretary of state described as 'a cargo of the most miserable and wretched convicts I ever beheld'.[28] Although nothing much is known of Tucker over the next few years, by January 1803, he was a secret passenger on the *Atlas* voyaging to China. Avoiding sanction, he eventually made his way to England, having made an opportunistic escape. But, just like many escapees, he was found out. Because of his age, he avoided the death penalty but was again transported on board another vessel anchoring in Port Jackson by June 1804.

After his term of imprisonment expired, and being an adventurous type of person, he joined the infant sealing trade. He is mentioned in an advertisement inserted in the *Sydney Gazette* in March 1805, as being one of a crew voyaging to New Zealand on the *Governor King*. That ship was owned by the entrepreneurs Kable and Underwood who were keen to exploit the eastern Fishery. The owners of such vessels generally advertised to the public the fact that certain sealers were about to leave the colony in case anyone wanted to press a claim against them for debts which needed to be paid out, Tucker's name was listed. The vessel was probably headed for the Antipodes Islands to the south of New Zealand, which had recently been visited and found to have abundant seal rookeries thriving there. By 1807, William was part of a crew voyaging back to England on the *Sydney Cove* with the sealing master Daniel Cooper, who had wrested control of the vessel en route, but nothing is known of the purpose of his visit.

Two years later, Tucker was on the Robert Campbell-owned *Brothers*, making his way to the east coast of the southern island of New Zealand to what is now known as Dunedin. He and a gang of sealers were left to fend for themselves by the master. It would appear most of the crew abandoned their camp because when a vessel was sent to recover the men, skins and oil, only Tucker and another sealer Daniel Wilson were found. Sent by Campbell's representative in search of the missing crew, Tucker was diverted

---

[28] Governor Hunter to Under Secretary King, 28 July 1799, in *Historical Records of Australia*, Series 1, Vol. 2, 1797-1800, 378.

from his task as he allegedly seized hold of a preserved Māori head. This, he secreted in his possession as he saw opportunities to sell it back in Port Jackson, but not before the local inhabitants, who had become aware of the theft, set out in pursuit of the surviving sealers. Luckily for the sealers, Tucker and his gang outwitted them and rejoined the *Brothers* in Otago. This incident itself unfortunately led to an escalation of violence between Māori and Pakeha[29] that was further triggered by a Māori chief stealing a red shirt and other property belonging to another crew.

After returning to Port Jackson, Tucker was employed on vessels going to Macquarie Island between 1811 and 1815, including the Underwood-owned *Aurora*, which was one of the first boats to anchor there. He would have faced extremely adverse environmental conditions, including excessive wind, ice, snow and dangerous seas, making it difficult to land at any time. Notwithstanding those harsh conditions, he spent many months on the island managing to survive. Unfortunately, on his return to the settlement, he was in trouble with the law again. On conviction, he was transported up to the harsh penal settlement at Newcastle for recidivists and served two years hard labour there. On his release, he eventually decided to leave the colony and finally settle down. Like many of those who became sealers, in 1815, he established himself on a reasonably isolated location ominously called Murdering Beach near present day Otago. There he partnered with a local Māori woman, living in a dwelling he built himself, raising goats and sheep. Fortuitously, he found another source of income. The region was well known for the *pounamu*[30] that could be extracted from its surrounding topography. Tucker, along with what the editor of the *Gazette* later described as 'groupes of sealers', was soon involved in mining the stone and then trading it in New Zealand and in Sydney as it acquired considerable value. While there, William also enjoyed good relations with the local people, no doubt assisted by his partner. He was named *Taka* or *Wioree* by the Māori.

Realising other opportunities could present themselves, and

---

[29] The name the Māoris gave to Europeans who came to New Zealand.
[30] The Māori word for greenstone or jade.

being an opportunist, Tucker voyaged back to Van Diemen's Land, probably in 1817, and encountered the intrepid James Kelly, whom he would have known in the trade. William was persuasive, as he must have convinced Kelly to organise a crew including himself to voyage on the *Sophia* back to Otago with European colonizers and encourage them to settle in the region. Unfortunately, by now, many of the local Māori were distrustful and hostile towards mariners as an outcome of their previous troublesome conduct and behaviour. Tucker was under the impression that the local people would be friendly, as he had "gifts" to hand to them. It turned out not to be the case. One of the local chiefs, with a long memory, had planned revenge against the mariners as a tit for tat reprisal following two Māori casualties. Kelly, Turner, Griffiths, a sealer called Veto Viole and two others voyaged in the longboat across to meet some of the locals ostensibly to trade. Kelly encountered a lascar who spoke the local language and promised to assist him to negotiate the sale of some potatoes. Suddenly, 60 of the Māori rose up and ambushed the crew. Most of the sealers rushed to the longboat near the shoreline, but Tucker was speared in the leg and cut quite badly falling into the surf. He cried out: 'Captain Kelly, for God's sake, don't leave me!'

But it was too late. Only the captain would survive with William and the others being hacked to pieces. Sensational reports appeared in the *Gazette*. The editor described in graphic and grisly detail what happened to Tucker:

> Mr. Kelly made the boat, and was dragged by her through the surf, calling on Tucker to follow who, however, would not attempt to do so till too late, a number of savages immediately rushing down on the beach armed with spears and hatchets. Tucker kept calling to them not to hurt "Wioree", but regardless of his entreaties, he was first speared in the right thigh, by the man who Mr. K. had wounded on the head, and who was then covered with blood, and immediately knocked down in the surf, where Mr. K. and his three men in the boat saw the unhappy "Wioree" cut limb from limb and carried away by the savages![31]

---

[31] *Hobart Town Gazette,* 28 March, 1818, 2.

From this, it would appear that Tucker was somewhat of a rogue and scoundrel, but that was only partly true. The reality of his life became clear after the publication of a manuscript in the 1840s by the Reverend Charles Creed, who recorded intelligence supplied by two Māori. They informed the clergyman that William was generally liked by the local inhabitants who enjoyed trading with him. He was just in the wrong place at the wrong time due to previous poor conduct on the part of some desperate mariners. Notwithstanding his criminal background, he was probably the first European to trade in greenstone between New Zealand and the new colony, establishing himself as a recognised dealer in Māori art. His history speaks of the daring diversity and challenges that such mariners faced in the industry, particularly early on in Aotearoa.

Many of the sealers were the first point of cross-cultural contact for First Nations people living along the southern Australian coastlines during the early 19th century. Initially, the encounters were reasonably friendly. First Nations people perceived the benefit of developing an exchange system whereby they traded their women and skins for dogs, seals and later, Western commodities. . Later that changed as various colonial parties including bushrangers, settlers and some sealers sought to take advantage by raiding First Nations tribes' campsites for their women.

One who was both a part of this aggression, but then transcended it, was the sealer George Briggs We do not know if Briggs was "native born" or a convict. He was described as being about 5' 9" tall with hazel eyes, light red hair and with a fair ruddy complexion covered in freckles. By the age of 16, he was employed by the merchant Kable in sealing gangs visiting Bass Strait. Shortly after his arrival there, Briggs formed a friendship with the northern Van Demonian Aboriginal leader, Mannalargenna. This enabled that nation's peoples and the sealers to have a cooperative relationship. The liaison was ultimately very useful as the sealer established himself in the surrounding islands, partnering with several First Nations women who would have helped to procure seals for him. He fathered children from the relationships and kept in touch regularly with local Aboriginal leaders.

Around 1815, Briggs formed a close business arrangement with the intrepid, multi-talented and versatile mariner Kelly referred to previously. When Kelly was funded to conduct a voyage circumnavigating Tasmania, Briggs would have been an obvious choice to him to deal with the northern First Nations peoples. It was a significant adventure for several reasons, not the least of which was the geographical and cultural observations made during the voyage and the development of friendly Aboriginal and colonial relationships. During the course of the journey, Briggs again met with Mannalargenna, who was chief of the Pairrebeenne clan on the northern coast of Van Diemen's Land and entered into an agreement to use Aboriginal women to hunt for seals. The chief also was instrumental in negotiating with other Tasmanian First Nations to secure a safe passage for his colonial friend. This was despite simmering tensions with settlers and disputes between warring clans. Most importantly, Kelly's personal journal provided a unique record of the methodology employed by the First Nations women in procuring seals and noted their significance as frequent collaborators with these mariners.[32]

Briggs certainly was not without blemish. He had at least two First Nations wives, and, during a decline in trade around the Straits in 1820, 'sold' his common-law wife to the sealer John Thomas for a guinea. He continued in the sealing and whaling trade, serving on vessels such as the *Glory* and *Nereus* mainly on voyages in the Straits and around New Zealand.

Thereafter, not much more is written about him, until G.A. Robinson records his employment as a seaman on 'Griffith's schooner'. Living in Launceston, by 1831, Briggs probably took no further part in the sealing trade as nothing of note is heard about him until his demise. That occurred in 1854, when he drowned while acting as a cook on board the *Sarah*. He is of key relevance because of his early cross-cultural encounters and relationships that he developed across the spectrum of the First Nations peoples in Van Diemen's Land.

---

[32] See K. M. Bowden, *Captain James Kelly of Hobart Town* for extracts from Kelly's diary.

Arguably, the man who was perceived to be the most settled, sedentary and respected of the sealers was James Munro. Born in England in 1779, Munro was convicted of stealing, and was sentenced to transportation to the colony on the *Lord Admiral* in 1800. On this voyage, were proselytizers from the London Missionary Society and, given his strongly held Christian beliefs that he seemed to adhere to later in his life, Munro probably was influenced by them. Described as being of medium height and light complexion, Munro developed strong political and physical survival skills. As best as can be determined, he first voyaged to the Bass Strait islands as an ex-convict in or about 1819. He found immediately that Preservation Island was an ideal destination.[33] The island is situated near the southwest coast of Cape Barren Island.

On the smaller island called 'Rum', Munro constructed a home with outbuildings and gardens. Here he lived with several First Nations women, including Margery Munro, until his demise in 1845. A painting by the colonial artist Henry Laing depicts his 'farm', which consisted of two thatched dwellings surrounded by trees, which he would have planted, and an enclosed 'garden' painted in the foreground. In 2024 I flew above the two islands. Not much has changed since colonial times, except for the lack of any obvious buildings or structures or anchorages. The vegetation is low windswept and sparse. Waves constantly pound the coasts that surround them. They are largely uninviting.

Working from this isolated and harsh base, Munro was able to trade his agricultural and maritime produce with passing vessels. At regular intervals, he sold or bartered commodities by voyaging to the markets on the main island. His enterprise reaped the rewards of organization where his First Nations partners and some itinerant mariners worked as a team during the sealing season and otherwise relied on agriculture and mutton birding[34] at other times.

Sealers lived and laboured on the margins of colonial society. They were often the subject of adverse reports and speculations in

---
[33] Lyndall Ryan. *Tasmanian Aborigines A History since 1803*, 61.
[34] 'Mutton birding' is the common name given by the First Nations and colonial maritime men to the seasonal harvesting of the chicks of petrels particularly the sooty shearwater practised by the First Nations people for thousands of years.

dispatches from press editors, and they came under scrutiny and sanction from the authorities. Munro was no exception to this, but, of all the sealers, he appears to have been the most successful at walking the fine line between adventurer, rogue, entrepreneur and diplomat. More telling was the fact that he was able to adapt to changing circumstances throughout his later life. Even though he had a close and continuing relationship with several men wanted by colonial authority, he must have been trusted by those occupying positions of power. He was appointed as a constable for the Straits in 1825 and continued in that role almost until his death.

Known as 'The King of the Eastern Straits',[35] Munro was instrumental as a leader of the sealers in successfully representing their best interests. In particular, he was proactive in preventing Lieutenant Governor Arthur in 1831 from attempting to follow through with his threat to remove all First Nations women from the maritime men living with them on the islands. That attempt arose following the persistent lobbying of Governor Arthur by Robinson. His interviews with the First Nations women of Van Diemen's Land led him to believe that the sealers were primarily responsible for their 'demise'. He determined that several women were being held against their collective will and secreted away from authority by the sealers.

When the mariners found out about Robinson's policy to remove their life partners from them, Munro and another Straits man travelled to Hobart to lobby the Governor to let them "keep" several women. This was successful despite Robinson's best endeavours to the contrary.[36]

Because Munro had earned the respect of mainstream colonial figures and was seen as a leader of the sealing mariners living in the Straits, other colonial traders, mariners and authorities sought him out and used him for various purposes. One was to gain access to "intelligence" about both seal rookeries and other resources that existed in and around the islands in the Straits. Another was to

---

[35] See Harry O'May, *Hobart River Craft and the Sealers of Bass Strait*, 20.
[36] Brian Plomley. *Friendly Mission: The Tasmanian Journals and Papers of George Augustus Robinson*, 355.

pin down the location of escaping convicts who were hiding out wherever they could to avoid capture. Munro trod a fine marginal line operating between valued and respected settler on the one hand and mischievous aider and abettor on the other. Two versions of this man paint a divergent portrait of him.

A man named Skelton reported of Munro:

> On Preservation Island I found a man named James Munro who harbors various characters visiting the Strait, apparently without any check on them... Two years ago he left Hobart Town. He owned a boat and seems to have gone to the islands in quest of adventure.[37]

The Christian missionaries, Backhouse and Walker, visited Preservation Island in 1832, and after meeting Munro they later recorded in their diaries:

> We paid him a visit and also interviewed three sealers and three female aborigines casually here on their way to the coast of New Holland, where on a number of small islands they still obtain seals. James Munro raises wheat potatoes and other vegetables near his huts... He also rears goats, pigs and fowls and by means of these added to the collection of birds obtains subsistence...

Munro was a chameleon-like character who lived a life on the edges of the colony, both literally and figuratively. He operated only just within the accepted parameters of behaviour and changed his demeanour to suit the circumstances. On the one hand, there is no doubt that he actively participated in nefarious activities, such as assisting runaways and escaping convicts. On the other hand, he was respectable enough to entice authorities to appoint him to positions of power and responsibility. But he almost faced a catastrophic end to his chequered career.

In 1840, the *Britomart* foundered in Bass Strait. Although there was never any direct evidence to link Munro with the circumstances causing the barque's demise, serious suspicions were raised against his party of sealers. A Captain Gill visited Preservation Island in his search for the missing vessel and found some flotsam from the barque in Munro's camp. Later, Munro handed over the

---

[37] Letter of W. H. Skelton, *The Australasian*, 9 March, 1826, 2.

ships' register and requested that Gill deliver it to the authorities in Hobart. Munro provided Gill with an explanation of how he came into possession of the plant and equipment from the barque. Shifting the blame, he told Gill that a gang of sealers led by a person called Drew had taken coin notes and other valuable items from the missing vessel to Launceston. There were rumours of mariners with substantial sums of money living beyond their means in Van Diemen's Land. Despite this, neither Munro nor anyone else appears to have ever been prosecuted. Others also avoided sanction. One who was particularly sinister was known as 'Black-Jack'.

Probably the most notorious of the sealers was John Anderson, probably an African American sailor who arrived in Western Australia on a whaling vessel near Albany in about 1826. He "jumped ship" and sought refuge on Kangaroo Island. There, he allegedly set up his own trade in sealing and salt with a divergent gang of sealers originating from the colony, Europe and the Americas together with some South Australian women. He was also known to have supplemented his income from that trade by "going on account" as a pirate. Given the name 'Black-Jack', Anderson appeared to terrify all he encountered over a 10-year reign of terror. A sketch reveals a tall man with an angular face having a ring inserted in his right ear from which dangles a threaded cord and keepsake. Around his neck is a kerchief, and near his waist is secured what was described as 'a brace of pistols'. Colonial writers described him as a 'stout and powerful man' who dealt severely with any dissenters.

Apparently, he ruled by creating fear and dread in his crew as much as by any leadership qualities he may have possessed.[38] He spent most of his time sealing between Kangaroo Island and King Georges Sound, especially around Mandurian Island. Anecdotally, he 'amassed a considerable fortune' from his nefarious activities.[39] Black-Jack came to prominence in early colonial discourse for various reasons. Primarily, this was because of his fearsome reputation and ability to cause distress and anxiety in the hearts

---

[38] 'Remarks respecting the islands on the coast of S.W. Australia', in *The Perth Gazette and Western Australian Journal*, 8 October, 1842, 1.

[39] *The Perth Gazette and Western Australian Journal*, 8 October, 1842.

and minds of the colonial traders around the southwestern fishery. With his armoury of weapons and fearsome appearance, he would have presented as a frightening foe to anyone who crossed him. Like most pirates, he was keen to display his ferocious demeanour to all who he encountered. His reputation was further enhanced following his trial in Albany on charges of stealing, and, finally, the nature of his demise.

Anderson carried on his "trade" for over a decade without ever being successfully prosecuted for piracy. This was despite the rumours that persisted about his illegal activities. On one occasion, two men, namely Manning and Newell, who had lived with Black-Jack on Kangaroo and Middle Islands, had to be rescued by colonial officials. The rescue party were horrified to find the two in an exhausted and malnourished state near Albany. They had been travelling on foot hundreds of miles across the Great Australian Bight and were close to death. With trepidation they blurted out to their rescuers that Anderson and his partner had marooned them on the coast of South Australia. Black-Jack had accused them of stealing some of his valuable ill-gotten coins and sought to punish them by forcing them onto the remote coast. In an ironic twist, the law enforcers prosecuted Black-Jack for stealing, but he was acquitted after a lengthy trial before the Honourable Sir Richard Spencer in 1835. His acquittal was due to the conflicting statements of the prosecution's unreliable witnesses. Notwithstanding his success, the local editor published a report of the trial in which he complained about the 'outrages of these lawless assassins', including Anderson.[40]

That all came to an end around 1837. What happened to Black-Jack is fraught with uncertainty. On one version, while he and his crew were sealing around Mandurian Island, he jumped overboard with an First Nations woman who 'died of cold'. Both were never seen again. At least that's what the crew reported when they returned to King Georges Sound. But it was rumoured by the colonial press in 1835, that Anderson had amassed a considerable fortune in gold and silver coins, on his person and concealed elsewhere, as buried treasure. This gave the fearful but avaricious

---

[40] *The Perth Gazette and Western Australian Journal*, 3 October, 1835, 575.

crew a strong motive to mutiny and dispose of him.[41] But, despite rumours of his demise, according to the editor of *The* Perth Gazette, 'no information was ever laid before the authorities'. This may mean that he perished from natural causes or from foul play, but it is difficult to confirm. His reputation as a pirate may be more myth than fact. He developed an ability to live on the margins of colonial society, beyond the reach of the authorities, and operated a significant enterprise as a black entrepreneur who had the respect of his crews, even if this was obtained by force and duress.

There have been at least two fictional accounts about Black-Jack, which add to the mystery and notoriety that surround him.[42] He is known to have had several differing reputations: as one of Australia's most notorious pirates, as a petty criminal, as a participant in a resistance practice against colonial authority, or he may have just been a successful maritime entrepreneur. He is arguably the sealer that best fits the description of criminality portrayed in the general historical discourse about those I describe as mariners on the margins.

Tucker, Briggs, Munro and Anderson were seeking a living, and sometimes adventure, from participating in the sealing trade. They lived far from most settled communities and away from the scrutiny of colonial authority. They were operating often in a cross-cultural network with Australasian First Nations peoples while exploring the coastlines and islands that made up much of the Fishery. At the same time, they were thumbing their noses at the mainstream traders who had often treated them poorly. From the late 1790s until about 1840, these men were participants in, and observers of, the demise of many First Nations people and the seal populations. The lives lived by the maritime characters described in this chapter were chosen as somewhat representative of the Antipodean sealing industry but are far from the only stakeholders. All the marginal mariners referred to in this chapter figure prominently throughout this work.

---

[41] *The Perth Gazette and Western Australian Journal*, viewed on 21 12 2015 at http://trove.nla.gov.au.
[42] Sarah Hays. Skins, and Elaine Forrestal, *Black Jack Anderson*.

While most chapters in this book focus on the traders, masters and sealers, no history of this period can be properly contemplated without reference to the First Nations men and women participating with the colonial mariners in the trade. They very rarely have a voice in that history. The sealers learned much from the First Nations peoples right across the southern Antipodes. This learning was not only about the methodologies involved in procuring seals but also about long-term survival in the difficult and harsh environments. Some Indigenous men and women played key roles as partners or crews on whaleboats supporting the sealers and, in some cases, such as Tommy Chaseland, went on to operate their own enterprises. Others, like the female warrior Walyer, endeavoured to protect their people and culture from the increasing violence that was being perpetrated against her nation, mainly by white settlers. She also sought, to some extent, the protection and assistance of the sealers in difficult times. After the early profitable sealing period, it would be the Australasian First Nations peoples who would increasingly occupy important roles in not only the industry but the cross-cultural networks and hybrid cultures that would emerge from it. The experience, knowledge and practical methodologies employed by First Nations peoples to hunt seals and passed on to European mariners were primarily acquired prior to the arrival of the colonizers. After all, it was these peoples who had procured seals for millennia.

Chapter 3: Diving into the Deep Past

Flensing[1] seals for their skins and oil by colonial mariners as a commodity to trade was somewhat inevitable. The colonists were aware, following the reports received from Dutch explorers in the 17th century, and later Cook and other English mariners, that seal rookeries existed in the Antipodes.[2] Even before the Bishop voyage, anonymous sealers had been procuring pinnipeds but probably had kept their locations a secret. Also, "intelligence" may have been passed onto colonisers by First Nations inhabitants on first encounter or as these local people visited the various settlements. But once Bass and Flinders undertook their now famous voyage to Van Diemen's Land, they provided the mainstream colonizers with glowing descriptions that would have excited the entrepreneurs.

In about October 1798, on his return from the Straits, the great navigator provided this to his colonial supporters:

> The rocks toward the sea were covered with Fur Seals of great beauty. This species of seal seemed to approach nearest to that named by naturalists, the Falkland Island seal.[3]

Of greater relevance is Flinders' observations when finding these mammals at The Patriarchs:

> the seals .... seemed to be the lords of the domain. Mr. Bass revealed with surprise... the males, who possessed a rock to themselves, where they sat surrounded by their numerous wives and progeny, on us drawing near to them, hobbled up with a

---

[1] The removal of the skins from the body of the animal but normally associated with whaling.
[2] In 1629 and 1727 respectively, the survivors of the two Dutch vessels, the *Batavia* and *Zeewijk*, both wrecked off the Western Australian coast, ate sea lions to survive. Later, in 1642, Abel Tasman observed a seal in the Great Australian Bight. In 1773, Cook reported seals off the New Zealand Coast. John Hunter in the Sirius also recorded seals off the Tasmanian coast in 1788.

> menacing roar... the seal is reckoned a stupid animal but Mr. Bass noticed many signs of sagacity in them... the seal appeared to branch off into various species... he did not recollect to have seen them previously alike upon any two islands in the strait, most were of that kind, called by the sealers, hair seals but they differed in the shape of the body or of the head, the situation of the fore fins, the color and very commonly in the voice, as if they spoke a peculiar language...[4]

This insightful statement suggests some fondness for the mammal. It also implies that sealers had by the late 1790s already been fishing in that region, unimpeded by anyone.

Equally so were the journal entries made by James Kelly when anchoring near King George Island off the north-west coast of Van Diemen's Land in January 1816. The sealers had exchanged some seal carcases for kangaroo skins in a friendly barter with the local First Nations inhabitants. But the next day the locals wanted more. Briggs, who was one of the few colonisers fluent in the local language, informed chief Tolobunganah that the seals were becoming 'scarce'. The 'old chief', realising the lack of skills displayed by the mariners, suggested using some of the local women to 'assist' in the hunt.

After agreement was reached, several women were chosen. They jumped enthusiastically into the whaleboat and accompanied the mariners in their quest. Keen to display their prowess, the First Nations people demonstrated an ancient cultural practice they had developed as expert seal hunters by mimicking the behaviour of the pinnipeds to lull them into a false sense of security. They swam out to the seals on rocks without seeking any help from the colonial men. The seals, basking on the rocks, turned their heads to smell the new creatures now lying beside them in the sun and ignored them, scratching themselves. After waiting for some time, the women rose up and clubbed the mammals, conveying the carcases through the surf to the boat. When they arrived back on shore, the women went to a hill and made a fire. Smoke billowed into the air which operated as a signal to their people that they had caught their prey.

---

[4] Matthew Flinders. *A Voyage to Terra Australis*, Vol. 2, cxxix.

This was answered by a corresponding smoke signal from afar.[5]

The two colonial observations referred to above are descriptive of both the prey being sought by the sealers and the pre-colonial seal hunting practices of one of the local people that procured seals as part of their culture. Unfortunately, there has been a lack of focus on the seal itself and the First Nations pre-colonial involvement as sealers in their own right in the historiography. Much of the written history that deals with the subject of the early colonizers sealing experience does not pay due regard to the culture and methodologies used by First Nations peoples to exploit the mammals prior to the first cross cultural encounters on the littoral frontiers. Missing is also any focus on the object of the sealing industry: the seal itself.

The word seal is generic in nature and refers to all pinnipeds, phocids, otariids and obodenids, although true seals are regarded as the 'phocids'.[6] There are several species of seals inhabiting the coastal marine environments of Australia and New Zealand. These mammals can be broadly categorised as Australian fur seals,[7] New Zealand fur seals and sea lions, although other species have ventured from further regions into this environment.[8]

When the colonial ships' captains and sealers first explored the islands around Tasmania, there were vast numbers of elephant seals inhabiting these areas.[9] It is now also known that there may have been ancient species of the seals still called 'monachines', which were smaller than their modern counterparts. They were similar to monk seals that exist in the waters of the Mediterranean. These more primitive southern seals lived apparently three million years ago in the Port Phillp Bay area near Melbourne, but little is known of them as the fossil evidence is not overwhelming.

---

[5] Bowden, 40-41.
[6] Roger Kirkwood and Simon Goldsworthy, *Fur Seals and Sea Lions*,18.
[7] *Arctocephalus pusillus odoriferus, Arctophoca fordsteri* and *Neophoca cinerea* are the scientific names that apply to these animals.
[8] For example, the Southern elephant seals originate from Macquarie and Heard Islands; Leopard Seals from Antarctica; Crabeater, Weddell, Ross, Sub-Antarctic and Antarctic Fur Seals in Antarctic and Sub-Antarctic waters.
[9] The elephant seal is scientifically classified as *Mirounga leonina* and is the largest of all seals, with adult males weighing up to 3,500 kilograms.

As a general rule, seals live in herds called rookeries. They thrive in and around littoral environments particularly on rocky outcrops and boulders surrounded by water and on beaches. The Australian fur seals inhabit the rocky shores around Tasmania, southern Victoria and South Australia. Occasionally, this species will be found as far west as Esperance and as far north as Port Macquarie. They come ashore at these locations from September, with females arriving later to breed. The pups are born in the summer months when the food supply is abundant. The males are larger than the females, often weighing up to 100 kilograms. They have large sharp teeth similar to those of large dogs or bears, and their bite can cause serious injury as experienced by unwary sealers in colonial times. By January, the males have departed, leaving the females to feed the pups for some months. The New Zealand variety's mating season commences later in spring. This species is also found off the south-west coast of Tasmania. Sealing crews were well aware of these facts and adjusted their activities to what they called the 'sealing season' accordingly.

In general terms, the seal is a carnivore, having adapted its thoracic and pelvic appendages to enable it to more efficiently glide through water. The mammal thrives in a rocky marine and, to some extent, a coastal environment. It has certain distinct characteristics. These include its elongated and spindle-shaped body, relatively symmetrical trunk, internal sexual organs, and a thick layer of fatty blubber beneath the skin, covering its whole trunk. Their bodies are adapted for speed, enhanced by their flippers, particularly the hind limbs, which propel the animal through the water. Their ability to catch prey is assisted by their flexibility and the strength of their necks. The Australian fur seal can dive to depths of up to 200 meters in pursuit of the fish, octopuses and squid that are their primary diet. The main predator that a seal has to avoid now is the shark. In the colonial period, it was humans. In that regard, its agility in the water makes it difficult for man to catch it in the ocean, but on land and/or close to the ocean's edge it is a different matter. This is because it is restricted on land.[10] As a seal's limbs

---

[10] Nigel Bonner. *The Natural History of Seals*, 9.

cannot support its weight out of the water, it must heave its body on land. It does this by using its forelimbs, or by way of a humping action, wriggling along to gain propulsion. Gaining momentum through this wriggling, the seal can build up speed.

The agility of the seal is also dependent on its senses. Although less effective on land, a seal's eyesight is highly valuable to its success in the wild. A seal on land can identify a predator, including man, by any slight movement. To do this, it will frequently raise its head to scan the surrounding environment. Light is limited or almost non-existent in the water, so a seal is reliant on touch, hearing and smell. Unfortunately, not much is known about a seal's sense of smell.[11] That sense is presumed to be a necessary component of the seal's armoury in seeking prey and defending itself from attack. Of more importance are its senses of touch and hearing. Sound travels faster and more effectively in the water and seals are alive to its effects. In addition, the seal uses its touch, including the use of whiskers, in low light conditions to sense and source food.

It became clear early on in our colonial history that the seal is a relatively intelligent mammal. When Flinders circumnavigated Australia in 1802, he anchored in the refurbished warship *Investigator* at Kangaroo Island. Apart from the plethora of kangaroos inhabiting the shoreline, he observed numerous seals located around its coast.[12] Flinders and his crew caught many seals, with the skins employed creatively in rigging on the vessel. But one seal took exception to the mariner Richard Staley. When approaching a colony of seals on the island among rocks with his wooden club, Staley came too close to one before striking at it. The seal latched onto his lower leg and bit into it. Blood spurted out everywhere, and the sealer fell to the ground crying out in severe pain. His crew successfully intervened and treated his leg as best they could with limited medical knowledge, but Staley was never the same, and apparently maimed for life. Sealers, like Robert Wyld, referred to earlier, and Staley were both bitten and severely disabled by male seals. They were among several who faced

---

[11] Bonner, 17.

[12] The island was unihabited by humans, and so wildlife thrived.

the possibility of a slow and agonising death if they had not been treated properly. Humans that were subject to injury and death by seal attacks included First Nations people evidenced by narratives given to Robinson by Woorady in 1831.

Flinders, though, was more interested in the seals. He thought they were more intelligent than kangaroos. Demonstrating his sense of humour, he wrote:

> Never perhaps had the Dominion possessed here by the kanguroos[13] been invaded before this time. The seals shared with it upon the shores, but they seem to dwell amicably together... The Seal, indeed, seemed to be much the more discerning of the two; for its actions bespoke of knowledge of our not being kanguroos, whereas the kanguroos not infrequently appear to consider us to be seals.[14]

Apart from observing the behaviour of the pinnipeds, the explorer noticed how fertile the land was compared to any region that he had chanced upon across the Great Australian Bight and was surprised to learn there was no sign of any human occupation. No wonder the seals and kangaroos were easy prey to his crew!

But Kangaroo Island was only one of many places in the Antipodes where seals thrived and came to be exploited by the sealers in the period considered. The pinnipeds established themselves in the Southern Hemisphere around 40 million years ago, and the ancestors of the sea lions colonised the Southern Fishery 4-6 million years ago. The predecessors of the New Zealand variety of fur seal arrived during the last million years and the Australian fur seal first inhabited the Australasia via an African ancestor some 18,000 to 12,000 years ago.[15] Humans, who adapted themselves to a marine environment, in New Holland, New Zealand and elsewhere, started procuring the mammals as a resource well before

---

[13] The Indigenous people of Northern Queensland called the marsupial Gangurru meaning large black hopping animal although some other academics have written that it meant 'I don't know' which is unlikely. Cook described the marsupial in his journals but had difficulty settling on the spelling for the animal naming it 'Kangooroo or Kanguru or Kangura.

[14] Matthew Flinders. *A Voyage to Terra Australis,* Chapter VII, Tuesday 23 March 1802, Vol. 1, 172.

[15] Kirkwood and Goldsworthy, 11.

the arrival of the colonists in the Antipodes.

It is reasonable to assume that the exploitation of seals by early man was an attractive proposition, even without the advanced Western technology used by colonial mariners. Those colonisers who first encountered the original inhabitants of the southern Antipodes were first-hand observers of the pre-colonial sealing practices and cultures undertaken by First Nations peoples. They found that, for local peoples, the seal was a mammal large enough to feed a family for some time. Not only that but it provided oil that could be rubbed on bodies for warmth or used for cooking and lighting in conjunction with fire. In addition, the skins were sliced off the carcases and wrapped around shoulders and torsos providing an additional level of comfort in cold climates. Some huts were also partly cloaked with them. Moreover, the seal did not pose the same danger that more aggressive and ferocious land animals did. Of more importance was the fact that the mammal was easily speared, clubbed or incapacitated when immobile on rocks or shores. The migratory patterns of the pinnipeds were closely monitored by First Nations people, who developed hunting weapons, craft and methodologies designed to slaughter the mammals during what they termed 'the proper' season.

Hunting seals was a communal activity in the widest sense of the word. This meant that a nation would organise to build huts and/or camps close to the places where seals would congregate at certain times of the year. Sometimes, other nations would be invited to join in the sealing venture or to act independently following invitations given to them by a neighbouring clan. Often watercraft was employed in regions where nations built such vessels. After setting up camp, men would construct canoes out of bark, tied with ligatures with resin acting as waterproofing. In Australia, the women would be employed in manoeuvring these vessels to paddle to rocks away from shorelines where the rookeries were located. In other locations, where no canoes or rafts were used, the natives would swim to these rookeries and lull the seals into a false sense of security.

Mariners on the Margins

Once the seals were clubbed or speared, they were immediately taken to the expectant crowd on the beach. There the mammal was flensed, and the skin removed with stone cutters. The carcass was then cut up into chunks and thrown onto a fire and partly cooked. Hungry families would then devour the part raw food. After they consumed the seal meat, the oil of the animal would be rubbed over their bodies. Generally, nothing of the seal was left over. In Australia, the pre-colonial sealing ventures and culture associated with it had been incorporated into each nation's Dreamtime, handed down by the ancestors and adopted religiously.[16]

In the Antipodes, there is not much written historical evidence to demonstrate when seals were first exploited by man, although there was some First Nations oral narrative to rely on. At Rocky Cape on the north-west coast of *Trowunna*,[17] archaeologists found two caves with material evidencing the local people hunted seals from about 8000 years ago. Here, remains of the pinnipeds were found in deep middens. More recently, ancient seal bones were discovered in middens on the western side of the island near West Point. Archaeologists believe that the Northwest peoples established villages and temporary dwellings in this region during the breeding season to take advantage of seal colonies arriving and thriving in that location. Those same experts believe that seals were often killed on shore except when the women, with their swimming skills, disposed of them in the water.

In pre-colonial times, all along the western coast of *Trowunna*, in the Tarkine region, the Peerapper peoples lived in semi-sedentary camps and moved about as the seasons changed. They built large domed huts constructed of timber, plant material and hides. This accommodation was suitable to house more than 10 men women and children over several months to take advantage of the marine life, including seals sheltering in the bays, rocks and beaches.

---

[16] The Dreamtime concept has been described as "a complex code for how life is to be lived, how food is to be gathered and how marriage, trade and disputes are to be regulated. It recognises that people are part of the land they inhabit, and the land is part of the people. In Dreamtime, all of the past present and future exist at the one time. The anthropologist William E.H. Stanner called it 'everywhen.'

[17] One First Nations' word for Tasmania.

These people inhabited only the narrow coastal strip of western Tasmania but allowed inland nations onto Country with whom they exchanged precious ochres for seals and other seafood. They possessed watercraft like canoes, rafts and, apparently catamarans, which enabled them to voyage from the mainland over to Robbins and Hunter Islands in pursuit of the pinnipeds and mutton birds. In particular, during the summer months, they sought out the elephant seals around Sandy Cape.

It appears that the people developed a special system based on catching seals, shellfish and fauna rather than boned fish as there is little nor no evidence of the latter in the various sites. This has been confirmed by the discovery of seal bones, shells, stone tools and relics in several depressions made in middens in the sands on cobble beaches.

A seal elephant colony noted by Plomley at West Point (known as *nongor*) was a target for the First Nations people to gather in summer at that place in ancient times. The specialized sedentary nature of these sites seems to also have been replicated along the southern Victorian coasts. Sites where the villages stood have been recorded for posterity on maps provided by the Australian Government as a permanent reminder of this pre-Colonial past.[18] The prominence of the west coast region of Tasmania as a location for the gathering together of the Peerapper people was noted by Professor Lyndall Ryan as well.[19] But it was not only the Northwest nation that maintained a strong desire to catch the pinnipeds. There were several coastal nations in Van Diemen's Land who exploited the sea for food. Firstly, vast numbers of fur seals were located along the southwest, northeast and northwest coasts of Tasmania, and arguably made up a significant part of the hunters' diet in the warmer months.[20] Secondly, the Nuenonne people of Bruny Island were keen fishers. In December 1831, Woorady, a prominent First Nations storyteller, sat around a fire with G.A.

---

[18] See Report: "Western Tasmania Aboriginal Cultural Landscape," Arthur River Rd, Arthur River, TAS, 13 February, 2013.

[19] Lyndall Ryan, *Tasmanian Aborigines*, 37.

[20] Lyndall Ryan, 'The Struggle for Recognition: Part-Aborigines in Bass Strait in the Nineteenth Century," in *Aboriginal History*, 1977, 29-30.

Robinson. While entertaining his listeners about stories of hunting prowess, he informed the Conciliator that his tribe 'subsisted in a great measure on the seal of which they were very fond'. But, just like several unfortunate sealers, hunting them was not without risk. He gave examples of frequent attacks by seals on the hunters. These included pinnipeds who "flew" at tribesmen, dragging them under the water, biting legs, and, in one case, breaking an arm.

Apart from the results of archaeological digs, there are also both the oral stories told by First Nations descendants in song and dance as well as the observations on first encounter that provide us with information about pre-colonial sealing. Woorady confirmed how fundamental the seas were for the First Nations peoples when Robinson recorded this statement:

> Those nations to the southward of this island was (sic) a maritime people. Their catamarans was large, the size of a whaleboat, carrying 7 or 8 people their dogs and spears. The men sit in front, the women behind.

Prior to the full impact of colonisation, colonial explorers and traders, in early encounters, recorded their observations of local peoples employing marine vessels, mainly canoes and rafts, to catch seals in Tasmanian and mainland southeastern waters. The sealers who first sought to exploit the pinnipeds in Bass Strait were successful in establishing trading relationships firstly in the northeast by mariners such as George Briggs and later in the northwest of Van Diemen's Land. Local clans would arrive at locations they knew the mariners would visit including Cape Portland, often in November. The colonisers would be welcomed before a ceremonial dance was performed for their benefit and then trade negotiations would begin. An exchange of women for seals, dogs and other commodities would take place. Like Kelly's crew, other mariners realised how skilful the women were as sealers and adopted some of the practices used by the First Nations people not only in procuring the pinnipeds but also to survive. In their encounters with the Tasmanian people, they observed first-hand the watercraft that each nation utilised to access islands off the mainland where seals predominated.

While First Nations people inhabiting the Queensland littoral environment constructed the dugout and stitched bark seafaring canoes, their southern counterparts adopted a different approach. using a 'folded end' bark canoe unsuitable for sea travel, They employed an ancient bark technology dating back 7,000 years, which was implemented in making watercraft in and around coastal lakes, estuaries and bays. On the other hand, the Tasmanians were more adventurous. The First Nations people used reeds and bark tied together with vegetable fibre cords in a criss-crossed secured pattern in their manufacture of their canoes.[21] They became familiar with the currents, tides and weather conditions in voyaging out to islands to procure seals and mutton birds. There is speculation that the First Nations peoples use of seafaring craft came to prominence about 6,000 years ago. Realising they needed a team to pursue the seals, Aboriginal Tasmanians constructed canoes designed to carry up to eight people 'with dogs and spears'.[22]

The early colonial French explorer Antoine Bruni D'Entrecasteaux, described a Tasmanian water vessel while exploring the island in the early 1790s:

> On the edge of our little bight, we had found some kinds of pirogues, seven to nine feet in length, equally flat at the bottom as at the top. They measured three or four foot in the middle, becoming narrower at the extremities and finishing up in a point. They were constructed with very thick tree bark, assembled and tied across their length with reeds and other ligneous herbs. They are in fact very small rafts, which have been given the shape of a pirogue [canoe].[23]

The watercraft observed by the Frenchman would have been constructed locally by the men for general use.

In most colonial Western societies, it was the men who seemed to be the main fishers. There are very few references to Western women hunting marine life during this period. In stark contrast

---

[21] Dr Stan Florek, *Tentative Chronology of Indigenous Canoes of Eastern Australia*, 26 June 2012.
[22] There is some speculation that Indigenous boat and canoe designs may have been copied from those of Southeast Asia going back more than 50,000 years.
[23] Edward Duyker and Maryse Duyker (eds). *Bruny D'Entrecasteaux Voyages to Australia and the Pacific 1791 to 1793*, 55.

is the reality of pre-colonial exploitation of the sea, particularly around the coastal environments of southern Australia. While the men constructed the canoes used in seal hunting, such as those described above, it was mainly the women who caught them. Once the colonial sealers discovered the dexterity displayed by these women in hunting marine life, it was almost a fait accompli that they would utilise their services. There is no better example of how the mariners exploited the skills of First Nations women to procure seals than that in Kelly's account written after his circumnavigation of Van Diemen's Land in 1816.[24]

When Kelly and his crew visited the First Nations clever man and leader, Tolobunganah in early January, the mariners had been trying to fish for the mammals with no real success for some weeks. The harbour master wrote that Briggs had:

> ... gone over from the island to Cape Portland to barter for kangaroo skins with the natives, and also to purchase the young grown up females to keep them as their wives, whom they employed, as they were wonderfully dexterous in hunting kangaroo and catching seals.[25]

On his return, Briggs complained to 'Tolo' (named as such by the illiterate sealers) they were frustrated trying to catch seals due to their scarcity at the time. The chief helped George solve his dilemma by selecting the stronger women of his nation to assist the mariners. Kelly wrote that the chief:

> ... considered that we had better take some women over to the island to assist in catching them, as they were very dexterous at sealing. Tolo ordered six stout women into the boat. They obeyed with alacrity, evidently delighted at the prospect of the trip... The women perceiving some seals on the outer rocks were anxious to commence operations.[26]

Then Kelly graphically described the methodology and skill employed by these 'assistants':

---

[24] Kelly's notes and records of the voyage were printed in serial form in the *Hobart Town Courier* in 1854 and reprinted as a parliamentary paper in 1881.
[25] K. M. Bowden, 37.
[26] Bowden, 40.

> We gave the women each a club that we had used to kill the seals with. They went to the water's edge and wet themselves all over their heads and bodies, which operation they said would keep the seals from smelling them as they walked along the rocks. They were very cautious not to go windward of them, as they said 'a seal would sooner believe his nose than his eyes when a man or woman came near him'… Two women went to each rock with their clubs in hand, crept closely up to a seal each, and lay down with their clubs alongside. Some of the seals lifted their heads up to inspect their new visitors and smell them. The seals scratched themselves and lay down again.
>
> The women went through the same motions as the seal, still imitating every movement as nearly as possible. After they had lain upon the rocks for nearly an hour, the sea occasionally washing over them… all of a sudden, the women rose up in their seats, their clubs lifted up at arm's length, each struck the seals on the nose and killed him in an instant, they all jumped up as if by magic and killed one more each.[27]

It was clear from Kelly's and his crew's observations that the women had talents other than seal hunting:

> The women then commenced to cook their supper, each cutting a shoulder of the young seals… They simply threw them on the fire to cook and when about half done commenced devouring them and rubbed the oil on their skins, remarking that they had had a glorious meal.[28]

The killing of a seal had other purposes than simply to feed a tribe or clan. Basically, all of mammal was put to use. In particular, the use of the oil to cover bodies helped warm them and prevent chills and sickness from developing in harsh conditions. This practice often offended mainstream colonizers as it gave off unpleasant odours and smells but still served its primary protective purpose.

Over the next few days, the sealers secured the employment of the women where possible to hunt seals. They realized they would have much more success by utilising the female hunters than if they tried catching the pinnipeds by themselves. The activity noted by Kelly was replicated elsewhere in Van Diemen's Land. For example,

---

[27] Bowden, 41.
[28] Ibid, 41.

on the far south coast of Van Diemen's Land at Maatsukyer Island, Australian men had been constructing canoes at a bay opposite the island for generations. Their role then ceased as it was the female hunters who used the finished watercraft as a means of voyaging to the island and catching seals to feed their families.[29]

After a successful catch, the First Nations people would celebrate on shores by performing ceremonies involving the beating of skin drums to the sound of singing and the stamping of feet in dances that had been performed for centuries. Often, the ceremonies would be given a name derived from the nature of the activity that was being celebrated, such as the seal, emu, kangaroo and later, horse dance. This cultural practice was observed by the Kelly gang in 1816, when, several days after sharing the half-cooked seals with the mariners, Briggs informed Tolo the chief that they had to depart the next morning. According to the master, the local inhabitants all began to cry. By this time, several women had been employed in procuring seals, which they accomplished not only by boat but in swimming out to the islands in pursuit of prey. On hearing the wailing come from the assembled multitude, the chief called his entire nation of more than 300 people down to the beach. On his signal, they formed up into three lines of men, women and children and commenced to dance.

Kelly observed of this ancient cultural practice:

> The women in the centre division began a song, and joining their hands, formed a circle, dancing round the heap of dead seals. They then threw themselves upon the ground, putting themselves into the most grotesque attitudes, beating the lower parts of their bodies with their hands, and kicking the sand over each other with their feet. …The men then commenced a sort of sham fight with spears and waddies dancing afterwards around the heap of seals and sticking their spears into them as if they were killing them. The game lasted about an hour.[30]

The very close cultural connection that First Nations women had with seals was further reflected in oral story telling. Tales were told

---

[29] See Cassandra Pybus, *Truganini. Journey through the Apocalypse* (St Leonards: Allen & Unwin 2020), 33. Seal bones have also been found on the island hundreds of metres below sea level predating European encounters by centuries.
[30] Bowden, 42-43.

whereby the females involved would deposit seal flippers into holes dug beneath their huts celebrating a successful catch. The experience noted by Kelly would be repeated not only on the Taswegian coasts but also elsewhere during the early colonial sealing years.

The women and men that inhabited Van Diemen's Land were not the only First Nations people who had developed methodologies to procure seals. In Western Australia, different practices were adopted along the coasts by the Noongar peoples to catch what they called the *manyina*. Over at King Georges Sound, the main types of pinnipeds that abounded were the New Zealand fur seal and the Australian sea lion, although other species were also present. The intrepid naval officer, hydrographer and surveyor Philip Parker King had voyaged to that region in the cutter *Mermaid* in 1818 but without coming into contact with the local people. King led a second mission to explore and survey the Sound in the 170-ton brig, *The Bathurst*, accompanied by Blundell, a seasoned and very useful First Nations mariner. He anchored there again on Christmas Day, 1821. At the time, there had only been a few explorers and gangs of sealers who had visited the region.

Parker King had the opportunity to observe and write about the Noongar procuring and eating a seal and some cultural practices associated with these activities:

> Finding we had no intention of sending a boat for them they amused themselves in fishing. Two of them were watching a small seal that, having been left by the tide on the bank, was endeavouring to waddle towards the deep water; at last one of the natives, fixing his spear in its throwing-stick, advanced very cautiously and, when within ten or twelve yards, lanced it, and pierced the animal through the neck, when the other instantly ran up and stuck his spear into it also, and then beating it about the head with a small hammer very soon despatched it.
>
> This event collected the whole tribe to the spot, who assisted in landing their prize and washing the sand off the body; they then carried the animal to their fire at the edge of the grass and began to devour it even before it was dead. Curiosity induced Mr. Cunningham and myself to view this barbarous feast and we landed about ten minutes after it had commenced... Ongoing

> to the place we found an old man seated over the remains of the carcass, two-thirds of which had already disappeared; he was holding a long strip of the raw flesh in his left hand, and tearing it off the body with a sort of knife; a boy was also feasting with him and both were too intent upon their breakfast to notice us or to be the least disconcerted at our looking on. We however were very soon satisfied and walked away perfectly disgusted with the sight of so horrible a repast, and the intolerable stench occasioned by the effluvia that arose from the dying animal, combined with that of the bodies of the natives who had daubed themselves from head to foot with a pigment made of a red ochreous earth mixed up with seal-oil.[31]

It is worthwhile noting that, for First Nations inhabitants here, the slaughter of a seal was also a communal and cultural activity that involved many hands. Also, it is striking how the methodology employed to kill the mammal was similar to but not precisely that which many coastal Australasians resorted to throughout the Fishery. King wrote about the weaponry, including spears, hammers and knives used by the local inhabitants and how they were specifically adapted for seal hunting.[32] Despite the explorer being revolted by the use and smell of seal oil smeared over bodies, it was a friendly encounter, no doubt facilitated by Blundell, who had been chosen partly for his skill as an interpreter even though he would have been totally unfamiliar with their native tongue:

> Their faces and sometimes their whole bodies were daubed over with a mixture of seal oil and red pigment that caused a most disgusting effluvia; but the only colouring matter that our friend Jack used, after his acquaintance with us, was the carpenter's chalk, which he thought particularly ornamental.

Across the Tasman Sea, the local Māori, who had arrived in *Aotearoa* from about 1250 AD, came bringing a seafaring culture and economy. From then on, throughout that region, and down to first colonial encounters and beyond, marine creatures, including the seal, were the most prominent form of meat consumed in the people's diet. Although sealing was an activity pursued throughout

---
[31] Phillip Parker King. *Narrative of a Survey of the Intertropical and Western Coasts of Australia*, Vol. 2, 126.
[32] Either he or one of his crew drew pictures of these objects which became part of his narrative.

the waters of the coastal regions of the two islands, the hunt for the pinnipeds predominated in the central and southern regions. Accordingly, my focus is on that region.

By the time Cook anchored in Pickersgill Harbour in *Tamatea* at the most southerly tip of the South Island in 1773, there was a limited amount of sedentary sealing activity being pursued by the Māori. In journals kept by Cook and some of his crew, there is reference to only about four huts on islands in the Sound occupied by up to 20 'permanent residents', according to the archaeologist P.J.F. Coutts in 1969.[33] This may have been because the explorer arrived there in late autumn when the weather had cooled, and the conditions were difficult for human occupation.

To access the Sound, most Māori seafarers lived in more hospitable conditions and would have had to voyage there by use of sophisticated watercraft they had constructed for centuries. These included the more stable and substantial prow-like canoes called the *waka tete* and large rafts, which were part of their maritime culture. In these craft, the Māori accessed the islands inhabited by the seals.[34] In the Foveaux Straits, the local peoples relied on catching fish for their very survival. When Abel Tasman explored the south coast of New Zealand in December 1642 in the *Heemskerk*, he was both alarmed and surprised when two vessels joined together, carrying 13 First Nations men, rowed within a stone's throw of his vessel in Murdering Bay.

He described the vessel in the following terms:

> Their boats consisted of two long narrow prows side by side, over which a number of planks or other seats were placed in such a way that those above can look through the water underneath the vessel: their paddles are upwards of a fathom in length, narrow and pointed at the end; with these vessels they could make considerable speed.[35]

Later, seven boats, including one containing 17 men, left the shore in pursuit of the Dutchmen, after some of their comrades had been killed by irate local inhabitants.

---

[33] Peter Coutts, "The Māori of Dusky Sound: a review of the historical sources," in the *Journal of Polynesian Society,* Vol. 78, no. 2, June,1969, 194.

[34] A seal is known as *hiri* in the Māori language.

[35] Jan Ernst Heeres (ed.) *Abel Janszoon Tasman's Journal*, reviewed at 19.

When the First Nation mariners anchored in the Dusky Sound islands and bays, such as Facile Harbour and Sealer's Cove, they would erect semi-circular huts. These were constructed of such wood and bark that was either carried on board or available locally. Pits were dug and fires lit in front of the huts, and it was from these temporary littoral places that they would operate for a few months of the year.

The sealing master Wiliam Raven, one of the first European to set up camp in the region, observed the Māori canoes and huts when he arrived in the Sound in 1793. He noticed that they employed bone hooks and flax netting in their pursuit of marine life. When he visited several coves and bays in the region, he found huts were generally about four feet high and six feet wide that had been built and occasionally occupied by Māori. Caves were also a haunt for local seafarers as temporary dwellings.

Once a seal was killed, it was flensed and the carcass cooked and eaten. Skins and oil were then used as clothing and for warmth as was the case over in Tasmania. Occupation mainly occurred in the summer months. Archaeological evidence has established that a wide range of prey was sought, continually over the centuries using fishing gear which included fishhooks made of seal teeth.[36] Apart from the pinnipeds, many varieties of birds, rats and dogs were consumed including mutton birds. According to one archaeologist, 'birding' formed a major part of the hunting activity of the Māori in that region and had some similarities to that pursued by the First Nations people in Van Diemen's Land.

Further east near the limits of the Fishery, the Moriori peoples on the Chatham Islands had, since 1500 CE, adopted a sustainable and restrictive practice in fishing for the many varieties of the pinnipeds that inhabited the rocks surrounding the two islands. They sought seals and marine birds, which formed their staple diet as there was little on the islands by way of fauna or vegetation to sustain them. The islanders imposed a cultural and religious code

---

[36] See for example archaeologist Ian Smith's article "Māori, Pakeha and Kiwi: Peoples, cultures and sequence in New Zealand archaeology," in G. Clark, F. Leach and S. O'Connor (eds.) Islands of Inquiry: Colonisation, Seafaring and the Archaeology of Maritime Landscapes. *Terra Australis 29*, 2008, 370.

that limited the killing and prevented over-exploitation of the mammals. Although Lieutenant William Robert Broughton of Gloucestershire was the first European to encounter the islands on 29 November 1791 in the British brig *Chatham*, it took a further 13 years for sealing crews from Port Jackson and Hobart to take advantage of the seal rookeries there.[37] The local people had been isolated from most other peoples for centuries and had developed strong kinship and other systems to ensure their maritime resources were never depleted. That changed after 1800.

For it was the case that before the arrival of the maritime colonisers in the Antipodes there had been little impact on seal populations. The First Nations peoples of New Holland, Van Diemen's Land and elsewhere, who procured seals for food, clothing, light and warmth had done little to adversely affect their environments. The First Nations peoples living across the wide expanse of the Fishery were not in the habit of depleting seal rookeries. They generally depended on procuring the mammals for their own personal use and that of their families and adopted sustainable economic and cultural practices. There may have been some trade, barter or exchange systems in place prior to colonial sealing. These arrangements occurred between nations or neighbours where invitations were extended to share in the spoils as a sign of amity. This is borne out by the observations of the colonisers and European navigators and explorers once they encountered the seals inhabiting the rocks, bays and beaches across the southern Antipodes. First Nations peoples used their knowledge of the seal habits to ensure the mammal was not over exploited.

In contrast with these sustainable practices, the gangs of sealers employed by avaricious masters sought to make quick fortunes for themselves and the Sydney Traders and had an almost immediate adverse impact on the Fishery. Once "intelligence" was disseminated to these traders about the seasonal, migratory and breeding habits of the mammals and the knowledge that seal skins and oil could command significant prices in the Asian and European markets,

---

[37] Sealing crews employed by Lord Underwood and Kable in vessels such as the Antipode and Commerce were the first to visit from about 1804.

it was open slather. The seal populations were quickly depleted by the mariners over a few years in three key periods. But there was another factor at play. Unlike whaling and other marine enterprises that were expensive and inconvenient to operate, what made these mariners occupation much easier to implement, in these otherwise testing environments, was the relatively cheap technology that could be utilised in the industry, allowing the sealers to easily butcher these mammals. That as well as the ease by which the mammals could be disposed.

The docility of the mammals was noted by Cook, while in charge of the *Resolution*, writing that the seals…*were all so tame or rather so stupid as to suffer us to come so near as to knock them down with a stick.*[38]

Once the Sydney Traders discovered the pinniped rookeries, the seals became scarce over the course of about 12 years.[39]

---

[38] See Alan Moorhead, *The Fatal Impact*. (Harmondsworth Middlesex: Penguin Books,1966), 238.
[39] John Robert. McNeill (ed.), "Environmental History in the Pacific World," in *The Pacific World,* Vol. 2, 82.

Chapter 4: A Polyglot Cluster of Maritime Peoples

In November 1820, the Russian explorer, Captain Thaddeus von Bellingshausen, in command of the corvette *Vostok*, anchored off Macquarie Island. Coming ashore he and his Russian crew encountered some sealers. He noticed they had some 'rowing boats' and were 'engaged in melting down blubber of seal elephants' in a metal container. As he spoke to the mariners, it became clear to the captain that these men had been on the island well beyond the length of time retained under their articles. The explorer described barrels with iron hoops and mud huts with fixed doors. He wrote about men disposing of sleeping seals with ease, using wooden clubs with metal bolts to strike them across their noses. These weapons were four and a half feet long, two inches thick, with bell-shaped ends studded with sharp nails. Once the seals were killed, he was present when the mariners cut off their blubber and dropped it into a boiler. The oil produced was poured into barrels, some of which were shipped to Port Jackson and the remainder to London, 'where it command[ed] a very remunerative price', according to the Russian.

Bellingshausen developed a friendly arrangement with the mariners and rewarded them with some provisions, including rum which was always much sought after. The men were by then feeding off the flippers of young elephant seals, penguin (and other bird) eggs, and any adult birds that they could kill 'with a stick', as they had run out of food. These birds were likely to have been shearwaters and penguins, which had flocked to breed on the island. To catch prey, the men informed the Russian commander that there was 'no need of guns and powder'. They had avoided the dreaded scurvy by eating the wild cabbage that grew abundantly over the island, boiling it up to make into a soup. There were several dogs about who assisted the mariners enormously in their hunts, but nothing was more effective than their clubs.

The graphic descriptions of these men by Bellingshausen largely mirrors the lives and operations of the sealers in the Antipodes over the early colonial period. But, unlike other colonial commentators, the Russian did not make any comments about their origins. It is the origins and nature of those lives and operations that are crucial to an understanding of the main subject of this work.

When the Sydney Traders advertised in the local press for mariners to man their boats to voyage to the Fishery, several men would answer the call. Finding their way to the wharves, they sought out the trader or his master to seek a passage. In 1806, there were more than 150 men wanting employment in the sealing industry according to the Musters of New South Wales.[1] Most were from a British background, primarily from England. For example, Charles Bishop of Nautilus fame came from a lower middle-class family living in Hampshire. Like many of his peers, his maritime career commenced when he joined the English navy while still a teenager, reaching the rank of mid shipman before voluntarily leaving and seeking employment elsewhere, in his late 20s.

But this does not give us the full story. There were others born in the colony, such as James Kelly and several other "currency lads". Other mariners included those who were born from a liaison between a white European father and a First Nations mother such as Thomas Chaseland. Further, there were First Nations people such as Maroot, who were either chosen by masters, to help in the hunt for seals or to assist in acting as liaisons or navigating coastal regions.

Some First Nations people later crewed on vessels with the sealers who operated small scale enterprises. A not insignificant cohort came from more diverse backgrounds. Those men were African Americans such as Anderson and Mytye from New Zealand, while others were from the Pacific Islands and America. Many, such as the Englishman John Boultbee, were free men who just wanted a life of adventure on the seas. Lower on the colonial scale were others who had served their time as convicts at His Majesty's Pleasure and were now emancipated. When Captain Beveridge gave evidence before Bigge in 1821 about the sealers on

---

[1] Musters were records kept of people living in the colony from 1795 to 1828.

Macquarie Island, he informed the Commissioner that 'many are free and emancipated'. Some had fled from mainstream traders, leaving behind harsh and intolerable conditions imposed by their masters. What is clear from the primary sources is that there were men and a few women, either employed by traders or operating on their own account of a polyglot multi racial and amorphous nature originating from all parts of the globe.

Many crews were in fact substantially multinational. Take, for example, the mariners who were reported by the editor of *The Sydney Gazette* when leaving the colony in the Campbell owned brig *Favourite* in 1809. Apart from Captain Arnold Fisk, there appear to be seven Anglo Saxon men and a boy called Charles Hoppy, who may have been Indigenous. In addition, the crew included the following men of diverse racial and ethnic backgrounds, namely Juan Francisco, Antonio Bectro, Daniel De Cruse, Augustine Ferrara Antonio, Augustine De Cruse Juan, Lawrence De Grasse Beecho, Ambrose Paul De Silva, Pedro De Luzo, Lence De Luza Hassam, Mensa, Serang Tindal, Boxew Salbian and Jarula Hyderally. Some of these men were of Portuguese or South American origin while one probably came from Africa. At least two were 'lascars' from the sub-continent. The term originated from the Portuguese in the early 1600s to describe Muslim sailors. It is not clear from the primary sources as to how these men became crew on ships in the Fishery. These men were either persuaded or contracted through an agent to accompany European crews on sealing voyages. They often received few benefits for their troubles other than food and lodgings. Most would have come from India, Bangladesh or South-East Asia. Given the significant colonial sea trade that was conducted between New Holland and the Indian seaports by Sydney traders, it is likely that the men from the sub-continent were a significant part of some of the crews voyaging to and from the colony, in the first decade of the 19th century.

Pacific Islands men also figured prominently in gangs frequenting the Fishery. After 1820, John Mirey who came from Otaheite,[2] and John Myteye of Māori descent were leaders among

---
[2] Now known as Tahiti.

the independent sealers. The part-First Nations sealer and whaler Tommy Chaseland was employed on many vessels early on in his maritime career accompanied by these Polynesian mariners as he voyaged to and from the southern Antipodes. While on the *King George*, he was part of a polyglot crew from Fiji, the Solomon Islands, the Sandwich Islands, the Marquesas, Tahiti, and likely other nationals including local First Nations men. These men were designated as 'half-caste', 'lascars' or 'mulattoes' by European masters and traders.

The American sealing masters who were directed by Yankee merchants to exploit the southern Fishery and did so for a few years in the first decade of the 19th century came with crews primarily made up of men from Boston, New York, Nantucket and Connecticut. Some of these men and others, who became aware of opportunities in New Holland, were enticed to join colonial sealing boats. They included those who had abandoned the Delano brothers in the Straits lured by Murrell to "jump ship" on promises of better lays and conditions. Others, such as 'Black-Jack' Anderson, the notorious pirate and sealer, needed no such enticement. He had allegedly "run from" the employ of an American whaler and commenced his sealing adventures on Kangaroo Island. While establishing himself, he came to rely on his partner John Bathurst, another African American, in something of a joint enterprise to successfully pursue his sealing (and other far more nefarious) activities. After Black-Jack's demise, Bathurst continued to live and operate a small-scale maritime venture from Kangaroo Island for some considerable time.

Apart from Black-Jack and Bathurst, other Americans, white and black, were prominent within the sealing trade. Samuel Rodman Chase, John Baker and John Taylor are three that come to mind. Chase (sometimes called 'Chace'), a white mariner, originally joined Bishop's crew on the *Nautilus* from Hawaii in 1798 before voyaging to the Straits. On the way back, he and 13 other sealers demanded the captain release them and pay them out when they reached Cape Barren Island. After his return to Port Jackson in May 1800, he was enterprising enough to enter a partnership of sorts with the Sydney traders Kable and Underwood. Chase was given charge of the sloop *Diana*, voyaging to and from the Straits. Like many masters, he managed to have the traders agree to give him a large minority share of each catch. This enabled him to purchase a sloop called the *Intent*. He was shrewd enough to hire the vessel out at a huge profit to others while continuing to partner with Kable and Underwood. He became a master mariner commanding several vessels operating mainly around the Tasmanian islands. Sadly for him, his vessel went missing off the east coast and, like many a colonial mariner, he was never seen again.

Baker, probably an African-American, came to prominence as one of the sealers who seemed to have spent his time voyaging between the Bass Strait and Kangaroo Islands hunting seals and living with several First Nations wives and some children. He was mentioned in despatches by Robinson as one of the more notorious of those mariners who abducted Bruny Island women. John Taylor was a mulatto from America who had voyaged extensively across the Fishery but by the time Robinson wrote his journals was living in the Kent Group with a First Nations woman. Yankee mariners made up the largest sector of those calling themselves sealers in the relevant period. As far as can be ascertained, from 1786 and 1828, almost half of all persons engaged in sealing in the sub-Antarctic region were Americans. The British accounted for a further 20 per cent and the rest originated from New South Wales, Van Diemen's Land and other nationalities.[3] This is not surprising as there were between 500 and 600 "people of colour" who resided in Van Diemen's Land from colonisation up to 1850 according to one historian.[4]

Many First Nations people were engaged in the sealing trade in one form or another during this period. The most prominent was Chaseland, who straddled the two most prominent maritime trades. There was another part-Aboriginal man who succeeded on

---

[3] Lorne K. Kriwoken and John W. Williamson, Hobart, 'Tasmania: Antarctic and Southern Ocean connections', *Polar Record*, Vol. 29, no. 169, pp. 93-102.

[4] Cassandra Pybus, Statement to the Legislative Council Select Committee on Aboriginal Lands, 10 April, 2000.

both sealing and whaling. Edward Tomlins was born in 1813 to a colonial sealer Samuel Tomlins and a First Nations woman, *Bulra*. By 1830, Ned, as he was called, was 'a fine stout well-made young man', according to Robinson, when he observed him operating out of the Hunters Island. There, he lived with other sealers, including Robert Rew. According to Robinson, Ned was badly influenced by those older men and, by 1832, was addicted to alcohol and 'immoral pursuits'. The poor perception Robinson had of Ned, however, did not stop him succeeding in life as he was by then already turning his gaze elsewhere. Like many of the sealers who were operating when the pursuit of the seals was on a downward spiral, he found better opportunities in whaling. He joined forces with William Dutton on the Victorian south coast at Portland. In that role he became what one colonial historian described as 'the best whaler in the colonies and the smartest man ever seen in a boat'.[5] Like Tommy, he became a leader of the mariners who worked out of Hobart and was active in trying to prevent crews from being badly exploited.

There were many other First Nations men who were employed gainfully in the sealing industry by sealing captains on either a temporary or more or less permanent basis. Three of them – Colbee, Tom and Jack Richmond – were engaged on the brig *Glory* in the trade around Port Dalrymple, Bass Strait and Kangaroo Island during the early 1800s.[6] In 1809, the boatswain Maroot (sometimes described as 'Merute' or 'Boatswain' by the colonists) of the Kameygal (or Gameygal) people, was only 16 years of age. He left on a voyage on the *Sydney Cove*, owned by James Underwood, for Macquarie Island. Unfortunately, he and another two sealers were left by Underwood's master to survive on that island with limited means for several months. They ran out of supplies and had to subsist on fish, penguins and mutton birds. Finally, when the island was visited by the brig *Concord*, Maroot and his fellow secretly stowed away on board.

---

[5] Dunderdale, George. *The Book of the Bush*. (London: Law Lock and Co, 1898), 3.

[6] William Charles Wentworth. *William Cox, Journal*.

When that vessel reached Sydney in October of 1810, Maroot fled and petitioned the Governor, claiming his sealing master had breached an oral agreement with him by abandoning him to his own devices. He was the initial First Nations man to do so. In presenting his petition, Maroot emphasised that he worked twice as hard as any white man and should be properly compensated. For his trouble, he was awarded £10 partly paid in cash and otherwise in goods.[7] Nothing much is heard of Maroot again until an advertisement appeared in the *Sydney Gazette* in February 1822 for claims to be 'presented' against him as he was departing from the colony on the brig *Mercury*. The next year, he and Bulkabara (chief of Botany) were sailing to the Straits on the same brig to slaughter seals. Like Chaseland and Tomlins, Maroot worked across whaling and sealing industries. When whaling in New Zealand near Otago, he and one other Aboriginal man, Dick, were described as boatsteerers. This was a position well up in the maritime hierarchy. As such they were able to claim the same lay or wage as their white counterparts. When giving evidence before the Select Committee on Aborigines in 1845, Maroot described the work of a sealer and whaler as being 'hard and dirty'. Questioned by a Dr Lang, he admitted that sometimes he'd earned up to £30 for each voyage, but then went out drinking with other sailors until all the money was spent, as was the custom, before returning to the public houses later when further wages were paid.

Other First Nations maritime men namely Bull Dog, Bidgy, Bundelll and Bloody-Jack were all described by Governor King's clerk David Dickenson Mann in 1811 as Aboriginals who had 'made themselves extremely useful on board colonial vessels employed in the fishing and sealing trade, for which they were in regular receipt of wages.'[8] This statement implies that these men, just like Maroot later on, may have been treated as equals with their white crew mates. It would suggest that these men were rewarded for hard toil and their abilities, rather than for their race. The overwhelming diverse racial nature of crews criss-crossing the

---

[7] See Regina Sutton, *Mari Nawi Aboriginal Odysseys 1790 to 1850*, 18.

[8] David Dickenson Mann. *The Present Picture of New South Wales*, 46-47.

wide expanse of the Fishery spoke of opportunities for non-white men to seek employment on boats and be treated fairly at times or sometimes even better than their colonial counterparts where ability was rewarded. It is not surprising that, in this period, when slavery is coming to an end in some parts of the Empire, black men were succeeding also in leadership roles. Most (if not all) of them came from a nautical background, having seen, or been given, opportunities at sea that were not likely to be available to them on land. They could see that not only could they earn a reasonable living but be part of culture where they might earn respect for their skills. They were able to demonstrate their talent at various tasks. This meant that black men were paid on an equal footing to whites, often being selected on merit rather than racial grounds.[9] But this would only ever apply on the high seas and regrettably was often not the case for First Nations women.

The diverse and hybrid nature of those men and women engaged in the sealing trade is further illustrated when considering those who barely subsisted by living off the sea along the south-western coastlines of Western Australia. The two abandoned sealing crews manning whaleboats the French commander and explorer Jules Dumont D'Urville in the corvette *Astrolabe* encountered when he entered King Georges Sound in 1826 were composed of men and women from various nations. In the first was a Māori, and at least one Aboriginal who might have been nicknamed 'Pidgin'. In the second was Richard Simon, an African-American, who was later chosen by D'Urville to assist him in navigating their way across southern Australia.[10] Shortly thereafter, Major Edmund Lockyer, in the *Amity*, on his official expedition to the same place in 1827, also met with two sealing gangs that included Robert Williams, a 'black' man; 'Pidgin' another Indigenous person called Thomas Tasmein; and William Hook, a native of New Zealand.

Pidgin was so-called by the colonists. His native name appears to have been 'Beewhurher' or 'Warroba'. He originated from the

---

[9] See W. Jeffery Bolster, *Black Jacks: African Americans in the Age of Sail*, 75, 76, 78 and 101. See also Grenville Mawer, Ahab's Trade, 168.

[10] Jules Dumont D'Urville. *An Account in Two Volumes of Two Voyages to the South Seas, Vol. 1, Astrolabe 1826-1829*, 32-34.

Shoalhaven area in New South Wales but had lived in Port Jackson for some time. After Lockyer observed and reflected on these motley crews, he realised that Beewhurber had the skills required not only to assist the Major in navigating around the region but also by acting as a liaison with the local First Nations people. He used the Aboriginal man's services as an interpreter. Lockyer described him as 'intelligent' and happy to be employed by him.

The history of the mariners on the littoral edge recognises to some extent the roles played by the Australasian men in the industry. But there appears to be very little recognition of First Nations women who partnered voluntarily (or otherwise) with sealers and who often trumped their white mariners in hunting seals. I have already referred to the significant skill displayed by these women to procure seals observed by Kelly on his circumnavigation of Tasmania in 1816. The abilities of the women to stalk, mimic and finally dispose of the pinnipeds did not go unnoticed. Many of the male sealers operating from whaleboats utilised the skills of these women to great effect. Woretemoeteryenner, Tolo's daughter, with whom George Briggs partnered for a time, was adept. Apart from working with George in his sealing endeavours, she was one of three First Nations women who crewed on a vessel going to King Georges Sound and later St Paul Island in the middle of the Indian Ocean, independent of any male partner. She later returned to the Straits and joined a gang of mariners involved in small scale seal hunting. But she was not unique. All around the Fishery, particularly in South and West Australia, crews observed by either explorers or official colonial representatives, such as Lockyer, often included several Aboriginal women. A good example of the gendered make-up of crews is illustrated by those under the command of Black-Jack Anderson around Middle Island and King Georges Sound. In his watercraft, he used several female companions for their maritime skills and knowledge of the various seal locations. Another such crew, where women were predominant, was utilised by James Everett in his whaleboat sealing expeditions around the southwest regions of the Fishery.

Most of the sealers who hunted the pinnipeds were uneducated and illiterate. Those who sought employment from the Sydney Traders would scratch a cross on articles of agreement. Sometimes, these documents were read out to them but not always. There are very few records of journals or letters being written by these men. One was by the adventurer John Boultbee. He had attended good schools in England and was able to read and write. He kept a journal of his travels, which has been the subject of analysis by the Begg Brothers.[11] Boultbee sailed from Van Diemen's Land to the Bass Straits, lived with Munro for a while, voyaged with a gang of sealers up to Westernport, surviving on some islands there; and eventually moved to New Zealand, before finally ending his journey in Ceylon. His journals make interesting reading and demonstrate the wide diversity of the men who made up the sealing community. Others who were unable to write told their tales of adventure to those who were literate. One such mariner was John Nunn who was employed on the *Royal Sovereign* in the 1820s as part of a crew that voyaged to the sub-Antarctic Kerguelen Islands and was marooned there. A professor of Botany and medical practitioner from Cambridge University who was mainly interested in the science of the plant life on the islands met with him. He grabbed an opportunity to tell a rollicking tale of Nunn's 'sealing adventures' to earn substantial royalties from sales of his book to an enthralled colonial readership.

One person who kept more or less meticulous records of the Straitsmen inhabiting the Bass Strait Islands in the early 1830s was Robinson. Historian Brian Plomley has meticulously copied Robinson's extensive journal and notes and tried to decipher them. His version of Robinson's journals, *Friendly Mission*, is a unique and primary source.[12] This insight into the sealer's world provides an opportunity to piece together a character portrait of the mariners who occupied the Southern Fishery between the late 1820s to 1840.

Despite the large minority of mariners of multinational or First

---

[11] A. Charles Begg and Neil C. Begg. *The World of John Boultbee*, 22.

[12] (Brian) *Plomley Friendly Mission* (Kingsgrove: Halstead Press Pty Ltd, 1966).

Nations backgrounds, most engaged in the sealing trade came from Britain. They found their way to the colony having previously either been employed in the maritime trade or as part of the British navy or had served their time as convicts and were now emancipated. There was a smaller cohort who had escaped lawful custody who were described as 'runaways'. An examination of the records kept by Robinson of the islander mariners in the early 1830s, when the industry was in decline, revealed that the vast majority of sealers described as 'seaman' were from a nautical background. Whether they came voluntarily or deserted their ship (such as in the case of Black-Jack Anderson or John Morgan who abandoned his vessel in Port Jackson in 1813), or left on a broken promise to collect them by an unscrupulous master, does not necessarily mean, as Robinson would imply or express, that they were therefore all men of bad character. For the terms and conditions under which men became sailors on boats in the late 18th and early 19th centuries were often extremely restrictive and oppressive. Some men were pressganged into service or had no other alternative source of employment available to them after the end of the wars with France or America.[13] They sought a better life in the Antipodes, initially working for lays on merchant vessels and/or later independently.

These sealers, who lived away from mainstream colonial society, were often perceived as criminals in the colonial press. But, from examining the Robinson material,[14] of the 42 sealers still inhabiting the southern Fishery, 29 were described as coming 'free' when they arrived in the Fishery, and another seven were from a convict background. A further six were non-white and of indeterminate status. A large majority of the mariners in the Straits were said to have lived with one or more First Nations women as their partners

---

[13] Pressganging or 'impressment' had become part of the maritime culture of Great Britain by the time of the French Revolution. The British Navy regarded it as a legitimate way to add large numbers of men to their ranks to enable Britain to pursue its war with France and other enemies. It essentially meant that naval authorities sought the assistance of paid gangs to capture and force sailors into His Majesty's Service.

[14] Plomley and Robinson almost speak as one voice and, as we are so dependent on Plomley's interpretation of the Robinson notes, I have linked them together.

or companions either voluntarily or following an abduction. Several had children living with them in their communities.[15] If this relatively small sample was representative of all those who came under the umbrella of 'sealer' then, probably over 80 per cent of all the sealers including the non-white men could not be categorised as convicts and some 15 per cent were from a non-British background.

The irony was that Straitsmen like Munro and others also assisted authorities in providing valuable intelligence and resources to bring runaway convicts to justice. A good example of this occurred in October 1803, when a gang of sealers inhabiting the Furneaux Island group encountered runaways under the command of a J. Duce. This gang had absconded from Risdon Cove by pirating Lieutenant Bowen's prize vessel. The sealers captured and restrained all of the pirates except their leader. Duce managed to flee. The mariners handed their captives over to a Mr Stewart, master of the schooner *Edwin*. What happened to Duce is not known; he may have been one of many convicts to escape condign punishment. However, his notoriety was enough for Lieutenant Governor Collins to write angrily to Governor King on 29 February 1804 about the escapee. Collins informed King that if he was ever to capture Duce, 'a full and proper example' would be made of him.

In locating the sealers geographically, much of the focus of the colonial primary sources has been on those who inhabited the islands of the Bass Straits. One might conclude that all of the sealers' economic and social activities took place within a radius of less than 100 kilometres just north of the Van Diemen's mainland. The reality was entirely different. The mariners employed by the Sydney Traders and other commercial merchants generally lived in the settlements like Sydney and Hobart, coming and going depending on their engagements. They could be away from their lodgings for months and sometimes years at a time. These mariners voyaged extensively looking for the seals in commercial vessels to which whaleboats were attached, not only along the length of the southern Australian coastline but to the west and east of

---

[15] Plomley. *Friendly Mission*, 1010-1017.

this continent. Often, they crisscrossed vast expanses of water over weeks and months to hunt down seals with varied degrees of success. Most of the employed sealers would have encountered each other on the remote habitats where seals were found or on the docks, wharves and public houses in the settlements. As most of the seal rookeries were located in cool or cold environments, these sealers had to dress for all types of weather events. Normally, they wore broad hats or caps and clothed themselves in long trousers, buttoned shirts with a kerchief around their necks. They always wore coats and either leather shoes or boots, if they were lucky enough to have them. While left to their own devices in remote locations, sealers had to adapt to their environment, as they often did not have very sophisticated equipment. For example, in the Recherche (near King Georges Sound), mariners found that a 10-foot Mallee tree, which they called the 'Seal Club Tree', was an excellent source of wood to cut and shape for the clubs they used to kill seals.

The independent sealers were different. Although they anchored off islands and coasts garbed in the attire described above, their clothing became ragged torn and unwearable after some months or years. This was due to their fishing activities and rough lifestyle. Unless they purchased gear from a passing ship (which would have happened only occasionally), they adopted the practice of clothing themselves in whatever resources they had available to them. Many adapted to clothing supplied or stitched together by the Aboriginal women. Such garments included pelts and skins flensed from animals including seals, kangaroos, wallabies and possums. Footwear came in the form of skin moccasins cobbled together in a rudimentary manner.

Captain Sutherland anchored at Kangaroo Island in 1819 and, in what can be only described as a disparaging observation of the islanders, wrote: 'They dress in kangaroo skins without linen and wear sandals made of seal skins. They smell like foxes.'[16] Smell like foxes they might, but on Kangaroo Island, the sealers and

---

[16] George Sutherland, *Report of a Voyage from Sydney to Kangaroo Island*. Appendix to Wakefield's report, 73.

Aboriginal women blended traditional and Western forms of dress as the need arose in what was a cross-cultural adaptation to suit the families. W.H. Leigh, an English ship's surgeon, artist and raconteur, visited the island in 1837. While there he sketched a somewhat comical night campsite scene, in which individual family members including men and women were dressed in animal skin garments, with moccasins on their feet. Otherwise, they were garbed with European maritime apparel like hats and coats while sitting around a fire.

Prior to the first decline in the industry, crews manning commercial trading vessels were extremely busy and mobile at times. Those employed on ships out of the settlements were in constant demand during profitable seasons. Often the anchorages around Sydney Harbour were full of brigs, schooners, sloops and other ships anchored to either load or offload seal skins and oil into the warehouses of Campbell, Lord and Underwood. Having done so, these vessels quickly departed either north to China, India or later London or south to the Fishery. The frenzy of maritime activity involved many crews, criss-crossing the oceans of the Antipodes in search of the pinnipeds.

Once they reach their destinations, the whaleboats that were carried on the ships and sometimes shallops were hoisted down and launched by crews to make the more difficult and tricky journeys required in pursuit of seals. Take, for example, those who were on board the Lord–owned *Caroline* under the command of Captain Daniel Taylor. He and his gang voyaged to the south end of Macquarie Island in April 1823 to seek out sea elephant oil.[17] After several months, its lucrative cargo was transported to Sydney, with the boat anchoring on 11 July 1823. By 25 September 1823, the *Caroline* was in the Derwent River returning to Port Jackson from a subsequent voyage on 1 January 1824. Its crew unloaded another substantial cargo of oil. Embarking for Macquarie Island again on 4 March for a third trip there, Taylor navigated his way back

---

[17] By the 1820s, sea elephants, as the mammals were called, became the main focus of the mariners going to Macquarie and Campbell Islands as the fur seals had by then been almost decimated.

to Sydney on 22 April 1824. It sailed again to the sub-Antarctic islands on 17 November reaching them by 15 February 1825. Unfortunately for Lord and his mariners, the boat was eventually wrecked at Macquarie that year while hunting for sperm whales.

Even in the mid-1820s, despite the fact that the seal rookeries had been reduced by over-exploitation, there seems to have been sufficient numbers available to entice crews. The editor of *The Australian* newspaper reported in late 1824 there were eight brigs and four sloops and schooners involved in the sealing trade. They were valued at approximately £3,000 each and could accommodate gangs of up to 30 men.[18] These comments did not take into account those operating independently of the mainstream trade in their whaleboats in the southern islands.

The mainstream traders had the money and/or colonial connections available to own, hire out or obtain on credit, boats such as brigs, schooners and sloops – all worth a small fortune. For the independent small scale sealing fraternity, the only asset of any worth they had use of was generally the whaleboats. They became the vessel of choice for the independent sealing communities, in particular, because of their manoeuvrability and expendability.[19] These vessels were normally up to 35 feet long and made of cedar or Huon pine. This meant they were extremely light. It enabled sealers to easily navigate difficult maritime terrains where their lives sometimes depended on their abilities to control boats in treacherous conditions. These vessels were so light that the mariners could even carry them over land. They had at the stern a housing storage area for the long oar required for steerage. Many were equipped with sails and a pot used for heating and cooking.[20] This mirrored, to some extent, what First Nations peoples using canoes and rafts had been doing from time immemorial. Most of these whaleboats would have allowed up to eight people to man them,

---

[18] *The Australian*, 28 October 1824.

[19] See Ian Stuart, 'Sealing and Whaling Seascapes', Susan Lawrence and Mark Staniforth (eds), *The Archaeology of Whaling in Southern Australia and New Zealand*, 99.

[20] See O'May, 41.

sometimes more.[21] These boats gave the mariners greater mobility to hunt seals across the wide expanse of the Fishery. The vessels were employed to pursue seals as far west as the French islands of St Paul and Amsterdam and, as far east as the Chatham Islands being the eastern and western limits of the southern Fishery.

Between 1828 and 1830, there were reports of collectives of sealers living on islands in the Spencer Gulf. There is anecdotal evidence of sealing camps right along the Great Australian Bight. Others had been stranded but were managing difficult circumstances in King Georges Sound. Another sealer, with two First Nations partners and their family, was located on Saint Peter Island near the Eyre Peninsula. A further collective was operating at Portland Bay prior to the area being settled by mainstream colonial settlers.[22] Then there was 'Old Scott' who had established a sealing camp with others at Westernport. All had as their main asset a whaleboat.

One example of the sealers who were very mobile, voyaging extensively to follow a trade in sealing, was James Everett. Robinson refers to him in his journal as being a resident of Bass Strait, living on Kangaroo Island in 1824, and active in King George Sound in 1826. He crewed a whaler between 1834 and 1835, before returning to live in Port Phillip by 1837. He was famous for employing First Nations crews for their sealing skills and used whaleboats to sail over vast expanses of sea to find seals.

While mobility was a key component for all mariners, they maintained bases where they set up camps, built huts and sometimes dwellings or lived in caves on or close to the coasts, like those Bellinghausen met on Macquarie Island.[23] The Russian made detailed entries regarding the sealers housing in his journal:

---

[21] See, for example, a good analysis of the whaleboat technology by Michael Pearson: The Technology of Whaling in Australian Waters in the 19th Century' in *Australian Journal of Historical Archaeology*, Vol.1, 40-54.

[22] Phillip Clarke, "Early European interaction with Aboriginal hunters and gatherers on Kangaroo Island," 51-81.

[23] Trevarthan asserts that the geography of the Antipodean mariners is defined more by points and places than land. Cora Trevarthan, *Trans-Tasman World. The Social and Cultural influence of the sealing industry in Australia, 1792 to 1842*.

> The foreman of the sealers invited us to his hut, which was 20 feet long by 10 feet broad. Inside it was lined with skins of seals and outside was covered with a kind of grass which grows on the island. At one end there was a small hearth, and a lamp was kept always alight. On the hearth, as wood and coal were unobtainable, there was burning a piece of sea elephant blubber and melted fat was used for lamp. Beside the hearth was a bedstead. Provisions were stored at the other end of the hut. Inside it was so black and dark from the smoke that the smouldering light from the lamp and from the holes in the wall over which bladders were stretched scarcely lit the interior of the hut, and until we got accustomed to the light the sealers had to lead us by the hand.[24]

As described by the Russian, often sealers, both mainstream and independent, lived in island or coastal huts for several months at a time, while procuring oil and skins throughout the Fishery. Sutherland observed the Kangaroo Islander habitations in 1819 describing them as 'complete savages living in bark huts like the natives', Sometime after 12 November 1826, Louis de Sainson, the French artist on board D'Urville's vessel, painted a work depicting several mariners – who had been sealing near Westernport on the south coast of Victoria – below a triangular-shaped dwelling roofed completely to the ground with reeds. This was supported by a wooden undercarriage with bark walls and a timber pole construction that would have been used to dry clothes and seal skins. The French artist and crew also found the sealers had been growing crops such as wheat and maize which was tended by their First Nation female companions. Other sealers, such as Munro on Preservation Island and Nathaniel Thomas on Kangaroo Island., constructed more permanent dwellings to house their extended families. Dogs were also constant companions of the mariners and used extensively by them to hunt prey.

Survival was key for mariners who were either left to fend for themselves at the directions of captains on remote islands and bays far removed from the settlements. It was also key for the

---

[24] Frank Debenham (ed.) *The Voyage of Captain Bellingshausen to the Antarctic Seas 1819-1821.*

independent sealers living with families or collectives in the southern Australian islands and coasts. Several of the independent mariners set up camp well removed from any sign of Western civilization. In doing so, some adopted an alternative lifestyle of sorts. From this, a perception developed in the early colonial period that these mariners were indolent and anarchic by nature, living a carefree and idyllic existence.[25] Those few who actually fit that description probably made use of First Nations women to undertake most (if not all) of the work, but the majority were not like this. Eking out an existence in many of the remote environments around the Fishery was hard work for all. Survival depended on their collective actions.

Similarly, for those sealers who were employed for long periods by traders to live on remote islands, life usually turned out to be very difficult. Take, for example, the several gangs of mariners left on Macquarie Island who were articled to procure fur and elephant seals. Captain Douglass, on his return from that island in the *Mariner* in December 1822, provided a report to the editor of the *Sydney Gazette* about the appalling state of the sealers, and the conditions in which they existed:

> As to the island is the most wretched place involuntary and slavish exilium that can possibly be conceived: nothing could warrant any civilised creature living on such a spot were it not the certainty of industry being handsomely rewarded; thus far, therefore, the poor sealer bids farewell probably for years, to the comforts of civilized life, enjoys the expectation of ensuring an adequate recompense for all his dreary toil.[26]

Douglass described the gangs of men as the 'very refuse of human species, so abandoned and lost in every sense of moral duty'. He found they were rebellious in nature, often refusing to follow the orders of the 'overseers' of the traders. But his observations were not completely negative. He extolled the virtues of 'the youths of this colony' as they maintained the character from industry and

---

[25] See, for example, Patsy Adam Smith, *There was a Ship* (Melbourne: Penguin Books,1995) where she describes the sealers as 'rude, wife snatchers, free booters, rum swillers and sea wolves' *inter alia*.

[26] *The Sydney Gazette and New South Wales Advertiser*, 12 December 1822.

attending to their employer's interest. Presumably, he was making a distinction between native-born and ex-convict youth. In praising the abilities of the native-born Australian men who made up part of the sealing crews, the captain was ahead of his time when he offered the following:

> This is a character, we trust, that the Australians in every sphere of life, will endeavour to preserve from the very appearance of blemish.

Douglass's comments reflect the rugged and determined nature of the employed sealers while maintaining the stereotype that was prevalent in the colony at the time. Unlike present day men employed in remote and dangerous locations, the sealers received little remuneration. Sealers may have earned as much as one pound a week on a successful voyage to the Fishery, but perhaps a more realistic figure would be about £38 over, say, a 17-month period.[27] Many non-European mariners were paid less, or were given supplies and provisions in lieu of skins or cash.

Food for the employed sealers was provided on board ship and was typical of that supplied by English maritime traders. The mariners who crewed on boats owned by people like Kable and Underwood were fed on a typical nautical diet, called by all and sundry 'victuals'. Normally, the ships were loaded with the staple which included 'hardtack' biscuits and beer that were consumed daily. Other provisions provided included cheese, oats, peas and salted meats like pork or beef. The biscuits were so hard that it was almost impossible to eat them without breaking teeth. To make them edible, "tars" as sailors were called, dipped them into hot tea or coffee or ground then down into a powder to make a broth. They were kept bone dry in the holds of boats to stop them becoming mouldy. Often, however, this did not stop weevils and other creatures infesting the food, but a hungry sailor turned a blind eye to any infestation. The main dangers that a mariner faced when consuming such a diet was spoiled, rotten and infested food or scurvy. But incidence of the latter illness lessened over time as

---

[27] David Roger Hainsworth, 'Iron Men in wooden ships the Sydney Sealers 1800-1825', in *Labour History* No. 13 (1967), 19-25.

masters learned to carry sauerkraut and other commodities which reduced its incidence. However, once a crew was deposited on islands and coasts for months at a time, although given victuals to see them through, these became depleted particularly in circumstances where promises to return were not kept by unscrupulous captains. In those cases, they had to resort to whatever was available, including parts of dead seals. For example, the mariners Bellinghausen met on Macquarie Island were forced to eat 'carrion and penguin's eggs' as well as seal fins to survive.

The independent sealers fared a little better at times. Initially, they depended on killing seals to feed themselves, sought passing trading vessels or sailed to the settlements to exchange their catch for such commodities as salted meat, tobacco and rum. They expanded their industry to include prey other than seals, particularly during the off season, and also to grow crops such as corn, cereals and potatoes. Fauna such as kangaroos, shellfish, other marine life and mutton birds were common fare. The latter were as easy to catch as the pinnipeds and became a substantial part of the islander diet. French explorers realised the ease with which those birds could be killed and eaten. François Peron, the zoologist on board *Le Geographe* in 1802, while in the islands of Bass Straits, wrote:

> These birds are not very bold, and only defend themselves by making a few blows with their beaks, at those who attempt to take them... Roasted or rather broiled on live coals, these birds have a taste similar to red herrings; this was the only way of dressing them, which rendered them eatable.[28]

After the sealers on the southern Fishery formed their own independent enterprises, they also varied their diet by establishing gardens, growing crops and acquiring sheep and goats. Many used dogs to catch prey like seals. Just like the First Nations peoples, such mariners used oil from the seals for lighting and heat, skins stitched together for clothing, caps and moccasins and traded these commodities for European goods supplied out of Hobart and Sydney from passing vessels or from visiting settlements such as

---

[28] Francois Peron, *Voyage of Discovery to the Southern Hemisphere* (London: Richard Phillips, 1809), 266.

Hobart, Port Dalrymple or Dusky Sound,[29] including tea, sugar, tobacco, alcohol, clothing and the like.

The collective small-scale enterprises and composite family groupings were often led by mariners who assumed significant leadership within their singular and more broader communities. Munro from Preservation Island, Thomas Tucker on Gun Carriage Island in the Straits, and James Everett in the Great Australian Bight were Europeans who were instrumental in either representing sealers, commanding crews in the hunt for the pinnipeds or in organising resistance to mainstream colonial authorities and their subordinates in the Fishery. Thomas Tucker (whom Robinson detested) was regarded as the "lawyer" of the Straits, advising and advocating for sealers in their disputes with traders, owners, and authorities. James Munro, respected by his colleagues, was appointed a constable in Bass Strait by Governor Arthur to maintain the law among the islanders and to keep an eye out for escaping convicts. The appointment enabled Arthur to use Munro as observer and informer and to monitor runaways who temporarily secreted themselves on the islands from time to time. Munro also acted as negotiator for the sealers when dealing with the attempts by Robinson to remove their partners.[30] From the outset, sealers were used to being organised into gangs by the traders and masters who originally employed them. So, it was only a small step for many of them to be part of a collective system under the command of leaders such as Anderson, Tucker, Everett, Munro, Daniel Cooper, and Murrell.[31] Apart from men such as Thomas Chaseland in New Zealand, other non-white men assumed significant leadership roles,

---

[29] See Peter. Cunningham, *Two Years in New South Wales,* Vol. 2, 103.

[30] Munro had to overcome the strong colonial perception that the Straits were 'infested with numbers of prisoners or illegal characters' as portrayed in *The Australian* on 9 March 1826 or, alternatively, that the sealers were associating with other 'miscreants' such as escaped convicts and the servants of the Van Diemen's Land Company who had a poor reputation in colonial circles as many of these men had engaged in brutal attacks on the Indigenous nations that inhabited Tasmania.

[31] Iain Stuart, 'Sea Rats, bandits and roistering buccaneers: What were the Bass Strait Sealers really like?' in *Historical Archaeology,* University of Sydney, *JRAHS*, Vol. 53, Part 1, 1997, 99.

such as Black-Jack Anderson, in his nefarious operations. Mytye, a New Zealand Māori, was regarded by Robinson and others as the sealers' 'headsman' and was considered 'most honourable'.[32] Richard Simons, who plied his trade with others around King Georges Sound, was chosen specifically by D'Urville to accompany him for exploration and other purposes eastwards to Port Jackson. Simons played a significant role, not only in the encounters D'Urville had with First Nations peoples on his journey, but also in dealing with other sealer settlements and gangs.[33]

While sealers hunted seals from whaleboats and on coasts and were subject to mainly adverse publicity in the press there was not much written about their hunting operations, the methodologies they adopted to kill their prey, and how they were rewarded for their efforts. John Nunn, the sealer who was part of the crew of the *Sovereign* on a mission to the Kerguelen Islands referred to above, gave a graphic description of sealers in action through his biographer. He informed Clarke that the men anchoring in the 'seal fishery to the south' conducted operations in 300-400-ton vessels. These boats were normally crewed by 24 mariners with each vessel carrying about six boats and materials to build a shallop. In April 1825, Nunn left London on board the *Sovereign* after he and his colleagues were informed that the islands abounded with all types of seals ready for the taking.

When the mariners reached one of the islands, Nunn and his crew were ordered to offload the sealing gear. Once anchored in a safe harbor they transported 'furnaces for boiling the blubber' and 'the cooperage'[34] onto the beach. The furnaces were commonly called iron trypots. They were also observed by Bellinghausen at Macquarie Island and were utilised by mainstream and independent sealers throughout the colonial period. One side of these objects was flat with a spout protruding from it from which oil was poured. In general, they were about 3 x 3 feet and were heavy to lift. The

---

[32] Plomley and Henley, 57 and 180.

[33] D'Urville, 33.

[34] The place where the work of a cooper, such as the construction of barrels and casks, is carried out.

pots were placed on fires and heated up. Oil or blubber from the dead seals was deposited into these containers and, once boiled, was poured out into copper containers and left to cool. The "coolers" could hold up to about a ton of oil. Meanwhile, the shallop was constructed and the men then rowed that vessel and the whaleboats to shore ready for the hunt.

Some men were tasked with manning the shallop. Their main role was the collection of blubber from the men in the whale boats, who were responsible for killing the seals and then flensing them, before 'rafting' the blubber to the beach 'where the oil is extracted'. Nunn is not backward in describing the sealing environment as a 'danger', where the men were distressed not only by their tasks but often by the lack of provisions and amenities available to them.

The old sealer then in graphic and excruciating detail explained the methodology involved in the killing of the seals during the hunt. He assured Clarke this was 'the method adopted by our party, and I believe, by all sealers'. The mariners were always equipped with a 'seal club' and a quantity of knives. Once a herd of fur seals was approached, the sealers with the clubs would strike the intended victim with a blow to the bridge of the nose which, in general, would 'stun' the animal and render it an easy target. Others would be equipped with knives, which were plunged into the chests of the victims, 'being careful' not to damage the skin, which was the sealer's primary object.[35] Once the seal was skinned, the body was tied up and taken back to the ship where the fat and oil were removed. The body was then salted two or three times before normally being stored aboard the vessel as food for times when other commodities were in short supply, which often was the case.

Nunn described a different method employed in the capturing of the elephant seal, in which the main purpose was securing oil. He informed Clarke that these animals, which weighed significantly more than a fur seal, were killed using a lance because a club and

---

[35] Apparently, colonial sealers were not that interested in the blubber from hair seals but would take oil from the elephant variety. John Nunn, *Narrative of the Wreck of the Favorite*, 26.

knife would not achieve the desired result.[36] The lance was thrust into the chest of the mammal. However, Nunn was keen to point out, if the seal seized the implement there was no point trying to retrieve it. He provided anecdotal evidence of a sealer who died after the lance was ripped from his grasp and somehow plunged into him by the elephant seal, causing instant death. So, occasionally, seals were victorious!

Once the mammal was killed, flensing would take place by cutting the animals into sections known, unusually, as "horses", which were about one and a half feet long by one foot wide. These pieces were transported and loaded into the shallops by a complicated procedure using ropes. The blubber was taken to the ship, cut up into smaller pieces, and placed in the trypots for boiling, having been secured on wooden panels also curiously named "horses".[148] From all relevant sources, it is clear that Nunn's narrative replicated closely the methods used by the sealers to kill most seals in the Fishery.

Jorge Jorgenson, a Danish mariner of sometimes dubious repute, found adventure and trouble in the Antipodes and abroad. He arrived in the colony around the turn of the 19th century. Active in the naval service, he looked the part. In Australia, he anglicized his name to John Johnson. He seems to have been present at most of the important events unfolding in the Fishery. The Dane wrote about his observations of the sealers employed in procuring seals in the work called 'A Shred'. In 1804, he described the process adopted by himself and his crewmates:

> We killed several thousand of these harmless creatures. It is indeed astonishing with what eagerness the sailors entre into this pursuit, knocking down the animals with their clubs, stripping them of their skins, and pegging them out to dry or salting them down with casks, with the greatest zeal and perseverance. At that time these skins sold in London for a guinea each.

The process took several days to complete before the skins were available for transportation back to Sydney. Although there is no

---

[36] Nunn, 28. The lance is described as about eight feet long with a foot long cutting blade.

reason to doubt the methodologies and sealing practices described by the Dane, he was what can only be described as a colourful identity in the history of the Antipodes. For Jorgenson was not only a sealer but a chameleon-like character who strode the maritime world across two continents. He had roles as an ordinary seaman, naval sailor, explorer, whaler, convict, prisoner, farmer, police officer and confidence trickster over 46 years. Perhaps he is now best remembered as the 'usurper' who helped overthrow the government of Iceland. He had installed himself as some sort of regal monarch there before being deposed after the British military intervened.

Over time, as the sealing grounds became depleted, those describing themselves as sealers decreased substantially. Early on, there were hundreds if not thousands of colonial mariners employed across the southern Antipodes. But from 1812 until about 1820, there was a lull in the industry and the traders basically left a vacuum in the Fishery that was filled by those sealers who chose to remain on islands and bays along the southern Australian coastlines. It has been estimated that, by 1820, there were about 50 sealers who resided with approximately 100 First Nations female partners and children on islands between Bass Strait and Kangaroo Island. Although there had been a resurgence of active seal hunting to the east and west of Bass Strait by traders for a few years in the 1820s, by late in that decade, there was little profit in the industry.

By 1830 the trade was finally abandoned by mainstream merchants. The numbers of mariners who lived independent more or less self-sufficient lives in the Fishery had also dropped by that time. Previously, according to one source, there were over 200 men calling themselves "sealers" inhabiting Bass Strait, Kangaroo Island and the Recherche Archipelago. Other historians and biographers have identified over 100 mariners who operated in the southern Australian domain. Robinson's "estimate" referred to above relies heavily on his narrow scope "intelligence" and does not portray the full extent of the demographic and extent of the operations of the sealing mariners.

Mariners on the Margins

The mariners who ventured into the remote littoral locations around the Fishery came to be pilloried in the colonial press and in despatches. But in the initial period, when the traders dominated the industry, most reports presented by that press and through official channels were sympathetic to the plight and difficulties faced by employed sealing crews. However, when parties of sealers began operating independently across the Southern Fishery and competing with mainstream commercial interests, such early sympathy steadily evaporated. It was replaced by a developing antipathy leading to a fixed and immutable stereotype that still dominates historical discourses about the sealers down to the present day. Sealers were described as 'bushrangers',[37] 'marauders',[38] 'sea rats', 'bandits', 'lawless assassins' or 'pirates'.[39] Alternatively these mariners were lazy, anarchic, white English male criminals, escaping colonial authority to avoid prosecution, living on a few islands in the Bass Straits, and conducting a slave trade in Australian women. An example of this mentality was portrayed by the editor of one newspaper in 1826.[40] Indeed, it is hard to find any objective description of them from the primary sources, except in some French and Russian explorers' accounts, and later in the accounts of foreign masters on scientific expeditions. Due to the lack of such information, and, as the sealers left no records themselves with few exceptions,[41] who these mariners were, and what they were like, is a complex matter. But Bellinghausen's account and description at the beginning of this chapter, gives us a good insight. The facts and fantasy of lives lived by the mariners is the subject of a later chapter.

---

[37] William Stewart, 'Letter to Colonial Secretary Campbell 1815' in *Historical Records of Australia*, Series III, 575-576.

[38] Editor, 'Remarks respecting the Islands on the Coast of Western Australia', *Western Australian Gazette* 8, October, 1842.

[39] A slave trader is defined in the *Encyclopaedia Britannica* as a person involved in the capturing, selling and buying of enslaved persons.

[40] 'The Islands between Van Diemen's Land and the main are infested with numerous gangs of runaways, whose piratical outrages render the navigation of Bass Straits dangerous to all unarmed vessels', *Colonial Times* 10, February, 1826.

[41] The adventurer John Boultbee kept a journal of his employment in the sealing trade in Bass Strait and elsewhere in the 1820s. See *Journal of a Rambler: the journal of John Boultbee*.

Chapter 5: Australia's First Enterprise

It took several years after Governor Phillip anchored off Sydney Cove in 1788 before any of the colonisers realised that sealing could become the colony's first industry. The focus of Phillip and those military and naval men who followed him, before Hunter took control in 1795, was on other concerns. Controlling and supervising convicts, trying to establish sufficient resources to feed the nascent population and keeping a close eye on "incursions" from the other European powers such as France, Spain and Russia, took priority. However, at the turn of the century, it quickly became apparent that the fledgling colony needed a staple resource to enable it to not only feed the colonisers but to thrive. There had been some attempts to till the land and create some sort of agricultural enterprise to supply food, but these had failed miserably.[1] It was not surprising then to find that prominent colonial men turned outward to the sea to find solutions to this problem.[2]

Prior to Bishop's famous voyage, seal sightings had been made to the west and east of the Australian continent. As early as the 17th century, pinnipeds had been sighted on St Paul and Amsterdam Islands[3] in the middle of the Indian Ocean some distance from the Western Australian coast by Dutch mariners. The Ile de St Paul and Amsterdam Island, which is in reasonably close proximity, are volcanic masses in the Indian Ocean some 3,200 kilometres from anywhere, including Australia. The potential of these islands for

---

[1] See David. R. Hainsworth, *The Sydney Traders Simeon Lord and his Contemporaries*, 114-115.

[2] By the late 1790s, most of the English colonists and convicts would have lived within about a radius of 150 kilometres from Sydney Cove.

[3] Amsterdam Island was first discovered in 1522 by Juan Sebastián del Cano, a Spanish explorer who had served under Magellan. A century later, Harwick Claesz de Hillegom sailed into the Indian Ocean and was the first European to observe a smaller island now called Ile Saint-Paul.

sealing was recognised early on. By May 1789, a lieutenant of the English marines, George Mortimer, on a "fishing" expedition, had command of a snow called the *Mercury*, under the employment of Englishman and former Canton merchant John Henry Cox. That ship flew the Swedish national colours in an endeavour to circumvent the harsh restrictions imposed on independent traders by the ubiquitous Company. The vessel arrived at St Paul's Island, where Mortimer found:

> the shore covered with such a multitude of seals that we were obliged to disperse them before we got out of the boat… we secured nearly a thousand skins of a very superior quality… besides several casks of good oil.[4]

After slaughtering the seals and hauling the skins on board, Mortimer recognised the future potential there and wrote:

> I am very much assured that the information respecting it in the following voyage has induced some adventurers to fit out vessels for the purpose of sealing… and I make very little doubt of their success…

Cox died on the voyage, and it was left to Mortimer to write about his observations read by others in the maritime industry. Within a few years, the destination attracted a variety of mariners from America, France and Asia. For example, in 1790, there were maritime visitors anchoring at St Paul's when a gang of European and Chinese sealers stayed for nearly two years until a ship could take on board the hungry and exhausted men and whatever skins they could save from their harsh existence on that fairly desolate island. When General George Vancouver passed by St Paul and Amsterdam Islands in September 1791, while on his voyage in the discovery to the South Pacific Islands and North America,[5] he was disappointed to find no seals, contrary to Mortimer's previous glowing reports. But, as he sailed across to the southern coast of Western Australia, he explored a sound near (present day) Albany that he would name after King George III, and wrote of its fauna:

---

[4] George Mortimer. *Observations and Remarks Made During a Voyage*, 10-11.

[5] The *Discovery* was a sloop of 340 tons built by Randall, Gray & Brent of Rotherhithe in 1789.

> Whilst on the coast whales and seals were frequently playing about the ship; of the latter we saw about a score at one time on Seal Island. The little trouble these animals took to avoid us indicated their not being accustomed to such visitors.[6]

Although no other comment was made by him about the seals in that region as an opportunity for commercial exploitation, his statement about the benign nature of the pinnipeds would have attracted the attention of colonial and American traders. By that time, Governor Phillip was aware that there could be opportunities to exploit the vast marine resources to the south and to establish some sort of fishing industry. Several English and American whalers had been voyaging into the cold icy waters along the southern Australin coastlines, extending their search for the leviathan there. In a letter to Colonial Secretary Stephens in 1791, Phillip focussed on the potential for a whale fishery:

> You will be pleased to inform the Right Honourable Lord Commissioners of the Admiralty that the Britannia, intended for the Southern Fishery, as mentioned in my former letter, has returned to this port after being out fifteen days, during which time the master says he saw a great abundance of spermaceti whales...

He later spoke of the endeavours of the crews on two whaling vessels:

> The Mary Ann and Matilda have returned to this port... Those ships had run southwards in search of seals but did not see any fish... The Britannia sails in a few days, and from information I have received from the masters of these ships, there is every reason to suppose that a fishery will be established on the coast.[7]

And so it was the potential to procure whales rather than seals that dominated colonial mentality and gained the attention of authorities and traders. Prominent among the later was the Enderby family. They had been operating whaling ventures in the southern oceans for some time and had been more than moderately

---

[6] George Vancouver. *Voyage of Discovery to the North Pacific Ocean and Round the World*.

[7] Governor Phillip to Secretary Stephens, Sydney, 18 November 1791, *HRNSW*, Vol. 1, Part 2, 556.

successful, as reported by the surgeon John Thomson in a letter to Captain Shanck in 1799.[8] However, marine resources were still not front and centre of the discourse in colonial circles when it came to establishing enterprises in the Antipodes. David Collins, who was appointed as first Lieutenant Governor of Van Diemen's Land, had presented his accounts of the colony to the English authorities but focussed on agriculture. It was only in a throwaway line that he stated:

> If, besides all this a whale fishery should be established, another great benefit would accrue.[9]

Although there appeared to be no sign of a potential for a fishery to be established anywhere east of King Georges Sound at this time, sealers were reaping the benefits of the rookeries Cox and others had found on the two Dutch islands. When the English *HMS Lion* and East Indian *Hindostan* reached Amsterdam Island on 1 February 1793, the crews encountered a sealing gang led by a Frenchman called Peron. He had with him two Frenchmen and two Englishmen who had adopted disguises as Americans, apparently due to the war between England and France at that time. Peron told the English sailors that the French and American traders jointly owned his vessel. The captain George Staunton observed the inhabitants had already flensed 8,000 seal skins, were subsisting on fish and fowl, and were establishing a vegetable garden. The men, who were described as living in a filthy state, had constructed a 'rude' hut, and were intending to stay for a further 10 months.[10] As was often the case where mariners were left to fend for themselves, the men had to abandon a substantial quantity of skins that were spoiled and were no longer saleable. The rotting carcasses, to which the skins were still attached, were piled high and the overpowering rancid smell disgusted the new arrivals.

---

[8] 'One of them belonging to Messrs. Enderbys, is expected to sail for England next month full of spermaceti oil', Mr John Thomson to Captain Shanck, Sydney, New South Wales, 8 September 1791, *HRNSW*, 717.

[9] David Collins, *An Account of the English Colony of New South Wales*, Vol. 2, 69-74.

[10] The men eventually arrived in Sydney on the Ceres in January 1796,

Chapter 5: Australia's First Enterprise

Three years after these men departed from the island, Captain Ebenezer Dorr of Boston sailed into the cove where the seal skins were stored and took possession of as many as he could fit into the American vessel named the *Otter*.[11] He then sailed for Port Jackson, reaching there in February 1796. While there he would have told the colonial men about his success. The sale of his skins did not amount to much and he was forced to sell a quantity of wine he had on board to cover his costs before departing for Nootka Sound. Previously, his employed master William Rogers had anchored in the port of Sydney to "refresh" before voyaging back to North America in the Dorr snow called the *Fairy*. While in port he informed the colonials of five seamen who had been left on St. Pauls Island some two years prior by their master. Relying on their masters' promise to return, these men had acquired 'several thousand sealskins'. Rogers reported to the Sydney officials that he himself intended to return to St Paul, where he had left a mate and two sailors after a visit to China. Having observed a plentiful 'harvest' of seals there, he expressed surprise that there was not a flotilla of vessels sailing there from the colony.[12]

Contrary to his expectations, it was New Zealand that became the initial focus of the seal trade for Antipodean colonial mariners. On 26 July 1792, the English master William Raven anchored the vessel *Britannia* in Sydney Cove.[13] He had been tasked by the English authorities to transport several convicts and a plentiful supply of much-needed clothing and food for the 4,639 deprived persons living there, according to Collins.[14] He was thought to be an enterprising and pleasant man who would succeed in whatever his employers, the Enderbys, would task him with. At the time,

---

[11] Collins. *An Account of the English Colony of New South Wales.* Vol. 1,452, according to J. S. Cumpston in his work *Kangaroo Island 1800 to 1836*, 5.

[12] Ibid., Vol. 1, 268-9.

[13] Raven had a licence which had been granted by the Company for three years (probably to trade and fish), according to Collins and was a part owner of the vessel.

[14] Op. cit., 204. Also see letter from William Raven, dated 19 November, 1791 *HRNSW*, 95-96.

obtaining a licence from the Company[15] was very difficult. By then, New South Wales was languishing and desperate for the arrival of supplies on ships which had departed from the mother country. While at Port Jackson, Raven was approached by officials who contracted with him for the supply of cattle, which were scarce and in demand. But Raven, like many in the trade, had other commercial plans in mind, mainly the exploitation of whales. That is why he had two vessels fitted out to voyage to Dusky Bay in late 1792 to explore the possibilities there. The vessel was away from Sydney town for about eight months, despite assurances that it would be returned prior to that time. Collins became concerned that she had met with misadventure; Raven's boat had supplied the colony with much needed provisions so her loss would have been severely felt. Imagine Collin's joy when the vessel sailed into the harbour at night on a chilly Monday in June 1793.

On arrival, the weary master gave a full account of his intrepid journey. According to Raven, he had left a gang on the southern New Zealand coast to procure enough seals and whales to fill his two boats. While there, he also found excellent New Zealand timber, which was very suitable for boat building, a trade still then in its infancy. Leaving his gang to their own devices, he then went elsewhere pursuing other trading ventures. Eventually, despite experiencing extreme weather conditions resulting in substantial losses, he made his way back to his crew now languishing at Dusky Bay. Such a voyage is indicative of the fact that the masters of sealing vessels were alive to all sorts of commercial opportunities that existed around the globe, and not just their quest for the pinnipeds. Masters would be instructed by their employers to carry all sorts of saleable commodities and exchange them for cash or other goods in whichever colonial port they were able to anchor. Ships carrying one type of produce going one way would return laden down with completely different cargo on their return.

Notwithstanding the success of mariners in islands to the

---

[15] The Company was established in 1600 by royal charter following the defeat of the Spanish in 1588 and thrived as a de facto 'regime' until well into the 19th century.

Chapter 5: Australia's First Enterprise

west and east of mainland Australia, the gradual trickle down of intelligence to Port Jackson of the potential for a sealing industry really occurred almost by chance. In late February, 1797, three of the survivors of the wreck of the Campbell and Clark Indian company owned *Sydney Cove* had reached Port Jackson following an arduous and somewhat treacherous journey on foot along the Australian east coast.[16] After being treated for malnourishment and exhaustion, they disclosed to the Governor and his officers that, while on Preservation Island in Bass Strait where the vessel had foundered, they had observed a plethora of seals thriving there and elsewhere in these Straits.

When you fly over the eastern part of this region you notice the numerous islands located within it and how close to each other many of them are. You also observe the reefs above and below sea level that lurk close to the pristine bays and beaches that abound surrounding these outcrops. Preservation Island has its share. It is easy to imagine how treacherous this environment would have been in rough conditions in colonial times when many a ship came to grief.

It was early the next year, Flinders and the surgeon Bass were authorised to voyage into this dangerous region and locate the wreck of the *Sydney Cove*, its cargo and any survivors. They were also tasked with conducting explorations down the south coast of New South Wales and along the coastal regions of Van Diemen's Land, primarily to search for a channel separating that land from New Holland, but secondly to seek opportunities for a staple economic enterprise.

In January 1798, Bass arrived at Seal Island in the Furneaux Group to see if there were any 'commercial advantage to be found there.'[17] But that was as close to the discovery of a marine resource or "staple" that anyone had been. Approximately one month later, Flinders voyaged southward to collect any remaining cargo from the wrecked *Sydney Cove*. When he reached Battery Island, he

---

[16] Mark McKenna. *From the Edge Australia's Lost Histories*, 1-63.

[17] Entry in the diary of George Bass, Voyage in the Whale Boat, Saturday, 27 January 1798, *HRNSW*, 325.

observed that 'large hair seals on rocks were found there'. Flinders took advantage of the docile mammals and taking aim, shot at one, noting that the seal's weight 'was equal to that of a common ox'. When he anchored near Cone Point, he journalled that fur seals located there numbered far more than they had witnessed ever before. His "sailors" slaughtered as many of these 'harmless and not unamiable creatures' as they could. In a sign of events to come, and perhaps with a guilty conscience, he noted in his journal: 'We then left the poor affrighted multitude to recover from the effect of our inauspicious visit'.

It may have been inauspicious, but it was also portentous. Following his discovery, Flinders anxiously reported his findings to the authorities in Port Jackson. It was this primarily which encouraged Charles Bishop and his deputy Simpson to fit out the brig *Nautilus* for a 'sealing speculation' and to have Flinders and Bass join him in the voyage of discovery to the south. Flinders had already informed colonial traders and the authorities in Sydney of the potential maritime gold mine that existed around Van Diemen's Land.[18] Later, Collins reported to the authorities in London:

> At the same time the *Nautilus* Brig and *Norfolk* long boat sailed for Van Diemen's, the two young men [Flinders and Bass] were determined to try, during this season, what the seal fishing among the islands to the southward might produce...[19]

But, by then, Bishop had already made his commercial intentions abundantly clear.

Charles Bishop was no ordinary mariner. After reaching the rank of midshipman in the English navy, he became disillusioned and dissatisfied. Like many other mariners, he turned his gaze to private trade and what some called 'the swing to the East'.[20]

---

[18] See Geoffrey C. Ingleton, *Matthew Flinders Navigator and Chart maker*, 37.

[19] Collins, *101*. Flinders and Bass (as often was the case with such missions) had another purpose to find out if Van Diemen's Land was actually an island so that traders from England could shorten the distance from that country to the new colony.

[20] See, for example, Michael Roe (ed.), *The Journal and Letters of Captain Charles Bishop on the Northwest est Coast of America, in the Pacific and in New South Wales 1794-1799*, xv-xvi.

Chapter 5: Australia's First Enterprise

He gained employment as a master with the English merchant Sydenham Teast, who was active in whaling, gum copal and the wood trades (mainly out of Africa). Teast was unusual at that time in that he abhorred slavery. At the time this nefarious trade was by far the most lucrative source of profit for the English traders.[21] During the late 1780s, Sydenham realised that a better outcome might be obtained from seeking otter furs in North America, which had interested many traders since the 1600s.[22] He purchased the *Ruby*, an American-built vessel and placed Bishop in command to seek his fortune in procuring the mammals.

The trader had appointed a very capable second-in-command, Roger Simpson, to assist Bishop. But neither man had any idea about commercial matters, let alone about the trade in otters. Unfortunately, the naïve Bishop engaged the services of a former clergyman and rogue John Howel to assist in his enterprise. It was all smoke and mirrors as the cleric went missing in action. Howel had become a part-owner of another vessel, and, tempted by the allure and opportunities that awaited colonisers elsewhere, spent most of his time in the Sandwich Islands rather than assisting Bishop.

In addition to the misleading and deceptive conduct of Howel, Bishop also had to contend with trading restrictions. Frustrated, he was ready to abandon fishing. To add to his anguish, the Ruby became less than serviceable. Bishop thought he had solved his dilemma by offering to buy the Nautilus. Excited by the prospects, he wrote that it was a 'beautiful little brig, 4.5 years old built at Calcutta, by Colonel Kidd'. This he purchased for 4,000 Star pagodas[23] by Indenture and Bill of Sale dated 23 November 1796.[24]

---

[21] Teast's vessels operated with surgeons on board. He was well regarded by his crews in ensuring a much better chance of survival in a hostile marine environment.

[22] Apparently, the Japanese had discovered the otters in North America before 1600, and other nationalities had voyaged there including the Russians, Spanish, French, Austrians and later the English and New England traders.

[23] USD6,200.

[24] The purchase from Major Alexander Kydd, a Bengal Engineer in the service of the Company, represented a change in fortune for Bishop as the vessel had previously been sold for £7,000 but the purchaser had not paid Timmins defaulting on

Bishop had every intention of going to America to pursue the otters and was on his way in the Nautilus when he anchored in Matavi Bay at Tahiti to replenish supplies and careen the boat.

While there, two crewmen absconded and stole a smaller watercraft. They were captured 'by the natives' and stripped naked. With them facing almost certain death, 'the King's father' somehow intervened and secured their release. By then, despite his kind intervention, it quickly became apparent from conversations Bishop had with some of the London Missionary Society clergy on the island that all was not as it appeared: some "natives" were going to kill the men of God. Without hesitation Bishop made a decision to leave and headed for Port Jackson. At that time, the vessel was leaking badly. Bishop later wrote to his employer:

> It was resolved… to proceed to Port Jackson in New South Wales and repair the vessel there during the winter months in the southern hemisphere and take such farther steps as the necessity if the case should require. That the step having been previously resolved on, application by the Society of missionaries as they conceived their lives eminently in danger from a proposed attack of the natives that we would receive them and their families on board as much of their effects as we could conveniently and with safety of the vessel carry, agreeing that they would make good any extraordinary expense of provisions… which we acceded to as well on the score of humanity as a return to the kindness we have previously received from them.[25]

The *Nautilus* limped into Port Jackson in May 1798. Fearing the worst, Bishop organised for the boat to be assessed for damage. The captain was shrewd enough to understand that he would need to do this before he spent any of Teast's money. The master arranged for a builder and carpenter to undertake the work. Covering his tracks, he also organised a document to be executed by those tradesmen. This referred to the necessity of undertaking numerous repairs so that 'the Nautilus [could] be put in a fit state to proceed to sea on her voyage'.[26] The materials required for the repairs were very

the contract.

[25] Captain Charles Bishop's report to Teast as set out in Roe (ed.) *The Journal and Letters of Captain Charles Bishop*, 161.

[26] The 'deponents' effectively swore to the truth of the content of the document.

Chapter 5: Australia's First Enterprise

expensive, and Bishop was forced to rely on Government support to supply him 'with pitch and other necessary stores'. Writing to Teast sometime later in a quaintly titled document called a "Copy of Protest" the master outlined the events leading up to the 'shattered and leaky' state of the vessel when arriving at the colony.

In this correspondence, it is already clear Bishop had received much intelligence[27] about the abundance of fur seals in the Bass Straits. He expressed confidence to his owner that he would be back in China 'in seven or eight months with a large cargo of dry seals skins'. His excitement at the potential waiting there was palpable. The gravitas of his mission to make the most of this opportunity (and effectively remove the stigma of his previous failed adventures in Asia and elsewhere), is made clear in his letter:

> …we learn that the islands thereabout abounds with fur seals, and it is our intention to proceed from here about the 25th of this month for those parts with a strong crew of 25 men and two whaleboats to kill and dry skins for China, and boil out seal oil for this market, proposing 1st to secure the ship in a good harbour and then divide the people in separate parties, to the different islands under the command of myself and officers, keeping a few of the crew boiling oil which we expect to procure for the quantity of 3 or 4000 gallons which will doubtless sell well here at least five shillings per gallon perhaps more, and it is further proposed that when we have got about 2000 gallons and 10,000 skins to leave 2/3 of the crew under the officers and proceed here with both articles we have procured, sell the oil, and lodge the skins as so much property secured, then to take in a fresh stock of provisions and return to the seal islands, the distance not being more than 3 or 4 day sail…[28]

The crew he hired were the most experienced colonial mariners available and were on 'shares' of the proceeds of sale of the skins and oil rather than wages. Articles of agreement were drawn up

---

Report of a Survey held at Sydney 19 May 1798 on the barque Nautilus by Messrs. Thomas Moore, Master Builder. The carpenter was a George McClay.

[27] It was common in the colonial circles of the time to call information that was received 'intelligence'.

[28] Captain Charles Bishop to Mr Sydenham Teast, viewed in J.S. Cumpston, *First Visitors to Bass Strait* (Canberra: Roebuck Society Publication No.7 1973), 7, and Roe, Op. cit., 29.

between Bishop and his gang which reflected the new employment arrangements for their maritime venture. It was made clear in the articles that the crew would only be entitled to their 'lay' on completion of the voyage *provided they fully performed their duties*. The document set the pattern that was put into place by the Sydney Traders with their crews until the sealing industry declined.

Probably of more interest were conditions giving the crew a right by majority vote to fine any member who was found to be 'indolent, slothful or idle' who did 'perform his or their proper task share or proportion of work in a suitable and seaman like manner'. These rights reflect a level of democracy that was present in the maritime industry that was not available to those employed on land. But it was subject to veto by Bishop. To some extent then democracy was alive and well in the maritime industry, something akin to the rules governing the conduct of pirates during the golden age of piracy in the early 18th century.[29]

Like many sealing crews, the crew Bishop had assembled for the task was multi-national. It included the American Samuel Chase and the Englishman Daniel Cooper (also known as 'Cowper'). These two men became leaders of maritime crews operating in Bass Strait and elsewhere during the relevant colonial period. Others who were chosen included John Boxo of Bengal, Chinese Taylor and Amowee both of Oriental origin, and two named Namahama and Oneehehow, probably from Owyhee or perhaps Otaheite as they were then called.[30] Once Bishop had undertaken the logistics required to prepare the boat for the mission, the crew had expanded to 33. The diverse *Nautilus* crew became the first of many who came to be identified as the sealers.

Bishop commenced his voyage from Port Jackson on about 7 October 1798 on his brig. He was accompanied by Flinders and Bass in the sloop *Norfolk*, which Governor Hunter had supplied, probably at little cost. This vessel had only eight crew and its primary purpose was discovery, not sealing. When Bishop and Flinders in

---

[29] See, for example, Marcus Rediker, *Villains of All Nations Atlantic Pirates in the Golden Age*.

[30] Called that by Captain James Cook and is the present-day Hawaii.

their respective boats reached Waterhouse Island, an arid slightly elevated treeless outcrop 11 kilometres off Van Diemen's Land, later that month, they observed it was almost completely covered by birds and hair seals. Flinders noticed there were no 'natives' on the island and mistakenly believed they were not capable of getting there as there were no canoes 'upon this part of the coast'. The *Nautilus* then separated from Flinders and Bass and Bishop went off on his own to seek seals. On 24 November, the boats were reunited, with Flinders 'finding Captain Bishop proceeding successfully in his sealing business, though slower than he might have done...'[31] When the two vessels eventually reached Preservation Island, they were shocked to find the remaining survivors of the *Sydney Cove* in a most deplorable drunken state. Flinders reported that if they had not eaten birds and seals they may well have perished.[32]

In any case, the principal purpose for which Bishop voyaged to the Straits was achieved. By 20 December, the gang had flensed 5,200 skins and poured 350 gallons of oil into barrels. Hauling up the anchor, Bishop left 14 'able hands' under the command of a John Harbottle to continue collecting skins in his absence. As was often the case on such ventures, there were more opportunities for the sealers. Bishop and Flinders found an abundance of seals in Kent's Bay. The crews proceeded to set up a camp of tents there with some men remaining in the Straits until March 1799 where they slaughtered in excess of 9,000 seals. Even at that stage, the explorer expressed his concern about the environmental consequences of aggressive sealing. Flinders recorded for posterity that 'unfortunately this species (seals) of fishery is soon exhausted', noting by then the plethora of sealing vessels that had commenced to frequent the Fishery.[33]

---

[31] Matthew Flinders. *A Voyage to Terra Australis*. Here Flinders was indicating that Bishop had been slower than if he was undertaking the hunt for seals.

[32] Matthew Flinders, reported in Collins, Op. cit., Vol. 2, 1238-1242.

[33] Flinders noted "Nine thousand skins of the first quality, with several tons of oil, were procured by the Nautilus, and Furneaux's Islands have since been frequented by small vessels from Port Jackson upon the same errand. Unfortunately, this species of fishery is soon exhausted in any one place; or it would have been the means of raising up a useful body of seamen, and thus proved of advantage, both

Before returning to Sydney Cove, five of Bishop's crew surprised him by declaring they wanted to remain in the Straits. They terminated their articles with him and their master paid them in kind the equivalent of USD545.25 for each of their lays, a small fortune in those days. Four of these men, namely Cooper, Chase, Joseph Oliphant and William Sparks, formed what may be regarded as the first gang of sealers in the islands. In the meantime, Bishop sailed back to Sydney with his booty. Lieutenant David Collins wrote:

> On the evening of the 25th, which had been duly observed as Christmas Day, the Nautilus arrived from the southward. She had been at Preservation Island, where, and among the neighbouring islands, she had been tolerably successful in seal catching.[34]

After arriving back in Sydney, Bishop gloated to Teast about the skins 'of the best quality' that he had secured. He was emphatic in underlining that he had spared 'no pains or exertion either of body or mind to bring the difficulties [...] encountered in this disastrous voyage to a happy issue.'[35] No doubt Bishop had shared his employer's anxieties following the master's own previous failures to derive a profit. Collins had understated the success of the voyage, as Bishop was more than tolerably successful, it seems with the complete catch selling at auction in only a few days. Unlike the difficulties that would beset other sealing captains in the Antipodes, he had only lost one man. That mariner was Edward Hogan who had sadly passed away at Cape Barren in December 1798.

Bishop had almost broken even on his voyage to the Fishery. Of more importance was that he had signalled to the world at large the opportunities that now existed for sealers in the southern seas. He left for Macao in about May 1799 to trade skins with the Chinese. The master was even more enterprising. He added to his commercial armoury by obtaining 'Letters of Marque' to enable him as a private operator to plunder any vessel belonging to enemies of

---

to the colony and to the mother country."
[34] Collins, Vol. II, 108.
[35] Bishop's letter to Teast from Port Jackson, 4 January 1799.

Chapter 5: Australia's First Enterprise

the King that he should come across in his travels.[36] He was the first to make such an aggressive application in the colony and was followed by others seeking another source of bounty. Writing to the authorities on 15 May 1799, he sought a commission and requested muskets, bayonets with pistols and cutlasses.[37] Leaving the colony soon after, he found his way back to England in the company of none other than Bass. The men had become friends. The surgeon was considering a career change from His Royal Highness' navy to a trader of various products in the Antipodes.[38] The friendship was not to last. Like many other such arrangements of the time, Bishop's venture with Bass was underwritten financially by men who had ties to the military and the colony. These included Naval Officer Kent, the colonial surgeon Thomas Jamison and James Williamson, the Deputy Commissary. But matters went from bad to worse for Bishop. Falling out with Bass, Charles suffered a mental meltdown and was declared insane. His estate was placed in the hands of the pastoralist John MacArthur and clergyman Samuel Marsden and sold off.[39] A sad end to the pioneer of the sealing trade in the colony!

Word about Bishop's sealing success soon spread far and wide. Excited by the potential in the Straits, the Sydney Traders started advertising for mariners to crew their vessels going to the southern Fishery. In particular, Robert Campbell, John Palmer, Simeon Lord and Kable and Underwood were actively seeking men who 'have references for sobriety and integrity' or 'exemplary character'.

---

[36] See Request of Letter of Marques Commission to Governor Hunter dated 5 May 1799 as recorded in Roe, Op. cit., 314.

[37] Bishop and Bass had purchased the brig Venus for various purposes, and it would appear had obtained the Letters of Marque from the authorities when they set sail on 9 January 1801 for the Canary Islands anxious to secure a Spanish 'prize' but had returned to Port Jackson by August.

[38] Bass and Bishop's partnership proved a disaster, so that by 1803 both the brig and Bass went missing, never to be found again.

[39] The following advertisement appeared in The Sydney Gazette and New South Wales Advertiser on Sunday 9 March 1806: "All persons who may have Claims upon the said Mr Charles Bishop are required to substantiate them before the Civil Court at its first Opening, that if Judgement be awarded they may be discharged; And all persons indebted to him are desired immediately to discharge the same, and deliver up to us any property of his they may now have in their possession."

A typical advertisement in late 1803 stated:

WANTED

> Ten or twelve able men to engage for a limited term on an expedition to the Southward, for the purposes of sealing, oiling etc. Persons of good character qualified to enter into such Engagement, are required to make application to John Palmer Esq.[40]

Many men from diverse backgrounds answered advertisements such as these, signing up articles with the Sydney Traders to crew vessels going to the Straits. They had a sense of adventure and foreboding. It soon became clear that some traders wanted the men to also remain on the islands on a whimsical promise to return and collect them often at an uncertain time. Left to their own devices, usually with a 'headsman' in charge, the mariners would set up camps and ply their trade seeking to slaughter the abundant Bass Strait seal populations. In doing so, they would increase the number of skins and preserve the oil from the seals by establishing additional means of production in difficult and sometimes extreme circumstances.

From 1798 until about 1809, the Sydney Traders' ships focused mainly on Bass Strait. It was effectively a 'gold rush' of activity that netted thousands of seal skins and gallons of oil. In so doing, it provided staple commodities that enabled several entrepreneurs to achieve significant wealth. So, by 1805, the Port Jackson merchants had earned sufficient profits from sealing to start building larger vessels. For example, in that year, Underwood built the first colonial vessel primarily for maritime purposes, according to Peter Cunningham.[41] Nearly all of the Antipodean environments where seals thrived had been exploited by 1810.[42] A report from a naval officer on 19 August 1806 indicated that nearly 120,000 seal skins had been landed from vessels since 1800, with 14,750 more coming

---

[40] *The Sydney Gazette*, 4 December 1803, 2.

[41] Peter Cunningham. *Two Years in New South Wales*, Vol. 2, 67.

[42] Other than sub-Antarctic Islands such as Heard Island which was not discovered apparently until 25 November 1853

Chapter 5: Australia's First Enterprise

from British whalers and sealers.[43] To maximise the anticipated profits and completely fill a boat, it was not unusual for vessels to voyage to many islands to secure a decent catch before returning to the settlements. So, Samuel Chace, who had set up on his own account after leaving Bishop, sailed his boat around the Kent's Group, anchored at Seal and New Year's Islands, flensing 500 seal skins before returning to Port Jackson.[44]

This commercial hunger for skins and oil was driven by eager and greedy traders keen to make vast profits selling valuable commodities. Even before the advent of the Antipodean sealing frenzy, on the eve of the industrial revolution, the oil from the elephant seal was valued in the Western World as an odourless and smoke-free fuel for the purpose of lighting houses, streets and commercial enterprises. It also functioned as a lubricant and applied in the painting trade. However, in what came to be known as the 'China Trade', it was the skin from the fur seal that was most in demand. The fur could be cut away from the body of the seal and used to make felt. The pelt could be employed in the manufacture of clothing, provided certain steps were taken to remove the soft part from the coarse outer shell.

By the mid-1780s, the Americans were trading dried fur skins in Canton for other goods such as tea and spices. The British joined the party in about 1793, through mariners such as Cox and Raven. That trade continued until about 1803, when the market slowed due to an oversupply of seal commodities. However, this did not prevent American and English traders from supplying the London market, particularly after 1796, when an industrial process was invented to separate the soft fur from the coarse outer layer.[45] Skins also could be better preserved in salt rather than by drying. Later,

---

[43] John Harris Naval Officer, *Historical Records of New South Wales*, 19 August 1806,169.

[44] *The Sydney Gazette,* 28 August, 1803, 3.

[45] Thomas Chapman was the inventor of this process according to the historian Hainsworth, *The Sydney Traders,* 149. Petition to the House of Commons Number 701 Seal Skins "A narrative of the case of Mr Thomas Chapman who first discovered the means of making the fur of the seal available to the manufacturers of hats shawls & super fine cloths."

another market opened when it became fashionable to use these maritime products in the manufacture of hats and other clothing.

For the first twelve years after Bishop's voyage, the focus remained on the rookeries in the Straits. Initial reports of those navigators who went exploring elsewhere and found any seals was not promising. By 1803, Flinders had voyaged around New Holland in the *Investigator* and had noted seals in various regions on his journey. When he arrived at Kangaroo Island, Flinders observed a plethora of pinnipeds but was principally unimpressed, commenting in his report:

> All of the islands seem to be more or less frequented by seals; but I think not in numbers sufficient to make a speculation from Europe advisable on their account; certainly not for the China market, the seals being mostly of the hair kind, and the fur of such others as were seen was red and coarse.[46]

But that assessment would change after 1809.

Seals were not the only creatures Flinders found in that region. Anchoring in Encounter Bay, to his surprise, he came upon a French expedition under the command of Nicholas Baudin. The meeting between the two commanders was pleasant enough, and Baudin was left to voyage to Port Jackson. On his arrival there, he was surprised to find Sydney Harbour in a frenzy of marine activity. By then, a boat-building industry had begun to thrive. Twenty-seven-year-old Francois Peron, the sole surviving zoologist with Baudin, kept a detailed journal of the voyage of discovery and exploration writing:

> A croud [sic] of objects, equally interesting, demanded our notice in every direction. In the port we saw, drawn up together, a number of vessels that had arrived from different parts of the world, and most of which were destined to perform new and difficult voyages. Some of them had come from the banks of the Thames, or the Shannon, to pursue whale fishing on the frigid shores of New Zealand… Several smaller vessels were on their way to Bass's Straits, to receive skins, collected by a few individuals, who had established themselves on the isles of those Straits, to catch the marine animals that resort to them…

---

[46] Flinders, 56.

The zoologist noticed that also American ships were a familiar sight anchored in the Harbour:

> Here they were preparing an expedition, to carry on a skin trade, with the people of the north- west shores of America. In short, in this period the harbour at Port Jackson had become familiar to the American navigators, and their flag was continually flying in it, during our residence.[47]

It is interesting to note that despite the hostilities that existed between the English, French and Americans following the two revolutions, at the margins of the Empire, there existed a degree of harmony which transcended nationalist zeal in the political sphere. At that time, opportunities to seek out pinnipeds existed across the globe. Many American traders were actively criss-crossing the seas from the southern to northern hemispheres in search of pinnipeds. Their aggressive approach was not to endear the Yankees to the colonial mariners. But economic rewards for some would be realised. The exploitation of the pinnipeds was about to explode.

While the French were ostensibly exploring, watercraft were constantly making their way to and from the sealing grounds in the Straits. The local press often reported in the *Ship News* on the arrival and departure of boats, and on their catches once they had returned. From that, we can ascertain just how successful an industry it was, certainly up to about 1810. The following reports in *The Sydney Gazette* are illustrative:

> On Monday also arrived the schooner Governor King, Messrs. Kable and Underwood owners from King's Island with 37 tons of oil and about 700 skins.[48]

> On Thursday arrived from King's Island, the schooner Endeavour with 1400 seal skins and 600 sea elephant teeth, the latter of which are said to be in high estimation among the natives of the Fejees.[49]

---

[47] François Peron. *A Voyage of Discovery to the Southern Hemisphere*, Chapter XIX, 276.

[48] *The Sydney Gazette,* Sunday, 1 January ,1804,1.

[49] Ibid., Sunday, 3 July, 1808,1.

> On the same day arrived the Pegasus Capt. Bunker belonging to this port with about 12,600 skins... Same day arrived the brig Fox, Captain Cox, with between 13 and 14000 skins and 190 whales' teeth...[50]

The Sydney Traders were the originators of these advertisements and were making a killing. The partnership between Kable and Underwood was particularly prominent. By the middle of 1804, they were employing an average of 63 men on at least three vessels to secure a total of over 28,000 skins, 40 gallons of 'elephant' oil, and 220 gallons of seal oil from their exploits in the Fishery.[51] The historian D.R. Hainsworth estimates from analysing a source document, the colonial muster, that over 200 men were employed as sealers by only three traders out of Port Jackson by 1805, perhaps representing 10-15 per cent of the colony's freemen.

Sealing became the colony's principal economic pursuit. Given the lack of an alternative staple, Governors Hunter and King fully supported the enthusiasm of the Sydney merchants. This was despite the restrictions on exporting skins and oil imposed by the English authorities and the ubiquitous Company. For example, even before Governor Phillip embarked on the First Fleet, on 25 April 1787,[52] he had received the following fairly prescriptive instructions:

> ...every sort of intercourse between the intended settlement at Botany Bay, or other place which may hereafter be established on the coast of New South Wales and its dependencies and the settlements of our East India company, as well as the coast of China and the islands situated in that part of the world, to which any intercourse has been established by any European nation, should be prevented by every possible means...

And further:

> you do not on any account allow craft of any sort to be built for the use of private individuals which might enable them to effect such intercourse, and that you do prevent any Vessels which may at any time hereafter arrived at the said settlement from any of the Ports before mentioned, from having communication with

---

[50] *The Sunday Gazette,* Sunday, 19 March, 1809, 1.

[51] Ibid., Sunday, 22 July, 1804, 2.

[52] See William Bradley, *A Journal of a Voyage to New South Wales,* 12.

Chapter 5: Australia's First Enterprise

any of the Inhabitants residing within your Government without first receiving especial permission from you for that purpose...⁵³

The importance of those instructions, influenced in part by the directors of the Company, is illustrated by the fact that they were provided to each successive governor of the Colony for some considerable time.⁵⁴ Those inclined to seek a living from the sea found it difficult to overcome the tight restrictions imposed by the Government and Company during the first 20 years of the colony. But this did not stop enterprising individual traders and others managing to do so by other means including using loopholes in the system. Some appointed agents with vessels registered in London. Others sought out partnerships of sorts with Yankee mariners who were free to ply their trade. Finally, the more savvy relied on lobbying prominent men such as Joseph Banks.

Early in 1802, Hunter had suggested to the Colonial Under Secretary that the sealing business would be 'better off' in the hands of the traders 'if permitted to build vessels for that purpose.'⁵⁵ They had the support of Banks who commanded significant political influence over Imperial policy. But it took him until June 1806 to write to the British authorities about allowing the local colonial traders a chance to prosper from sealing.⁵⁶ This happened after several complaints had been made to him by the Sydney Traders and "shippers" about the constraints placed upon them by the Company monopoly. In his letter, he informed the English officials that mariners had already entered into the seal trade with 'spirit and activity'. But the botanist was concerned that, once the good citizens of Sydney had established their own democratic rights, they would also seek the benefits already afforded to English traders through their navigation legislation. He had come to believe that

---

⁵³ See John Bach, A Maritime History of Australia. Sydney: Pan Books, 1976 ,71. See also a transcript of Phillip's instructions at https://www.foundingdocs.gov.au/item-sdid-68.html

⁵⁴ See J. S. Cumpston, Shipping Arrivals and Departures Sydney 1788-1825.

⁵⁵ Governor Hunter to Under Secretary King, in *Historical Records of New South Wales*, 22 March, 1802.

⁵⁶ Joseph Banks, 'Some remarks on the present state of the colony of Sidney [sic] in New South Wales, 4 June, 1806 (series 35.35) No. 0002.

colonial traders would be forced into piracy due to the Company's harsh restrictions, or, heaven forbid, into trading with other nations such as France and America.[57]

Banks was clearly aware of the vast seal rookeries that were located in the Fishery. He was savvy enough to know the uses to which the fur, skin and oil of the pinnipeds could be employed at considerable profit. A Captain Wilson had written to him expressing his concern about the restrictions imposed on colonial maritime trade once the sealing industry gained momentum.[58] In his letter, Wilson asked Joseph to support the move to lift Company sanctions. This would have enabled colonial traders to build many larger boats and increase the prospects of trading profitably. It would mean avoiding the sinister consequences of piracy and any alternate trade.[59]

The local trade was also encouraged by the wholehearted support they received from Governor King. In 1804, King wrote a gushing report to Lord Hobart. In that document, he informed Hobart of the successes being enjoyed by 'individuals' engaged in the 'Basses Straits' sealing industry. He noted that the pursuit was 'very profitable', and as such was 'an advantage to the colony in the number of men and small vessels employed'.[60] He went further, informing Hobart that several 'individuals' had built vessels 'larger than His Majesty's instructions', but only on the basis that they stay within the limits of the territory. He explained that he had already allowed Robert Campbell permission to build but only on condition that he paid a bond as security against any default on the part of the merchant.

Governor King was obviously concerned about promoting a breach of the original instructions and fearful of repercussions from the Company. He had asked Hobart for advice on how he should

---

[57] *Historical Records of New South Wales*, 4 June, 1806, 87.

[58] He was the London Agent for the Reverend Samuel Marsden and Messrs Campbell and Co and had command of the ship Royal Admiral when it visited the colony in 1800.

[59] *Historical Records of New South Wales*, Captain Wilson to Sir Joseph Banks, Monument Yard, 27 June, 1806, 89.

[60] See Letter from Governor King to Lord Bathurst, 1 March, 1804.

Chapter 5: Australia's First Enterprise

best extend Campbell's liberties to others. But, in practice, King turned a blind eye to the restrictions. Not only did the Governor encourage the industry, he also assisted it. For seven shillings a skin, he contracted traders to supply him with seal skins for shoe leather. Not only that, but he permitted other traders to load their catch onto government vessels for export. In his letter to Hobart, he confirmed that he actively encouraged boat builders and traders like Campbell to build vessels without having to obtain his consent. This was subject to operating within the limits of the territory so as not to offend against the monopoly of the Company.[61] The Company directors in London would have been furious and angrily sought to prevent interference with the monopoly.

King ignored them. Under his liberal and encouraging governance, traders started shipping skins to China where the demand for seal commodities remained high. But this was not so in England where the East India Company maintained tight controls over the trade. That was until January 1805, when Campbell arranged to export 14,000 skins to London in the 500-ton ship *Lady Barlow*. He was outraged when, on arrival at the docks in London some months later, the Company men seized his cargo. This resulted in him suffering significant financial loss. But the outcry occasioned by that loss, the support the Sydney merchant received from Banks and Campbell's lobbying, eventually led to an easing of restrictions. By June of that year, the Company 'in consideration of the increasing activity of this distant colony [Sydney]' permitted the vessel Sydney to enter the London docks. By this action, the Company reluctantly acknowledged 'an important and an improving industry'.[62] Effectively, the colonial traders managed to avoid the harsh restrictions that were imposed by the Company, and significant rival competition from the Americans and French, who were active in the pursuit of seal in Bass Strait, and many of the colonial traders prospered.

---

[61] *Historical Records of New South Wales* Vol. 5 (1803-1805), 335-36, 1 March, 1804.

[62] Ibid., The Board of Trade to the East India Company, 30 June, 1806, 103.

One of the mariners to benefit from this change of heart by the British authorities was a Captain W. Wilson who had visited the colony in the *Royal Admiral* in 1800. He had later become the agent for both the persuasive Reverend Marsden and the Campbell House and kept in close contact with Banks. In his 1806 correspondence, he outlined the controversial history of the colonial sealing vessels that had voyaged to London in the previous year or so and the impediments that had been overcome by Bank's intercession. In particular, he blamed the mercantile interests of what he described as the 'old whalers', like the Enderby family, as driving the prohibitions that had been imposed by English Customs and the Company. After praising the encouragement given by King to the colonial industry and setting out the various clothing that could be made out of fur skins, he focussed on Campbell's losses in graphic detail. These losses were not limited to skins and oil. Wilson emphasised that many other commodities were shipped by traders on a regular basis to maximise the profits. Trading all manner of goods from sealing vessels was a common occurrence in the colonial period designed to reward captains and boat owners with additional income to line their pockets. For example, apart from a bounty in seal skins, on Campbell's ship there were quantities of what were called tuna oil, 'beef-wood' and 'cabinet-wood' being carried. Once the English authorities opened up the trade to the colonials, vessels came laden with all manner of bounties. For example, the *Honduras Packet* docked at London first with a cargo of '30,000 salted and 6,000 dry fur sealskins belonging to the colonists' and the owners had organised insurance for another 30,000.

After that, the Antipodean sealing trade prospered for a time with the additional assistance of restrictions placed on foreign traders such as the French and Americans. These colonial mandates created their own level of tension and disharmony. Notwithstanding that fact, the colonial traders would not be denied. By then, mariners were voyaging far and wide searching for the mammals with vessels and their human occupants being sacrificed in the pursuit of profit. In addition, whenever sealing became unprofitable, such as the lean years after 1813, several traders, masters and sealers began to

Chapter 5: Australia's First Enterprise

supplement their income from other pursuits such as whaling, the collection of salt and flax, and agriculture.

Some of the main victims of this avarice were the crews that operated the sealing vessels. Entrepreneurs were finding significant value in the practice of leaving mariners behind on sealing islands to fish. The gangs were enticed into these arrangements by promises of a greater percentage of the catch. At least, that is what the crews were promised. In reality, sealing gangs were frequently left in various littoral and far distant islands to live on their own for several months – sometimes years. This meant the exploitative Sydney Traders had opportunities to harness significant manpower without need to maintain the welfare of their men at little or no cost. Many crews left to sealing in the islands by masters ran out of provisions. After a while, this sort of nefarious practice came to the attention of the colonial authorities, and, though some attempts were made to correct the practice, it continued.

An early example of this practice was broadcasted to all and sundry when the master mariner Samuel Chase informed the editor of the Sydney paper that, while sealing in the Straits he had met the sealer Mr Cooper: 'formerly the second mate of the brig *Margaret*... in quest of seals but out of provisions'.[63] Another report from May 1806 in the same publication, probably from the captain of the *Estramina*, mentioned that the ship 'fell in with the sloop *Raven* belonging to Messrs. Raby and Wills, with her people in great distress for want of provisions, having from some unknown causes considerably overstayed their time'.[64] Later still, the *Ship News* announced the arrival of the *Eliza* from Kangaroo Island. The editor reported that its crew had encountered seven sealers on that island, led by Joseph Murrell. They had used up their provisions within the first three months and were eating 'wild animals', having received no additional supply from their employer.[65]

After several years and many reported cases of neglect and exploitation of the stranded mariners by ship masters travelling

---

[63] *The Sydney Gazette and New South Wales Advertiser*, 15 May, 1803, 1.
[64] Ibid., 4 May, 1806, "Ship News", 4.
[65] Ibid., 16 April, 1809, "Ship News", 2.

through the Straits, the practice of crew abandonment came to the attention of the Lieutenant Governor at Port Dalrymple. Firstly, he was informed about this problem when a boat crew arrived there seeking supplies to 'relieve their distresses and those of 20 other people in the employ of Henry Kable and others'. Secondly, a gang of men who signed articles with Sydney Trader Campbell complained that they had been 'ten weeks without provisions and languishing with cold and hunger'.[66] As this was not the first time the authorities had been made aware of the mariners' plight, they decided to do something about it. They vainly tried to censure the conduct of the Sydney Traders, and they accused them of acting 'negligently' towards their fellow human beings due to 'perplexing and unwarrantable conduct'. By order of the Acting Secretary on 30 March 1805, owners of colonial vessels were required to enter recognisances to ensure that the 'gangs' of sealers were left with adequate provisions in the various islands where languishing or face stiff penalties. In addition, if there was sufficient evidence of further exploitation then the owner would also face the prospect of being restrained from leaving the various colonial ports at Sydney, Port Dalrymple and Hobart. The ultimate penalty would mean the termination of their contract.[67]

Whether any of these measures resulted in the sealers being properly and adequately provided for or compensated is debatable. Towards the end of this first period of the sealing industry, little sympathy was being displayed for the plight of these mariners. They were later the subject of significant adverse comment, by colonial authorities and the press of the time, particularly after the handing down of the *Bigge Reports* in 1822 and 1823. Certainly, both the Sydney Traders and foreign entrepreneurs, from France and the United States in particular, managed to use the sealers to the best of their advantage as they continued to procure seals without restraint. Some sealers took matters into their own hands and brought proceedings seeking damages in the Civil Jurisdiction

---

[66] *The Sydney Gazette and New South Wales Advertiser*, 31 August, 1805, 4.

[67] Garnham Blaxcell, Acting Secretary in *The Sydney Gazette*, 5 September, 1805, 4-8.

of the Supreme Court of New South Wales against the traders who had left them without adequate provisions. An analysis of these cases would reveal they had mixed outcomes from such litigation, as will be demonstrated.

Some historians tend to assert that the industry declined rapidly by the end of the first decade of the 19th century. But reports, letters and editorials after that time illustrate this assertion maybe somewhat misconceived. During the early to mid-1800s, seal skins sold well at Canton and Macao, but, by 1807 the market was oversupplied. The initial colonial "golden age" of sealing almost came to an abrupt halt[68] in about 1809 once the rookeries in Bass Strait had been almost entirely wiped out. But that just meant mariners went further afield. Traders compelled masters and sealers to voyage far and wide in the search for new killing fields. In so doing they crisscrossed the Antipodes and found fresh rookeries, which generated excellent revenue there for three years before the trade became saturated.

Then the British and colonial governments attempted to put another nail in the sealing industry's coffin by imposing hefty taxes on imported oil and skins. This became more important after the Company no longer held a monopoly over the sealing industry in the Antipodes. Its stranglehold was replaced by port charges introduced by the colonial authorities in Sydney and Hobart. This led to a groundswell of complaints by traders in those settlements who lobbied those same authorities to abolish the imposts.[69]

Notwithstanding these restraints, the industry continued to thrive and reward the colonials and the foreigners well beyond the peak of the first decade. This is illustrated from reports in *The*

---

[68] The Sydney Traders had already foreshadowed the decline of both sealing stocks and markets when they began organising, at great expense, voyages of economic 'discovery' to the east of Sydney Cove to unknown places beyond New Zealand. They were soon rewarded for their efforts once the Campbell and Macquarie Islands were encountered in 1810.

[69] James Kelly complained to Bigge about the port charges when giving evidence before the Commissioner in 1820. Also, several 'merchants' had passed a resolution to the effect that duties were 'highly detrimental and injurious to the commercial interests of this island and is particularly oppressive in the colonial craft'. See Bowden, 57.

Sydney Gazette. In the "*Ship News*" of Sunday 19 March 1809, the editor recorded at least six boats whose masters had secured from 2,000 to 30,000 seal skins, and vast quantities of seal oil.[70] Not long after, once adventurous crews found the rookeries at Macquarie and Campbell Islands, there was renewed interest in the locations to the south of New Zealand, and sealing as an industry thrived for a few years. Cunningham, who spent time as the Naval Surgeon on convict transports during the 1820s, wrote letters about his experiences in the colony. They were, on the whole, gushing in his support for it. He informed his readers that even by the early 1820s there were at least six sealing vessels operating in the Fishery.[71]

Apart from the hurdles imposed by the Company monopoly, imposts of the colonial authorities and depletion of seal rookeries, the colonial sealers had one other challenge to the free reign they enjoyed in the first decade of the 19th century. That came from the foreigners who had "discovered" the bounty available for the taking in the southern Antipodes. The early good nature of the relationship between the colonial traders and sealers and their American counterparts were tested on many occasions, particularly during this first period. While the Americans and colonial sealers and masters, often competed aggressively at similar locations for the same prize, the French were less inclined to assert themselves in disputes with the local maritime men.

---

[70] *The Sydney Gazette*, 19 March, 1809,1-2.

[71] Cunningham, Vol 2, 75. There were only four whaling vessels operating at the same time.

Chapter 6: Foreigners at the Tipping Edge

Even before the seal rookeries along the southern Australasian coastlines were revealed to the colonial mariners, French and American sealers, whalers and explorers were already active in seeking marine creatures to exploit. During the late 18th century, several foreign mariners were operating globally. Ships were voyaging from the Atlantic and Pacific Oceans up to China, Russia and into Europe, trading in skins and oil in exchange for Asiatic provisions. Dominating was the trade exchange system in place between the Americans and China. The Canton Factory Records demonstrate that the Yankee boats supplied over 90% of seal skins and oil to the Chinese markets from 1800 to 1804. Previously reports from the English explorer Vancouver,[1] of seals inhabiting the islands near present day Albany following his 1791 voyage, had reached Yankee shores. As early as 1792, a few American whaling and sealing vessels had visited Shark Bay in Western Australia, Adventure Bay on Bruny Island and Port Jackson.[2] They were on their way to Canton to trade otter skins. However, many of these traders did not just specialise in procuring seal products but brought with them other provisions which they sold to the colonials. The colony was in dire need and were keen consumers of these commodities. Despite these friendly encounters, colonial authorities, entrepreneurs and sealers had deep seated concerns about the arrival of American boats anchoring both in strategic locations and the sealing grounds being plundered.

Prominent among these foreign visitors were vessels owned by Ebenezer Dorr, a mariner from Boston. He owned a flotilla of

---

[1] Vancouver, 173.

[2] The vessels *Asia* and *Alliance* had been to Shark Bay and *Hope* and *Providence* had been to Sydney. See Nigel Wace and Bessie Lovett, *Yankee Maritime Activities and the Early History of Australia*, 2.

vessels, including the snow Fairy and the sealer Otter, anchoring in Port Jackson in 1793 and 1796, respectively. They carried skins flensed at St Paul's Island. After word of the Bass Strait sealing grounds spread following Bishop's voyage, a plethora of foreign boats, mainly from America, came to the Antipodes. They were stocked with "stores" of every kind. When they arrived, the Sydney traders realised the opportunities to make money, not only by dealing directly with the Americans but also by engaging them to transport products, including seal skins and oil, to the Chinese market. This avoided the severe restrictions imposed by the British East India Company and the imperial navigation legislation and led to a cosy and profitable relationship for some. But significant negative consequences also threatened.

At the time, colonial authorities were suspicious of the intentions of the international visitors. America had won its war of independence against England, and the French people had overthrown their monarch in a revolution from 1793. The western world was in a state of turmoil and upheaval, with disputes and wars breaking out between England and three other key powers, namely France, America and Spain. The colony could be in dispute with any of these nations. There was an underlying concern that any of them could try to claim a part of New Holland as a colony. Apart from this xenophobic fear and uncertainty that the visitors engendered in officials, another matter caused the colonial trader even greater concern. This was the aggressive competition from Americans and, to a lesser extent, the French, that arose as a direct outcome of the foreigners pursuing the sealing trade in the Fishery. This competition led to an escalation of tensions around Bass Strait, leading to violence. It also resulted in the imposition of legislative restrictions mandated by the colonial authorities on the detested international traders. During the first few years of the avaricious sealing period, disputes between the colonial and American sealers were intense, causing upheaval and turmoil. But they were short-lived with the more aggressive Yankees leaving disgruntled. Traders from the United States continued to sell carry and exchange goods around the colony as they did not pose any threat because they were not competing with any sealing ventures. It would be several decades before mariners from Boston and Nantucket would return to seek marine mammals, in this case to pursue another marine staple, the whale.

Between 1792 and about 1812, more than 60 American vessels visited the colony. Most came from Boston, New England, Rhode Island and New York. By 1803, some sealers, previously operating in the Straits, had left and set up camps in small communities on Kangaroo Island. They were joined by other adventurous mariners who sought a life free from the reach of colonial society and its officials.[3] It was in that year that the first significant American trader commenced sealing activities around *Karta* and encountered the colonial sealers occupying it.

At the time, Edmund Fanning, the American merchant, had risen from a simple cabin boy on his first voyage in 1792 to become a marine vessel owner and trader in his own right. His familiarity with Vancouver's journals excited his curiosity to pursue a trade in the Antipodes. Fanning arranged for his master Captain Isaac Pendleton to skipper the 99-ton brig *Union* to undertake an intrepid sealing voyage from New York to the colony. Fanning recorded later that 'Never, perhaps, was a voyage entered upon with brighter prospects, and never did a vessel sail with more encouraging prospects than this brig'.[4]

Pendleton was initially tasked with finding the Crozet Islands in the southern Indian Ocean. This opportunity came from intelligence freely given by French mariners who anchored there in 1772, finding a plethora of seals inhabiting the rocky outcrops. Unable to locate these bare volcanic land masses, the American changed directions and headed for King Georges Sound, eventually anchoring at Seal Island. The American was disappointed to find a rookery of only 30 seals. He attempted to voyage to Bass Strait, but hostile weather conditions prevented it. In rough seas, he sailed

---

[3] Kangaroo Island was named by Matthew Flinders on his circumnavigation of Australia when he observed the large numbers of the hopping quadrupeds there. The island was called *Ultima Thule* or 'land at the end of the world'.

[4] Edmund Fanning, *Voyages around the World*, 314.

towards Kangaroo Island in mid-1803. On entering the safe still harbour later called American River, he decided to seek shelter. He found the island and its coasts teaming with 'game' of all kinds, including both fur and hair seals. The Americans remained there for four months, decimating seals and other animals. The Yankees had come towards the end of the sealing season and wanted to maximise profits. As Pendleton had a great deal of spare time on his hands, he persuaded his crew and some of the resident colonial sealers to build a schooner from local timber resources. Once completed, it was 35 tons and named the *Independence*. Keen to take advantage of other opportunities, the master ordered one of his mariners, Owen Folger Smith, to sail to King Georges Sound in the newly constructed boat to hunt for more seals.[5] Meanwhile, the master further developed his cordial relationship with the local sealing community. This gang was headed by the sealer Daniel Cooper.

By January 1804, Pendleton had laid on board about 6,000 seal skins which he transported to Port Jackson via the Straits, becoming the first Yankee to do so. But, by then, his countryman Samuel Chace, now a successful entrepreneur in his own right, had informed the Governor and Sydney traders, with whom he had a close relationship, that the Americans were coming to monopolise the trade in the Straits.

On arrival at the Port Jackson docks, Pendleton encountered the Sydney trader Simeon Lord. By then, word had reached the colony about the abundant rookeries inhabiting the Antipodes Islands. Once there, Pendleton left a small crew of sealers to join in culling the islands of their seal populations. Greedy to make greater profits, he set sail for Kangaroo Island. When the Yankee returned to Sydney, he was persuaded by Lord to deposit with him in his stores for safekeeping 14,000 skins flensed on that island by the Americans. Convinced by the trader's persuasive nature, Pendleton entered into an unfortunate joint venture with Lord to travel to the 'Feejee Islands' to procure sandalwood. I say unfortunate for two reasons. En route, the American and his crew were 'all most

[5] Fanning, 317.

inhumanly massacred', allegedly by some local men.[6] No trace was ever found of his vessel. Then, once Lord found out about Pendleton's demise, he voyaged to the Antipodes Island. Here he located the crew that the captain had left behind and found, to his delight, they had accumulated near 60,000 seal skins of 'very superior quality'. By duplicitous means, he loaded the skins and then sailed to Canton to trade them for Chinese goods which he eventually disposed of in the United States. Greed got the better of Lord. He never accounted for the skins and profits derived from the trade to the rightful owners being Pendleton's estate trustees. Indeed, Lord had obtained a benefit by deception, a criminal offence then and now. Simeon was never charged, thus avoiding any adverse consequences.[7]

At about the same time as Pendleton was plying his trade across the Fishery, another American was also active. Captain Percival, in the 35-ton ship *Charles* of Boston, owned by Dorr and Co., went fishing in King Georges Sound. After some success, he turned his attention to the Bass Strait islands. Sailing across the Bight he anchored with a 35-man crew in the Kent Group of islands. Unlike the friendly Pendleton crew, these Americans were enterprising and aggressive in their approach. In their three-month stay, they upset many of the colonial mariners by fishing where the colonials had previously faced no competition. This led to physical violence. On 26 December 1803, George Howe, editor of the Sydney Gazette,[8] expressed anger and indignation in an article following a report from a Captain Moody sailing the *Governor King*. Moody had just returned to Port Jackson from the Straits with 37 tons of oil and 700 seal skins. He made it known how the Americans there had acted with 'the greatest violence' being 'offered to the schooner's people, some of whom were treated with unexampled inhumanity'. One of the colonial crew was so badly beaten about the head that

---

[6] Fanning., 320.

[7] Ibid., 326. Fanning says that the owners of the Union never received 'one farthing'.

[8] Howe was a convict who managed to establish *The Sydney Gazette* with assistance and support from the colonial authorities in March 1803 and apparently operated the *Gazette* until his demise in 1821, when his son Robert took control.

splinters from the butt of the musket remained embedded in his skull! As an outcome of the melee that occurred, when each crew sought to assert rights over the sealing grounds, the Americans triumphed, seizing Moody's vessel. The colonial men were forced onto an island and marooned without water. Only when Moody acquiesced and agreed to go elsewhere were they released.

Percival was well known by then as an aggressive and deceptive character who had already enticed several colonial men away from their employers' vessels to man his armed boat, contrary to their articles. The American endeavoured to explain the behaviour of his crew as being a necessary consequence of protecting his boat. This explanation lacked credibility. He was not to be the last to act in such a manner. Percival's conduct was described as 'unbecoming', and, after a short stay, the *Charles* left the Straits to voyage to the Ile de France with a huge 400 tons of seal oil. This early skirmish was a sign of more serious conflicts to come between colonial sealers and the Americans.

While Percival posed a threat to one colonial sealing gang, it was of minor significance when compared with events that would unfold after the arrival in the Straits of the Boston-based Delano brothers and their crews. Captain Amasa Delano and his two brothers were tasked by Boardman and Co, the owners of the *Perseverance* and *Pilgrim*, to voyage between the United States and the Pacific Islands on a sealing mission. Amasa had been in the maritime trade since 1789. He and his brothers had followed his father into that calling. A clean-shaven, multi-talented portly man who traded as a ship builder, whaler, sealer and explorer, he was ambitious. Nothing would obstruct his profit-making ventures. The voyage to the Antipodes would be the last of three voyages he undertook around the globe. Making his way to Van Diemen's Land with a multinational crew, including men from Portugal and Chile, he exploited the Bass Strait Island seal rookeries between about 1803 and 1804. Towards the end of his mission, in February 1804, he and brother Samuel anchored at Kent's Bay King's Island.

His brig *Perseverance* was impressive. Built in Massachusetts, it had two large masts, a bowsprit displaying numerous sails and a fifteen-star flag. Together with its sister ship, it was carrying several whaleboats. On the way to the Fishery, Amasa and his crew demonstrated their pugnacity by capturing a Spanish slave ship known as the Tryal. Reaching Kent's Bay, the two Yankee vessels had some unfortunate encounters with colonial sealers. Here, they encountered Joseph Murrell and his crew. Delano recorded his experiences in a book he wrote some 13 years later.[9] The portrait he paints of the local sealers is one of aggressiveness, brutality and deceptiveness, while claiming he had been maligned and deceived. However, his version of events is probably only partly true. Unlike most mariners, Murrell was literate; he was outraged by the behaviour of Delano and his crew and wrote about it. At the time, there were newspaper reports and correspondence between the Governor and Delano about the encounters. Murrell also complained to his employers Kable and Underwood about the bellicose Americans. Reading all the primary sources leads to a more balanced view of what happened between the sealers and the Delano brothers.

The events that occurred after first contact reflect the conflicts that arose between very competitive and aggressive mariners. Delano, his brothers and their crews stayed in Kent's Bay at King Island for nearly eight months. While there, Delano made some excursions into Hobart and around the south of Tasmania, leaving his brothers Samuel and William to seal. The Americans were enthusiastically seeking out the rookeries in and around most islands in the Straits. Delano highlighted their purpose in being there when he wrote:

> Having a greater part of the time from four to seven boats exploring the islands in all directions in search of seals which were the principal object of our pursuit.[10]

While sealing, the Americans were 'visited' by 'six different gangs of sealers on the same business' as themselves, 'all of which were out

---

[9] Delano, *A Narrative of Voyages and Travels in the Northern and Southern Hemispheres* (Boston: E.G.House, 1817).

[10] Ibid., 460.

of provisions'. This is not surprising given the number of complaints and reports of the poor treatment received by these mariners from their employers. Delano complained that, despite his providing the colonial mariners with supplies and other assistance, the sealers did everything in their power to 'injure' him. Further they prevented him from hunting seals because of their aversion to 'foreigners'.[11] The injuries that he complained of in his book and to the colonial authorities were a litany. The colonial mariners allegedly stole from him, induced the American crews to abandon him, set his boats 'adrift', and frightened the seals away in an attempt to spoil the Yankees' chances of a good catch.

Agitated and angry at the actions of the colonial mariners, Delano wrote a long, querulous letter to Governor King.[12] Delano singled out one particular sealer, Murrell, as the root cause of his problems.[13] He reported that Joseph was the ringleader of a gang employed by Kable and Underwood in charge of the brig *Endeavour*. He emphasised that the colonial sealer was trying to drive the Americans out. Clearly, he had underestimated Murrell. Initially, Delano thought him a man of little significance, but when the sealer started to have some success in enticing the crews away from Delano, and 'stealing' from him, he changed his mind.

Delano wanted King to interview relevant witnesses and sought his opinion about the nefarious conduct of the mariners. He was at pains to stress that it was a 'delicate matter' and did not want it to become a dispute between the colony and the United States.[14] The Governor had a different point of view. Murrell had already managed to get intelligence to him via his employers, complaining about the Yankees. To the American's dismay, his complaint fell on deaf ears. This was partly because of a previous incident in which he charged a colonial captain a fortune to transport his rudder to Hobart. By then, the tide had turned, A general disquiet developed

---

[11] Delano, 461.

[12] Ibid., *Letter to His Excellency Governor King from the ship Perseverance*, 4 August 1804.

[13] He was also called Joseph Morrill.

[14] Op. cit., 463.

Chapter 6: Foreigners at the Tipping Edge

about the Americans, not only by the sealing parties but also from the Sydney traders who were concerned about competition for both the pinnipeds and the leviathans.

While this was going on, there was an escalation of the dispute which ultimately resulted in violence back in the Straits. Murrell and his gang had had enough. They decided to confront the Yankees. Well-armed with muskets, they voyaged by whaleboat to where the Americans were camping. A skirmish then occurred with Delano later recording his men were successful in the fight, partly because 'the other party could not make their guns fire'.[15] Although this fight ended quickly, it was not the end of the dispute. The Americans wanted revenge. Shortly afterwards, they surprised the colonials at their camp and took Murrell and some of his men hostage. As described by Delano, the local mariners were tied to a tree and whipped with 'a cat o'nine tails' for the perceived injustices brought upon Americans by 'convicts'. After getting free, Murrell immediately wrote a letter to his employers to give his version:

> At four in the morning on the 17th I was suddenly seized by the chief mate of the Pilgrim, and three other American ruffians two of whom caught me by the hair, the other two by the arms. They dragged me out of bed and trailed me in this fashion along the ground till they came to the sea beach. Here they beat me with clubs, then kept me three-quarters of an hour naked whilst they were searching for the rest of my people.
>
> Then they began to sport away with their bloody cruelties, until some few Englishmen belonging to other [sealing] gangs out of Port Jackson, stung to the quick to see the cruelties exercised upon me without humanity, law, or justice, determined not to suffer it, and began to assemble. This occasioned the Americans to face about, at which instant I got my hands loose and ran into the sea, determined to be drowned rather than be tortured to death. I was followed by a number of Americans to the seaside, who stoned me... [I] was then dragged on shore and left lying on the beach, the men remarking that they supposed I had had enough, but that there were more of their country's ships expected, who would not let me off so lightly. Then they took away some of my people, rescuing from my custody a King's prisoner.[16]

---

[15] Delano, 465.
16 Louis Becke, *The Americans in the South Seas* (1901) from "The Tapu of Banderah and Other Stories" viewed at http://gutenberg.net.au/ebooks/fr100233.txt

Murrell managed to escape only to be chased down again by a 'Sandwich Island' man. The Pacific Islander must have struck him severely as Murrell was reported as bleeding profusely. His employers were informed that his arm was broken in three places.

But if the colonial sealer was hoping that Kable or Underwood would assist him in seeking redress from the Americans, he would have been disappointed. Instead of pursuing Delano, the Sydney partners were more concerned about some of their crew, led by a Robert Pawson, who had been enticed away from their employ by the Yankees. Abandoning their vessel, they stole some sails and rigging. Underwood placed an advertisement in the local newspaper offering rewards of up to £100 for the capture of the renegade gang and retrieval of his property.[17] It was unlikely that anyone would ever have claimed the rewards given that the 'delinquent' sealers would have left with their new employer.

The only sympathy Murrell received was from Delano, who later expressed some regret but otherwise vented his spleen to any prominent colonial who would listen. Apart from the skirmishes between the Delano Brothers and the sealers, there are few records demonstrating that some other Yankee boats clashed with the colonial gangs.[18] Relationships with other ships coming from around the globe including French visitors was, on the whole, different.

The encounters between the French who visited New Holland and the sealing community were mostly friendly. The first French visitor, La Perouse, had been given a warm reception and enjoyed the hospitality offered by Governor Phillip when he anchored at Port Jackson just after the English in 1788. But, as the two countries were often at war, particularly following the French Revolution and the rise of Napoleon, any friendly relationship was tempered with doubt and suspicion.

To provide some exceptions to the possibility of being restrained and held captive by the English on account of hostilities, the

---

[17] See advertisement entitled *"Reward"*; *Sydney Gazette*, 11 November, 1804.

[18] Lloyd Gordon. Churchward, *Australia & America 1788-1972 An Alternative History*.

French explorers and navigators were issued "passports" of a kind by English authorities. This enabled these voyages of discovery to take place, provided that the French were conducting "scientific" business.[19] In June 1800, two passports were approved for the vessels *Le Geographe* and *Le Naturaliste*, under the command of Captain Nicolas Baudin and Captain Emmanuel Hamelin respectively. They informed London they were only going to undertake a 'voyage of discovery' to New Holland. According to Peron's journal, the purpose was scientific and geographic (rather than strategic or political). Bonaparte had given his approval.[20]

During their Antipodean voyage, the French reported observing numerous seals off the coast of Western Australia, and again at Maria Island off Van Diemen's Land. On their voyage to Port Jackson, Baudin lost a small boat and its crew. It was feared the boat was wrecked and men drowned. On 10 March 1801, after leaving Maria Island and sailing north on the road to Sydney, the French encountered on a 'small ship' captained by an unknown mariner. This captain informed them his vessel was bound for Bass Strait and was seeking out 'Sea Cows'.[21] He also flagged to the French that the 'English' were expecting them in the port while making preparations with 'consideration and respect' due to the nature of their expedition. In exchange, the French told the colonial master he could expect to find Bay Fleurieu abounding with seals. Given the treacherous seas in the Straits, he warned the mariner about the loss of their 'chaloupe'[22] and its crew in harsh and dangerous marine conditions. Pleasantries were exchanged and the two vessels went on their way.

Shortly afterwards, the French arrived at the Furneaux Isles where they 'fell in with' the *Harrington*, a brig under the command of the Sydney trader Campbell. After complying with a request

---

[19] David Hill, *The Great Race,* 165.

[20] Francois . Peron, 3. Peron informed his readers in Chapter 1 that the purpose was: improvement of navigation, geography above five thousand leagues of coast that was hitherto but little known were to be explored.

[21] This is the name the French gave to elephant seals.

[22] Literally, a small French boat or harbour boat

to supply the visitors with substantial provisions, the merchant informed the explorers he was on a mission to Bank's Strait to recover 'seals and sea-cow skins' collected by a crew living on King and Furneaux Islands.[23] Peron described Campbell as 'generous' and willing to accompany the French to Port Jackson. These two encounters were important in that they illustrate the openness and friendliness which existed at the time between the French and the colonists when it came to matters of trade and exploration. This was notwithstanding the hostility that existed between them on a political level. It shows that both the colonisers and French were willing to share information which the other party could use to their commercial advantage.

After anchoring at Port Jackson, Captain Baudin purchased a sealing schooner, the *Casuarina*, from James Underwood in July 1802 in exchange for various chattels and a small sum of cash. It was intended to replace the *Naturaliste*. That boat had been forced to return to France over laden with curiosities and exhibits. As Baudin assured the Governor that it was for 'the advancement of science and navigation', Governor King granted approval for the acquisition. But they hid from the Governor one of the main reasons for the purchase. The French left Sydney for the Straits on 17 November 1802. They visited Elephant Bay to be greeted by a sealing party under the command of their experienced leader Daniel Cowper. The latter mariner was of American origin having been recruited by traders from the Sandwich Islands as he had vast experience in the otter fur trade. To give a level of security to the colonial sealers, Baudin immediately hoisted the English flag.

The French remained at the mariner's camp for about three weeks. For the most part the visitors found themselves participating in a friendly and cooperative relationship with the gang. Cowper agreed to supply the new arrivals with oil from the seals, and with marsupials and emus as the French had run short of 'victuals'. Indeed, so well did these two parties get along that, when the French left, they were gifted a large quantity of seals.[24] Unfortunately, this

---

[23] Peron, Book 3, Chapter XVIII, 264.

[24] Mr. Thompson, in his letter to the Governor referred to several other sealing

Chapter 6: Foreigners at the Tipping Edge

particular relationship soured a little when Baudin was surprised to find three convicts, whom he had previously deposited on King Island, had secreted themselves on his ship. Apparently, the same sealers who had been so generous in assisting his crew had also disposed of their own unwanted runaways. This angered him.[25] But the French were not necessarily without blemish.

After a time, another sealing gang, under the authority of the Sydney ship builder and merchant Thomas Palmer,[26] 'fell in' with Frenchmen from *Le Geographe*. They had found the shores of a bay in the Straits that were 'covered with innumerable legions of various species of seals'. Palmer's gang rendered every assistance to the French to enable the foreigners to profit from the venture, contrary to the express purpose of their mission.[27] The friendly relationship that developed between maritime crews when England and France were often at war appears to be unusual, to say the least. It may have arisen because, unlike the Americans, the French were mainly on scientific voyages of discovery and lacked the will to compete aggressively with colonial mariners over seals. However, when sealing became the object of French mariners, particularly one who teamed up with an American, it would prove a different matter.

The French Captain, Alexandre Le Corre, entered into an "arrangement" with an American, Nathaniel Cogswell, in Mauritius in 1802. This required these partners to fit out a schooner *L' Enterprise* for a joint secret sealing venture to Bass Strait. Once the purpose of the mission became known in the colony, it caused

---

vessels in and around the islands when the French were there including those left by the captain of the Margaret who had acquired 6,000 gallons of elephant oil but few seals and another gang under a Mr. Palmer located some distance away.

[25] It was common for convicts to attempt to escape the confines of the settlements in Sydney and Van Diemen's Land by endeavouring to stow away on vessels either with or without the consent of the masters.

[26] Thomas Fysche Palmer (1747-1802) was originally a convict who was transported for sedition as one of the Scottish martyrs. He spent seven years in the colony making the most of his opportunities and, along with two others, had built several smaller vessels employed in both the seal and whale trades. He is an interesting character as he was a zealous political reformer as well as a merchant and spent time in prison for his public comments about Governor Hunter.

[27] Op. cit., 22. Peron reports that on departure 'they even forced him to accept some of their best skins'.

significant alarm. Unfortunately for the joint venturers, the vessel was partly wrecked off Cape Leeuwin. In need of significant repairs, the damaged vessel was forced to sail to Port Jackson. By then, the owners had anglicised the name of the boat to Surprise, in an attempt to disguise its French origins. But it was the Frenchman who was surprised. A furious King refused him permission when he went a step further and pleaded to be allowed to seal in the Straits.

He was ordered to depart immediately. Luckily for Le Corre, Baudin was in town and had some influence with King. After the French explorer interceded, the Governor begrudgingly allowed Le Corre to fish to the north of the Furneaux Group on condition that he go nowhere near the Straits. He warned both Baudin and Le Corre that no further permissions would be granted to any Frenchman who wished to hunt seals.[28] The limited nature of the rights granted were reinforced by a naval officer (under instruction from King) writing to Le Corre:

> His Excellency the Governor... observing from your clearance from the Isle of France that you are bound on a sealing voyage on the coast off New Holland... he does not consider himself authorized to grant any general permission until he has received instructions on that head from His Majesty but as it appears that your vessel has been fitted out on a speculative voyage... he does not withhold his permission for your vessel sealing on the coast of this country which is to be clearly understood as confined to your vessel alone and not as a general permission...[29]

The restrictions on such foreigners had their genesis in the fact that King had granted several Sydney traders expansive rights to seal. An example of this was the exclusive open access given to Kable and Underwood to fish out of Cape Barren and the adjoining islands, while Campbell enjoyed sovereignty over King Island. However, in the case of the deceptive Le Corre and his crew, the colonial mariners need not have worried. The French captain and most of his crew drowned after their vessel was smashed to pieces on rocks in the Straits on 4 October 1802. The wreck became the

[28] Cumpston, *First Visitors to Bass Strait*, 15.
[29] John Harris to Le Corre, *The Sydney Gazette*, 27 November, 1803.

Chapter 6: Foreigners at the Tipping Edge

subject of a salvage operation. Kable and Underwood were favoured and appointed Murrell to undertake the mission sometime later.[30]

The demise of Le Corre did not earn any sympathy from the Governor. The political climate had changed. Shortly after, England and France were at war again, with King reporting to the Colonial Secretary:

> The French schooner I mentioned in a former letter which arrived here from the Isle de France to catch seals etc. in the Straits, was lost among the Cape Barren Islands, which may stop any more adventurers from that quarter.[31]

There is no doubt that the Sydney merchants would have been pleased.

The fierce competition, particularly from the Americans, and the complaints and lobbying from the Sydney traders also led to official intervention from the colonial authorities. Such intervention became urgent when the Yankee mariners, enticed, by fair means or foul, several colonial sealers to abandon their masters and join the crews from Nantucket. The colonial press editors were in the vanguard of the chorus of criticism of the Americans. One singled out Captain John Percival for particular attention in his newspaper when he reported:

> An interference with our colonial concerns it was his duty to avoid but on the contrary, he chose to take away some of the most useful people from the gangs for which he could not avail himself of necessarily as a plea, his ship being already more than sufficiently manned, and this proceeding has been highly prejudicial to the interests of our own Adventurers.[32]

By August 1804, the Governor had become increasingly worried by American activity in the Bass Straits. The Delano brothers were front of mind. He wrote to Lord Hobart after receiving intelligence

---

[30] Peron, Op. cit., 1, 5 and Cumpston, 16.

[31] *Historical Records of New South Wales*, Vol. 5,132.

[32] The Editor, *The Sydney Gazette*, 3 December 1803, 4, where Percival, the captain of the Charles of Boston is mentioned as having informed a Mr Stewart that up to 20 American vessels were due to hunt for seals in the Straits and already vessels' crews had dispatched 'all the elephants that they knew of' to the detriment of the colony.

from Collins, who was in command of the settlement in Sullivan's Cove, of a ship being built by the Americans in Kent Bay. It became the third Yankee vessel constructed in the Antipodes strictly on a mission to hunt seals for the Chinese market in the past 12 months. At the time, the English authorities had appointed Lieutenant Governor Paterson to command an expedition to Port Dalrymple (now Launceston) for the purpose of establishing a settlement there. Governor King used Paterson to order the Americans to cease the construction of their vessels. Not only that but mindful of their aggressive nature forbad 'the said commander or the commander of any ship belonging to foreigners of any nation... from building any habitation whatever... without my previous consent'.[33]

Their fishing activity came to the attention of King, probably through the intercession of the Sydney Traders. He formally complained to Under Secretary Cooke in London. Explaining that the pursuit of an agricultural industry was adversely affected by the many men procuring seals on vessels in the Straits, King warned the authorities and sought intervention:

> ...I am sorry to say that if the most decided checks are not given to the introduction of Americans and American vessels any benefit to this colony may possess will become the property of Americans at the expense of England.[34]

The complaint more or less fell on deaf ears. King received no support from the British. In the absence of action from abroad, increasingly frustrated by the behaviour of Yankees, and constantly harassed by complaints from Sydney traders, King was forced to act. On 30 March 1805, he issued a 'General Order', mandating that masters of ships of all nations had to provide a bond of 800 English pounds. In addition, they had to find two other 'freeholders' or 'well-known merchants or dealers' to put up an additional 50 pounds each and comply with other more draconian measures.[35] But the colonial authorities' attempts to curtail the activities of the

---

[33] King to Paterson, *HRA* 1.5.23, 1 June, 1804.

[34] Governor King to Under-Secretary Cooke, 1 November 1805 in *Historical Records of New South Wales*, Vol. 5, 717.

[35] General Order of Governor King, 30 March 1805, *HRA*, Vol. I, Series 5, 315.

foreigners' hunting seals and competing with the Sydney traders failed. When it came to trying to stop the Americans and French from luring the sealing crews away from their colonial masters, they had even less success. This was despite the fact that the General Order contained sanctions against that behaviour as well.

But it was not only the competition from the Americans and their enticement of colonial crews which was a problem for the English; London was also afraid that the Yankees, growing increasingly confident after independence would claim part of the colony. This is evident in the instructions given to Governor Bligh by George III. The Governor was directed to 'give them notice of His Majesty's right to sovereignty and in all cases warn them to depart' if any tried to establish a 'settlement' anywhere in the colony.[36]

Even after the first decade of the 19th century, the colonial authorities continued to be concerned about foreign intrusion into the maritime regions of the colony. Soon after Macquarie arrived to take up his position as the new governor in 1810, he instituted a revised set of port regulations mandating that no 'ship or vessel, whether British colonial or foreign', after arriving in the colony from anywhere, was to discharge any part of their cargo unless by special authority of the Governor. Orders had also been promulgated requiring vessels to provide a written report from the naval officer or his assistant to the Governor once they docked in Port Jackson.

After April 1814, there was a relaxation of the sanctions. This only applied to 'his Majesty's subjects', which enabled maritime merchants to trade within the East India Company limits on ships of over 350 tonnes. In some areas, a licence was required. However, so far as American and other maritime nations were concerned, even as late as 1815, the Secretary of State for the Colonies was writing to the Governor to remind him that trading with foreigners was 'at variance' with the Navigation Laws of Britain. Effectively, there was a gradual relaxation of the maritime laws. However, it was not until 1819 that it was lawful for any local or foreign vessel to trade

---

[36] See Cumpston, *First Visitors* 13. Also see *HRA,* Vol. I, Series 6, 18.

between the United Kingdom and the colony of New South Wales and its dependencies.[37]

While the Americans mostly vacated the Fishery and turned their attention elsewhere after the first decade of the 19th century, the French kept coming back, mainly on scientific missions.[38] They encountered various sealing gangs at the tipping edge of the colony. Often these meetings were beneficial to the French and the colonial mariners. In one such encounter, the French explorer Jules Dumont D'Urville anchored the vessel *L'Astrolabe* in King Georges Sound in early October 1826. He was tasked primarily with visiting and carrying out scientific studies in New Holland. One night, the French were surprised to observe a boat with an 'English' sealing crew come alongside. D'Urville was astonished to find sealers operating in the Recherche Archipelago.[39] One of the crew informed D'Urville that they had been left by the master of the *Governor Brisbane* while in Coffin Bay. They were subsisting mainly on a diet of fish. When D'Urville offered to take them to Port Jackson, they at first declined, so the Frenchman assumed they were escaped convicts. However, eight gladly accepted D'Urville's invitation to stay the night. For reasons unknown, three of them changed their minds and decided to leave on his ship. The captain expressed compassion for their plight, recording in his journal:

> What an extraordinary fate for eight Europeans to be abandoned like this with a frail skiff on these deserted beaches and left entirely to their own resources and industry![40]

The 'skiff' was the ubiquitous whaleboat. Once on board, one sealer volunteered to assist D'Urville as a navigator. The following day, the French were approached by another whaleboat with a different crew. One of this crew told D'Urville they were from the vessel *Hunter*. The Frenchman allowed one mariner from this

---

[37] The freedom for all vessels to trade became available after the passing of the Act of the British Parliament known as *42 Geo III, C 77*.

[38] There were no less than seven such French voyages mainly of discovery, exploration or scientific observation into Australian waters from 1815 to 1840.

[39] American mariners were also sealing in the region during this period.

[40] D'Urville, Vol. 1, 31.

whaler to come aboard, despite his concern and the suspicions of the two crews he had now encountered. He need not have worried. The two whalers, full of sealers, later returned with a significant catch including fish, petrels, oysters and penguins, gifting the catch to the French crew. All they wanted in return was gunpowder and rope yarn. The French noticed they had with them five First Nations people, two from Van Diemen's Land and another two from Kangaroo Island, who had all been living with the mariners for several years, and a young girl. The sealers also informed the French there were two 'native' women on Breaksea Island, where they had been camped. The French Captain expressed his 'wonder' at the fact that the sealers came from many different backgrounds and had been thrown together in a very difficult environment. He was surprised that they had only survived on the produce of the sea, with their boats as their only valuable worldly possessions.

This circumstance mirrored the multinational nature of many of the sealing crews and communities living in the Fishery. The French also noticed the sealers also had dogs on board. It is interesting to note that the sealers who inhabited King Georges Sound also made significant use of these animals as part of their hunting armoury as did many other independent mariners in the Fishery. They gave the Frenchmen access to several to hunt kangaroos. No doubt the owners of the dogs would have informed the French of the usefulness of such animals in assisting them to exist in difficult circumstances.[41]

But it was not just the dogs and whaleboats that the French observed which had assisted the sealers to survive in the Recherche. Other Frenchmen on the D'Urville voyage kept diaries of their observations. One, M. M. Quoy, recorded his observations concerning the invaluable assistance that their First Nations partners had given sealers:

> These women are indeed very useful to them getting sustenance for them, either by catching fish, shellfish, lizards and so on, or by hunting with dogs or even with guns. They quickly become

---

[41] The irony was that, despite the use of the dogs, no kangaroos were captured at all when the French and their sealing companion went out hunting the next day.

very skilled with the latter... The women were an enormous help, and that without them they would perhaps have died of starvation.[42]

The women had become familiar with the white man's ways, something that was common across the southern Antipodean sealing collectives. Unlike the colonial press, Monsieur Quoy was objective in his observations of the relationships between the sealers operating out of King Georges Sound and the First Nations women. Although he was concerned that the sealers had abducted women, he believed that, having observed relationships between First Nations sexes, many of the women would have been better off with the sealers. He thought this was because they had been 'ill-treated by their husbands' and had more freedom in the sealing game. There is some anecdotal evidence supporting this.

After several days, *L'Astrolabe* left King Georges Sound with four sealers on board, One named Hambilton was instrumental in helping the French find Westernport on the southeast coast of the mainland in November 1826, He guided the French into the same harbour where Flinders had once anchored. On their arrival, D'Urville met with another crew of sealers. They clambered aboard, with the "skipper" offering his services to the French. He presented papers to them as to his capacity and experience. But the French were not interested. It was there that French artist Louis de Sainson painted what is now regarded as a great symbolism of the mariner's life, *Sealers in Western Port*. It was later displayed in Paris in 1833. Depicted are three sealers in the foreground carrying a seal being led by a 'foreman' and accompanied by dogs. In the background is a large sealer's hut.

The French observed that the sealers had vegetable gardens from which they supplied radishes to their visitors. The foreigners gratefully accepted the gift, along with several seals slaughtered by their hosts. Some mariners accompanied the French when they went kangaroo hunting, a sign that the relationships were cordial, if not very friendly. Quoy was concerned about the lack of 'natives' residing in the area. He thought this was due to hostility that existed

---

[42] D'Urville, *King Georges Sound: Officers Diaries*, 45.

Chapter 6: Foreigners at the Tipping Edge

between the Westernport sealers and the local nations as a result of the mariners endeavouring to abduct First Nations women.

Leaving their friendly hosts, the French voyaged to Port Jackson. But, unlike the harmonious relationships they enjoyed elsewhere across the southern part of Australia, the reception the French received at Port Jackson was tense if not downright hostile. At the time, the authorities had sent two vessels on separate journeys, one to Westernport and the other to King Georges Sound, in an endeavour to establish settlements in those regions. These missions were directed partly by the authorities' fear that foreign powers might attempt to establish sovereignty in those places. Governor Darling expressed his amazement that D'Urville had managed to navigate his way into so many maritime harbours without the use of a pilot. He did not apparently comment about the assistance given to the French by the western sealers. The Governor's focus was elsewhere. He was agitated by the fact that the French had not encountered any English vessels on their expeditions.

Quoy expressed amusement that the English authorities thought the French wanted to establish a colony in New Holland. It seems the English colonial authorities might have only partly misconceived this. The French Minister for the Navy and Colonies had written to King Charles X in late 1825 seeking approval for the D'Urville expedition. One purpose was to look for bays where French warships could dock to give some advantage against the English. D'Urville would be tasked with doing 'what he [could] to satisfy himself whether France could freely take possession of the territory indicated or any other suitable place'.[43] The French vessel did not stay long at Port Jackson and left for New Zealand, much to the relief of Governor Darling. D'Urville would return to New Holland one more time in August 1837, but, on that voyage, it appears that he did not have any contact with the sealing communities.

Despite the violent disputes and conflicts that occurred between some over-zealous American mariners and their colonial

---

[43] D'Urville, Appendix III, *Conclusion of a Letter to King Charles X signed by Comte de Chabrol*, 4 December, 1825, 285.

counterparts over a short period in the first decade of the 19th century, most of the foreign sealers who came to the Antipodes operated either successfully on their own account without much interference from anyone or chose to continue their maritime careers in the colonies. After that first decade, tensions that had previously existed dissipated. Competition for seals no longer became an issue when most mariners abandoned the Bass Strait rookeries to ply their trade elsewhere. Many of the Yankee sealers who chose to stay in the colony were mainly employed by the Sydney traders. Furthermore, the political hostility that previously existed declined once it became clear that the Yankees simply wanted to trade and not conquer the colony. Apart from the intrepid mariner Chase and Daniel Cooper and the African Americans Anderson Baker and Bathurst, other Yankee men became residents of the settlements enjoying varied success in a variety of trades. Prominent among them was George William Robinson who came from Boston on the *General Gates* in 1819. He led several sealing expeditions to Kangaroo Island on the *Hunter* during the 1820s, later settling in Hobart where he owned and operated several hotels.

Other American sealing vessels voyaged to the colony on various missions. This included trade in provisions and chattels that the colonisers were desperate to acquire. These boats sought out and carried seal skins and oil and other commodities to sell or exchange on the Chinese market. The arrangements were mutually beneficial to all concerned. The colony needed Yankee trade. Even as early as 1791, American Ebenezer Bunker,[44] in charge of the convict transport vessel and whaler *William and Ann* probably caught several seals off the New Zealand coast. When it returned to London, its cargo included 8,468 skins from 'New South Wales and the Fishery'. Later, Governor Macquarie described Bunker as 'a very able and expert seaman... and a most respectable character'. He had a full and varied career as a maritime sealer and whaler, mainly around Bass Strait and New Zealand.[45] Being entirely reputable,

---

[44] 1761-1836.

[45] He was described by John Cumpston in 1966 as 'the father of Australian whaling' in the *Australian Dictionary of Biography*.

Chapter 6: Foreigners at the Tipping Edge

he was tasked with pursuing the pirated brig the *Harrington* in May 1808 by the colonial authorities. The brig had been seized by escaped convicts led by a ringleader Michael Stewart. The pirates stole away on the vessel right under the nose of the owner, Captain William Campbell, who was asleep in his harbourside house. Their mission was to reach China. Sailing across the Tasman Sea in the *Pegasus*, Bunker unsuccessfully searched far and wide for the vessel, including in the islands of Tonga and New Caledonia. Meanwhile, the pirates were intercepted off the island of Luconia in the Phillipines. All but the ringleader managed to escape. But the leader had the last laugh. Stewart was arrested and transported back to England, but being an enterprising rogue, he fled from his captors and, following in the footsteps of his notorious crew, vanished from the pages of history.

As the first decade of the 19th century closed, the mainstream sealing traders and merchants chose new 'roads'[46] to pursue their sealing enterprises. No longer able to make a living out of the Bass Strait Islands forced enterprising merchants to look elsewhere, relying on capable and experienced masters and crews that led the way to regions mainly east of Australia. These new regions presented avaricious traders with many opportunities to make profits. But the pursuit of seals came with many adversities and at a significant cost.

---

[46] A 'road' in colonial times was a sea route chosen by maritime men to voyage to and from their destinations.

Chapter 7: Opportunity and Adversity in the Eastern Fishery

In September 1809, several maritime men gathered together in Campbell's counting house[1] on a Sydney wharf. One of these men was Frederick Hasselborough, (aka Hasselburgh). Frederick had been appointed master of the brig *Perseverance* by the Sydney merchant. All the sailors were there at the request of this captain. Among the crew were two 'Otaheitans', one quaintly known as 'James Brown'. There was some uncertainty about their mission. The vessel was to voyage into the sub-Antarctic in search of new sealing grounds. Articles of Agreement were read out to all of them before each sealer signed or marked the document. As was the case with many of these documents, the terms included the "lay" that each man was entitled to, with the sealers and landsmen commanding the best portion of the potential catch. The crew was informed they would be sailing to the islands off the coast of New Zealand or 'elsewhere for the purpose of procuring oil, seal skins, other animals or substances the produce of the sea or islands'. Thus, Hasselborough had a wide brief to take the men wherever he saw fit in pursuit of the pinnipeds and whales. Not one of those present had any idea where they might end up. But all knew, by reason of the demeanour of Hasselborough, that there was a sense of desperation pervading the docks now that the Bass Strait sealing grounds had been depleted.

As a sign of the commercial value in slaughtering marine mammals, Campbell agreed to pay the men £20 sterling per ton of right whale or elephant oil, six shillings for each merchantable fur seal skin, and three shillings for each salted hair seal skin.[2] A

---
[1] A room or office used by businesses in the old days for accounting and bookkeeping purposes.
[2] Cumpston, *Macquarie Island*, 2.

small fortune might have favoured this gang. But there was a level of mistrust that existed between merchants and sealers at the time. This meant the crew's "lay" would be forfeited if they deserted the boat with a financial penalty of £100 of 'good and lawful money' imposed if they breached their agreement. Jumping on board the brig,[3] Hasselborough then invited his crew, which one author described as 'one of the most experienced sealing gangs ever',[4] to sail out of Port Jackson and into the icy waters south of New Zealand.

When reaching the Auckland Islands, they encountered the 185-ton ship *King George* owned by Henry Kable. This boat, the merchant's pride and joy, was under the command of the American S. R. Chace. The crew returned to Sydney by 1810 with a cargo of between 7,000 and 8,000 seals. More relevant was the large size of the vats full of 1,800 gallons of seal oil. Perhaps Chace gave Frederick some intelligence which assisted him in his mission. This was because, on 4 January 1810, when voyaging further south, and quite by chance, the mariners anchored at an island, never visited by Europeans. Here, they were astounded to find an abundance of seals wherever they looked. In recognition of his employer, Hasselborough named it Campbell Island.[5] This heralded the beginning of a new chapter in the quest for sealing grounds, which would bring huge profits for some. Others would suffer the consequences of a dangerous trade when taking up the challenge.

The "discovery" by Hasselborough and his crew of the volcanic outcrop, Campbell Island, is not as well known by Australians. That is because, when one considers colonial sealing, most people think of those who plied their trade in the Bass Strait islands, where much of the mainstream history of the sealing is focused, and, to a lesser extent, Kangaroo Island. But other opportunities presented themselves to the colonial mariners to both the east and west of Van Diemen's Land after the obliteration of the rookeries in the Straits from 1810. Many of the Sydney and Hobart traders fitted

---

[3] Owned by Campbell & Co.
[4] Op. cit., 3.
[5] The Māoris later called it *Motu Ihupuku*.

out vessels controlled by experienced masters. They employed crews anxious to make some sort of living from the sea, often in very difficult circumstances. Fortunes were made by the more enterprising of the traders. Over a few years, there was a constant stream of maritime traffic in the "roads" voyaging between Sydney or Hobart and the icy islands to the south of New Zealand. For a few years some boats filled to overflowing with elephant seal oil and fur seal skins destined for the Chinese and London markets would come and go from Sydney.

But other maritime merchants and masters were not so fortunate. Several suffered both financial and personal loss. Many a vessel was wrecked on rocks, sometimes resulting in the entire loss of their cargoes and crews. Death by misadventure, drowning and starvation were common. Many others would have, too, but for their ability to adapt and use what resources they could find to remain alive on the icy cold islands. These mariners lived on beaches and coves for months or years at a time. There they constructed boats and huts, grew food or hunted prey, and, where First Nations peoples lived, sought partnerships, if any local inhabitants were amenable. Some crews were left in difficult circumstances or sometimes even abandoned in perilous and hostile environments. On their return they received little financial benefit from their employers. Disgruntled mariners subjected to such difficulties started to tire of their unrewarding ties to mainstream commercial traders. Some left to pursue a life of independence and perhaps adventure in remote littoral places and spaces.

While Hasselborough's success in locating Campbell Island to plunder seal rookeries was fortuitous and timely, it paled into insignificance following a further "discovery" soon after. After a short stay at that outcrop, Frederick parted company with some of his crew and returned to Port Jackson. Excited by his success, he wanted to extend his search for the pinnipeds in the sub-Antarctic islands and had to reprovision the brig and attract further sealers for what he had in mind. A gang of six was left behind, including the second officer John Wood, Martin Bryant, a cooper, and Joseph Murray, a prisoner of the crown. On his return to the settlement,

Chapter 7: Opportunity and Adversity in the Eastern Fishery

Hasselborough was surprised to learn Campbell had decided to quit Sydney for London with his family. Robert left his maritime empire under the control of a Charles Hook. While the captain was anxious to seek further 'discoveries, Hook was worried about costs. He was prompt in giving Hasselborough clear instructions:

> Proceed direct to Campbell Island... and then make no delay in taking on board what skins they may have procured and then make the best of your way back to this Port. I have only to add that I hope every economy will be observed in the expenditure of your stores and provisions as you must be aware of the very heavy expense at which the vessel sails...[6]

Hasselborough ignored him, voyaging by a different route. On 11 July 1810, some 700 kilometres south of Campell Island, they chanced upon a unique land mass that had been formed following a meeting of two tectonic plates. The ridge resulting was found nowhere else in the world. Hasselborough and his crew observed a long thin island which had peaks at either end. At that time of the year, it would have been covered in snow. There were no trees but many indigenous low-lying plants covering most of the higher land, some of which were found to be edible. Birds and seals proliferated everywhere. It was to become the panacea for a failing industry. But finding a safe harbour was extremely difficult owing to the many reefs and jagged rocks that surrounded it. While anchoring off the outcrop Frederick named it Macquarie Island after the new Governor of the colony.

Attempts to land on the island were thwarted by the freezing and treacherous conditions. A few days later the mariners finally found a way to avoid drowning while attempting to land. On 18 July, Miles Holding, the first mate and seven crewmen, reached the shore carrying many of the provisions originally intended for Campbell Island.[7] The sealers were delighted the island abounded in fur and elephant seals. Holding reported later that 'there were a sufficiency of skins on the island to employ four or five

---
[6] These were Hook's instructions to Hasselborough on 19 June 1810.
[7] The provisions were supposed to keep the men in 'victuals' for nine months but there developed significant disharmony, with legal proceedings being commenced by several sealers against Campbell due to their treatment.

gangs'. Excited by the prospects of a new golden era for sealing here, Hasselborough immediately set out in the *Perseverance* for Sydney to obtain fresh provisions and salt. Arriving back in port in August he was met by Hook who expressed his surprise to see him. Campbell's man tried to keep the "discoveries" a secret. The only mention in *The Sydney Gazette* of the arrival of the *Perseverance* was underwhelming: "From the southwards, having left part of her crew for the purposes of procuring skins."[8] No mention of the location or coordinates of this island at this point.

Hasselborough sailed for Macquarie Island sometime in September in the *Perseverance* again. Concerned about other traders locating this outcrop, he did not dally. On his arrival, he was relieved to find no other vessel anchoring in the vicinity. The crew left behind were restless. Frederick was immediately approached by the steward James O'Burne. After he lobbied the master hard for a greater share of the catch by reason of him being the first of the crew to announce to the gang the "discovery" of the island, Hasselborough gave him a certificate:

> I do hereby certify that by directions of Charles Hook Esq. I have re-entered James O'Byrne ship and cabin steward in the articles of agreement registered 216 and set opposite his name the 60th lay share or proportion in lieu of the 80th. The latter I have crossed.
>
> Gov Macquarie's Island, October 1810
> Witness: Robert Murray Frederick Hasselborough

Keen to take further advantage of the island's resident seal population and loaded with skins, Hasselborough set off quickly and voyaged back to the docks in Sydney. An advertisement appeared in the *Gazette* almost immediately. The notice had the desired effect. Thirteen experienced men signed fresh Articles of Agreement with the Campbell merchants. Once again, Hook was anxious about the costs and somewhat annoyed with Frederick. He directed Hasselborough to:

> Proceed direct to Macquarie Island... and you will on no account suffer any new discovery you may make in your Rout(e) to

---
[8] *The Sydney Gazette,* 18 August, 1810.

deviate from the above instructions. The Perseverance is most liberally fitted out and victualled for 12 months and I have every confidence in your care and economy in the expenditure of stores etc. Wishing you well and a speedy return...[9]

When Hasselborough departed the docks of Sydney on his third voyage, he was accompanied by a young woman, Elizabeth Farr. It was unusual to find a female on a colonial sealing vessel. That is, unless she presented as a male, as was somewhat customary. The maritime space was seen in such times as a masculine domain where women aboard would bring bad luck to the sailors. If permitted to voyage, a female companion was strictly under the control of the master. Elizabeth was aged only about 16 years, and, at the time the master was separated from his wife. Elizabeth was probably taken on board by Hasselborough as some sort of 'comfort' girl and provided personal services in a maritime environment far removed from the gaze of the officials and settlers of the colony. She came from Norfolk Island and was the first European woman ever to set foot on Macquarie Island.[10]

When the vessel anchored there in July, there was a confrontation between the men on the island and those on board the *Perseverance* over the division of the catch of seals. Fortunately, the dispute was resolved, as all 24 men commenced to reside together at the camp until departing on 17 October for Campbell Island to join the six men surviving there since January. By now, the sealers at Campbell had exhausted their rations and were eating wildlife. This may have contributed to a dispute that occurred between the mariners Bryant and Wood as the former was taken into custody and sent to Port Jackson sometime later. He was charged with mutinous conduct while serving on board the *Perseverance*. Luckily for Bryant, the charge was dismissed. But this was not the end of adverse outcomes for the remaining gang.

Meanwhile, Hasselborough had returned to Campbell Island. Whether he was conscious of the plight of the sealers he had left

---
[9] Hook to Hasselborough, 4 September, 1810.
[10] There may well have been several women secreted on board sealing and whaling vessels enticed by promises, adventure, monetary or other rewards and once at sea were only subject to the master.

there previously or not, he would have wanted to check on the sealing endeavours of his men. Unfortunately for him, on 4 November 1810, he and his crew of five were sailing back towards the island in a jolly boat[11] when a sudden gust of wind caught it awry. The boat quickly filled with water and sunk. As so often happened, the master, a 'little boy' and the girl Farr were all drowned. When the *Perseverance* arrived back at Port Jackson on 8 January 1811 with its cargo of elephant oil, Hook was informed of Hasselborough's fate. The sad circumstances appeared in the next edition of the local press, with the editor publishing a graphic description of his demise:

> The weather being somewhat cold, Mr. Hasselbourgh had very heavily cloathed himself, and wore a thick Flushing boat cloak, together with a pair of strong high water-boots, the weight of which must have baffled every personal exertion when necessary to his preservation... Bloodworth, regardless of himself, sprang forward to the assistance of the woman, whom he considered most likely to be in need of it; and finding that she could swim, he cheered her with the assistance of his ready aid, and turned towards his Commander, who was imploring his assistance; but who, alas, after struggling some minutes to sustain himself with an oar and boathook, before he reached him, sank into the abyss of eternity. His next object was to save, if possible, the little boy whose danger was most imminent; and he, unhappily, sunk as he approached him. Thus sadly mortified by the disappointment of the hopes to which his generosity had aspired, even at the moment when his own safety was in doubt, his female charge remained alone the object of his attention. The poor creature was exhausted and had not the power of contributing to her own deliverance. With one arm supporting her, however, he swam upwards of a mile, through a rough sea, and with her gained the sand; but vain had been his labour, for respiration had for ever ceased... A boat was the same evening sent in search of the body, which darkness prevented from being found. The next morning, however, it was discovered, and the day following interred on shore, with every decency the circumstances of the case admitted. The bodies of the other two were not discovered when the vessel came away.[12]

---

[11] A jolly boat was a small four-oared ship's vessel often carrying a triangular sail. They were attached to the stern of a ship and were in general use throughout the 19th century.

[12] Elizabeth was buried at Perseverance Harbour on the island, see Robert McNab, *Murihiku: a History of the South Island of New Zealand and the islands*

Chapter 7: Opportunity and Adversity in the Eastern Fishery

Later, a notice was published in the form of an application by Charles Hook to be appointed administrator of Hasselborough's estate in 1811. Frederick's fame as a maritime explorer and discoverer is not well known, although the Hazelburgh Islands off Ruapuke are named after him.

While all at Campbell and Co. mourned the loss of Hasselborough and the other two victims, their main focus was on keeping the location of Macquarie Island a secret. Clearly, they saw the huge potential to plunder the huge colony of seals that abounded there. Hook inserted an advertisement in *The Sydney Gazette* seeking 12 to 14 seaman and sealers 'clear of every embarrassment to proceed on a voyage to the southward'. In a letter dated 23 October, Hook flagged how important the island would be to the sealing trade without revealing its location. He sought the assistance of the Governor, and Macquarie was happy to oblige him. Given the need to store huge number of skins for long periods, he gifted Hook 12 tons of English salt from the New South Wales reserve. The *Perseverance* and 80-ton schooner, Elizabeth and Mary were tasked with seeking an abundance of seals in what he described as the 'Penantipodes'. He wrote:

> By the Perseverance and Elizabeth and Mary with two gangs I have sent salt enough to cure 70 or 80 thousand skins. The situation of the island is only known to ourselves at present if we could keep it for two seasons, we shall be able to cover the many heavy losses you have hitherto met with…

It was clear the purpose of *Elizabeth and Mary* was not only to land the salt on the island but to also collect the skins and oil procured by Miles Holding and his crew. The fresh gang were to continue sealing there in anticipation that the island would yield up enough skins and oil to make trader Campbell a huge profit. Hook gave a letter addressed to Holding to the master of that vessel, James Gordon. Given the previous hostilities between the crews, and Hook's familiarity with how disputes can quickly arise between rival gangs, he made his position clear:

---

adjacent and lying to the south, from 1642 to 183,173-174.

> The gang which Mr Gordon will leave on Macquarie Island are not to interfere or mix with the gang under your charge and the skins procured by each must be kept separate and distinct in order that no disputes may arise in future in settling the different lays. Wishing you well…

When the *Perseverance* anchored back at Macquarie Island on 31 December 1810, the crew complied with their instructions and slaughtered 17,037 seals for skins, returning to Sydney on 2 March 1811. Hook was surprised to learn from Gordon that at least three other vessels were fishing at the outcrop despite Campbell House's endeavour to keep its location a secret. The *Sydney Cove, Unity* and *Star* had all been there with crews, with the last vessel leaving with what Gordon described as 'a tolerable cargo of skins' for England. So much for trying to keep quiet about this island.

Efforts to keep the destination a secret did not become apparent until James Gordon gave evidence when called to testify in a case brought against Campbell on 3 February 1812. The assertive O' Burne sought damages against his employer arising out of a promise to increase his "lay" from an eightieth to a sixtieth part as a reward in consideration of him keeping the island's location a secret. When called as a witness, Gordon swore:

> I recollect the plaintiff applying to Mr Hook either to have his lay increased or to have some reward for secrecy… The overseer of the gang (Kable and Underwood that is) told me that O'Bern had given Mr Underwood the situation of the island.

Contrary to that evidence, James Underwood was called to the stand and quizzed by his barrister as to whether the plaintiff disclosed the situation of the island to him or anyone else he knew of. His answer was a firm: 'No. Not to Captain Cooper. I disclosed it to Captain Cooper'. [Daniel Cooper had command of the *Unity* referred to above.][13]

Notwithstanding these allegations, there were other rumours circulating as to how other Sydney traders found out about the location of the island. Probably the most interesting is a story by Thomas James in the book *Six Months in South Australia*.[14] In about

[13] James O'Burne v Robert Campbell (1812) *NSWSupC*, 3.
[14] Thomas Horton James, *Six Months in South Australia*.

1838, Mr James voyaged to that colony and purportedly met two sawyers. He informed them that early in the rule of Governor Macquarie, when the little town of Sydney was 'as dull as ditchwater', a flag was hoisted on Signal Hill announcing the arrival of a vessel with a few hundred seal skins. It was rumoured that the vessel had come from a destination abundant with pinnipeds. This rumour was reinforced when it became known that the vessel required the large quantity of salt referred to above [at the time selling at £20 per ton]. Also, the quality of the skins aroused much interest, and efforts were made in discovering their origins.

By ruse or otherwise, a mariner based in Sydney arranged for some of the *Perseverance*'s crew to attend a party of friends and acquaintances at his home. The host had purchased sugar lemons and cigars and other victuals for the occasion, and those present were encouraged to drink to excess. Once many of the guests were intoxicated, the host organised a game whereby a wager was placed to see if anyone could accurately write in chalk under the table the latitude and longitude of the secret island. The winner would take away the proceeds. The very drunk captain of the vessel wrote the correct location under the table which the host secretly observed. The deceptive host announced to all and sundry that he had lost the game. The naïve captain was very pleased and collected all the money. Little did he know that he had disclosed the location for about £20, which turned out to be worth '£30,000', according to Mr James.[15] In any event by then, a plethora of colonial boats were outfitted and set sail for the island to 'cash in' on the seal colonies.

In the meantime, foreign mariners had also been active. The Virginian brig *Aurora*, owned by New York traders, arrived in Sydney on 19 July 1810 under the command of Captain Owen Folger Smith. He hired the services of Chase, the intrepid sealing identity who had recently returned to Sydney on the *Governor Bligh*. At the time, Chase had successfully landed crews in the Foveaux Straits and Stewart Island but had not returned to collect them. He sailed with a crew of 36 men on the *Aurora* and reached Campbell Island in November 1810. There he tried to extract the location

---

[15] Cumpston, Op.cit., 12.

of Macquarie Island from the acting master of the *Perseverance*. Despite his being given some information in return for an alleged bond of £200, the coordinates provided were incorrect, much to the fury of the American. The *Aurora* left Campbell Island with its crew and, again by chance, eventually located the larger island in early December. By then, her crew was reduced to 17, and Captain Smith had reported the death of Captain Hasselborough and his companions.

On his return to Port Jackson, Chase supplied 'intelligence' about the island:

> This island is of a moderate height nearly flat on top of which there are several lagoons of freshwater; it is about 20 miles in length and five in breadth lying nearly in a north and south direction a straight shore on each side with reefs extending from the North and South point; there is no harbour but good anchorage is to be found under the Lee of the island... Captain Smith saw several pieces of wreck of a large vessel on this island apparently very old and high up in the grass probably the remains of the ship of the unfortunate de la Perouse.
>
> The above islands (Campbell and Macquarie) were discovered by Captain Hasselborough in the brig Perseverance belonging to Messrs Campbell and Co, during the last year there are a few seals on either of them but there is an immense number of Seal Elephants on Macquarie's Island.[16]

The American sealer's focus on the plentiful seal elephant colonies meant that those mammals became the principal target of mariners for the next few years. In particular, Folger Smith took advantage of this intelligence, returning to the docks in Sydney via the Aurora in May 1811 laden with 60 tons of seal elephant oil and a few seal skins. By then, the location of Macquarie Island, and its abundant sea elephant rookeries had become well and truly known to all interested parties. Until May 1811, other vessels such as the English brig *Concord*, under Thomas Garbut's command, the *Oriental Navigator*, the *Mary and Sally*, captained by Charles Feen, and the *Governor Bligh*, owned by the Sydney trader Simeon Lord and captained by John Grono, had all voyaged there to procure

---

[16] *The Sydney Gazette*, January, 1811.

Chapter 7: Opportunity and Adversity in the Eastern Fishery

elephant oil and seal skins.

In the meantime, the provisions of Miles Holding and the crews on that island were about to run out. There was no real relief in sight from their employers in Port Jackson. The men had to forsake sealing to search for food to remain alive. News had already filtered through to Sydney of the dire circumstances of this crew. By early June, Hook was giving instructions to James Gordon to sail the *Perseverance* there with an experienced crew and supply all on the island with equal quantities of victuals and other provisions. The word "experienced" is an understatement given the make-up of the gang that went on this voyage. Illustrative of the demographic and diverse nature of such mariners, the crew included one Portuguese named Joaquin de Santos, the sought after 'Ohaetian' Straitsman, Mahomet Cossum from the Middle East, a 'man of colour' named 'Brownie', and Catherine Rook, the second woman to visit the island. She may have been the wife of William Rook, who had been employed by the Campbell company to lead one of the two gangs left on the island. Hook was by now more concerned about the possibility of disputes between crews and, to a lesser extent, the health of the surviving sealers. He gave clear directions to Gordon:

> Immediately on your arrival at Macquarie Island to give the command of the brig Perseverance to Mr Miles Holding late mate of that vessel under Captain Hassellburgh and to take upon yourself the agency. You will then give such directions to the different overseers as you may think best adapted for landing stores, casks and oiling gear and getting on board the skins at the island with the greatest expedition. All the stores casks et cetera you will equally divide between the two gangs under Rook and Murray who you will inform are considered as complete separate gangs and not attached to any vessel whatever but you will assure from me that they shall be equally attended to and supplied with all necessaries and also to remove them to any other island that may be thought more eligible for a vessel which I will provide for that purpose.
>
> On the skins et cetera being all shipped you will then take on board those of the crew of the vessel who are present on the island and whose term of agreement expired and immediately proceed with them to Port Jackson. PS. Should you see that either of the gangs are too weak I leave it entirely to yourself to

strengthen them from the people whose times are expired should any be desirous of stopping...[17]

Prior to the *Perseverance*'s arrival at the island, the difficult circumstances the Rook and Murray gangs experienced initially finding conditions favourable to land and whilst on the island were felt and observed by others. When Captain Garbutt on the *Concord* reached Macquarie on 12 July 1811, he was forced to spend a further six weeks before he could find safe anchorage. Then after three days, when the vessel became adrift, frustrated, Garbutt gave up his quest and headed back. He reported that 'the people of the island' were in a 'deplorable condition for want of food and other necessaries'. Further, there had been significant falls of snow covering the whole island and all were bitterly cold.

One unnamed vessel had attempted landing a crew, and almost overcame the challenge, but it was not until about 25 September that the mariners on the *Perseverance* succeeded in landing provisions. The surviving sealers must have been utterly relieved. When Gordon reached the island, he was astounded to learn the two gangs had slaughtered in excess of 50,000 hair and elephant seals for skins and oil. The crews worked together and secured on board 35,740 skins. There was a changing of the guard as the fresh crew replaced the malnourished and exhausted resident sealers. Immediately the captain and the original sealing crew left for Sydney just as the weather conditions deteriorated. On 31 October, the vessel finally reached the Campbell wharf. Hook would have been delighted as this cargo would have fetched a huge profit for his employer and no doubt a reward for the second in charge. But not everyone was satisfied.

Shortly after arriving at the docks, Hook distributed the proportion of the catch due to each returning crew member. But some of the employed sealers were disappointed with their 'remuneration'. The calculation of the lays was disputed by some sealers from the *Perseverance* and the *Elizabeth and Mary*. This led to several legal actions being brought against Campbell and other traders in the Civil Jurisdiction of the Supreme Court in

[17] Hook's letter to Gordon, 2 June, 1811.

Sydney. The most infamous was the case initiated by John Wood Mariner. He claimed a fortieth lay or share of oil, seal skins and other substances taken by the two vessels, and in addition sought wages and damages of £100. The main issue to be tried was the quantity of skins to which Wood was entitled to make up his lay. Campbell was no fool. He lined up his witnesses carefully and chose powerful friendly traders. They all gave evidence that the custom in the sealing trade was for the skins to be divided proportionally among the separate gangs and not treated as a whole.[18] The court gave judgement for Wood for a paltry sum of £16, 19 shillings and nine and a half pence plus costs of £2, 4 shillings and 10 pence. Unfortunately, the judges gave no reason for the decision, but it would appear that Wood failed to convince the presiding justices, Ellis Bent, and Gregory Blaxland (the explorer of the Blue Mountains), of the justification of his full claim.

In other cases, brought by many disgruntled sealers against masters and traders, verdicts followed a similar pattern. Although many of the plaintiff litigants were successful, the amounts awarded by the courts were either paltry compared to the claim or minimal. Take, for example, the case of James O'Burne, referred to earlier. He sought from Campbell the sum of £700, to cover his wage and the 'money paid, laid out and expended for the defendant at his request'. On 3 February 1812, he was only awarded damages of £141.13 shillings, four and a half pennies and costs of £3.11 shillings.[19] Other mariners were entirely unsuccessful. Patrick Cullen, employed by Folger Smith, brought proceedings against the American, seeking damages for an overdue bond of £200 allegedly for revealing the location of Macquarie Island. It was not surprising that the court found in favour of Smith, following evidence given by several sealers that helped establish Cullen had given false or misleading information. The case was thrown out with an order for costs against Cullen.[20]

---

[18] Appearing as witnesses for Campbell were Henry Kable, James Underwood, Simeon Lord and Mr Kable's clerk John Archer, being men who were generally regarded as pillars of the colony . See Cumpston, Op.cit., 21.
[19] Apparently, a notice of appeal was filed by Campbell, but the outcome appears to be unknown.
[20] Patrick Cullen v Owen Folger Smith, 2 July, 1811, Court of Civil Jurisdiction.

Despite these disputes, by November 1811, it had become clear to the maritime world at large that Macquarie Island would be capable of filling the vacuum that had existed in the trade since the demise of the Bass Strait endeavours. Hook was delighted with the progress being made there by the Campbell crews, reporting:

> On Macquarie and Campbell Islands 1000 tons of elephant oil may be procured annually, I have brought the business of oiling and skinning on these islands into such train, and have plenty of casks and salt both here and on the islands that two vessels such as the *Perseverance* may be employed for two years to come and be sure to find cargoes at least and of skins according to the quantity of seals which come up during the pupping season.[21]

On that basis it was no surprise that he and others continued to pursue their maritime interests on that island. By 1812, the Campbell crews who were staying there had acquired about 120 tons of oil and 50,000 skins, according to one author. Even in November 1820, when the Russian Bellingshausen visited there on his voyage, he observed:

> the shore of this island was covered with huge sea animals, called 'see elephants' and penguins; seabirds flew about in great numbers... At 5 o'clock a large sea elephant covered with blood slid past... We wounded it with another two shots and its blood ran red in the sea for a long time. I wanted to launch the ship's boat in order to give chase; however, the sealers said it was impossible to kill in the water but that there were many on the shore for which we could take our choice.[22]

Notwithstanding the plentiful colonies of the elephant seals that still were there for the taking, severe difficulties experienced by the resident mariners still persisted. Some complained to the Russian 'they had been for four months without employment having filled all the barrels having no empty ones'. Bellingshausen and his Russian crew enjoyed a friendly relationship with the sealers while they were there, describing them as 'good people'. Further, they were very grateful for their assistance as they 'fulfilled our commission even at danger to their lives'. Appreciating the mariner's efforts

---

[21] Cumpston, Op.cit., 24.
[22] Ibid., 44.

and realising the gangs were experiencing significant personal difficulties, they gave them provisions and rum. As the Russian had been informed of their desperate plight, he even gifted a compass, and provided them with information to enable the sealers to seek a suitable return to Port Jackson if ever they were 'rescued.'

Shortly after this encounter Charles Hook was called to give evidence before Commissioner Bigge in 1821 about the nature of the sealing industry. The inquiry proceeded in the following manner:

> Bigge: At what Islands was the greatest quality of seals taken?
> Hook: Macquarie Island and Campbell Island, Kangaroo Island and those in Bass Straits.
> Bigge: From what places in those seas is the elephant oil principally procured?
> Hook: Macquarie Island where there is now from 150 to 200 tons of oil already prepared.[23]

Another to give evidence was a Captain John Beveridge. He was employed as master of at least two vessels owned by Underwood involved in the seal trade.[24] The captain told the Commissioner that thirteen mostly 'free and emancipated' men inhabited Macquarie Island procuring elephant oil at that time. He asserted to Bigge that these men had a 'supply of provisions for six months!'

These two testimonies, painting a rosy picture of the life of mariners in the Fishery, was at complete odds with reality. For, apart from the consistently large number of disputes that arose between the various Sydney traders and their crews over the payment of lays or wages that often found their way into the colonial courts, there were other more serious incidents. Some involved vessels which were unable to land on the island at all. Worse still were the boats vanishing without a trace or lost due to shipwreck, But, by far the most serious, were the loss of lives.

When William Stewart in the *Cumberland* arrived at Campbell Island in early 1812, he found only one of the sealers left by the *Mary and Sally* still alive. The survivor, a cooper by the name of

---
[23] Ibid., 40.
[24] These were the *Campbell Macquarie* and *Elizabeth and Mary*.

Henry Neale, told Stewart of how all his comrades had boarded a boat but never returned from a sealing expedition.[25] On 18 March 1812, William 'Earl' Lutrell, the carpenter on the *Elizabeth and Mary*, died probably of natural causes, gifting most of his estate to his "gang" in his will. By far the most serious incident occurred when the 135-ton brig *Campbell Macquarie* under Richard Siddons, with James Kelly as chief mate and a crew of 50, struck rocks near the island at 1.30am in May 1812. The vessel was a total loss. The survivors endeavoured to save what they could. All seal skins, salt, and water casks were lost or destroyed in the storm. The captain, Kelly and 11 other survivors, were collected by the ever-reliable *Perseverance*. But left for dead were one luckless European, four 'sea cunnies and 26 lascars'.[26] By then, four Indians had already died.

Another vessel, the *Sydney Cove*, had been at the island for two months in the same year when it lost its anchors and cables. In treacherous seas, it foundered. When the *Perseverance* again left Port Jackson in April, the whereabouts of the *Sydney Cove* remained unknown. Ironically, in early 1813, the dependable *Perseverance*, destined for the eastern Fishery, itself disappeared at sea with the loss of all on board.

The dangers to life and limb posed by vessels being wrecked on the reefs around the island or lost completely were some of many life-threatening possibilities. When a Mr. Thomson, the master of the *Betsy*, owned by Underwood, arrived safely at the island in early 1815, he was directed to proceed to the Auckland Islands. En route, two crew members, a European and Indian, died of scurvy while several others were affected. That was not the end of it for the crew on the *Betsy*. In a subsequent voyage to the island, they lost their rudder, and several sealers contracted scurvy. Running out of victuals, the remaining men were reduced to meagre rations. Shortly after that, two Portuguese mariners died, namely Reza and Mendoza followed by two other mariners and an officer William Grubb. All bodies were deposited into the sea. The surviving crew

---

[25] This was the second such tragedy on the island.
[26] A 'sea cunny' was a helmsman or steersman employed in a vessel manned by lascars.

jumped ship and sailed a whaleboat several hundred kilometres to New Zealand. But that was not the end of this dystopian ordeal. The hapless exhausted survivors were captured by the Māori and held by them until finally being rescued in February 1816.

In addition to the problems of foundering vessels, legal disputes, death and disease, there were also many crews left for extended periods on a promise to return, resulting in near-starvation. This mirrors the experience of mariners who had been left to their own devices elsewhere in the Antipodes. Often, crews were given provisions based on estimates by the traders of how long they would need to stay on the island. For example, a crew that had been left on Macquarie, possibly by the *Cumberland*, had exhausted their provisions by October 1815 and were not removed until well into 1816. It is open to conjecture how this crew endured in such circumstances. Their enforced diet was likely a predominance of the island's seal meat and the local wild cabbage. Another crew from the *Emerald* arrived in November 1821 and found sealers who had been left there in circumstances where they were about to mutiny. Some had threatened the trader's overseer with death. The men appeared to be living off a variety of bird life as there were 'no refreshments' remaining.

By April 1822, the sealers on the island also faced the prospects of starvation, as by then the *Emerald* had departed. One, Joseph Price, had to beg to secure a berth on the *Elizabeth and Mary* to return to Port Jackson. He pleaded with the ship's master to be collected. Then, he implored him to secure a boat to come to the rescue of the other starving inhabitants. When he left, the crew on the island had no provisions from their masters in Sydney but had acquired a quantity of 427 tons of elephant seal oil. To rub salt into the wounds, some sealers were deprived of their lays. Disgruntled they sought legal redress against the merchant Nathanial Thornton in the Courts. Some recovered damages of between £62 and £100.[27]

Even as late as April 1830, the vessel *Faith*, under the master Willett, sailed out from Port Jackson to effectively 'rescue' a crew

---

[27] The men who brought proceedings were Joseph Price, John Morgan and Thomas Eldridge.

who had been working for a John McQueen, before he passed away. As the rescue vessel approached the island, the resident cook, who was suffering more than most, collapsed and died, possibly from heart failure. He was probably over-excited at the forthcoming prospect of his rescue. When Willett reached the island, he found that the gang left by McQueen 'suffered every probation from hunger'. So weak were they that he observed how they failed to reach into burrows to catch mutton birds, a reasonably easy task. The sealers had been there for 30 months and had accumulated 200 tons of elephant oil for their employers despite their parlous state and condition.

Macquarie Island, in particular, and, to a lesser extent, Campbell Island, remained the principal focus and destinations of the Sydney traders during the second decade of the 19th century. But the hunt for seals extended elsewhere in the Eastern Fishery. One such destination was the southern tip of New Zealand, called *Murihiku* by the Māori,[28] and the surrounding islands, particularly those in the Foveaux Straits. William Raven's early voyage in the *Brittania* in 1793 had only yielded 4500 seal skins and was considered a reasonably small return for the time spent at Dusky Sound. Captain House, the commander of the schooner *Francis*, had accompanied Raven across the Tasman Sea. He parted ways with the Brittania and returned to the wharf at Sydney Town. The report he gave to the military ruler of the colony Lieutenant General Francis Grose was a bleak one. David Collins wrote that:

> Nothing appeared by this information from Dusky Bay, that held out encouragement to the Government of Port Jackson to make use of that part of New Zealand......; a seal fishery there was not an object with it at present, and besides, it did not seem to promise much. The time the schooner was absent however, was not wholly misapplied, it proving the event of having, as Mr Raven had done, left 12 people for 10 months on so populous an island, the inhabitants whereof were known to be savages, fierce and warlike.[29]

---

[28] The word in the local language means something like 'the last joint of the tail.'
[29] Collins, Op.cit., Vol. 1, 322.

Chapter 7: Opportunity and Adversity in the Eastern Fishery

As an outcome of this most negative assessment and due to the lack of ships available in the colony for some time after this date, not many attempts were made by mariners to voyage across the channel in search of seal rookeries for several years. The only early substantial effort was in 1795 when the 800-ton *Endeavour* and the 150-ton brig *Fancy*, under the commands of Captains Bampton and Dell, respectively, sailed for New Zealand. These masters were probably on a sealing venture but also wanted to examine the partially built boat constructed by the Raven crew. Leaving Port Jackson, the two captains were unaware of two facts that would come to haunt them. Firstly, 45 convicts including a woman had secreted themselves on board, and, secondly, the bigger vessel was unseaworthy.

When they reached Dusky Sound the only good news was that they found the Raven boat in a reasonable condition. The *Endeavour* was ill fated from the start. It foundered shortly after they arrived. By then there were 240 mariners and others residing in difficult conditions at Luncheon Cove. The voyage was a complete disaster with Bampton and Dell salvaging what they could from the wreck. The runaway convicts, who had also caused headaches for Bampton, were eventually returned to face the punishment awaiting them! The news of this maritime catastrophe would have had a negative impact on any trader seeking to pursue New Zealand as a sealing destination. Until early in the 19th century, only one other vessel, the American snow *Mercury*, sought to trade in the southern tip of that country according to McNab. It is unknown whether sealing was part of their mission.

It took until 1803 before several ships crewed by mariners sought the pinnipeds. In doing so the mariners focussed their attention on the southern tip of *Aotearoa*. After a time, the islands and bays in the Foveaux Straits became the most popular destinations. That region was to provide an economic rollercoaster ride for mainstream and independent traders during periods of boom and bust over the next 30 or so years. In particular, peaks were experienced between 1803 and 1813 and gained new impetus again from the late 1820s until about 1830.

One historian estimates that over 60% of all sealing boats coming to the eastern Fishery made the southern tip of New Zealand their main focus during those years. In doing so, the mariners adopted different technologies and strategies to catch the seals. Some vessels would anchor off the coasts and bays where the mammals frolicked on rocks and conduct raids on the rookeries without venturing on land. Under this type of strategy, the sealers were completely mobile, relying on their boats to supply all their wants. Jules De Blosseville, the French baron explorer and navigator, made observations about this methodology in his journals in 1823:

> When a ship is fitted out for an expedition of this kind, it is provisioned for the whole duration of the campaign... Having arrived on a shore which appears promising, they embark in boats, and leaving the ship sometimes for several days, they explore the smallest bays and storm beaten rocks, knowing that where the sea is the most stormy, there will the animals, which they pursue, be the most numerous. The least useful men are left on the ship as a guard. The vessel remains in a safe haven and receives any necessary repairs...[30]

Other mariners chose to operate out of caves and camps, while there was a smaller but increasing cohort who chose to make the local environment their home. Some of these sealers had broken their article agreements by "jumping ship" and deserting. Most of these "immigrants" were "adopted" or "accepted" into the Māori families or clans in the region. However, by 1825, a collective of mariners had established themselves independently on Codfish Island in the Straits on a more or less permanent basis.

Once a particular strategy was put into place the mariners went to work on the pinnipeds. The mammals were killed in a similar manner as those in other parts of the Antipodes. Sealers used elementary equipment such as a knife, club, hook or lance to slaughter the mammals. Occasionally, a gun was employed. Once the seals were disposed of and skins cut and dried, they were loaded on the boats and destined for either the Chinese or London markets. From time to time, they commanded high prices.

Several sealers from the colony and elsewhere were prominent

---
[30] McNab, Op.cit., 220.

Chapter 7: Opportunity and Adversity in the Eastern Fishery

during the early colonial phases of the sealing industry in New Zealand. However, few kept any record of their ventures. Two who did were the Dane Jorgen Jorgenson,[31] and the Englishman John Boultbee. Another whose exploits were chronicled was Thomas Chaseland referred to earlier. Through the records kept by or written about these men and other journals, logs, newspaper articles, Māori storytelling and archaeological digs and surveys we find out about the nature of operations of the mariners in this region during this period. Jorgensen was an intrepid adventurer. He sailed extensively on sealing and whaling ventures across the Fishery during the early 1800s. Sometime during 1804, the Dane was employed to take command of the 44-ton sloop *Contest* and sail to New Zealand to seek out new sealing grounds. The Dane was excited by the prospect and, in his 1807 *Observations*,[32] wrote:

> Thereafter I accepted command of a small vessel belonging to the firm of Underwood and Kables which went sealing to New Zealand and other islands.

If we can believe Jorgensen, it appears he was successful in both his exploitations and discoveries. Jorgen managed to secure a healthy catchment of seals while also noting newfound fiords in the southwest of the New Zealand coast. He reminisced about his journey around that country, in particular noting 'four quite new harbours as well as several islands where there were seals'. The Dane was a prolific writer of journals and books, although prone to exaggerate from time to time. In his *Shred of Autobiography* referred to below, he described the methodologies employed by the sealers hunting the mammals in New Zealand:

> It is indeed astonishing with what eagerness the sailors enter into this pursuit knocking down the animals with their clubs,

---

[31] Jorgen Jorgenson (1788-1841) anglicised his name to John Johnson at some stage during his voyage around the Antipodes.

[32] Jorgensen wrote about his maritime adventures in at least two works: *Observations on the Funded System: Containing a Summary of the Present Political State of Great Britain, and the Relative Situation in Which the Colony of Van Diemen's Land Stands Towards the Mother Country* (1831) and *A Shred of Autobiography, Containing Various Anecdotes, Personal and Historical, Connected with these Colonies.*

stripping them of their skins, pegging them out to dry, or sorting them down in casks, with the greatest zeal and perseverance. We filled our little vessel and returned to Sydney.[33]

Notwithstanding his early success, he failed to voyage any further due to his leaky vessel that continued to plague him even as he limped back to Port Jackson. This mariner who, according to several historians, was prone to exaggerate, alleged he returned with '7,000 articles'. However, in 1805, *The Sydney Gazette* reported that Jorgenson anchored with perhaps '5,000' seal skins. Like most histories surrounding the discovery and exploration by such mariners, little is known about Jorgenson's charting of the southwest coast. As was the custom. he and his employers would have benefited from keeping certain destinations a secret. Jorgensen then spent some time in Van Diemen's Land and undertook further sealing voyages before leaving the Antipodes entirely. He led a very colourful life. Jorgen was employed by the Danish Government in command of a war vessel, was captured by the British and incarcerated as an enemy of the state and later usurped the throne of Iceland and installed himself as "King'"before being deposed.

Far more descriptive of the lives lived by sealers and their industry in the south of New Zealand was Boultbee.[34] He was one of the few well-educated literate sealers to keep a record of his sealing life in the Antipodes. He set out his experiences in the *Journal of a Rambler*. Originally from a middle-class English family, he sought to escape the tedium of a dull career by voyaging overseas. He was one of the few who clearly fitted the description of an "adventurer".

Initially. he was destined to pursue agriculture as a career in the West Indies, trying his hand at planting crops in Barbados. This did not last long, and he departed after a few months disgusted by the consequences of slavery there. Coming to the southern Fishery in about 1823, he was an unusual individual as he did not fit the developing negative stereotype attributed to sealers at that time. During his 10 years in the Fishery, he encountered and joined

---

[33] Jorgensen, *A Shred*, 14.
[34] 1799-1854.

sealing gangs wherever he went. Although he and his brother came to Van Diemen's Land first and signed up as part of a sealing crew there, they disliked the characters in their gang and left.

By 1826, John was employed by the sealer Daniel Cooper and the trader Solomon Levey on the brig *Elizabeth*, which voyaged to the southern island of New Zealand. He stayed with his crew in a hut constructed by mariners previously. His journal gives a vivid description of the life that he lived among the mariners and his encounters with the Māori. In doing so, he complained about the wet miserable nights he experienced and the violence of certain First Nations people that attacked and plundered vessels in the sealing grounds. Early on, clashes between local Māori and mariners were commonplace resulting in much bloodshed for both Europeans and the original inhabitants. But he also recorded the friendly meeting the mariners had with two boat crews in Milford Sound, the encounter with the mariner Jacky Price and his Māori consort at Pahia, and how he joined in with the local community.

While in the southern regions, Boultbee wrote down an extensive vocabulary of the Māori language for posterity. Encountering the Māori chiefs, Te Whakataupuka of Ruapuke and Te Wera of Bluff, he sketched their portraits for posterity while participating in the Maori lifestyle. Tiring of life in the Foveaux Straits, he joined another sealing crew on the *Samuel* before landing in Port Jackson in 1828, without any financial rewards for his troubles. That was an outcome typical for many men in the trade.[35] He spent two years there before deciding to journey to the new Swan River colony in Western Australia in 1829. He departed from that colony in 1833, when he joined a whaler bound for Timor, and eventually settled in Ceylon in 1834.

Boultbee's journal entries of his life as part of the early sealing community in New Zealand is an important resource for historians endeavouring to piece together an accurate record of the early colonial culture of that period. In the account of his life as a sealer, he described one of the main strategies adopted by the mariners to hunt seals. This essentially involved a very flexible and mobile

---
[35] Starke, 18-30.

approach. Mariners and supplies were left at a few different depots or camps to seal while the brig or schooner in which they were transported, sought other commodities. In the south of New Zealand, this involved a base camp where the main provisions were stored in huts constructed for that purpose. Having landed the mariners at strategic locations, the principal boat would sail away to pursue other tradeable commodities seeking flax or pork to exchange at the major colonial settlements. According to Boultbee, distances of up to 50 miles would be completed in a day to seek out the seal rookeries and commercially viable produce or timber. Sometimes on these journeys a whaleboat would be beached on shore and left ready for future visitors.

This adventurer also commented on the accommodation at the various camps. He observed huts built by mariners at Arnott's River, Open Bay Island, Milford and George Sounds and Anchor and Codfish Islands and caves occupied by them elsewhere. Conscious of the extreme weather conditions, he expressed delight at the large fires burning fiercely at night. At one camp, he ate vegetables his predecessors had grown there in a garden established, with 'a few celery plants, cabbages, potatoes, and turnips'. Apart from these "home grown" supplies, the sealers consumed flour, salt, salted pork, sugar and tea they either carried with them or sought by trading with passing European vessels. Added to this diet were local seafood and anything they could trade with the Māori. To take advantage of the seals and other food, Boultbee was present at well-established campsites where muskets, a keg of powder and balls, water buckets, grindstones, cooking pans and large iron pots and blankets were utilised. Just like sealing gangs who were dropped off by masters at remote locations in other parts of the Antipodes, many sealers were left for long periods in these camps and suffered physically and mentally from the actions of unscrupulous traders. Other risks emanated from more visceral events. The dangers of misadventure by drowning, starvation, attacks by the local hostile inhabitants and other misadventure and piracy were ever present. By the summer of 1827, Boultbee had been accepted as a crew member of the collective gang living out of Codfish Island. Here he spent much of his time sealing around Stewart Island and Foveaux Strait.

Around this time, the First Nation's mariner Thomas Chaseland was already earning a reputation as a prominent sealer and whaler over the two years he had lived in the region. He was able to straddle the two maritime pursuits with relative ease. Chaseland exercised a degree of flexibility that was common to some of the sealers in that region particularly as the sealing industry declined over time. Given the relatively small size of the European sealing community at the time, it is highly likely the two men encountered each other, although Boultbee does not mention Tommy in his writings. Thomas, like many mariners, was illiterate and left little or no written records of his life-time adventures.[36] But his reputation as an experienced, strong, and capable sealer, able to spot prey from great distances was recognised in the local press, colonial journals and oral Māori tradition.

Surveyor Frederick Tuckett recorded a positive and telling memoir about his eyesight:

> [The] Australian half-caste named Chaseland [is] gifted with such extraordinary powers of vision that once, when stationed on the lookout, he gave notice of a whale being sighted although the master after reconnoitring with his glass declared he could see nothing – Chaseland however still persisted in his statement adding it was a dead fish [a whale] with a harpoon stuck upright in his back with several fathoms of line attached – on pulling in the direction pointed out – the whale was found under the exact circumstances he had described – they say he sees land when fully thirty miles from it.

But it was his relationships with the local Māori peoples that is more telling about the complexity of his character. For, although he enjoyed two harmonious and monogamous relationships with local First Nations women and actively participated with the menfolk in sealing and whaling ventures, he, like several colonial sealers, was also involved in violent confrontations. His role in a sealing gang that killed local people in two separate raids on villages earned him a fearsome but poor reputation among the Māori. The second raid,

---

[36] The only writing may have been some notes on a map that was later found in the possession of his relatives upon his demise in 1869.

which occurred at Whareko near Milford Sound, resulted in all 30 of the local inhabitants being slaughtered. Indeed, there were numerous incidences in which sealers and Māoris used violence during the 1820s to redress wrongs allegedly committed by one against the other.

Apart from Chaseland's violent experiences, there were others. One occurred in 1833, when about 200 Māori secretly anchored at Codfish Island intending to rid the region of the sealers once and for all. Luckily for the mariners, they were warned in advance. Armed with muskets, they confronted the First Nations men on the beach. This was enough to ultimately persuade the hostile locals to reach a settlement with the sealers. There is some evidence that, due to the adverse effects of these violent confrontations, the Māori chiefs located in the Foveaux Straits tried to placate their colonial opponents. They did this by setting aside parts of Codfish Island for the sealers and their local partners, which may have assisted in finally resolving some of the conflicts.

But it was not just skirmishes with the local inhabitants that was a cause for concern for the sealing industry. There were other risks. One of the greatest dangers was shipwreck. This is well illustrated by the plethora of boats that foundered off the coasts of the Fishery's islands, including New Zealand. Take, for example the mariner William Wiseman. He arrived in Sydney Town in 1806 with his family. Well-connected, he married the daughter of Captain John Grono. The captain was engaged not only in sealing but the ship-building trade in Port Jackson, where the brig *Industry* was built in 1826. Grono sent that vessel on a mission under the command of Wiseman to seek oil and skins between the southern coast of New Zealand and Sydney. Despite early success, the brig was lost at sea off Stewart Island in a storm. All but two on board were to perish.[37]

Despite these difficulties, and even as late as 1824, there were still good opportunities for mariners to make a living out of the seal trade around some islands. At this time the French naval corvette

---

[37] See Mick Roberts, 'Three Times Buried' in *Time Gents, Australian Pub Project*, 14 July, 2016,

Coquille under Captain Duperrey was on a scientific expedition of discovery. The ensign on board, de Blosseville, noted in his personal diary:

> Besides providing excellent ports of call, New Zealand offers brilliant possibilities for the sealing trade. Fur seals are very numerous on her coasts and in her bays. The skins of the Fur Seals sell for three piastres in America and three and a quarter piaster in China…

However, pointing a finger at the English, he believed the pinniped numbers would be substantially reduced within a few years if 'the ardour' of the sealers did not cool. Preying on the seal colonies all over the Antipodes Fishery was to become a major issue throughout the relevant colonial period.

Apart from the southern tip of New Zealand and Macquarie and Campbell Islands, there were other remote and isolated locations where mariners pattern of behaviour was similar to that experienced elsewhere in the Antipodes Fishery. In general terms, on encountering coastal environments where seals thrived, there would be a plethora of sealing ships packed with crews and equipment that would voyage to and from the newly 'discovered' rookeries. Once a new island inhabited by seals was "found", it did not take long for the Sydney traders to direct their masters to voyage there. In so doing, it was not unusual for several ships to anchor off bays and beaches at any one time to compete for what became scarce resources. Boats would then be loaded with slaughtered seals and masters would hasten back to the ports in Sydney and Hobart for shipment of skins and oil to Chinese or London markets. From time to time, significant profits were generated from such trade. At other times when markets were not favourable, there were scarce returns.

Over 460 kilometres to the south of New Zealand lie the Auckland Islands.[38] Between 1806 and 1840, numerous sealing and whaling vessels had voyaged there to hunt for seals with crews

---

[38] The Auckland Islands were apparently discovered by East Polynesians circa AD 1200. This was the southernmost latitude ever recorded (to date) of East Polynesian/early Māori exploration. They were 'rediscovered' by Captain John Briscoe travelling in August 1806 in the the *Ocean* owned by the Enderby family.

from many nations including America, France, England, Portugal and New Holland. After Captain Abraham Bristow observed seal colonies in and around these outcrops in late 1806, one of the first masters to visit there was the American Samuel Chace. He was given command of the 185-ton *George* then the largest vessel built in the colony. Chace was tasked with voyaging to the islands with crews on three separate occasions in 1807. It was a sign of the potential for large scale sealing there and the American was keen to oblige the Sydney traders.

When Captain Sirone in the *Commerce* arrived there in 1807, he thought he would be alone to procure seals undisturbed by others. To his annoyance, he discovered two other gangs of mariners there on the same account. Disgruntled, he created a more favourable environment by arranging for the rival gangs to be plied with rum. Once they were inebriated, Sirone found he had no competition and, while the gang attempted to recover from their stupor, he proceeded to kill 3,000 seals for their skins. No doubt the pelts sold well in China.

Chace returned two years later when he encountered Hasselburgh in the *Perseverance* who needed more crew to assist on his voyage to the sub-Antarctic. Chace arranged a swap with the desperate captain. While Hasselburgh sailed south to encounter Macquarie and Campbell Islands, Chace headed north to the Bay of Islands. Within three years, Chace's fortunes had been dashed, and he was open for any maritime work he could find. By then, he was in command of a vessel that returned to the Bay of Islands delivering the first of the Christian missionaries to preach to the Māori.

But there were better times ahead. By 1823, there were at least two American vessels sealing in that area, One of those, the *Henry*, a New York-based ship, returned to that city in 1824 with 13,000 skins from the island. The captain Benjamin Morrell described the seals as having 'good fur seal skins as ever were brought to the American market'. The same vessel later voyaged into more southern waters to seek other resources and returned to New York with another 3,000 seal skins.[39] In August of the same year, the clergyman Dr. John Dunmore Lang and other passengers in the *Midas* anchored in Sarah's Bosom, a bay being part of Bristow's Island. They were on their way back to England. The captain of that vessel was tasked with delivering much needed provisions to a desperate sealing crew who had been left there procuring skins and oil for the London market. The *Midas* gang were to arrange for the procured booty to be taken on board and shipped to London. Lang observed that the mariners living on the island had established a stone home with a thatched roof and wooden American door covered with a seal skin. In a sign that sealers had a wry sense of humour, over the entry was written that visitors were welcome to their "mansion". But that sense of humour evaporated when, to the seal hunters' dismay, their whaleboat which they had lent to the *Midas* crew, had come adrift and was floating out to sea. Fortunately for them, it was found the next day partly stoved in on rocks. To satisfy the angry sealers, Lang and others gave the sealing men cedar from the *Midas* which was used to effect much needed repairs. In his journal, Lang wrote that nearby was Rowe's Island which was 'the resort of numberless seals at particular seasons and was traversed in all directions by the tracks of these amphibious creatures.'[40]

The high point of the sealing trade there was in 1825, when at least six sealing boats were hunting the pinnipeds. After that, it appears there was little success for any vessel which anchored at the island. Quite the opposite; many of the Auckland Island vessels not only failed to load enough pelts for their anxious traders, but many were wrecked by treacherous conditions, with several crewmen losing their lives.[41]

About 840 kilometres directly east of New Zealand are islands called the Chathams by Europeans. The First Nations peoples

---
[39] *New York Evening Post,* 18 April, 1826.
[40] John Dunmore Lang, *Reminiscences of My Life and Times from auto biographical cuttings*, 51.
[41] For example, in 1830, John Biscoe was again at the islands but one of his vessels was wrecked there while another boat came to grief in 1833. There was evidence of a third ship being destroyed in 1834. He knew the risks involved.

call them Rekohu.⁴² They were originally populated in 1500 CE by a Polynesian race, the Moriori.⁴³ These original inhabitants lived as hunter-gatherers. They relied on sealing to provide an essential component in their diets. Undisturbed by foreigners for generations, a Lieutenant Broughton of the British Navy anchored there by accident in 1791. His vessel, *The Chatham*, had accompanied Vancouver's *Discovery* on a mission from England and had lost contact with the larger vessel after leaving Facile Harbour near New Zealand.⁴⁴ Shortly after Broughton berthed his boat, he made some observations of the topography, describing the land as 'very pleasant'. Through his glasses, he spied the local inhabitants working on their "canoes". Reaching the shore in a cutter with some of his crew, Broughton acted to create a friendly discourse (like most Europeans on first contact). He offered the usual supply of "trinkets" and, by gesture, advocated the English wanted to trade. As often occurred on first encounters, the locals were reluctant to enter into any exchange of objects. Then the history follows a predictable pattern: the locals became wary and retreat from any bartering. The colonial mariners grew suspicious and mistrustful. In the hours that followed, one of the Moriori was shot by a musket ball. All potential for peaceful intercourse ceased in an instant.

During the encounter, Broughton observed the canoes and dress of the local people, noting they clothed themselves partly in seal skins and relied mainly on the produce from the sea.⁴⁵ The Englishman assumed he was the first white man to set foot on the island. Thinking of his own historical importance in the scheme of events, he ordered the British flag to be unfurled and erected, taking

---

⁴² Essentially, there are two main islands called Chatham and Pitt, with some smaller uninhabited ones with a total area of approximately 966 square kilometres. There are also several lagoons and lakes on the two main islands, which were subject to much volcanic activity over the millennia.

⁴³ It may well be that the date of first human occupation occurred somewhere between the thirteenth and fifteenth centuries.

⁴⁴ Vancouver and Broughton had already discussed the possibility and had agreed to make for Otaheite if such an event occurred.

⁴⁵ See Vancouver, *A voyage of discovery to the North Pacific Ocean, and round the world*, 230-245.

Chapter 7: Opportunity and Adversity in the Eastern Fishery

possession of the island for King George III. Somewhat unusually he named the islands after his vessel. To create further immortality, a piece of lead was suitably inscribed and tagged to a tree, with a bottle being placed close by containing similar claims in Latin. Broughton had by then had time to reflect on the tragedy of the first encounter and expressed regret, stating in Vancouver's journal:

> I have to lament that the hostility of its inhabitants rendered the melancholy fate that attended on one of them unavoidable, and prevented our research extending further than the beach, and the immediate entrance of the adjoining wood.[46]

At the time the Chatham Islands were outside the territory of New South Wales by about three kilometres. This meant they came within the jurisdiction and control of the monopolistic British East India Company. It prohibited traders such as sealers and whalers from conducting any operations without their express permission, which would not have been granted. Despite this, most of the visitors to the islands (until at least 1840) were mariners who defied the Company's sanctions and managed to avoid penalty, mainly by keeping their activities a secret. Accordingly, there are few written records such as journals and letters from the early maritime adventurers on which one can base any degree of certainty about what happened during the early years of the sealing trade there. In addition, no Māori or Moriori artifacts are available to assist researchers to piece together the maritime jigsaw puzzle of what occurred. There are, however, some records that appear to show there were two periods when sealers came to procure the pinnipeds. The first was from about 1800 to 1810, and the second from about the mid-1820s until the late 1830s, when there was another frenzy of activity involving sealers from Australia and New Zealand. This pattern replicates what occurred throughout most of the Antipodes. Notwithstanding the unfortunate circumstances of the first encounter, the Moriori later welcomed colonial visitors. But this led to dire consequences for their future survival.[47]

---

[46] Ibid., 242.
[47] The First Nations inhabitants thought the English had descended from the sun, but they may have been in awe of them. In addition, the fact that the white men

More recent historians estimate (with some doubt) that the first sealers to visit the Chathams arrived in about 1804. Certainly, by 1807, there were reports of several sealing gangs hunting the pinnipeds for their Sydney employers out of the islands. This included those arriving in the *Commerce*, owned by Lord, Kable and Underwood, whose crew apparently disposed of 300 seals. This event was later recorded by a nine-year-old local boy named Marmon, who later recollected his eye-witness account as an adult. He remembered the visit at the time of Hororeka, a local First Nations man. This Moriori male acted as a liaison between the First Nations people and the crews, having previously voyaged to the Bay of Islands and being familiar with both native languages.

A new Chatham economy had been forged by the mariners in the period concluding in 1810. Visitors included the intrepid sealer Samuel Chase captaining the *Pegasus* and the *Antipode* commanded by Scott. Americans such as Captain Mathew Folger, also arrived on the *Topaz* shortly before he had an encounter with Fletcher Christian and his mutineers on Pitcairn Island. All this occurred on islands that were populated by the original inhabitants whose generally friendly demeanour meant that the visitors could exploit the natural resources at will. The European mariners probably formed temporary sexual liaisons with the local females, which introduced diseases. The diseases themselves led to disastrous outcomes for the locals. For many decades to come, any contact made between the Moriori and their visitors was fraught with difficulty and, worse, death.

Fortunately for the Moriori, the sealing trade ceased between 1810 and 1825, with only a handful of vessels arriving at the Chathams, including the *Sophia* in 1818. This meant that the First Nations peoples had their monopoly on the resources of the sea restored. As the pinniped rookeries recovered, they could again rely on the sea to provide food and clothing. But the hiatus in Western sealing did not last. When the mariners returned to these islands,

---

left the body of the deceased where he fell and did not try and make claims on their land meant that they were prepared to let 'sleeping dogs lie'. However, the relationships with the Māori were different after their mini 'invasion' in 1835.

Chapter 7: Opportunity and Adversity in the Eastern Fishery

the local people's lives were changed forever. New diverse teams of sealers arrived starting with the Americans in the *Henry* in 1825, followed by the colonial lads from Australasia.

There was a revival in the sealing industry after the mid-1820s, with prices rising sharply to average 20 shillings or more per skin, which would have driven demand for more of the mammals. Although it may well have been that several hundred men visited the Chathams, the outcomes of their endeavours were relatively poor compared to those profiting from elephant seal oil at Macquarie. For example, in 1827, the *Glory*, owned by the trader Campbell and under Captain Swindells managed to collect a cargo of only 1,800 seal skins. Tommy Chaseland was one of the crew on board but separated from the gang with his partner and some others when the vessel was incapacitated. Tommy survived a treacherous voyage back to New Zealand Several more survivors were later transported back to Port Jackson by a Mr Drysdale as master of the vessel the *Samuel*. They arrived with 4,500 skins they had removed from the Fishery.[48] No other vessel after that time procured greater than 1,000 skins, according to Brett.[49] The seal colonies would have been over exploited.

During the second wave of visits, the newcomers started to settle permanently. Many international visitors remained at the Chathams seeking to make a living from the sea. Jacob Tealing settled in the islands and became a leader of a tribe of Moriori until his demise in 1855. They were far removed from any possible sanction and scrutiny, surviving on their own talents and the assistance of local peoples. There was no lawful authority being exercised over the islands until much later. That fact further fostered a completely indulgent and lawless environment. This led to an ideal climate for those wanting to avoid colonial authority. Towards the end of the sealing years, the American explorer Charles Wilkes visited the islands and found them inhabited by characters he called 'a nest of rogues'.[50]

---

[48] *The Australian*, 20 March, 1827, 1.
[49] See Andre Brett, "Australia and the Secretive Exploitation of the Chatham Islands to 1842." in *Journal of Australian Studies*, 106.
[50] Charles Wilkes. *Narrative of the United States Exploring Expedition, 1838-42,*

His descriptions may have been encouraged by the presence of William Walker [aka 'William Swallow], the most famous criminal among them. He, along with other convicts, had seized control of the brig *Cyprus* in 1829 while being transported to Sarah Island in Macquarie Harbour. After forcing the vessel's startled and frightened crew to remain at Recherche Bay, Swallow and his pirates set off for China under new pseudonyms to disguise them as American traders. Blown off course, they eventually found their way to the Chathams, where they ransacked a Moriori village before plundering the local sealing community. Ultimately, they were "found out" and faced prosecution in London, where most were found guilty of an 'abominable crime' and sentenced accordingly. Three of these pirates were executed.[51]

However, the main impact on the local peoples and the seal population did not come from the piratical criminal classes but firstly from mariners who, apart from sexual diseases, introduced measles and smallpox, and decimated the pinnipeds. It also came from the Māori, who conducted a war of attrition in 1835 when they travelled there en masse in an attempt to exterminate the Moriori. Not only did the local population decrease as a direct outcome of the ravages of disease and violence, but they were no longer able to rely on the seals to provide food and skins for clothing. Similar to what had occurred in other parts of the Fishery, those sealers who stayed the course and settled had to rely not only on the sea for survival but also agriculture. They produced such commodities as flax and potatoes, constructed piggeries and partnered with local Moriori women who assisted them in such endeavours, along with satisfying the mariners' sexual needs. Although over-exploitation of the seal rookeries, decimation of the local Moriori and piracy occurred in the Chathams during the colonial period, the sealers managed to eke out a reasonable living and were not abandoned. It was different in the west and southwest of Australia.

Vol. 2, 404.
[51] William Walker once again avoided the hangman's noose but was eventually convicted of further crimes , transported again to Van Diemen's Land where he was kept at Port Arthur dying there of natural causes.

Chapter 8: Rogues, Rapscallions and Survivors Haunt the Antipodes

While the colonial sealers who operated out of the Chathams mainly had to deal with the risks associated with shipwreck, piracy and depleted rookeries, there were others who faced starvation and death on the far western edge of the Fishery having been abandoned or remaining on false promises made by their master or even worse. Worst still were unscrupulous masters who took advantage of crews and rivals where there was an advantage to be gained. Some of the more telling accounts which fit the description of this pattern of behaviour occurred in the Auckland and Kerguelen Islands to the east and in the Recherche Archipelago and St Paul's Island to the west of Australia.

Some masters were particularly unscrupulous and profligate. One of the most notorious was Captain Abimeleck Riggs. He was an American from Boston who commenced on a sealing voyage from that port in October 1818 with a seasoned crew in the 180-ton brig *General Gates*. One of his crew was George William Robinson. On 12 April 1819, Riggs landed some of his employed sealers on St Paul or Amsterdam Islands with a promise to return. We know this is the exact date as one of the gang etched it in rock with a knife. During that time only one other vessel anchored there several months later. Robinson was one of the five sealers who disembarked. Little did he and his comrades know at the time, but Riggs was to become a notorious character who would offend, not only his crews, but also the Māori and the colonial officials.

The American master later sailed for Port Jackson, where he illegally seized 10 convicts he forced to assist him in sealing activity while in the Fishery. He was later arrested at the Bay of Islands and obliged to release the prisoners, who were found to be in a deplorable state as Riggs had imposed harsh physical punitive measures to ensure control and order on his brig. According to the editor of the *Gazette,* the *General Gates* arrived accompanied by the transport ship *Dromedary* in Sydney Harbour on the 13 May 1820. Riggs was detained as a prisoner and on arrival was placed under arrest 'for infracting the Port Regulations, by conveying from the Colony ten prisoners and one free man who had not obtained a clearance'. At his trial he was convicted and fined £6,000. After paying his fine, Riggs finally set sail for his isolated and starving crew on St. Pauls, but not before his cook a "Negro" by the name of Tristram Shephard, had absconded. The American master offered a reward of five pounds for his apprehension. No one claimed it. Meanwhile, the American vessel, the *Panther,* had been to St. Pauls. Its fresh Yankee crew found:

> A house built to our hands, by persons who had before been on this island killing Seals, and it was in tolerable condition— though not perhaps what would be called in tenantable repair by a lessee in England; but as we had not to pay either rent or taxes, we did not consider it requisite to find much fault...

According to George Robinson's testimony recorded years after, they had slaughtered 7,000 seals for their pelts but otherwise had survived by eating seal, fish, petrels and wild pigs while trying to keep an horrific mouse plague at bay!

Riggs sailed from Batavia to collect the disgruntled crew some 23 months later. After his malnourished weather-beaten men clambered on board, he headed to Kangaroo Island. On arrival, Robinson and his four comrades must have thought the island a paradise compared to the remote Indian Ocean outcrop. After a few weeks, Riggs returned to New Zealand, which was fateful for his crew many of whom were supposedly devoured by the Māoris. He popped up again in the shipping records, sailing between Canton, Manila, and Batavia, until he anchored at Hobart some time in 1822. By 1824, he had lost at least 20 of his crew to misadventure. This did not stop him making a killing on the Canton seal market. Strangely, by February 1825, there is no further record of him or any of his mariners. It might be not difficult to imagine the totality of the terror that Riggs' crew and his ten convicts would have faced

Chapter 8: Rogues, Rapscallions and Survivors Haunt the Antipodes

against the constant threat of death, be it by starvation, exposure to the elements, conflicts with and the cannibalism allegedly perpetrated by the Māoris.

Another example of the kind of deprivation and heartbreak endured by sealers at the hands of unscrupulous masters on remote Western volcanic islands was experienced by James Paine and Robert Proudfoot. These sealers had been left by a Captain Craig in the *Hunter* on Amsterdam Island in November 1827. Their story of betrayal, privation, resilience and determination became public when the *Calcutta Government Gazette* published an account of their ordeal, which was repeated verbatim in *The Sydney Gazette*:

> Their whole stock of salt had been washed away on the beach, they had not even a pocketknife, their only clothing was on their backs. They had a small store of bread and provisions, which they husbanded so well as to last them five months before it was all expended. The only vessel they saw was the late ship Hope, bound to this place in November 1826, which coming within a few miles of the shore, sent a boat out to fish, which they hailed, and the officer in the boat told them that when he returned to the ship he would inform Captain Cunningham of the circumstance; and act according to his directions. He did return to the ship, and the unhappy men had soon the mortification to see the boat hoisted up, and the Hope making all sail on her voyage. From that period to the appearance of the Palmira, twelve months after, they did not see a single ship. During the whole 14 months they had obtained only 7 seals… These poor men thus left entirely destitute, by accident found on the rocks a needle, an old knife, and a spike nail, with the last of which they made a hook, and a piece of coir rope formed a line with which they contrived to fish, but there being no barb at the point of the hook they had often the misfortune to lose their prey. The only sort of fish they caught was the trumpeter, and limpets. They were often much distressed for want of water… They therefore had to depend on pools of rainwater alone.
>
> The island is well furnished with wild hogs, but they could not manage to catch more than five. These they ran down and felled with a stick. 'You must have run very fast for your dinner', said the Captain. – 'Yes, we did, said they, but the pig had to run for its life.' … After their arrival they were obliged to burn the long grass which obstructed their proceedings, and the conflagration spreading over the island, continued burning for several months. They tried to make a bow and arrows, but the wood was not

> fitted for the purpose. They had a tinder box when they landed, but the tinder was soon expended, and they could find nothing dry enough to supply its place. The necessity of keeping their fire constantly alive, was therefore both anxious and difficult... There is no eatable vegetable in the island but parsley, which is plentiful. No snow fell during the winter months, but hail and sleet continually, and it was extremely cold at that season of the year. Proudfoot once got a severe fall from a rock, which confined him with a violent sprain in his shoulder for four months.

Such a tale of deprivation and ultimate salvation would have titillated a colonial audience that was thrilled by stories where fact trumped fantasy. It probably reminded the colonial settlers of other tales of resilience, such as those fictionalised by the English writer Daniel Dafoe. In this case, the master had, at best, simply forgotten about the distressed sealers or, at worst, deliberately avoided returning to Amsterdam Island. He curiously sailed near the more habitable St Pauls Island, a short distance away, and reaped the various benefits of his voyage without any concern for his destitute crew. Like many such masters, his boat was loaded up with a plethora of valuable commodities for sale in the colony as reported by the press soon afterwards:

> Same day, the Schooner Hunter of Hobart Town, James Craig, Master, 61 Tons, from the Isle of France, 14th August, touching St Pauls; with 126 bags containing 20377 lbs. Sugar; 226 bags, each containing164 lbs. Rice; 100 pieces blue Nankin; 72 dozen cakes shaving Soap; 1 case Hardware; 1 ditto Haberdashery; 25000 Cheroots; 60 pieces Bengal figured Bed-matts, 279 lbs. pounds Soap; 2 pipes Marsella Wine; 50 pieces blue Mahmoodies; 40 pieces tow Ducks; 40 pieces Flax Ducks; 20 bags Salt.[1]

No doubt he would have earned a considerable profit from his ventures while docked in Sydney town. In the meantime, the *Palmira* collected the two men languishing at the island and transported them back to 'civilization'.

Another one of the coastal places that became sought after by traders and sealers was King Georges Sound. Although explorers, surveyors and navigators such as Vancouver in 1791, Flinders in 1802, Parker King in 1818 and D'Urville in 1826, temporarily

---
[1] *Hobart Town Gazette*, 21 October, 1826.

Chapter 8: Rogues, Rapscallions and Survivors Haunt the Antipodes

anchored there, the sole resident European occupants were colonial and American sealers. Despite these occasional prominent visits, no thought was given to colonising this region until the colonial government became seriously concerned about French incursion in the late 1820s.

Mainly out of fear of their rivals, the Governor of the colony sent Major Lockyer in the 142-ton brig *Amity* there on a fact-finding mission in late 1827. But it still took another three years for a formal settlement to be established. In the meantime, there was a vacuum that came to be filled by adventurous and hungry mariners, who were deposited there either by chance or design. Following Vancouver's voyage of discovery and exploration, the American sealers were the first to commence sealing operations around the western Australian coastline after news of the explorers' voyage there became public. For, apart from the Yankees, perhaps one of the reasons why maritime traders and sealers, did not flock to the Recherche Archipelago early on to hunt seals was because the initial reports of explorers and traders were not promising. As previously written, Vancouver, Flinders, and Pendleton all reported their disappointment at not finding significant seal populations. In January 1802 (although compiled much later), Flinders journalised that, while seals occupied most of the islands, they were not in such numbers, and were not of the kind, that would attract exploitation, or were not suitable for the China market.[2]

However, on 20 January 1818, Phillip Parker King, while conducting his nautical survey of the entire continent, landed in King Georges Sound, observed:

> In the evening we landed on Seal Island, which we had much difficulty in effecting on account of the surf. Several seals were upon it, one of which we killed; and some penguins were also taken.[3]

King's observations would have come to the attention of the Sydney traders and others, such as the American whalers and sealers. The report may have contributed to a renewed interest in

---
[2] Flinders, 91.
[3] Parker King, 11.

that region as an opportunity for commercial exploitation of the marine resources there.

In any event, by the time King returned to the Sound in the *Dromedary* in November 1822, the Americans were sealing there. On 8 November, King recorded:

> A few days after our arrival we were surprised by the appearance of a strange vessel beating into the sound; she proved to be an American schooner on a sealing voyage and was coming in for the purpose of careening and cleaning the vessel's bottom in Oyster Harbour.

By the mid-1820s, economic circumstances had improved for many sealers, including those from other nations. This meant that several disparate gangs started to frequent many of the islands lying along the southwestern coast of Australia. For example, it has been established that the Belinda, a sealing vessel, was operating around the Recherche Archipelago in the early 1820s. Further, some sealers had established a base from a cave on Boxer Island, where the remnants of seal skins were located in the 20th century. There were also many camps found on Middle Island, a haunt of the notorious Black-Jack Anderson.

Apart from some records following the surveys by King, and the work of modern-day archaeologists, there is little recorded information about sealers who conducted the trade in Western Australia until the journals of D'Urville were written sometime after his arrival in the Sound in 1826. Those entries also give testimony to the fact that traders were not only operating there in the early 1820s but were also behaving in an appalling manner by failing to collect their sealers by the agreed timeframes. In October 1826, when D'Urville anchored in the Sound in the L'Astrolabe, he observed that the mariners there were clearly in distress from want of provisions. Desperate crew members were more than happy to join in with the French expedition.

This crew was probably part of a larger gang under a Captain Davidson. That master left 'on a sealing voyage' on the *Governor Brisbane* from Hobart Town around 29 September 1825.[4] The

---
[4] According to the editor of the *Hobart Town Gazette*, 1 October, 1825.

remainder of the mariners under Davidson abandoned those choosing to remain in the Sound and voyaged on to Batavia. There the vessel and its nefarious crew were detained by the Dutch government, which had 'intelligence' that the captain and his crew had 'gone on account.'[5] Davidson's conduct and behaviour was confirmed when a report about him circulated in the *Hobart Town Gazette* on 7 October 1826:

> Our Readers will not confound Mr. Baxter's schooner Brisbane of Sydney, Thomas Smith master, with Messrs. Kemp and Company's, the Brisbane of this Colony, which was piratically carried off by the master Davidson (formerly mate of the ship Phoenix) from Bass's Strait to Batavia, where it was seized by the Dutch Government, and Davidson and his guilty crew placed in confinement.[6]

By December of that year, D'Urville had sailed with several (but not all) of the abandoned mariners in the *L'Astrolabe* into Port Jackson. What the disreputable Davidson had arranged, prior to his hasty departure for Batavia, was for eight of the men to be deposited in the Sound and the remainder on Middle Island, 800 kilometres to the east on unreliable promises. The editor of the *Gazette* recorded the sad state of affairs:

> The Captain said he would take them in again in a day or two after. A vessel supposed by the crew to be the Governor Brisbane, was seen, in the offing three days after they were left. They had been on shore about eight months, when the Corvette hove in sight. On signals being made, the crew of the Astrolabe put off a boat and took them on board. When [they] left they had only two days provisions.[7]

Also on board the *L'Astrolabe* were some sealers who were part of the Captain J. Craig's crew on the Hunter referred to above. On the return journey, the *Hunter* had been anchored on the French Island of Mauritius. The unfortunate sealers had been forced to

---

[5] It is also alleged that Davidson had left four crew members at Westernport in a similar *modus operandi* according to Cumpston and Plomley.
[6] There is no further report available as to what happened to the 'pirates' who would normally have been handed over to the colonial authorities for trial, and if found guilty, executed.
[7] *The Australian*, 9 December, 1826.

voyage back to Western Australia on another vessel. Meanwhile the unscrupulous Craig had returned directly with a sweet cargo of sugarcane to Van Diemen's Land.[8] From all accounts, there may have been something like 20 people who had encounters with the French vessels who were part of a combined gang of abandoned sealers made up of a composite of races and nations at this time.[9]

It is probable that some of these mariners were part of at least two gangs of sealers operating out of King Georges Sound when Major Lockyer voyaged there in the *Amity* in 1827, ahead of those settlers who came with James Stirling[10] to establish a new colony. The *Amity* berthed in the Sound on Christmas Day 1826 and established a camp the following day. Shortly after his arrival, Lockyer encountered some sealers who were endeavouring to subsist by conducting small-scale operations, along with whaling crews, between Kangaroo and Rottnest islands over several years. It appears that we have only the journal of Lockyer to rely on in respect of those encounters, which were to some degree troubled.[11] Once again, these mariners sought out the visitors for provisions, although it is hard to ascertain exactly how bad their state and condition was at the time. It was the sealers who first approached the Major seeking either assistance or food. The latter quickly concluded that some of these men had been guilty of illegal activities in relation to the "natives". He proceeded to conduct his own extra-judicial enquiry into the affairs of these men, which resulted in the arrest of at least two of them. In April 1827, Lockyer, intent

---

[8] Previously, Craig had enjoyed some success as a seal trader in the Fishery, as evidenced by this short entry in *The Sydney Gazette* in 1824: 'Same day returned from a sealing trip, the brig *Perseverance*, Captain Craig, with 30 tons of salt and 4000 skins'. He continued to trade for seals in the Hunter in Bass Strait as late as November, 1826.

[9] Cumpston sets out the names and origins of the gang. There appear to have been 12 Anglo Saxons, one New Zealander named William Hook, two 'black men', possibly African Americans, Pidgeon, a 'Sydney Black', Harry, a 'native boy' and their female companions, Sally, Dinah and Mooney.

[10] Stirling (1791-1865) was later knighted for his naval and overseas exploits, but has more lately come under increasing scrutiny for the role he played in the Pinjarra Massacre, where several First Nations people were killed or injured by a force under his command.

[11] James Sykes. Battye. *Western Australia: a history from its discovery to the inauguration of the Commonwealth.*

on their prosecution, secured the offending sealers found to have perpetrated atrocities on the local Nyungar people in his vessel. It would appear from further investigation that none of the men faced any particular sanction. Once these sealers were removed from King Georges Sound, only a handful of mariners remained including the sealers John Williams and Robert Gamble. Little is known about the settlements that men such as these established while in the Recherche, but we do know that the sealers who lived there had been surviving on sealing for more than two years. They had built huts, and may have traded in seal skins, oil and salt from Manduran Island.

In early 1827, Stirling, a semi-retired naval officer, anchored near Rottnest Island in his brig the *H.M. Success* with the botanist Charles Fraser. Stirling set about exploring the Swan River area, leaving in late March. His investigation of that region fostered the establishment in 1829 of a settlement, with the first colonial men and women occupying it under the command of a Thomas Peel. This proved a difficult task and took time to come to fruition. In the meantime, though, the sealers were very active, despite a decline in the industry generally. Part of the reason for this appears to be the prominence in the region of American and French whalers. One of the main reasons the authorities sent Lockyer to the west was due to the threat these whalers posed to English sovereignty.[12] Vessels began to anchor off the coast around Rottnest Island and Perth and were probably also active in the Sound. Disgruntled crew members of these vessels would have sought to escape harsh and unpleasant conditions and one of those was John 'Black-Jack' Anderson.

After escaping from his American whaler in 1826, Anderson chose to head straight for Kangaroo Island. Over the next 11 years, he plied a nefarious trade, criss-crossing the southern oceans from there to the Recherche Archipelago. By stealth or force, he (and some others, such as Gamble) cobbled together a primarily female Aboriginal crew to pursue the sealing trade with considerable vigour. But, unlike many of the small-time maritime traders in

---

[12] In addition, the threat of French activity in the region would have also been perceived as potentially a larger risk to the Empire.

the Fishery, he quickly came to realise he could make a fortune by piracy. Most of his crews were terrified of him, and there were rumours that some plotted to mutiny and dispose of him when the chance arose. Anderson was no doubt aware of this and carried about his waist numerous pistols in a belt. He became legendary for his zealous raids on vessels and settlements in the west. There were also rumours that Anderson may have been responsible for the death of at least one mariner. The unfortunate sailor was found with his throat slit from ear to ear under a waterfall near Doubtful Bay Island. Although the finger was pointed at Anderson, he never faced any charges for murder. One has to wonder how he was able to avoid nearly all legal sanctions until his death in 1837.

For approximately 11 years, Black-Jack amassed a considerable fortune in gold and silver. He pocketed some around his person while the rest he secreted on Manduran Island. While on such a voyage to the island, in circumstances much like any other, Anderson and his First Nations female companion were "lost" in suspicious circumstances. Although the pirate had kept his crew together by fear of reprisal and force, it was only a matter of time before one of them would pluck up the courage to plot against him. The editor of *The Perth Gazette* told his excited readers the sorry tale:

> At last, one day when he was asleep in the tent, one of them entered and taking deliberate aim blew his brains out. The corpse was thrown into a hole and covered over with earth, they then shared the booty, killed the woman in case she should afterwards tell the tale.[13]

While Anderson occupies the pages of the history books as one of the most notorious and colourful of the marginal characters, there were other mariners who made a success of their ventures. This they did by diversifying their businesses. One example was the Henty family. In 1834 that family were sealing in the Recherche area according to reports by the master of the schooner Thistle. Like many independent sealers, they and men like Gamble and Red Jimmy Everett had expanded their mobile operations in well-organised multinational itinerant gangs. Operating to the east

---

[13] William Nairne Clark, in *The Perth Gazette,* 8 October, 1842.

Chapter 8: Rogues, Rapscallions and Survivors Haunt the Antipodes

of the Sound they found seals 'were abundant in that quarter' in contrast to the substantial depletion of the seals in nearly all other Antipodean locations.

As the Antipodean rookeries became depleted, other opportunities to find new seal rookeries arose as the traders became aware of reports from explorers returning from more remote sub-Antarctic islands. While many a master successfully completed a voyage there and loaded seal skins and oil ready for the Canton and British markets, some of their crews were not so fortunate. One of the remotest of outcrops near the Antarctic Circle was one called Isle de Kerguelen. This had previously been discovered by the French.[14] A few years later, Cook arrived there, having sailed from Cape Town in December 1776. He observed in his journal:

> The shore in a manner covered with penguins and other birds and seals, but these were not numerous but so fearless that we killed as many as we chose for the sake of their fat or blubber to make oil for our lamps and other uses...[15]

After the publication of Cook's journals, interest in the commercial opportunities of these islands mounted significantly. As a result, these isolated French outposts became an object of exploitation by other mariners.[16] In about 1800, Captain Robert Rhodes sailed there in the Hillsborough and was responsible for charting the entire group. These charts became an invaluable resource for other mariners. While on the islands, Rhodes and his crew killed sufficient elephant seals to bring on board 450 tons of oil, which he transported back to London. Subsequently, many vessels visited the islands. One of the early visitors was the crew of the *Frances*, which arrived there in 1818 or 1819. When they departed after a successful seal hunt, they left some vessels, including one shallop, later renamed the Favorite.

---

[14] The island was discovered in February 1772 by the French navigator Yves-Joseph de Kerguelen-Tremarec. Part of French Territory, they are also called Iles de la Desolation (Desolation Islands) and lie over 3,000 kilometres from the nearest human habitations.

[15] James Cook, in J. C. Beaglehole (ed.) *The Journals of Captain James Cook on his voyage of discovery, voyage of Resolution and Adventure 1772-1775*, 23.

[16] The names given to various geographical features in the islands indicate that, apart from the French and English, the Americans, Norwegians and Russians had also visited there over time. The highest point is Cook Glacier.

Although most of the sealing journeys to the islands were moderately successful, there were several ships wrecked there, including the same Favorite under Captain John Nunn, which came to grief in 1825. Nunn had been part of a crew under Captain Alexander Sinclair in the Royal Sovereign, which left London on a sealing voyage earlier that year. He was shipwrecked at Kerguelen along with three crew members when they ventured out alone in the shallop around the islands.

Many years later, Nunn had a chance encounter with Clarke, referred to earlier, who took sufficient notes from the old sealer to write a book about his misadventure referred to previously. Although the work was written with future economic and scientific opportunities in mind, it provides as close a primary source as one could want. This was borne out given that Clarke cross-checked a number of the "facts" related to him by Nunn, particularly in relation to the islands' geography and mineral composition. The most illustrative part of the book is devoted to the shipwrecks Nunn endured, and the methods by which he and his fellow sealers subsisted in appalling conditions.

While at the Kerguelen Islands, Nunn was the subject of two separate wrecking events. Following the first one where their shallop capsized, he and his drenched mariners were fortunate in finding their way back to the main vessel, the Royal Sovereign, just in time to rejoin the rest of the crew. On 25 November 1825, when Nunn, James Lawrence, the ship's mate John Richardson, and James Stillman were out hunting seals in one of the shallops, they struck rocks and the boat started leaking. Nunn describes this calamity in graphic detail:

> Few situations could be more distressing than ours, as we had no one at hand to assist us: furnished only with a scanty stock of provisions, if we had an opportunity of preserving it, which we much doubted, as the leakage was increasing and little probability remained that our shallop would continue long above water… The rocks were rugged and precipitous in the extreme, and amongst these we could scarcely expect to find a spot in which we should obtain protection from the inclemency of the weather. Upon looking around us we found we could escape and reach the

Chapter 8: Rogues, Rapscallions and Survivors Haunt the Antipodes

shore in safety, and all succeeded in doing so by the assistance of the oars and boathooks with which we swung ourselves from the shallop's deck. By a little manoeuvring and exertion, we obtained about a fortnight's provision, and several articles which we conceived would be of use in defending us from the inclemencies of the weather, such as the jib of the shallop and a spar or two, and, in fact, anything we could lay our hands upon to pitch ashore. We were obliged to do all this in the most hurried manner, as we observed our vessel was sinking fast: we secured our seal clubs and lances, knowing these would be required in obtaining provisions if we were not soon relieved from our present situation. We had scarcely time to remove what we wanted, for the vessel began rapidly to sink, and in a few minutes, she went down in about seven fathoms water.[17]

Nunn and his mariners managed to climb one of the nearby promontories loaded down with equipment they had salvaged. The sealers relocated to a cave where they set up camp until they were able to walk to where they found an old shallop in poor condition called the *Loon* located in Maryanne's Straits. One of Nunn's companions wrote a note in chalk with the words 'Look in the cabin'. Inside, he left another note to inform prospective rescuers of the location of the cave. All the men were rescued as one of their colleagues in the *Royal Sovereign* observing the sign. The exhausted men were eternally grateful.

The second incident was a much more traumatic affair. A month later, Nunn and three others were in another shallop, also called the *Favorite*. They were searching for water near Saddle Island when the boat sprung a leak through no apparent reason. As the vessel was sinking, Nunn and his crew were isolated from the shore on an outcrop, some distance away. Thinking laterally the mariners came up with a novel idea. They constructed a raft from various parts of their damaged and sinking vessel. Stillman and Nunn managed to paddle through masses of seaweed and kelp reaching the shore. Unfortunately, the hawling rope to which the raft was attached gave way. Before Nunn had even fully comprehended its importance to him and his crew, the raft quickly ran adrift and out to sea. John realised that unless he acted quickly, they were all doomed:

---

[17] Nunn, *Narrative of the Wreck of the Favourite*, 53.

> These thoughts induced me to hesitate no longer, and I removed such clothes as I found necessary and plunged into the water and got upon the raft, shoving it by the boathook to the shallop, and thus saved it and the rest of our party from the greatest inconvenience, and perhaps starvation. I had no sooner reached the vessel than I found my limbs completely set fast from the intensity of the cold: the mate upon this handed me a quantity of rum, and I drank about a quarter of a pint without feeling much warmth at my stomach; but probably it had the effect of preserving my life, which I feel convinced might have been destroyed from the effects of the cold immersion…….[18]

Fortunately for the mariners, they spied a 'young sea elephant', which they slaughtered, cooked and ate being the first food they had consumed for three days. After some time, they constructed a makeshift 'residence' by using the hull of the *Loon* and made it their home on Saddle Island for a considerable time. Despite their desperate circumstances and in a state of hopelessness, , they made use of provisions they were able to salvage from the wreck of the *Favorite*. They used a part of a 'bogy', normally used to boil blubber, to make a fire. Fortunately, there was a waterfall located close by, so they did not go thirsty. Fortune also favoured them when they discovered the remains of an old whaleboat which they converted into a watercraft of sorts. Using old timber they constructed some oars. When the weather permitted, the mariners sailed the vessel into Big Elephant Bay to what was known as 'Old Shoe Hole'. Luckily, they found an abandoned skiff. Desperate to rejoin the *Royal Sovereign*, they were dismayed to find that there was no sign of it or its crew. They were effectively marooned in the Kerguelens but found the means and resources to feed and protect themselves until rescued.[19] Nunn's story, told many years after the event, is telling. It illustrates not only the strong will of the mariners to survive in almost impossible conditions but also their ingenuity to adapt what resources were available to them in appalling circumstances.

Notwithstanding the risks and trauma faced by their employees, many of the colonial traders were able to make substantial profits from the trade. It has been estimated in the second decade of the

---
[18] Nunn, 66-68.
[19] Ibid., 69-72.

19th century that between 200,000 and 400,000 fur seals inhabited Macquarie Island. By 1812, 120,000 of them had been slaughtered for their skins. In addition, over thousands of tons of oil from the other mammals had been distilled from Macquarie and returned to Port Jackson. Despite a note in *The Sydney Gazette* in 1815 that, as a result of over-exploitation of the island, sealing could no longer be a profitable enterprise for mariners, the industry continued to exploit fur and elephant seals until 1919. An 1821 *Sydney Gazette* article is typical in its glowing reporting of the successes enjoyed by traders seeking seal oil:

> Arrived on Thursday from Macquarie Island the ship Regalia [Captain Dixon] with a full cargo of 260 tons of sea elephant oil. The Robert Quayle, barque, which sailed from here on September 8, had left for England on November 13, with upwards of 150 tons of oil. This getting of over 400 tons had been accomplished by a gang from Hobart Town.[20]

That island continued to generate significant returns for the traders. By June 1828, the prices for elephant seal oil skyrocketed. It was reported, for example, that it was trading at £30 per ton while the New South Wales elephant oil, which was regarded as inferior, was being sold at £22-28 per ton. Meanwhile seal skins were bringing in only 15-37 shillings each.[21]

While the exploitation of the seals in the sub-Antarctic Islands and elsewhere proved to be a financial bonanza for the traders and their masters, as foreshadowed previously, it came at a significant environmental cost. Concerns were being raised in the press by April 1815 about the wholesale slaughter of the pinnipeds and the damage sustained on Macquarie Island by activities of the mariners and their hunting dogs. Indeed, there were very few restrictions on the men employed in the sealing trade around Macquarie Island. The only laws the men had to be concerned about were the articles of agreement that they were bound by, and perhaps the merchant shipping legislation, but nothing restricted them in their pursuits of the mammals. Further, as is often the case in these environments,

[20] *The Sydney Gazette,* 17 March, 1821. The Russian vessels on Bellingshausen's expedition were there for both scientific and discovery purposes.
[21] See *The Australian,* 4 June, 1828.

their canines went missing in action, and became feral, devouring birdlife and seals at will.[22]

However, the good times enjoyed by maritime men from Port Jackson in the Southern Fishery were almost over. What stopped further decimation was over-exploitation of the pinnipeds. When a malnourished crew rescued from the island by Captain Willett reached Sydney in 1830, they informed their employer that the pinnipeds had abandoned the island due to their 'continued persecution'. Captain Benjamin Morrell circumnavigated all of the Auckland Islands in the *Antarctic* in 1829 and was unable to find a single fur seal. In early 1831, Samuel Harvey, master of the *Venus*, reported that: "Macquarie Island is entirely cut up. I landed at both ends of the island but could see no signs of an elephant whatsoever".[23]

As time went on, the economic outlook for the sealing trade became grim. By November 1834, Captain Robertson of the *Bee* made two voyages to Macquarie and the Chatham Islands. He collected 17 members of sealing gangs and found to his dismay that they had not been able to dispose of any seals. The only positive outcome for him was that he managed to capture eight or ten escaped convicts for which he was no doubt rewarded when he returned to Port Jackson. After this, not many sealers visited the south-eastern part of the Fishery. The islands were no longer a viable proposition for the Sydney traders to exploit.

For many of the mariners, diversity and flexibility became the key to continue making a living from the sea. Many of the sealing captains who plied their trade around New Zealand and its southern islands were also experienced in other industries. They sailed extensively between Australia, New Zealand, the surrounding islands and the commercial trading centres in India and China. One who operated across many industries while crisscrossing the wide Antipodean expanse was the whaler Richard Siddons.[24] Originally coming to the colony on the *Alexander*, he gained

---

[22] See *The Sydney Gazette,* 15 April 1815.
[23] Robert McNab. *Old Whaling Days*, 88.
[24] Siddons lived from about 1770-1846.

extensive experience in a fairly short period of time. He became the master of several vessels, and later a boat owner. Siddons criss-crossed the wide expanse of the Fishery, sailing in the *Mercury* to Fiji to collect sandalwood in 1809. The next year, he journeyed to the islands of Bass Strait and Kangaroo Island in the *Endeavour* on a sealing venture.[25]

In the following year, he was master of the *Campbell Macquarie*, which was under contract with the Underwood trading company and went sealing around Macquarie Island, until that vessel foundered in the icy waters of the Tasman Sea on 10 June 1812. But Siddons was undeterred. He was fortunate to gain a berth on the *Perseverance* back to Sydney. Employed as a crew member on the *Elizabeth and Mary*, he returned to Macquarie to collect any remaining shipwrecked sealers. There, he sought to salvage any remnant plant and equipment for which he was no doubt compensated. After one more year, he realized how depleted the seal rookeries were and sought to diversify by seeking his fortune in the whaling and the sandalwood trade. Voyaging between Calcutta and Madras in India and Port Jackson from 1813 and about 1820, he made those commodities his focus. By then, he was a part owner of the brig *Lynx*.[26] It is almost exhausting to read his exploits, but he was not alone.

An analysis of vessels like those manned by Siddons and other masters demonstrates that the skins of the pinnipeds, rather than oil, were the most substantial item sought out by the mariners, making up some 61% of all voyages. It is clear from the records that the coastlines of New Zealand and Macquarie Island were by far the most popular destinations for a sealer. They accounted for at least 261 of the 353 voyages that were undertaken by vessels involved in the search for seals in the eastern Fishery over the period.[27] Most interest from the sealing industry in exploiting the region ceased

---

[25] See *The Sydney Gazette*, 6 January, 1809.
[26] See, for example, the mention made of some of these ventures in *The Sydney Gazette* 19 June, 1819 and 17 June, 1820. See also Cumpston, *Shipping Arrivals and Departures Sydney 1788-1825*, 133.
[27] See, for example, Ian W. G. Smith, *The New Zealand Sealing Industry History Archaeology and Heritage*, 9.

by 1835. After this, there was a significant and long-lasting decline which, to a large extent, mirrors the historical pattern elsewhere in the southern Antipodes. But the wide-ranging exploitation of the seal populations across the expanse of the Fishery had disastrous consequences for not only the mammals, but also for the flora and several of the First Nations peoples.

Chapter 9: Preying on the Environment

On 8 December 1802, a colonial surgeon, Thomson, voyaged to what was then known as King's Island to the immediate north of the west coast of Van Diemen's Land. He encountered an officer and seven men sealing there. Like many sealers, they had been left to their own devices. Their master, in command of the *Margaret*, had left the Straits for Otaheite some six months previously on other business. Thomson had been informed by the mariners that they had slaughtered 50 elephants in less than a month, which yielded 6,000 gallons of oil. However, so far as flensing skins off the fur seals was concerned, they had only 'got about 600'. A gang of 231 maritime men, employed by the Sydney trader Palmer, were also on the island but the surgeon had no clue as to their catch. Concerned about the avaricious nature of the sealing industry, even at this early stage, Thomson wrote to the Governor:

> The seals, from continuing harassing, seem to have forsook the island and I am much afraid, from similar continued interruptions the elephant will be forced to seek some other haunts and from their being none of these animals found in any of the other islands in the Straits… if they are forced to abandon entirely, would be a great loss and detriment to the colony.[1]

The surgeon was an intelligent man, who could see that the industry was doomed to fail unless it could be properly controlled. He was most concerned about the economic consequences to the colony if the pinnipeds were annihilated.

Thomson's concerns would not have been alleviated by the sedentary nature of the mammals on land, for seals resting on rocks are easy targets for hunters. Their docility was noted by Cook, while in charge of the *Resolution* in his travels in the Antipodes, writing that the seals 'were all so tame or rather so stupid as to

---

[1] Extract of a Letter from Mr Thompson from King's Island, *Historical Records of New South Wales* 18 January, 1803, 8.

suffer us to come so near as to knock them down with a stick.'[2] Most of the mariners were able to despatch seals as they wished and without any repercussions. How significant this adverse impact of the colonial industry was on the seals is hard to ascertain. Not only that, but the negative effect of the colonial sealing industry on the environment has never been fully explored and the long-term consequences of it were not at all understood at the time, nor perhaps, even now. To date, there has been little written about this important subject. Many of the experts who focus on the adverse effects of the sealing industry on the pinnipeds have had to rely on secondary sources and shipping statistics. One expert estimated that over seven million southern fur seals were butchered and their skins transported from around the globe to the Canton and London markets by British and American traders, masters and sealers from 1788 to 1831 alone.[3] Another scientist calculated that more than 1,309,000 skins were flensed by mariners in the Antipodes up to 1830.[4] But this would be an underestimate as it does not take into account skins delivered directly to the markets by ships instead of voyaging via the colonial ports. Officially, just between November 1800 and August 1806, over 100,000 seal skins were transported back to colonial ports. However, the actual statistics during those years was probably far greater.

By May 1803, the Governor was writing to the Colonial Secretary expressing his doubts about the plunder in the Straits. After informing Nepean that over 16,000 gallons of oil and 27,000 seal skins had been off loaded from the islands in Sydney, he was adamant that he would need to do something immediately to 'restrain individuals from resorting there in too great numbers.'

To give readers some idea of the avaricious and rapacious nature of the mariners employed by the Sydney traders, in one

---
[2] See Alan Moorhead, *The Fatal Impact*, 238.
[3] See, for example, Rhys Richards, *Sealing in the Southern Oceans 1788–1833*, 15.
[4] See John Ling, "Exploitation of fur seals and sea lions from Australian, New Zealand and adjacent subantarctic islands during the Eighteenth, Nineteenth and Twentieth Centuries" in *Australian Zoologist* Vol. 31, No.2 (1999), 323-350.

week in March 1809, three vessels anchored near the docks in Port Jackson laden with up to 45,000 seal skins worth about 30 shillings each. The masters involved, Chace, Bunker and Cox in charge of the *King George*, *Pegasus* and *Fox*, respectively, had been fishing in the recently "discovered" Foveaux Straits and depleted the sealing stocks substantially.[5]

The prominent botanist Joseph Banks had been in the vanguard in promotion of the colonial sealing trade. He lent valuable support to the Sydney traders exploiting the seals in Bass Strait. As one of the most influential men in London , he gave those keen to take up the trade the impression that it was "open season" on the pinnipeds. In his elephantine titled manuscript "*Some Remarks on the Present State of the Colony of Sidney in New South Wales, and on the means most likely to render it a Productive, instead of an Expensive, Settlement,*" he gave all merchants a marketers dream enticement to go out and plunder:

> The importance of the seal fishery is yet little understood. All seals produce oil and skins of some value... This, by the invention of a Mr. Chapman, can be separated from the hair that covers it and is converted into a most valuable raw material for hat manufacturing and possibly a more advantageous article to the revenue when employed in that trade than any other of equal value... The island of Van Diemen's Land, the south-west coast of New Holland and the southern part of New Zealand produce seals of all kinds in quantities at present almost innumerable. Their stations on rocks or crags have remained unmolested since the Creation. The beach is encumbered with their quantities, and those who visit their haunts have less trouble in killing them than the servants of the victualling office have to kill hogs in a pen with mallets.

Inspired by men such as Banks, the Sydney Traders exploited the seal rookeries mercilessly. The activities of the mariners meant that the pinniped rookeries in the Antipodes became scarce over the course of about 12 years.[6] Following Flinders' and Bishop's discoveries, a fleet of ships, many new to the fledgling industry,

---
[5] See James Connal Howard Gill, *Notes on the Sealing Industry of Early Australia*. Read to a meeting of the Society, 23 February, 1967, 242.
[6] McNeill, 82.

joined the hunt for seals.[7] Traders and their ship captains were encouraged by officials, particularly Governor King, and by the profits to be made in the Chinese, Indian and UK markets.

Early on, the price for elephant seal oil was approximately £20 per ton. By 1820, seal skins were selling in London as high as 30 shillings per skin. The various reports and records of the time attest to the fact that King, of all the governors, was most passionate in encouraging the wholesale slaughter of the seals. The Governor assisted entrepreneurs to make it a viable industry by permitting them to overcome the severe restrictions imposed by the East India Company. Furthermore, he occasionally gave them tax free incentives. He even contracted with traders directly to purchase skins for use in the colony.[8] One expert estimated that, apart from generating many employment opportunities for mariners who were unemployed after the various wars which raged during the latter part of the 18th century and into the first decade of the 19th, it also achieved for the traders a significant income worth about $100,000,000 in today's currency! As the industry was keenly supported by Governors such as Hunter and King, and to a lesser extent Bligh, who to some extent underwrote the costs, it was destined to be a "goldmine" for the more enterprising mariners. But the depletion of and damage to seals almost led to their extinction in parts. Their recovery took over a century.

This wholesale slaughter of the seals arose alongside a near global reduction to duties paid on tea in England. Cheaper tea placed it within the economic reach of many ordinary people. This opened up significant markets for traders in England, America, India and elsewhere with the oriental powerhouse and tea producer that was China at the time.[9] A huge economic exchange system developed whereby merchants from New South Wales and elsewhere sold seal products either directly to China or via the mother country in exchange for tea and also silk. Even prior to the discovery of the

---

[7] 'The moment the seal fishery opened itself to view after the discovery of the Basses Straits, a large number of persons enter'd into it with spirit and activity. *Trade and Commerce Historical Records of New South Wales* Vol. 6, 4 June 1803, 87.
[8] New South Wales Trade. *HRNSW,* Vol. 6, 27 June 1806, 101.
[9] McNeill, 89.

seal populations in Bass Strait by explorers and traders, markets had already developed between American traders and the Chinese as a direct result of the culling of seals on the Juan Fernandez Islands near Chile. Although the Antipodean seal populations suffered significantly during this period, it was insignificant compared to practices of the rapacious Americans. The Yankee mariners flensed and sold over three million seal skins in just over seven years, exhausting the population by 1824.[10]

As surgeon Thomson noted when he wrote to Under Secretary Cooke on 28 June 1804, the seals were 'valuable on account of their fur, skin and oil' and several thousand skins had been taken to the Chinese markets over the past four or five years. By then, unfortunately, for the colonial trader, prices had started to plummet, driven by an oversupply of commodities exchanged by the Yankees and Russians. Selling a skin for four shillings each at the time was not going to bring any great recompense to the colonial mariners.

England was a better alternative. Here, by the middle of the first decade of the 19th century skins were bought for up to 14 shillings each. They were by then used in the manufacture of hats. Oil from the elephant seals was selling at up to 42 pounds per ton and used for lighting and in machinery applications. James Underwood was one of the first of the colonial traders to realise the value in the London markets. Despite the Company's monopoly on trade, he arranged for two cargoes on the *Rolla* and *Dart*, respectively, to anchor in English ports in the latter part of 1803.

Later, when Governor King directed David Collins to look at founding an 'Establishment' at King Island in the Straits to foster industry in that region, traders already sealing there lobbied hard against it. They argued such a settlement would drive away the 'seals and elephants'. Collins complained to King in a letter dated 29 February 1804. He asserted that it was the 'rapacity' of these very traders and their crews procuring the pinnipeds that 'will tend more effectually to extirpate these animals than could the Establishment of any System which might introduce regularity among them'. The pinnipeds were exploited with so much zeal and ferocity that, even

---

[10] The American sealing traders were active in these islands from 1782.

before environmental conservation became a popular concern, there were serious reservations expressed in official channels and elsewhere. This led to some steps being taken to endeavour to protect the pinnipeds, if only for commercial reasons.

Even four years after Bishop's voyage, colonial people were worried about the impact of the 'new' industry. For example, in *The Sydney Gazette*, a person describing themselves ominously as 'A well-wisher to Posterity' stated:

> The impolicy of killing the breeding seals will in time discover itself; the parties already complain of the scarcity occasioned by themselves, and unless new islands are discovered, a new employ must be.[11]

By late 1807, it had become crystal clear, from the paucity of the catch being offloaded in Port Jackson, that the industry was no longer viable and was in danger of being discontinued:

> A few of the ships that have arrived have had a home freight of whale oil and seal skins; but the latter trade is greatly on the decline, as the seals are nearly all destroyed on the southern islands on this coast, or, from the constant molestation they have suffered have abandoned the islands.[12]

The scarcity of prey available to the mainstream traders was corroborated by another Surgeon Luttrell who wrote to the Under Secretary on 8 October 1807 about the dangers of a failing industry. He bemoaned the fact that the seal fishery was greatly on the decline and called for new and more distant islands to be discovered. As we know, he did not have to wait long.

Before Hasselborough encountered Macquarie Island, sealers were being dropped off by ships in islands closer to the south coast of New Zealand. One of those was Thomas Brady. He and several others were left to their fate in bitterly cold conditions on the Isle of Wright by the master of the Campbell-owned vessel *Brothers*, for 13 months in June 1809. When Brady and the others were rescued and found their way back to Port Jackson, he filed a claim against the Campbell house. One of his witnesses, Samuel Pugh,

---

[11] *The Sydney Gazette*, 29 May 1803.
[12] A Surgeon's Letter, 5 October 1807, *HRNSW*, Vol. 6, 293.

gave evidence for Brady. He swore on oath:

> I and Brady and the rest stayed on the island for 20 weeks after the schooner left us. We fell very short of provisions and obliged to be upon short allowance. When we left the island, we could get nothing at all to eat, and before that were obliged to feed upon seal or what else we could get... We were there 13 months without provisions and obliged to live on whatever we could catch.[13]

The inference was that seals were in very short supply, having been almost wiped out. Judge Ellis Bent awarded Brady £25 in damages. Following in his footsteps were proceedings by other mariners who also appear to have been badly treated by masters and traders alike. These cases were all dealt with by the Courts, after the early killing seasons there when the cargoes of skins and oil coming from Macquarie and Campbell Islands were in decline and profits marginal.[14]

Although some in positions of power were concerned about the meagre prospects for the sealing industry, few, if any, would have done so with the environment in mind. They were worried about the loss of income and opportunities available to the influential traders in the colony. The rapacity by which mariners slaughtered seals in the Straits meant that by the end of the first decade of the 19th century, there were no further significant opportunities available to the traders in the islands to the north of Van Diemen's Land. At that point, the traders made no further attempts to commercialise the seal industry there and left a vacuum which was filled by the small-scale sealing mariners. As the independent sealers were more worried about surviving and operating small enterprises, these men were not concerned about the plight of the seals. This meant that the rookeries became further depleted. When James Kelly gave evidence on oath before Commissioner Bigge in 1820 in Hobart, he

---

[13] *Brady v Campbell* [1811] *NSWSupC*, 5.
[14] *Bryant v Hook* [1812] *NSWSupC* 2; [1812] *NSWKR 2* (31 January, 1812) where the sealer was totally unsuccessful; *Wood v Campbell* [1812] *NSWSupC* 1; [1812] *NSWKR* 1 (20 January, 1812) where Mr Wood was successful but received in damages a small sum of just over £16; *O'Burne v Campbell* [1812] *NSWSupC* 3; [1812] *NSWKR* 3 (4 February, 1812) when, in an extraordinarily interesting case, the Plaintiff was awarded only just over £14.

volunteered that the seal numbers had been exhausted. On being questioned as to why, he answered:

> From the frequent fishing, and from men remaining upon the islands and going to catch seals in open boats.[15]

Kelly, by now a "respectable" merchant, boat owner and whaler, who had crisscrossed the wide expanse of the southern oceans and was highly experienced, volunteered further intelligence to Bigge about the New Zealand 'Fishery'. The Commissioner grilled James asking him whether the seals were still found there in great numbers. Kelly replied: 'Not as much as formerly. The fishery has been too much occupied'.[16]

Despite the fact that mainstream traders had masterminded the decimation of the seals in the Straits and elsewhere in the Antipodes, it was only the islanders who were under constant attack by newspaper editors for their role in the demise of the seal populations. In 1826, the editor of the *Hobart Gazette*, in an attempt to enlist support from the Governor to sanction the activities of the islander sealers, pointed the finger in their direction:

> It is evident that the Legislative Government must enact a law to prevent the fishery for seals at improper seasons; else this most valuable source of colonial export will soon be lost. There are two species of seals in these seas. The early kind brings forth its young from 25th November to the latter end of December, and the reefs and banks should be left undisturbed until May following, when the increase will be grown up, and the skins well furred. The black seal, which is the most valuable, is a month later. The unthinking sealers, harass these useful animals at all seasons, and the consequence is, that many reefs are deserted, and inferior skins have been procured from animals too young, and imposed on the merchants.[17]

The seals were 'useful' as they were only a staple for trade or exchange in the colony. The merchants were 'imposed on' as they had spread their activities by then far and wide and wanted the better-quality skin available to the islanders to seek better incomes.

---

[15] *Historical Records of Australia*, Series 3, Vol. 3, 461.
[16] McNab, Appendix F, 350.
[17] *Hobart Town Gazette*, 25 March, 1826.

But, unfortunately, the mainstream trading houses did not learn from their own avaricious conduct and behaviour leading to the wholesale depletion of the sealing rookeries in the Straits. The resurgence of interest in sealing that followed the "discovery" of Campbell and Macquarie Islands in 1810 and the huge numbers of fur and elephant seals basking on the shores of these sub-Antarctic places attracted the continual passage of ships voyaging from Hobart and Port Jackson via New Zealand seeking out the mammals. Crews and gangs employed by traders such as Kable and Underwood, Lord and Campbell once again set out to fill the boats with skins and oil. But at what cost?

The pattern of aggressive plundering evident in the Straits was repeated here resulting in a similar decline in seal populations. In September 1821, a Captain Raine was asked if he could prepare a report on Macquarie Island. While there, Raine observed that although the island 'abounded with seals' at one time, it was 'now… a very rare thing to see one; only four were killed last year. The *Phocas leonina*, elephant seal or sea cow, however, is still plentiful and alone makes the island valuable in a commercial view.'[18] He wrote that sealers on the island were living off penguin hearts, livers and eggs, the tongues of female elephant seals and birds of various sorts. Not fur seals. Although some traders continued to send sealing crews to Macquarie Island after 1821, by 1830 the elephant seal population had become scarce on the island's beaches. The fur variety had almost ceased to exist there. McNab wrote that between 1830 to 1840 there were only three vessels that went to that outcrop which had as their sole mission the flensing of skins. Another three sought both skins and oil. None focused on solely pouring oil into barrels. Any other ships that anchored there were merely doing so as an adjunct to trading in other commodities such as pork and sandalwood.

Meanwhile, across in the Recherche Archipelago, early attempts by American traders to seek out seals from all around Western Australia's southern coast had not been very successful.[19] Little is

---

[18] See Cumpston, 52.
[19] Captain Isaac Pendleton in the *Union* undertook a sealing expedition there

heard about efforts by mainstream and independent traders and mariners to seal there until after 1826 when *D'Urville* anchored near present day Albany. From then until the mid-1830s, there were several sealing crews operating and successfully making a living along the west coast and islands nearby. However, so successful were they that it is estimated that by 1840 the seal populations in that region had been depleted by up to 90 per cent![20]

Back in Hobart, the depletion of the seal populations around Bass Strait and southwards from there was evident in 1839 when D'Urville, returned on the *L'Astrolabe*, accompanied by the *Zelee*. One of his officers expressed concern about 'businessmen' who were going to fit out a schooner to go exploring southwards towards Antarctica to procure seals. In his opinion, the seals were 'almost extinct in all other frequented places' with the venture described as very risky. He did not think the harvest would be 'very heavy'. This was because, during his exploration they 'did not see more than four or five of these animals.'[21] By 1850, the pinnipeds had all but been wiped out of the rookeries they had occupied for centuries south of Westernport as a direct consequence of participants in the sealing industry.

In the Far East, the Chatham Islands also experienced a substantial environmental disaster. Between 1807-1810, several maritime crews voyaged to the islands in vessels owned or controlled by New Zealand and Sydney traders. They set about procuring as many seals as would fill their boats without any regard either for the pinnipeds or for the local inhabitants and their culture. There was a brief 15-year reprieve from the exploitation as the sealing industry recessed, but sealing crews quickly returned during longer periods of growth. The island's environment was altered almost irreversibly. Seals that inhabited shores and rocks were almost exterminated. In addition, foreign animals such as cats and dogs ran riot by feasting on the local marine life, accelerating the decline of their population numbers. This was compounded by the arrival of the Māoris, who

---

during 1803 when they encountered Baudin's vessels in the Sound.
[20] See Ross Anderson, *Beneath the Colonial Gaze,* PhD thesis. University of Western Australia School of Social Sciences Archaeology, 2016, 99.
[21] Captain Jacquinot in Dumont D'Urville, Vol. II, 524.

Chapter 9: Praying on the Environment

conducted a full-scale bloody war against the Moriori in 1835.[22]

By the time Broughton arrived at the islands, the Moriori had already been hunting all kinds of seals undisturbed, for centuries. They had adopted their own codes of conduct to ensure the pinnipeds' sustainability over time. This meant they exploited only sufficient stocks for their immediate culinary needs. The local seafarers had made it a practice of removing the seal carcass well away from the seashore to "process" it. This also sent a message to its kin that they need not fear depredation at the hands of the local men. Employing this intelligent arrangement meant that the seals continued to inhabit the estuaries, rockeries and beaches around the coastlines of the two main islands. All that changed with the arrival of the colonial mariners.

However, it was not just the substantial depletion of the seals by men that was caused by the rapacious nature of the industry. There were other, less well-known, environmental impacts. Many of the more fragile ecological conditions that had been established over the millennia on many remote islands were adversely affected by the introduction of other species. One of the main predators were introduced canines. When the English first came to the colony, they imported hunting dogs used in Britain with success like the Irish wolfhound and greyhound. But these were found to be totally inadequate for the purpose. So, one coloniser came up with a bright idea. They would interbreed the canines. This led to the creation of the kangaroo dog. With its lightning speed, very strong jaw, muscular physique and weight up to 80 pounds, they were a match for any prey. It was an entirely successful hunter. Even the Reverend Robert Knopwood employed such dogs to hunt for him in Van Diemen's Land. Initially used to bring down kangaroos and wallabies, it was soon found to be a useful instrument in rounding

---

[22] One writer on the subject, Hirawana Tapu gave evidence to a Tribunal on 17 June 1870 that, after 1835, some Moriori were saved as slaves and after a long time in the settlement were killed by them [Maori] for meat, that is, for food They kept on killing like this until the gospel of Jesus Christ arrived, and then they stopped. Further the Maori killed up to 300 Moriori people being one sixth of the entire population of the island population by 1836. See *Deed of Settlement* dated 2003 between the Moiriori people and the Crown in 29 viewed on line at https://www.linz.govt.nz/resources/rfr-guide/moriori-claims-settlement-right-first-refusal

up seals and other wildlife such as mutton birds. After a while, most of the mainstream and independent mariners resorted to acquiring these animals as hunters and companions. So successful were these dogs as predators that First Nations people sought them from the mariners as a necessary part of an exchange process after first contact. Dogs became an integral part of Aboriginal and colonial maritime hunting armoury from early in the first decade of the 19th century. Over time, we find references to them accompanying mariners on sealing expeditions to the sub-Antarctic islands such as Macquarie as noted by Bellinghausen above. They became permanent companions to the independent sealers occupying the Bass Strait Islands, Westernport, the Recherche and Kangaroo Island. Colonial paintings of sealers, like the one from the French painter Louis de Sainson in 1826 often depict the mariners accompanied by dogs.

In the French painter's image of the sealers at Mangrove Creek near Westernport, four of these animals are depicted. Many became "wild", particularly where sealing gangs only resided temporarily or seasonally. On Macquarie, seals were not the only prey that the dogs salivated over. The canines also ravaged penguin and bird populations mercilessly. By 1815, reports appearing in the Sydney Gazette suggested that the seal population had declined significantly at the island, not only due to over-exploitation by the sealing gangs, but also the 'ravages committed on the younger seal by large numbers of wild dogs'. On Kangaroo Island, dogs became part of the islander 'family', but for the wildlife they were a nightmare. When naval surgeon Peter Cunningham came to converse with the old sealer George Robinson there, the aged mariner told him about the plentiful supplies of fish and kangaroos, but their stocks were 'decreasing' because of the dogs left behind by sealers who were 'breeding and overrunning the country.'[23]

While kangaroo dogs went on the rampage over much of the Antipodean Fishery, mariners unwittingly perhaps, and other introduced species such as rabbits and rats had an adverse impact on the flora of some islands. Take for example, the Ile de St Paul. It

---

[23] Cunningham, Vol. 1, 145.

was subject to a "golden age" of sealing between 1797 and 1809. During that time, the island became a sought-after destination for many crews voyaging from Europe and America to Australia or Batavia and back. Many sealers were Americans from Boston and Nantucket seeking a quick "kill" during the summer season. When the mariners first started to visit, they observed a mixture of trees and grasses, with the island enjoying an overall green verdure. But, by October 1811, a James Prior (no relation), who was a seasoned mariner, visited the island in the *HMS Nissus*. The sealer was shocked to find it was no longer green but

> A parched dirty brown appearance without trees or shrubs. Further that the seal populations were not so numerous as they were; vast numbers being killed annually to supply the European and Indian markets.

Fast-forward to 1816, and the only vegetation visible was 'coarse grass and reeds.'[24] Not a shrub was to be seen anywhere.

Although some traders such as Lord, Campbell and Underwood enjoyed some success as maritime entrepreneurs, it was mainly temporal. Despite being championed by Governors and influential officials as solving the problem of a regular 'staple' for the colony, it never really eventuated. Part of the reason for this was variable economic circumstances, including the oversupply of skins and oil into depressed markets. But, by far the main reason for its failure for the mainstream traders what one historian has described as the 'rapid extermination of fur seals'.[25] Targeting female and pup seals led to a decline in the populations. This resulted in the trade becoming an uneconomic industry for most with only a few boats operating from Port Jackson and Hobart by the 1820s. Anecdotally, the wholesale slaughter of pinnipeds fostered the mistaken belief that the seals, or at least some populations, had become almost extinct. Still, despite the decimation of Antipodean seal rookeries, they did not disappear. Perhaps, as Flinders asserted, the pinnipeds were far more intelligent than humans give them credit for. Sensing

---

[24] See John Purdy, *Oriental Navigator*, 83.
[25] Hainsworth. *Builders and Adventurers*, 98.

continual danger at the hands of zealous sealers, seal species sought refuge by migrating elsewhere. But it would take generations for the depleted rookeries to reach the numbers requited to avoid a catastrophe.

Many mainstream traders turned their attention to other industries such as whaling, pork, sandalwood and other commodities such as flax as the sealing grounds became depleted. Other mariners who were either left to fend for themselves or chose to occupy places abandoned by commercial operators chose an alternative lifestyle. Such a lifestyle had as its principal focus the pursuit of the remaining seal population, but their social and economic circumstances quickly changed, and they diversified. They had to. In October 1832 Robinson who, despite his misgivings about the independent Bass Strait sealers was spending a lot of time in their company wrote:

> The sealers live a miserable life. The seal skins they procure is not a quarter sufficient to support any one of them.

By then he had decided one of them in particular Thomas Turnbull was a decent man who had confided in George that he had been living with a crew of sealers, described as 'wretched' by Robinson, for 12 months and had only procured 24 skins! Notwithstanding their 'wretched' state these mariners became the subject of vitriol and negative stereotyping in the discourse that prevailed. In so doing, it became difficult to ascertain fact from fantasy.

Chapter 10: Fact and Fantasy in the Lives of the Independent Sealers

Prior to the first decline in the sealing industry from early in the second decade of the 19th century, some independent small-scale mariners had already explored and occupied remote parts of the Antipodean fishery. They were among the first Europeans to "discover" the pinniped rookeries, important geographic and strategic landmarks and were in the forefront of first encounters with First Nations peoples. Many either introduced or learned new methodologies to enable them to survive in harsh and difficult maritime littoral environments. After a time, their more positive roles in these activities were effectively forgotten. They became subject to severe criticism from many of the colonisers including but not limited to the press, government officials and others for what was regarded as their abhorrent conduct and behaviour. A very negative colonial stereotype developed, which portrayed these mariners as being lower on the rung of humanity than everyone. Everyone that is except the natives. Some of the negative stereotyping that occurred was to a large extent an accurate assessment. But the reality of the colonial independent sealer's existence was a complex and developing one. This complexity and progressive change can be illustrated by comparing the following differing colonial perspectives.

In the spring of 1819, George Sutherland was appointed Commander of the 132-ton brig *Governor Macquarie*. Its owner was an entrepreneurial woman by the name of Mary Reibey. George was tasked to lead an expedition to Kangaroo Island by her to examine any potential commercial "advantages" that could be gained there. When he anchored the vessel at Saltwater Creek near Cape de Couedic, he encountered 12 sealers. The mariners had been well settled in and around the island's bays.. With one eye on ensuring that his commercial employer received a glowing report on the possibilities of reaping the benefits from exploiting the marine and other resources there, he derided the local mariners:

> They have carried their daring acts to extreme, venturing on the mainland in their boats, and seizing on the natives, particularly the women, and keeping them in a state of slavery, cruelly beating them on every trifling occasion; ......[1]

Many other colonial writers, newspaper editors and historians were never to have a kind word to say about the independent and islander sealers.

But contrast these very pejorative 'observations' with D'Urville's who, in about 1826, encountered the two whaleboats manned by the abandoned sealers in King George's Sound. The French Commander had time on his hands and no axe to grind. In doing so, he observed the relationships between the mariners and local Noongar people and expressed no reservations:

> Aboriginal women found life with European men more pleasing than with men of their own race because European men treated them with much more respect.[2]

Fast forward to 1837 when the American explorer John Lort Stokes, was on his global voyage in the *Beagle* exploring the coasts of Australia. On this voyage he visited several of the sealing communities in the Bass Strait Islands. In doing so, he was more than pleased to record for posterity that:

> A sealer had established himself on the north island with two wives, natives of Tasmania. They were clothed in very comfortable greatcoats made of kangaroo skins and seemed quite contented with their condition. Their offspring appeared sharp and intelligent.

So we have both negative and positive perspectives about the independent sealers particularly when it comes to their relationships with First Nations peoples. Much of the negative stereotyping arises from the relationships that the mariners had with these

---

[1] Sutherland, 73.
[2] D'Urville, Vol.1, 197-198.

Chapter 10: Fact and Fantasy in the Lives of the Independent Sealers

peoples. But there were other pejorative stereotypes that were applied to them as well. This being the case, it may be difficult to dispel fact from fantasy when it comes to the colonial mariners who occupied the spaces and places vacated by the mainstream traders in the Fishery after 1813. Having said that, there were arguably several positive aspects to the lives lived by the sealers during the relevant colonial period. The fixed immutable binary that portrays independent sealers as all 'evil' and every other mainstream mariner as all 'good' is misconceived.

Firstly, it is worthy to note that many of the independent sealers were the first to explore and discover destinations where no European had ever been before in their quest for the pinnipeds. Historians have made little attempt to consider the roles that many of the mariners played in such endeavours. The lack of any real attempt to write the history of the mariners as explorers is partly due to the secrecy practiced by sealers looking to preserve their discoveries from other competitors. Furthermore, they were aware that colonial authorities and others may have wanted to curtail their activities to support the traders.

The mariners were often the first Europeans to voyage into certain remote southern Antipodean locations, often well before anyone else. Many were part of gangs aboard ships owned by the colonial traders when they were a party to finding their way to environments where no human in some cases, and no European in others, had ever been before. These included the sealing grounds in and around Antarctica, the interior of Kangaroo Island, some islands in Bass Strait, Macquarie and Campbell islands, the Chathams, St Paul and Amsterdam islands, and some parts of New Zealand.

One example of this occurred in 1793, when Captain Rogers of Boston anchored in Sydney from the island of St Paul. On arrival, the captain reported they "fell in with" a crew of five sealers, including a Frenchman called Perron. The marooned men had been on the island for some 18 months, having been left there by the captain of the vessel *Emilia*. They were among the first humans to explore the island and had established the initial huts and a vegetable garden there. Later, in 1798, when Flinders, Bass and Bishop were "discovering" the channel between the mainland and Van Diemen's Land, they were also maintaining to all who would listen that they and Bishop had "found" the abundant seal rookeries. The fact of the matter was that sealing crews were already occupying some of the Bass Strait Islands and hunting seals. These men had already developed a knowledge of the islands and rookeries but were keen to keep it a secret.

North from Bass Strait, the only Europeans who explored the channels of (what became known as) Westernport and Port Phillip Bay on the south-east coast of Victoria and set up camps were crews of sealers. They established some huts 'about 12 miles up' shortly after Bass had temporarily visited that location. Following reports from masters such as Lieutenant Grant, probably conveyed by isolated sealers to him, that seals abounded there, Governor King wrote to the Duke of Portland expressing his excitement about the prospects of establishing a fishery there:

> The important situation of that port and its relative connexion with this settlement (Sydney) points it out as a proper and necessary place to have a settlement at, not only from its convenient situation in the centre of the straits for ships to stop at, either by reason of adverse winds or any other cause, but also from its advantageous situation for a seal fishery, which will be more particularly explained on the chart sent by the 'Albion' which has been ably surveyed by Ensign Barrallier of the New South Wales Corps.[3]

Meanwhile, back in London, the Governor's predecessor Hunter, who maintained an interest in the fortunes of the colony, was lobbying hard to also have the fishery established there. On 22 March 1802, in a report to the Under Secretary, Hunter advised that 'small vessels' would be more suitable for establishing a fishery than the larger vessels such as barques and East Indiamen. The sealers living in that region were well aware of its great potential for a settlement from which to seek out the pinnipeds. Following information received about the sealers' fishing experiences, King wrote to Banks expressing his optimism about that part of the Victorian coast:

---

[3] The letter was written on 8 July 1801. See *Historical Records of New South Wales,* Vol. 4, 439 and 729.

> The great number of Seal Elephants, prime and other seals, that are throughout these Straits and all up the southwest coast, will make this (Port Phillip) a place of great resort, if the oyl of the elephant or skins are held in request....[4]

Later in 1815, the colonial authorities, having established settlements in Hobart and Port Dalrymple, were considering charting the entire Van Diemen's Land coastline. James Kelly had set out with his sealing crew in December 1815 to circumnavigate the island. Apparently he had been given the task by Lieutenant Colonel Thomas Davey, the presiding Governor at the time. George Briggs, who already had established family ties with First Nations peoples in the Straits and knew the geography of the main island reasonably well, was an essential and valuable part of Kelly's gang. Although no actual account of Kelly's voyage appears to have made its way to the authorities when he returned after 49 days, he was rewarded for his endeavours by receiving a land grant together with, what the colonial historian James Calder describes as, 'certain exclusive privileges'.[5] These rewards were an outcome of Kelly and his independent crew encountering as colonisers for the first time not one but two major geographically important sites. Briggs would have been instrumental in these discoveries by reason of his prior knowledge. The crew had anchored in a bay, in the almost inaccessible southwestern region of the island, which Kelly named Port Davey after the Governor. He then voyaged further north, and he and his crew were the first colonists to find access to a very large harbour which he named 'Macquarie'. Sailing down through what became known as 'Hell's Gates', he found an island in the heart of the harbour he called 'Sarah', apparently after the wife of T.W. Birch, who funded Kelly's voyage.[6]

The latter discovery would prove very useful to the successive governors of the colony when considering future economic and trade opportunities, in particular for boat building and extracting Huon pine trees. It later became the site of the notorious prison

---
[4] *HRNSW,* Vol. 4, 785.
[5] Calder (ed.). *Van Diemen's Land in 1815* by James Kelly and in 1824 by James Hobbs, 7.
[6] Ibid., 7.

for the more recidivistic convicts. Several years were to pass before Kelly provided a written account of his historic voyage in the form of a journal to the editor of the *Hobart Town Courier* in 1854.

Briggs acting as a navigator and explorer with Kelly was not unique. There were many sealers in the colonial period in the Fishery who acted in those capacities. They also provided valuable information to key stakeholders, including governments and settlers. When D'Urville voyaged from King Georges Sound towards Port Jackson in 1826, he transported abandoned but by then independent sealers with him as he realised some had talents other than procuring seals. Two of them, namely Hambilton and Simons, were employed by the French to pilot the *L'Astrolabe* into various safe anchorages on the way to Sydney. On the way, the two men helped the French to navigate into Westernport and Jervis Bay. Their skills were highly sought after, particularly in negotiating treacherous marine environments along the way.

The abilities they displayed as navigators surprised the French but amazed Lieutenant General Ralph Darling when they arrived safe and sound in the principal settlement. His reaction underlined the fact that sealers were not perceived as being able to fulfil any other function on board colonial vessels than that of a compliant mariner. Hambilton and Simon were just two of many sealers and masters who also became navigators with extensive knowledge of the southern coasts of Australia, New Zealand and elsewhere.

When Major Edmund Lockyer arrived some years later where D'Urville had been, he also encountered independent sealers who had chosen to remain in that region. While staying in the Sound, and, despite his generally poor opinion of the characters that he came into contact with, Lockyer was able to gain substantial maritime information from the mariners still there, about the Sound's weather, climate and interior. He also sought out information regarding the economic potential to the west of Albany and up towards Rottnest Island. From this intelligence he could convey to his masters' back at Port Jackson, information he clearly had been supplied with by the sealers, he wrote in his journal:

> From these men's account, the coast from Middle Island down round Cape Lewen [Leeuwin] to Rottnest Island off Swan River, there are boat harbours all the way at convenient distances from fifty to seventy miles and some less and many of them a vessel of good size would find shelter in, good anchorage, mostly islands along shore with deep water between them and the main. They described the weather on the coast as fine in general, with variable winds seldom blowing the same way longer than four of five days at any time of the year.[7]

The sealers also had the benefit of knowledge passed on to them by the Nyungar people, the local Australian nation about the climate and geography mentioned.

From the journals and reports of Lockyer and D'Urville, a reader would be forgiven for thinking that the only sealers inhabiting Western Australia were the two surviving crews of the *Brisbane* and the *Hunter* ships. However, other mariners had already explored (or were continuing to explore) the southern coastline, and some had provided their own important "discoveries" to other authorities. In 1830, Captain Collet Barker, the commander of the King Georges Sound garrison, received local information regarding whaleboats hunting for the pinnipeds at 'Palerongup' near Doubtful Island Bay, roughly two hundred kilometres to the east of the Sound. Following the information supplied, the sealer and whaler Captain John Hart from Van Diemen's Land undertook a voyage, anchoring in all of the possible bays between Bass Strait and Palerongup, and discovering what came to be known as Margaret Brock Reef off Cape Jaffa in South Australia.[8] This information proved important as it assisted in preventing further shipwrecks off that reef.

During the same year that Captain Hart was hunting for seals and exploring the southern coastline, the Colonial Surveyor's office was sending an expedition to find a route between Perth and Albany. While struggling to reach the coast, they crossed the Nornalup Inlet. One of the surveyors was a Mr Smythe, who obtained information subsequently that this particular inlet had a bay or port which was

---

[7] *Journal of Major Lockyer,* 38,
[8] 'Captain John Hart' in Thomas Francis Bride, *Letters from Victorian Pioneers being a series of papers on the early occupation of the colony, the Aborigines etc* (Melbourne: Heinemann, 1969), 55.

visited by sealers and was suitable for anchoring. A sealer by the name of Lane, who lived with a First Nation woman on Saddle Island, provided Smythe with significant amounts of information for the benefit of the colonisers.[9] When considering the possibility of opening up an overland stock route between Western and South Australia, the editor of the *Perth Gazette and Western Australian Journal* referred to the independent sealers as one of three sources of information about a section of the coast between Point Bell and Middle Island which was of great benefit to officials.[10]

Although there were very few sealers who could read or write about the first-hand explorations of newly charted waters and landforms, they left their mark in other ways. Many of the southwestern Australian physical geographic and topographical forms and features where the sealers operated were named by them. Later, this nomenclature was adopted by surveyors and government bodies.

The following are samples: Figure of Eight Island reflected its shape; Dome Island rises up straight from the water; Hospital Island is where sealers believed the pinnipeds recuperated; Monkey Jacket Island was named after a sealer known as 'Butty' who had left his monkey jacket there; Butty Head and Butty Harbour after the same man; and Sealers Creek near Cape Arid because sealers were known to camp there. There would be many more such places aptly designated. These mariners would have known all habitats frequented by seals, and the benefits to be gained or adversities to be avoided in the Esperance region.

Across the Tasman and from the time of the *Brittania's* arrival in 1793, independent sealing crews had found and explored just about every cove and bay along the coast of the southern island of New Zealand. Despite this, part of the coast was regarded as "unknown" even by 1844, something that Monro, one of the original settlers, was keen to correct when writing to the editor of *The Sydney Gazette*:

> Yet there are certain individuals and those not a few in number,

---

[9] *The Inquirer,* 25 August, 1841 and 15 September, 1841.
[10] *The Perth Gazette and Western Australian Journal,* 17 October, 1840, 3.

Chapter 10: Fact and Fantasy in the Lives of the Independent Sealers

> to whom nearly every harbor, cape and river mouth are familiar and the wilder and more remote parts of the coast are better known... Wherever seals were abundant, the pursuit of them was of great profit and many large boats carrying crews of hardy and daring men (unfortunately often reckless, licentious and ferocious) who annually visited the most remote parts of the New Zealand coast... Accordingly among these men an intimate and practical knowledge of the most remote parts of the coast is [still] to be met with.[11]

One of those to whom Monro was referring would have been Thomas Chaseland. In the southern part of New Zealand, Chaseland found new land features on his voyages in the hunt for seals and whales. Once, he was in charge of a vessel that reached a promontory that had not been explored by mariners before. To his pleasant surprise, the rocks had been claimed by an abundant rookery of fur seals. Unfortunately, it was late in the day and Tommy made the decision to wait until morning to go "fishing". When the gang arrived at the bluff the next day, all of the seals had vanished. Disappointed, Chaseland sailed away. In the nearest settlement, word spread about his folly. It came to haunt him as the cape was named *Chaseland's Mistake*. The region known as Chaselands in the Otago district is also named in his honour.

Exploring and providing intelligence to mainstream colonial authorities and traders was only an adjunct to the principal occupation and existence of the independent mariners. When several employed sealers chose to abandon life as employees working for the Sydney traders, they headed south to occupy islands in the southern Antipodes. This was partly sparked by their knowledge that mainstream traders no longer involved in the business of sealing in that region to any large extent and had left a vacuum. That vacuum was occupied mainly by these small-scale independent mariners who seized opportunities to make a living from the sea. These men set up and established camps, huts and settlements in remote locations on these islands and in bays where seals continued to frolic, albeit in reduced numbers. In general, the sealers operated as collectives to maximise the possibility of both

---

[11] G. Munro, *Nelson Examiner*, 20 July, 1844.

hunting down the pinnipeds and surviving in difficult climatic and personal circumstances. The independent colonial mariners developed ongoing relationships which were friendly and sometimes hostile with First Nations peoples. Those mariners who established friendly relationships entered into trading arrangements for the mutual benefit of both parties.

In the regions where seals had once flourished, the mariners were able to establish alternative societies and economies which were not subject to the scrutiny of mainstream colonial society and authority. Between the years 1810 to 1820, these marginal collectives were able to operate in isolation from the rest of colonial society, except when it came to their transactional relationships with mainstream traders in the Fishery. Although suspicions may have developed about the behaviour of these marginal collectives, there is little in colonial discourse about the negative nature of the sealers at this time. The sealers had organised commodity exchange systems and relationships with mainstream traders and First Nations across the breadth of the Fishery, without attracting sanctions or scrutiny about what became their unorthodox lifestyles. This is evident from the fact that, with one exception, there were very few adverse comments about these mariners at this time.[12]

One of the first gang of sealers to establish independent operations were those led by Jos Murrell. Early in the first decade of the 19th century. Murrell had been living and sealing on the western part of Kangaroo Island with a small gang. While enjoying a taste of a life free of constraints, Jos returned there in about 1810 establishing a sealers camp. According to Kelly, Murrell was soon joined by others, many of whom partnered with Australian women and fathered children. There were several family collectives on that island who had developed close ties and established settlements around the island. By 1826, the independent population on the island had grown substantially. There were reports in the colonial newspapers that 'two hundred' people were living in close proximity on the island. According to one editor, they were so well established

---

[12] This was because the sealing industry was generally in decline and the sealers were not being subjected to any sort of scrutiny or focus.

and independent of the mainstream colonies that they were going to set up their own monarchic dynasty with regulations to follow. They had various areas of land under cultivation, growing vegetables to supplement their income from the sealing trade, a fact that did not escape the attention of Commissioner John Morphett, who described the mariners as 'intelligent quiet men'.

Meanwhile, sealer George Briggs had formed strong relationships with several Australian tribes. He was regularly trading in the Straits and on the mainland with First Nation peoples and commercial traders earlier than 1815. By the 1820s, independent sealers had followed Brigg's example and had entrenched themselves at Preservation Island, Kent Bay, Islands of the Kent Group, King and Hunter Islands, Woody Island, Gun Carriage Island and elsewhere in the Straits. They became known in colonial circles as either 'the Islanders' or 'the Straitsmen'. Meanwhile, up at Westernport in Victoria, sealers had occupied camps close to the ocean and thrived on sealing and the exchange system that developed with commercial traders from Hobart, Port Dalrymple and Sydney. Over at King Georges Sound, D'Urville in 1826, and Lockyer in 1829, were surprised to find gangs of sealers who had been there for several years. Lockyer and D'Urville were sympathetic to the fact that many men had been deposited there by masters who had broken promises to return and collect them, resulting in the sealers becoming 'almost starved', despite carrying on some sort of sealing life. The difficulties experienced by the mariners at this time and the multi-racial nature of the crews is best illustrated by D'Urville's comments reported in his journals:

> A strange gathering of these wretched mortals of such different origins and education capricious chance has nonetheless gathered together in order to subject them to such a miserable and precarious existence.[13]

But despite the harsh and demanding conditions under which such mariners lived and operated, they had not sought help from passing colonial vessels. Perhaps this was because they chose independence and a sense of freedom over the stark reality of an

---
[13] D'Urville. Vol.1, 34.

employed sealer's life. That existence meant being on board boats commanded by tyrannical masters or tricky employers. They were no longer prepared to be dumped on islands on falsehoods to collect them. Nor were they tied to the trading houses where merchants advanced commodities to the sealers knowing they would never quite repay their debts.

Another reason why these mariners chose independence was the mobility they enjoyed on their only asset: the whaleboat. The mariners regarded whaling boats as superior to ketches and cutters since they were far more manoeuvrable. Manning such a craft made it easier to chase seals in difficult, tight and hazardous spaces. One sealer, Robert Gamble, was particularly enamoured with the concept of operating a thriving mobile industry in the islands to the east of the Sound.[14] Another was James Everett, (better known in the Fishery as 'Red-Headed Jimmy'). He commanded a versatile crew that arguably made the best use of their whaling boat during the 1820s. Everett's crew usually included some First Nations people , including 'Black Boy Harry', and women. Several gangs, including Everett's and Gamble's, were undertaking mobile trading ventures across the Great Australian Bight from King Georges Sound around to Westernport in Victoria. The trade did not just include seal skins and oil but also kangaroo skins, vegetables, copper, tin and salt, especially from around Kangaroo Island.[15] This is not surprising given the report by Sutherland in 1819 to Reibey, that the natural resources found on the island included not only seals but kangaroos along with an abundance of fresh water, limestone, granite and most especially salt [all very much in demand at that time].

While many independent sealers established themselves across

---

[14] He was also known by the surname 'Gambell' or 'Gemble' and had developed a sealing enterprise of sorts at King Island before eventually settling in the Recherche Archipelago. He was also charged with the murder of two Tasmanian women but seems to have avoided any conviction and may have voted with his feet by moving his operations across the Great Australian Bight in about 1831. See Bill Mollison and Coral Everitt, *The Tasmanian Aborigines and their Descendants*, December, 1978.

[15] The schooner *Liberty,* owned by Cooper and Levy, returned from the sealing grounds with 1,500 fur seals, two tons of salt, and some copper and tin in 1827.

Chapter 10: Fact and Fantasy in the Lives of the Independent Sealers

the southern islands and harbours of Australia, there were others who went further afield to New Zealand and its southern and eastern islands. Early on, ship builders like John Grono, working out of shipyards at Hawkesbury and Windsor, sent sealers such as Chaseland and Kelly across the Tasman in search of seals. Some of these hardened mariners, having negotiated the dangers of the Foveaux Straits, repelled attacks by Māori peoples and survived shipwrecks off reefs around previously unexplored sub-Antarctic islands. These mariners also decided to abandon mainstream colonial employment trying their hand as small-scale entrepreneurs. One place they called home was Stewart Island, called *Rakiura* by the local First Nations peoples. The Polynesians had populated it thousands of years before the arrival of the colonial men. By 1800, sealers had anchored there to fish. Finding the island an ideal base they had formed a collective and settled there partnering with some local Māori women.

Notwithstanding these camps and settlements occupied by the independent sealers throughout the Fishery, their world cannot be defined just by the lands and islands they inhabited. The scope of their activities took place across the wide expanse of the entire southern Antipodean oceans. Many criss-crossed over several hundred kilometres from island to island, coast to coast and from rookery to rookery. The whaleboats they used were mobile enough to form networks of marine and other economic activity involving sealers, their indigenous partners and commercial trading vessels. For example, several of the Straitsmen would seek out seals from around Bass Strait and Kangaroo Island in the season where the pinnipeds were plenty and then trade mainly skins and some oil in the markets and docks of Hobart and Port Dalrymple.

A reasonably objective analysis of this aspect of sealing life was presented by James Kelly, the former sealer and jack of many trades. When examined under oath before Commissioner Bigge in Hobart Town in 1820, he informed the Commissioner that sealers traded in small whaleboats of 40 to 90 tons in the summer season, but that the success rate of catching seals had dropped substantially.[16] Kelly believed this resulted from frequent fishing and 'men remaining upon the islands and going to catch seals in open boats'. He explained that the sealers who 'clear out' for the islands in these vessels subsisted on kangaroo, wombat and emu, and that some would 'seduce' native women who gave birth to their children. Kelly stuck by his previous 1816 observations telling the Commissioner the women were very skilled at sealing.

When asked how the sealers made a living, Kelly told the Commissioner they traded with commercial vessels that passed by the various Islands. He explained they had an exchange system in place where produce, skins and oil were traded for clothing, 'slop' and spirits. When asked about the resorts of the mariners he answered that the largest sealer population by far were those who resided at Kangaroo Island. When queried about the escaped convicts, he replied that many had escaped on board the vessels that passed through the islands. He informed the Commissioner that the sealers had assisted in recapturing a boat taken by runaways. To his knowledge, no sealer had ever been involved in pirating commercial boats in the Straits.[17] Certainly, Kelly had no motive to exaggerate his evidence before Bigge and portray sealers negatively. Under oath, he could be taken to represent a balanced and reasonably objective portrayal of those mariners who traded out of the southern parts of the Fishery. Essentially by then, these independent men were living on remote beaches and outcrops often partnering with First Nations women eking out what can only be described as a marginal existence in difficult circumstances.

While the above analysis reflects the more positive aspects of an independent colonial sealer's existence, they became subject to extraordinary negative stereotyping as the second decade of the 19th century came to a close. Some of this was warranted. In particular, their exploitation and abuse in their encounters and relationships with First Nations women up until about 1830. However, other stereotyping was wide of the mark. Exploring the colonial discourse

---

[16] Kelly told the Commissioner that by then the mariners were lucky to catch 1,500 to 2,000 in any season.
[17] Examination of James Kelly, in *Historical Records of Australia*, Series 3, Vol. 3, 3 May, 1820, 458-462.

Chapter 10: Fact and Fantasy in the Lives of the Independent Sealers

of the time demonstrates that there were at least four stereotypical tropes that were being disseminated in colonial circles during that period. The first was the fantasy that the mariners living on the edge of the southern Antipodean coasts and islands were an abandoned set of idle castaways living a Crusoe-like existence.

Although many of the independent sealers sought out a life free of the constraints imposed by mainstream masters and traders, some also wanted a life of adventure. This meant often completely abandoning the trappings of colonial society in favour of a more liberated form of existence. In adopting a new lifestyle, they came with the baggage associated with rugged and brutal lives lived on the high seas. The main change adopted by the men was the entry into polygamous relationships with many of the local First Nations women by exchange, force or otherwise. It also meant other lifestyle differences, including building huts (rather than houses) out of timber, rocks and grasses they were able to find scouring about the region. Further, it meant they made clothing and footwear from the skins and hides of mammals such as possums, wallabies, kangaroos and seals as Sutherland observed in 1819. Some of the methods used to make clothes originated from their life partners. It also resulted in them seeking other prey such as mutton birds out of the sealing season.

By the late 1820s, concerns were being expressed about the conduct and behaviour of these mariners by newspaper editors and officials. They fomented a perception among colonial settlers that the independent sealers had become savages or had adopted a 'Crusoe-like' existence. This perception was fuelled by a colonial audience keen to hear titillating maritime tales. Such tales had their genesis in England in the early 1700s. By then, English audiences had become fascinated by tales of maritime expeditions taken to exotic and little-known places across the globe. They were particularly interested in the stories of men who had been shipwrecked or men who had to discard their clothing for the skins of dead animals, a trope which had already survived a long literary history. By the mid-eighteenth century, these "adventure" tales had found their way into popular journals and newspapers.

The Christian-civilised shipwrecked and abandoned male mariner found a central place within Western colonial imagination. This fantasy thrilled colonial audiences across the Empire, including those in the new colony. It had its roots in Daniel Defoe's 1719 novel, *The Life and Strange Surprising Adventures of Robinson Crusoe of York, Mariner*.[18] Defoe, who had suffered many adversities in his life, suddenly found fame and fortune as an authentic storyteller. It was later established that the idea for Defoe's tale likely came from the real-life adventures of the Scottish sailor Alexander Selkirk.[19] After being left voluntarily on an island in the Juan Fernandez group off the coast of Chile, Selkirk had survived for about four years until rescued by Captain Woodes Rogers, commander of the *Duke*, in 1709. The circumstances of Selkirk's life on the island was initially broadcast to a British public by Selkirk himself (upon his return to England in 1711). Later Rogers's own extraordinarily detailed journal gave a more dramatic version.[20] Defoe is likely to have read about Selkirk's experiences and adopted them for his own novel. That is not to detract from the significance of Defoe's creative work, or its underlying themes of individuality, entrepreneurship, spiritual awakening and resolve.

As Australia's colonial press heard more about the exploits of the sealers around the Fishery, it became easier for its editors to titillate their audiences by wildly comparing the fantasy of Selkirk's fiction with the marginalised sealer living in remote circumstances. For example, Selkirk, when rescued by Rogers was dressed from head to foot in goat skins. This is the apparel in which Defoe eventually clothed Robinson Crusoe. Similarly, the sealers living permanently on the various coasts of the Fishery resorted to sewing seal and kangaroo skins as their original clothing gradually reduced

---

[18] The full title was *The Life and Strange Surprising Adventures of Robinson Crusoe of York, Mariner who lived for eight and twenty years all alone in an un-inhabited Island on the Coast of America, near the Mouth of the Great River of Oroonoque; having been cast on shore by Shipwreck, where in all the Men perished but himself. With an account how he was at last as strangely deliver'd by Pyrates.* (London: W. Taylor,1719).

[19] Alexander Selkirk (1676-1721).

[20] Captain Woodes Rogers. *A Cruising Voyage around the World* (London: Cassell & Company, 1712).

to rags. Their clothing was not only for modesty's sake but also kept them warm, particularly in freezing unpleasant conditions in winter. As time went on, sealskin moccasins and kangaroo vests were commonly used among many of the sealing communities. Visiting traders and settlers would have observed the men garbed in such skins before reporting back to the traders in Sydney and Hobart. Then it was only a matter of time before the press took hold of this information and liberally portrayed the mariners as they saw fit as Crusoe-like figures, lazy castaways, layabouts, or as 'strange abandoned creatures'. But this image never was going to fit that of the shipwrecked hero we observe in Defoe's tale. Crusoe never loses his identity as a civilised white English Christian individual who overcomes much hardship through determination, perseverance, and prayer.

Unfortunately for the sealers, already receiving very negative press, the editors were never going to give them the "hero" status that Defoe's character enjoyed. They had already been condemned as men who had become savage barbarians not fit for any Western society. Royal Naval Surgeon Peter Cunningham R. N., who sailed to Australia as medical officer in charge of several convicts on four separate occasions, wrote several letters about his experiences in the colony, published in 1827. This is what he had to say about the sealers on Kangaroo Island:

> A few years back the charterers of a small vessel bound thither from Sydney decoyed two young women from that town on board, with a view to exchanging with these Robinson Crusoes, for the commodities they had to dispose of but the wreck of the vessel in Bass Strait frustrated all of prospects of founding an independent white colony in that quarter...[21]

In the same letter, he refers to the indolence of other mariners who lived in the Straits:

> Many belonging to this class of beings submit to live in a state of abject wretchedness in the enjoyment of liberty rather than feast upon sumptuous fare to which the bare name of work or control is attached. Accustomed to a life of wild irregularity, their minds can never entirely be subdued into contentment with a state

---
[21] Cunningham, Vol. 1, 22.

wherein their bodily capabilities are urged into action, or their wills constrained.[22]

He went on to refer to the sealers on Kangaroo Island as leading a 'most slothful idle life.'

The discourse, which perceived the sealers as being lazy beachcombers who led relaxed lazy lives on islands far removed from other settlements was a common one. Even as the sealing communities began to decline in the late 1830s, writers, editors and reporters were keen to keep audiences engaged by tagging sealers, particularly on Kangaroo Island, in terms of the shipwrecked animal skin-clad castaways. For example, when the artist and ship's surgeon, W. H. Leigh visited Kangaroo Island in 1837, he described the mariners there as living a 'solitary Selkirk life.'[23] This was despite the fact that by then many had settled into permanent productive existences on farms or properties.

A travel writer in 1847 asserted that the sealers led a 'Crusoe-like life without law or constraint.'[24] Soon after, endeavouring to attract travellers and settlers to the *Ultima Thule*, Edward Snell reported in his journal that he fancied living on the island as it 'must be rather a Robinson Crusoe sort of life.'[25]

However, the portrayal of colonial sealers as courageous white pelt-wearing shipwrecked survivors only ran skin deep. It was useful only to those entrepreneurs endeavouring to attract colonial settlers and commercial traders to the shores of remote coastal and island regions, like Kangaroo Island, for a 'taste of the exotic'. As time went on, this image became an immutable one, dominating the histories written afterwards, mirroring the perceptions portrayed by the colonial and post-colonial press. For instance, the well-known and respected historian James Bonwick, writing in the late 19th century, reflected on the fact that the mariners had to seek

---
[22] Cunningham, 23.
[23] W. H. Leigh. *Travels & Adventures in South Australia, 1836-1838* (Sydney: Currawong Press,1982), 102.
[24] George. Fife. Angas. *Savage Life and Scenes in Australia and New Zealand* Vol.1 (London: Smith Elder, 1847) 184.
[25] Tom Griffiths (ed.) *The Life and Adventures of Edward Snell* (North Ryde: Angus and Robertson,1988), 42.

out sexual relationships with the Australian women (because of the lack of European female company). This meant that 'they were compelled to adopt the society of savages'.[26] The fact that white men, some of whom were former convicts, had dressed in animal skins and formed intimate personal relationships with native women, whether by force or otherwise, rendered them criminals, savages and libidinous sexual predators. They became demonised and relegated to the lowest rung of humanity.

Even well after the demise of the sealing communities in 1907, historian John Blacket described these men as 'descended almost to the level of the kangaroos'.[27] Perhaps some of the mariners fitted this description and were adventurers in the broad sense, but many did not. In general, living in remote islands without access to the comforts of mainstream colonial life and subject to harsh environments would not have been a picnic. The lives lived by sealers was much more difficult, complex, divergent, nuanced and developed over time.

The second trope that developed in colonial circles about the independent sealers was that they were plunderers, marauders and pirates preying on the mainstream traders. By the mid-1830s the Colonization Commission for South Australia was meeting to consider whether to promote and encourage the "settlement" of Kangaroo Island, which they wanted to populate with 'respectable' families. Sutherland's 1819 report to Reibey found its way into Edward Gibbon Wakefield's work which extolled the economic benefits of settling there. Slavishly adopting the concerns previously raised in the press and elsewhere about the characters of the mariners living in the southern Antipodean islands, the leading Commissioner was clear in his concerns about:

> the lawless squatters, the abandoned sailors, the runaway convicts, the pirates, the curse of savages that now infest the coast of New Holland and perpetuate against the defenceless natives, crimes at which humanity revolts.[28]

---

[26] James Bonwick. *The Last of the Tasmanians*. London: Sampson, Low, Son and Martson 1870, 295.

[27] John Blacket. *The Early History of South Australia* (Adelaide: Vardon & Sons, 1907); the historian referred to in Taylor's *Unearthed*, 55.

[28] Taylor, 78, quoting from that report of the Colonization Commission for South

He was not alone.

When Lockyer encountered the sealers at King George's Sound in 1826, the mariners had been operating free of any constraint for several years, conducting mainly sealing enterprises from their whaleboats. During his time in the Sound, the Major perceived the sealers as a threat to the Empire and its maritime traders. In his journal he described them as:

> a complete set of pirates, going from island to island along the southern coast from Rottenest Island to Bass' Strait in open whaleboats. Kangaroo Island is their principal resort... At Kangaroo Island a great scene of villainy is going on... several desperate characters... runaway prisoners from Sydney and Van Diemen's Land...[29]

Lockyer may have been influenced by his knowledge of the nefarious activities of 'Black-Jack' Anderson and his motley crew. Of all the independent sealers, it is arguable that only Black-Jack and his gang who could be tagged as pirates. Even as late as 1835, when most of the independent mariners were in their dotage and well settled, the editor of *The Perth Gazette and Western Australian Journal* published an article based on the report of a Captain Welch about the 'characters hovering around the islands of the Straits'. He urged the government to take action to repress 'a dangerous and increasing band of pirates.'[30]

This prevailing sealer stereotype was fuelled by at least two factors. Firstly, there was the zeal of colonial authorities to 'get tough' on all lawless elements operating throughout the colony. Secondly, colonial society and the press were fascinated by (and thirsty for) news which involved anything to do with piracy, marooned sailors, savagery or preferably all three. These were popular subjects for colonial newspaper editors, pamphlet publishers, and book sellers who fed on any hint of such primitive and barbaric practices taking place.[31] Tales of the golden age of piracy in the late 16th and early

---

Australia for Her Majesties Principal Secretary for the Colonies, 1836-1838.
[29] From Les Johnson, *Major Edmund Lockyer. Forgotten Australian Pioneer* (Perth: Western Australian Museum, 2002) 69.
[30] The Editor, *The Perth Gazette and Western Australian Journal*, 1835, 575.
[31] Daniel Dafoe's *Robinson Crusoe* and his *General History of the Pyrates* in 1724

Chapter 10: Fact and Fantasy in the Lives of the Independent Sealers

17th centuries had fascinated colonial audiences for over 100 years by the time mariners were occupying islands off the coasts of the Australian mainland. They continued to provide compelling reading in the colonies. Such tales of "daring do" easily found their way into stories perpetrated by editors of the colonial press and others seeking to marginalize the independent sealers. Although the "golden age" of piracy had long since passed,[32] there had been several incidences of piracy in New Holland up to 1835, mainly involving escaped convicts. Such incidences were reported in great detail in the press.[33]

One of the most famous was the pirating of the brig *Cyprus* from the southwestern coast of Van Diemen's Land in 1830, and the dangerous voyage undertaken by the pirates afterwards. The punishments meted out to the perpetrators of such crimes were keenly reported in graphic detail by the colonial press editors. For the practice of piracy, the first international crime[34] was punishable by death until that penalty was abolished in 1838.[35] Convicts in the Antipodes were the main perpetrators. They were escaping to avoid the consequences of the regime, a 'salutary terror', instigated by colonial authorities, but they had little in common with the marauders who operated during piracy's golden age. Nonetheless, the colonial press and authorities were determined to "group" the sealers in the same underclass of "miscreants" as those who had 'gone on account'. In particular, the communities on Kangaroo Island became a target.

---

became increasingly popular as time went on and were effectively compulsory reading right up to the middle of the 19th century and beyond and still find a global readership.

[32] Pirates operated almost with impunity from about the late 1650s until about 1715, particularly in the Atlantic and the southern American marine environment, until the authorities gained the upper hand after that time.

[33] See also, for example, the seizure of the just completed vessel the *Frederick* from soldiers by convicts in Macquarie Harbour in 1834 and reported in the *Sydney Herald* on 6 March, and the *William Cossar*, owned by the Government and cut from her moorings at Sydney in 1817.

[34] See Geoffrey Robertson, *Crimes against Humanity. The Struggle for Global Justice* (London: The Penguin Press,1999), 195.

[35] See Tim Castle, "Constructing Death Newspaper Reports of executions in New South Wales 1826 to 1837, *Journal of Australian Colonial History* 9 (2007), 66.

By 1820, that island had been identified by Wakefield as a place where a significant colonial settlement and commercial centre could be established.[36] Wakefield relied heavily on Sutherland's report. That captain had spent seven months there in 1819.[37] On the island, he and his crew interacted with and observed the sealers going about their daily lives while enjoying a plentiful supply of sufficient natural resources to adequately feed and clothe themselves. Sutherland was able to rely on "friendly" sealers who had been there for several years to assist him as navigators when he endeavoured to cross Kangaroo Island. In doing so, they supplied him with valuable assistance in the form of 'intelligence' and guided him and his crew around that island. However, despite the support he received, he initially painted a less than positive picture of the sealers.

After informing his employers that there were no First Nations people living there and the commercial prospects were promising, he described the mariners in unflattering terms. Having one eye on his own interests and the other on the interests of the merchants, he did hold back:

> Several Europeans assemble there, some who have run from ships that traded for salt, others from Sydney and Van Diemen's Land, who were prisoners of the Crown. These gangs joined after a lapse of time and became the terror of ships going to the Island for salt etc. being little better than pirates. They are complete savages living in bark huts like the natives, not cultivating anything, but living entirely on kangaroos, emus, and small porcupines, and getting spirits and tobacco in barter for the skins which they lay up during the sealing season. They dress in kangaroo skins without linen and wear sandals made of seal skins. They smell like foxes...[38]

The image portrayed by Sutherland of the sealers was utilised time and time again in mainstream discourse of every kind,

---

[36] Edward Gibbon Wakefield. *Plan of a Company to be established for the purpose of founding a colony in Southern Australia, purchasing land therein, and preparing the land so purchased for the Reception of Immigrants* (London: Piccadilly, Ridgway and Sons,1832), 34-37.

[37] See Sutherland's full report in Appendix in Wakefield, Edwin Gibbon, *Plan of a Company to be established for the Purpose of founding a Colony of Southern Australia* (London: Ridgway and Sons, 1832).

[38] Sutherland, 73.

including the colonial press, official reports and correspondence. Such an image has been indelibly written into the colonial record. After exploring the many reasons why this characterisation was adopted, and how it came to play a role in the attempts made to remove sealers from their various places of abode, it is quite clear that it does not provide any honest portrait of these mariners.

The reality was that the sealers had settled into communities or collectives on the island. They constructed many huts and used caves in which to dry and salt the skins of the pinnipeds they had killed. The salt was freely available in the interior of the island. Nepean Bay became a rendezvous for trading. Skins, salt and oil were exchanged by sealers for commodities from the vessels that anchored there.[39] That is why the editor of *The Australian* in March 1826 reported: '[there] are at present upwards of two hundred souls *vegetating* on this convenient spot' and that the sealers were about to appoint a king and pass their own laws.[40] After telling his readers about the stability and progress the mariners had made in establishing themselves there, he went on to portray them as 'hordes' who plundered, seized and pirated traders' vessels.[41]

What really happened was that agricultural and farming collectives developed on Kangaroo Island. During this time, some sealers and their families constructed dwellings in a valley near the salt lagoons where there were also huts, freshwater wells, and a thriving garden. The collective was 'led by' one Abyssinia Jack, who was able to employ First Nations men for the purposes of hunting, using the whaleboats, and their women for making clothing and other domestic tasks. The reality was that, by 1824, the island was subject to a thriving maritime and small farming sealer community occupying several settlements and camps dotted around the island making a marginal living from their activities.

Fast forward nearly 20 years, Sutherland was interviewed by the commissioners of the Colonization Committee in 1837. He was asked whether he was ever 'molested' by the sealers. His

---

[39] Taylor, 23.
[40] Editor, *The Australian,* 9 March, 1826.
[41] Ibid.

response was: 'No, I was never interfered with at all by them. They used to sometimes to come on board my vessel'.[42] This answer flies in the face of his very pejorative description given to Reibey and later Wakefield. Nothing remotely negative in 1837. The more balanced evidence given by Sutherland, Kelly and others led one commissioner to describe the sealers as 'intelligent quiet men having plots of land under cultivation'.

During the period, several escaped convicts and others had formed gangs which terrorised and plundered the 'decent' settlers who now occupied much of Van Diemen's Land. These were identified as 'bushrangers'. These men conducted raids across the island, ransacking farms and establishments and perpetrating abominable crimes wherever they went. They were particularly prominent before Colonel William Sorell became the Governor in 1817. Although Sorell took active steps to arrest, prosecute and execute them, there were still many at large in the 1820s. Reports about their exploits proliferated in the colonial press and other publications. Henry Melville, an editor journalist, and an opponent of Lieutenant Governor George Arthur, described their aberrant conduct:

> these marauders or bushrangers were constantly committing all kinds and descriptions of crimes and even most horrid murders were of common occurrence.[43]

Despite the efforts of Sorell and the colonial officers to bring these 'bushrangers' to justice, there was apparently an upsurge in criminal activity during 1825. According to many editors (including Melville) none of the severe legal sanctions had a salutary effect. It left a sense of anarchy and lawlessness pervading the colony.[44] Gangs controlled by the notorious Plumb, McCabe, and Brady continued in a systematic way to terrorise the settled communities.

---

[42] Commissioner John Morphett. *Supplementary Report to the Commission.*
[43] Henry Melville. *The History of the Island of Van Diemen's Land from the year 1824 to 1835 inclusive* (London: Smith and Elder, 1835), 4.
[44] Melville describes the status of lawlessness in the colony: 'Bushranging during this year [1825] was rapidly on the increase. At times one or two of the desperadoes were captured and executed, but all endeavours to bring the Colony into a state of tranquillity seemed unavailable', 46.

Chapter 10: Fact and Fantasy in the Lives of the Independent Sealers

Brady and his gang evaded capture for many years to the chagrin and embarrassment of the colonial authorities. These gangs operated on the mainland. Not one of them ventured to extend their influence on the high seas or on the islands occupied by the sealers. In addition, there was no intention formed or attempt made by the sealers to join in any enterprise with these bushrangers. The sealer James Kelly made clear his position when confronted with the possibility of an encounter with bushrangers on his voyage around Tasmania in 1816. James wrote his crew were hell bent on avoiding such dangerous characters.

But colonial traders, authorities and pressmen continued portraying the sealers as bushrangers. There were several attempts made to 'group' the sealers with the outlaws and to reign them in. For example, the sea captain, W. Stewart, when writing to Colonial Secretary Campbell, described them as 'a Banditti of Bushrangers'. Later, in March 1826, the editor of *The Australian* reported erroneously that there was regular communication between 'the runaways of the islands and the bushrangers of Van Diemen's Land'.[45] Even well after the decline of the sealing industry, Bonwick, in his history, went close to coupling the mariners with the outlaws by telling his colonial readers that 'on shore, they would have been bushrangers'.[46] Tagging the independent islander sealers as bushrangers like the notorious Brady and Howe, who were the terror of the colonists in Van Diemen's Land, would have given men like G.A. Robinson the ammunition necessary to approach the colonial authorities to take steps to remove the mariners from the islands. But the fact of the matter was that the sealers and bushrangers operated totally independently from each other.

Another common trope that developed was that these islanders were either associated with criminals and convicts or were former guests of His Majesty's prisons, either as felons or escapees. Shortly after Sutherland's 1819 report, and towards the latter

---

[45] In the same article, he reported that at Kangaroo Island 'Every sealing vessel suffers from hordes of men' in and about the Straits and 'by all accounts' the mainstream mariners 'may be considered particularly fortunate if they escape by being only plundered and are not altogether seized and pirated'.
[46] Bonwick, 191.

part of Governor Macquarie's term, a perception was fostered among influential colonial elites that Macquarie was too liberal in his approach to dealing with convicts. These elites, led by the pastoralists, believed the original purpose for which the colony had been established was being eroded. Moreover, they asserted, convicts were no longer being deterred from criminal activity and, as a consequence, they were not only escaping from penal servitude but profiting from the settlements, much to the detriment of the colony and its free traders.[47]

In 1819, as a result of pressure on the British Government from certain elites, Commissioner Bigge (a former Chief Justice of the slave colony of Trinidad) was appointed to inquire into the laws, regulations and usages of the colony and reform of its convicts. He regarded the fact that a colony should principally be arranged as a receptacle for prisoners, where punishment of any criminal conduct should be severe enough to deter any further criminality.[48] Bigge interviewed many colonial men over the course of several months before handing down his three reports.

After the commissioner returned to London and Macquarie's term as governor had ended, the colonial authorities were over-enthusiastic in their efforts to adopt Bigge's recommendations. From about 1822, significant wide-ranging and harsher sanctions were imposed in the implementation of the reforms, which have been described by more than one commentator as a 'reign of terror'. These were adopted by Governors Brisbane and Darling to allow authorities to impose stricter controls over their convicts, mainly to the benefit of settlers who capitalised on a generation of free labour.

At the same time, harsher laws were being passed in Britain to restrict freedom of association. The colonial authorities following in "lock-step" with London, also imposed draconian measures. From all of this, a trope developed grouping the sealers with convicts,

---

[47] The Editor, "Botany Bay" in *Edinburgh Review*, 32, 1819 Judith Johnson and Monica Anderson, *Australia Imagined* (Crawley: University of Western Australia Press 2005), 36.

[48] John Ritchie, *Punishment and Profit, The Reports of Commissioner John Bigge on the Colonies of New South Wales and Van Diemen's Land 1822-1823* (Melbourne: Heinemann,1970), 61.

Chapter 10: Fact and Fantasy in the Lives of the Independent Sealers

runaways and criminals operating outside the boundaries of the law. For example, the editor of *The Australian* complained that the Straits were 'infested with numbers of prisoners or illegal characters'.[49] The authorities often portrayed the sealers as associating with other 'miscreants' at large in Van Diemen's Land during the 1820 and 1830s.[50] The adventurer Boultbee, a "gentleman'", early on described his companions as 'the refuse of merchant ships' and 'formerly convicts, thieves and scoundrels fit for no society'. Only one of those in the collective escaped his negative description.[51]

Despite this perception, there was little evidence to suggest that criminals and escapees were involved in the sealing industry. Boultbee may have changed his mind after immersing himself in the sealer life. This may have been after an encounter with a crew of sealers who traded skins for alcohol with traders. He was surprised that 'they did not commit such excesses as might have been expected'. Although there were some instances in which escapees may have "assisted" some sealers or vica versa, by the late 1820s, the leaders of the sealing communities like Munro and Tucker, were actively informing officials of the activities of escapees in the Straits.

It is interesting to observe that the Conciliator Robinson could only identify seven out of the 42 sealers who were still inhabiting Bass Strait and Kangaroo Island as ex-convicts, and none as escapees from His Majesty's pleasure.[52] Finally, in 1833, John Jones, a colonial trader, met with several sealers and was convinced that none of them were escaped convicts. According to the elderly sealer George 'Fireball' Bates, who had nothing to hide when interviewed by the editor of the *Adelaide Observer* in 1895, no sealer he knew was a runaway convict on Kangaroo Island in the period.[53] More recently, some historians have taken the allegation of criminality to task. One has concluded that there is little evidence to support

[49] The Editor, *The Australian*, 9 March, 1826.
[50] See, for example, Extracts of the Minutes of the Executive Council, 14 March, 1831.
[51] Begg, 52.
[52] See Plomley (ed.) *Friendly Mission: 1834*. 1010-1017.
[53] Bates had been a sealer on Kangaroo Island for many years, was part of the Islander community there, outliving the other men. Referred to in Taylor, 52.

the notion that the sealing community was composed of many escapees, going so far as to describe this perception as a 'fiction'.[54] The one trope that found its way into the pages of colonial newspapers, journals, letters and reports that had more than some accuracy to it was that the sealers kidnapped and abused and exploited First Nations women. This theme was coupled with the view that these mariners were also slave traders. Early on, and then continuously right up to the decline of the industry, the sealers recognised that, if they wanted to survive on the islands, they would have to depend on the First Nations inhabitants of New Holland. The encounters and relationships formed with these peoples were sometimes friendly but often hostile. Many, but certainly not all, of the mariners were involved in the kidnapping and abuse of First Nations women, who were subject to various forms of violence, including forced abduction, assault and rape. Sometimes the men traded women with other mariners. Despite the early abuse and oppression of these women by several sealers, many of the local people partnered with the mariners in mutually beneficial relationships. Once the sealers realised just how valuable the women were to them, not only as sexual companions, but also as hunters, gatherers, and sealers in their own right, they settled into more nuanced arrangements with their female companions. These women were also knowledgeable about the procurement of other fauna and flora such as kangaroos, mutton birds, bark, tea tree and kelp for eating, medicinal and utilitarian purposes. The nature and complexity of the relationships between the mariners as perpetrators and partners of the First Nation women will be considered further in a later chapter.

The fantastical portrayal of the sealer as castaway, pirate, banditti, convict and exploiter and slave trader have become fixed over time, so it is difficult to find the voice of these mariners in the historical records to sift through and ascertain what really occurred. No doubt, as more than one commentator has stated, further evidence will be found to support a more balanced reflection of the life of the colonial sealers. A multi-disciplinary approach, which would also

---

[54] Taylor, 52.

include First Nations oral traditions and archaeological material, may assist in exploring this subject. Targeting sealers living a marginal existence on the fringes of the colony became a regular feature in colonial circles. After a time, it led to louder calls for these mariners to be subject to sever sanction.

Chapter 11: How Do We Remove the Banditti?

The labelling of the independent sealers operating out of the southern Antipodean coasts and islands as banditti, pirates, slave traders, escapees and the like was the start of a campaign to rid these same coasts and islands of these mariners. But, despite paying lip service to imposing sanctions on these sealers, nothing much was done. Nothing really until Robinson, appointed Conciliator, had interviewed, journeyed with and lived alongside the First Nations peoples in Van Diemen's Land.

His journals kept between 1829 and 1834 record interviews he fostered with these women. They paint a very negative picture of a typical Straitsman as being violent, abusive, promiscuous exploiters and slave traders of the worst kind in their relationships with the women. There is hardly a kind word that the Conciliator has to say about the men. Appalled by what he had been told and armed with this horrific "evidence" he approached the Lieutenant Governor on two counts. Firstly, to apprehend and remove the Straitsmen from the islands. Secondly to persuade the First Nations people to follow him to a yet to be chosen island destination But he did not realise that some of the women and nearly all of the sealers would resist his demands. For, as time went on, the sealers got under the skins of Robinson and his official supporters. These appointees became frustrated. It posed a serious question: hat could really be done to remove the banditti?

Prior to the Conciliator focussing on the 'sealer problem', colonial elites relied on reports about mariners such as commercial shipping captains and colonial masters trawling around the Fishery. They would have wanted to portray sealers in a negative way to satisfy the economic concerns of mainstream commercial traders.

Chapter 11: How Do We Remove the Banditti?

These entrepreneurs were anxious to gain a commercial advantage over those who lived outside colonial norms; they did not want the additional competition from independent sealers to deplete their profits. They were given an important boost to their cause once the Bigge's Reports were handed down.[1] Bigge had gravitas and his influential reports suggesting a much tougher approach being implemented to curtail criminal elements within the colony. His recommendations were adopted slavishly. Afterwards, the gaze of colonial authority shifted beyond the boundaries of the early established settlements and focussed on perceived miscreants. These included the independent Straitsmen.

The military was to first monitor, and then curtail, the mariners' activities. Despite this unwanted attention, no significant effort was made to sanction the sealers mainly due to the lack of financial and naval resources necessary to pursue them. By that time, there were probably at least 50 sealers and approximately 100 First Nations women and their offspring dwelling on islands the Straits. An unknown number of other mariners and their partners were existing in King Georges Sound, Kangaroo Island and other environments.[2]

After 1820, several official and commercial trading vessels, along with military personnel, were sent into many of the remote maritime places inhabited by the Australian independent sealing communities. Officials wanted to scrutinize their alleged aberrant conduct and behaviour. By then many sealing grounds were depleted, the price of seal skins and oil had escalated, and there was a fresh demand for such commodities. The commercial maritime traders were interested in expanding their trading opportunities in locations where seals and whales could be found, including around Kangaroo Island and King Georges Sound, as the diaries and reports of Sutherland and Lockyer attest. In their reports to their respective colonial masters, they were keen to point out the threat posed by the

---

[1] See John Thomas Bigge, *Report of the Commissioner of Inquiry into the State of the Colony of New South Wales 1822.*

[2] Attempts have been made to calculate the number of sealers with estimates ranging between 200 and 400 plus the Australian women and some Indigenous men, but this is not necessarily accurate.

sealers operating in these places. They called loudly for sanctions to be imposed. For example, Sutherland sought to make that point to his colonial masters. He asserted that to take advantage of the commercial trading opportunities on Kangaroo Island, including sealing, salt production and access to other resources, colonial authorities needed to appoint soldiers or constables immediately to effectively deprive the islander sealers of their liberty and send them elsewhere. In support of this proposition, he wrote: 'There are a few [sealers] even still on the island whom it should be desirable to have removed if a permanent settlement was established in the neighbourhood'.[3]

Sutherland and Lockyer were only two of several powerful colonial figures who sought a solution to the perceived problem of the sealers. Despite the attention given by authorities to sanction sealer conduct, the colonial elite became increasingly frustrated over their inability to achieve their aims. At the time, some criticism had been levelled at the colonial governments in Sydney and Van Diemen's Land that these settlements were developing an ideal climate for the criminal classes to live in with relative abandon. Further, that the sealers were prospering from their activity.[4] In 1820, Bigge travelled to Van Diemen's Land and interrogated several colonists including James Kelly, the former sealer, now a respectable citizen of Hobart. Kelly confirmed some escapees had attached themselves to boats in the Straits which, by implication, would have included those operated by the sealers.[5]

Steps taken to sanction sealer conduct were supported by the press. The colonial editors were keen to provide its reading public with as much information (often of an alarmist kind) as possible. Several articles appeared in the newspapers, including the *Sydney Gazette* and *Hobart Gazette*. They described the opportunities that the mainstream traders could exploit while also complaining about

[3] Sutherland, *Appendix to Wakefield*, 73.
[4] See Sydney Smith, "Botany Bay" in *Edinburgh Review* Vol. 32, 1819, 28-48, as reviewed by Judith Johnson and Monica Anderson in *Australia Imagined* (Crawley: University of Western Australia Press 2005, 35) where reference is made to New Holland as a 'school for criminals'.
[5] Although Kelly made it clear that 'none of the free people in the islands' had acted illegally.

the operations of the sealers. In doing so, they suggested ways and means that might be used to eradicate the independent mariners. The sealers were grouped with other miscreants including escapees and employees of the notorious Van Diemen's Land Company. The authorities were also keen to act. In 1831, the Executive Council singled out three classes of culprits:

> The only violence they [the women] may be exposed to, as there are no settlers in that quarter will proceed from convicts escaping from Macquarie Harbour, the servants of the Van Diemen's Land Company and sealers upon the Coast...[6]

At first, officials engaged the services of commercial traders to conduct voyages into the Straits designed to locate and remove runaway convicts in addition to monitoring sealer activity. These men may have also been retained privately for other purposes, such as sealing and whaling around the Fishery. Docking back in the colonial ports, the master mariners would usually report back to government officials their observations of the sealers they encountered. Often these reports found their way into the local press, with colonial editors urging the government to act against the Islanders for a variety of reasons. They also wanted them removed so that the 'honest' and 'upright' traders could profit unimpeded by those who had chosen to be independent of mainstream colonial society and its trading enterprises.

As time went on, the authorities became increasingly exasperated with the attempts to remove the sealers from the Fishery, and so they sought more pro-active solutions. This frustration was mirrored in the press. For example, the editor of the *Hobart Town Gazette*, when referring to information that had been obtained from the aged sealer George Robinson, commented on a report of illegal activity in Bass Strait:

> How appalling... received an alarming account of the increasing hordes... the evil is too formidable to be neglected and we are sensible the Government with where the power rests will take some special measures to remove it.[7]

---

[6] Extract from the Minutes of the Executive Council, 14 March 1831.
[7] *Hobart Town Gazette*, 1 July, 1826, 4.

Such was the level of colonial anxiety while searching for a solution to the sealer 'problem' that one editor took it upon himself to write no less than six methods that could be utilised to deal with it. In an article entitled "Kangaroo Island", he recommended that authorities begin issuing passports, creating new regulations, arranging for the appointment of a police officer to check and record all relevant details, placing restrictions on maritime activities, using a 'swift sailing armed cutter', and 'adapt[ing] speedy and efficient measures to check this serious and growing evil'. In a highly charged comment at the end of the article, probably designed to send alarm bells to the readers, and perhaps with one eye on his competition, he added that these measures would help 'annihilate these irregular characters'.[8]

Such constant badgering from the press appears to have had some success. The government did employ the services of at least two men to start removing so-called 'miscreants'. Captain Thomas Whyte, a former convict, sailed for Bass Strait in *The Duke of York* with a directive to 'apprehend all runaway prisoners and other illegal characters harbouring in the Straits'. He found and restrained about ten persons, including some who 'could not give any account of themselves'. Shortly afterwards, a Captain Skelton in the schooner *Governor Sorell* anchored in the Straits and "fell in with" Whyte on his journey where they exchanged 'intelligence'. Skelton came to the conclusion as a result of his surveillance expedition that an armed vessel should be employed to 'visit every island with every prospect of success in securing all suspicious and dangerous characters that *infest* these parts'.[9] However, despite the aggressive attempts by colonial pressmen to urge the authorities to apprehend the so-called 'dangerous characters' for unspecified criminal activity, it is clear that this was not the principal motive of those in power. Rather, it was the curtailment of the operations of the sealers because they were perceived as getting in the way of the mainstream commercial traders and inhibiting the opportunities of those traders to make a "killing" out of the Fishery. Indeed, in an

---

[8] *The Sydney Gazette,* 1 July, 1824, 3.
[9] The Editor, *The Australian,* 9 March, 1826.

Chapter 11: How Do We Remove the Banditti?

act of ventriloquy as the puppet of these same authorities, Skelton, in a letter to the editor of The Australian on the same day as that referred to above, made that purpose abundantly clear.

Notwithstanding the 'call to arms' that occurred, apart from capturing a few runaway convicts, the government had little or no success in sanctioning sealers. Any success they did have was in part due to the efforts of one of their number ,James Munro. By 1825, Munro had established himself as a leader among the Straitsmen. Despite later efforts by Robinson to portray him as a man of poor character that bordered on criminality, he was able to establish a reasonably good relationship with the colonial government in Hobart and authorities in Port Dalrymple. This was principally because he was playing a somewhat duplicitous double game.

While running his sealing enterprise and probably giving some help to some nefarious characters, he was assisting in providing valuable intelligence to the government about several escaped convicts who had stolen two vessels before relocating to the Furneaux Island group. The convicts had been found out by Munro and others.[10] As a reward for providing information to officials, Arthur appointed Munro to the role of constable. As part of his role, he was to seek the apprehension of criminals and provide further reports on their activities. Given the relationship that had developed between Munro and Arthur, the colonial government in Hobart perceived the 'free' sealers as persons 'whose interest it is to prevent piracy'.[11] This meant that the sealers continued to operate without any significant impediment during the years 1820 to 1830, carrying out their small-scale, now more diverse, trading activities. But attempts were being made by the colonial government to bring the mariners to account by legal sanction. Early in 1828, Arthur issued his Demarcation Proclamation which, in its preamble, inter alia, referred to attacks by sealers on First Nations women. It prohibited settlers, stock keepers and sealers from using 'force against any Aboriginal except in the presence and direction of a

---

[10] Begg,105.
[11] See letter from M. P. Musgrave JP to Captain Montagu, 3 October, 1825 (referred to in John Boultbee's journals).

magistrate'.[12] A curious and strange piece of legislation, it proved to be useless.

Meanwhile to the west of the Straits independent mariners, fishing for seals in locations around King Georges Sound and South Australia, were also targeted. But despite lip service, the government failed to prevent the sealers from operating their political economy. For example, when Lockyer encountered the sealers in the Sound, he became aware that two men had allegedly murdered an First Nations man. He tasked himself with bringing the accused sealers, Randall and Kirby, to justice. After capturing them and holding them for a short time, he suddenly let them go without further charge.[13] Given that First Nations people at the time were not permitted to be called as witnesses and the alleged victim was deceased, he may have had no other alternative. At the same time, Lockyer was also frustrated by the activities of the sealers on Kangaroo Island and expressed the view that something should be done about the 'lawless' people there.

However, the reality was that nothing of much significance had been done to curtail sealer activity until the rise of Robinson following the conclusion of what has been colloquially described as the 'Black War'. This conflict arose out of colonial concerns about a perceived increase in aggression on the part of the First Nations people of Tasmania. Increasingly louder voices called for sanctioning the Trowunna people, who were being accused of various crimes, including arson, rape and violence of all sorts, even murder. In 1830, Arthur decided to take action against these First Nations peoples. With the assistance of senior military officers and some settlers, he moved to force the First Nations people into certain restricted areas in Van Diemen's Land so that they could be 'protected' from possible further violence and controlled and monitored effectively. This was to enable the good citizens of the island to enjoy a greater level of security and other opportunities, particularly in those lands that would become freely available to them.

---

[12] Henry Melville. *History of Van Diemen's Land*, 72-74. This seems to be a very curious and odd law, and unenforceable.

[13] See Gordon Copland, "The Mysteries of Karta alias Kangaroo Island. Creation Colonisers and Crusoes", 25.

One of the tragic outcomes of the war was that many Aboriginal people were killed, along with fewer Europeans. Afterwards, Arthur (along with his masters in England) became increasingly alarmed about the hostility of and possible extinction of the First Nations people, who had already been decimated by frontier war and disease. The former aggressive mentality changed. Attention became focussed on the steps that needed to be taken to avoid these outcomes. Believing that the First Nations people of Bruny Island would be most amenable to conciliation, Arthur firstly decided to appoint a person to assist in improving relationships with them. In late 1829, Robinson commenced his role as Conciliator. He had no previous ethnographic experience or any dealings with the First Nations people or the Islanders.

Even though Robinson had never had any encounters with sealers, he had already made up his mind about them. His knowledge of them came mainly from the colonial government in Hobart and anecdotal evidence he obtained from First Nations women.. He set about a course of conduct, for altruistic and selfish reasons, designed to bring the sealers to account. In doing so, he always operated with one eye on the prize he would gain if he were successful.[14] It was always going to be in his interests to portray sealers negatively. It also fitted in well with the overwhelmingly adverse stereotype that had already developed.

Robinson engaged some "assistants", including a former sealer by the name of James Parish, to round up the Aboriginal people and to remove the women from the sealers in the Straits. James had been a sealer in the Straits and was familiar with the region and the independent sealer colonies. He had participated in seizing First Nations women in the past. In early 1831, Parish and some other men voyaged to Penguin Island, a sealer 'haunt', to remove the women from their mariner partners. The mariner John Williams lived there with other sealers and First Nations women including one called Walyer, who was most feared by the colonial authorities, settlers, sealers and other First Nations clans. Their menfolk had

---

[14] Arthur had promised him a substantial financial reward for bringing in the last of the 'Native People' and removing the influence of the sealers from the Straits.

become marooned at the time and had no way of voyaging to the island having been shipwrecked. Parish was no fool and seized his opportunity. Observing the sealers in distress, he hauled his boat out to the stranded men. The bargain he struck with them allowed him to remove their female companions in exchange for their rescue. Parish and his henchmen enticed all the First Nations people to leave for Swan Island, one of the first of Robinson's 'native settlements'.[15] He had no opposition.

Between about 1830 and 1835, Robinson also put into place a series of measures designed to nullify the influence of the sealers, with the aim of their ultimate removal. He perceived them to be the main perpetrators of First Nations exploitation.[16] A controversial figure in colonial Australian history,[17] the Conciliator had a very difficult relationship with the mariners. Ultimately, he failed in achieving his mission to bring them to heel.. In this task, he also failed miserably, though he had some support from the authorities, such as Arthur and John Montagu of the Executive Council.[18]

His removal strategy proved less than effective for several reasons. Some employees and military personnel on secondment either did not perform the tasks allocated to them or deliberately thwarted Robinson. Furthermore, the resistance by the sealers sabotaged any attempt by the Conciliator. This is somewhat ironic given that Robinson often had the cooperation of the Islanders. He managed to get some to consent to the removal of First Nations partners to Gun Carriage Island. On occasion, the men even provided assistance to him in the form of clothing, food, shelter

---

[15] The deceitful Parish maximised his advantage over the women and sealers by stealing their prey including mutton birds and kangaroo skins. See Lindal Ryan, *The Tasmanian Aborigines*, 150.

[16] This was despite a number of other groups such as settlers, bushrangers, whalers, convicts, farmers and employees of the Van Diemen's Land Company were major exploiters of the First Nations women along with several sealers. See Extract of the Minutes of the Executive Council in *Report from the Select Committee on Aborigines*.

[17] See, for example, various critiques of G. A. Robinson in Anna Johnson and Mitchell Rolls (eds), *Reading Robinson: Companion Essays to Friendly Mission*. Hobart: Quintus Press, 2008.

[18] Montagu was the one who suggested a government vessel be employed in the Straits to take 'native' women from the sealers. See extract from Minutes of the Executive Council in *Report from the Select Committee on Aborigines*, 84.

and trinkets for the people.[19] Early on and following his meetings with the sealers, Robinson had initially thought that the sealers would cooperate with him. But he was wrong.

In late March 1831, some mariners did deliver their female companions to Robinson 'with so little resistance'.[20] But such success was short-lived because, about two days later at Dog Island, one of the leaders of the sealers, Tucker, informed Robinson that 'he did not care for the government'. He boldly asserted the men intended to remain for as long as they could. In frustration, the Conciliator wrote:

> I regret I do not have a warrant to apprehend him. I told him that I would refer charges and put him in confinement aboard the cutter.[21]

But none of this occurred.

At other times, the sealers either resisted, defied, or undermined Robinson's orders and activities. They often did this collectively. The Straitsmen authorised Munro and Tucker to approach the authorities to complain about Robinson's behaviour. By acting in this manner, and with the assistance of many of their First Nations partners, the sealers undertook various resistance strategies. This ultimately led to Robinson abandoning his attempts at curtailing them. The failure of Robinson (and persons charged with sanctioning and removing the sealers) is in part due to the misconceived view of these men as anarchic Robinson Crusoe-type figures, itinerant criminals and layabouts, who would be an easy target.

For, by the 1830s, most of the sealers were part of stable collective economies based on islands where each had established partnerships, residences and gardens. Many of the women were

---

[19] Plomley, fns. 332 and 181.
[20] Ibid., 332.
[21] The colonial historian James Erskine Calder described Tucker as 'the most daring active and serviceable [sic] man'. Despite his poor reputation, he later received a government award of £25 in 1848. Stephen Murray-Smith, "Beyond the Pale. The Islander Community of Bass Strait in the Nineteenth Century", in *Papers and Proceedings of the Tasmanian Historical Research Association*, Vol. 20, Number 4, December, 1973. 175.

active and essential participants who by then had their own stake in these sealing economies. Removal was resisted strongly by many First Nations women as well.

One of the resistance practices employed by the Straitsmen to frustrate Robinson was to remove their female partners to other islands or conceal them. Writing in his journal throughout 1831, the Conciliator refers to those First Nations people that he managed to secure in his early Establishment and others who were concealed by the mariners. He enjoyed only partial success in his attempts at removal. There were at least 30 women who Robinson asserted had been concealed, but there were probably many more. Prominent among the sealers who resorted to this practice were those who resided on King's Island. The Conciliator was aware of at least 13 women who had been removed from that place and transferred by boat to Kangaroo Island allegedly by the sealer John Morgan (also known as Hughes) by May 1831. Other Straitsmen who actively sought to hide their companions included John Riddle and Tucker, both residing on Gun Carriage Island, James Thompson living on Preservation Island with Munro and John Anderson alias 'Abyssynia Jack', residing in the Kents Group, who had concealed one of his female companions and a 'lad' by the name of Praree.

While the sealers took active steps to thwart Robinson, the Lieutenant Governor acted. Arthur formed the 'Aboriginal Committee' to make recommendations about steps to remove the First Nations inhabitants in Van Diemen's Land. That committee proposed there not only be a resettlement of the surviving First Nations people at Gun Carriage Island, but also that (and this was a common plan of attack) a vessel be dispatched to protect the women from sealers.[22] Acting on advice received from Robinson that the sealers would abandon the Straits if they lost "the native women", a meeting of the Executive Council was held on 23 February 1831. That committee ordered the Conciliator to 'tell the sealers to deliver up the women'. The one caveat was that they should obtain the 'most express and unequivocal consent' of the

---

[22] *Report of the Aborigines Committee in Military Operations against the Aborigines of Van Diemen's Land* (Committee Room, 4 February, 1831), 76-77.

Chapter 11: How Do We Remove the Banditti?

women.²³ Shortly after this, Arthur wrote to the Colonial Secretary to confirm that Robinson had been so instructed. ²⁴

Over the next several years other legislation, regulations and sanctions were imposed by colonial authorities in an attempt to drive the sealers from the islands. These included *An Act to facilitate the Apprehension of Offenders escaping from the island of Van Diemen's Land and elsewhere*,²⁵ two public notices prominently displayed on selected islands, and an act requiring all occupiers of the islands in the Straits to have a licence. None of these legal sanctions imposed on sealers succeeded. This resulted in an underlying seething frustration, mainly for Robinson, and to a lesser extent, his colonial masters.

The ability of the Straitsmen to evade legal sanction is no better illustrated than by the fact that the Conciliator tried to convince them that legislation had been passed to drive them from the Straits when, in fact, no such act had been promulgated.²⁶ When Robinson tried to enforce other legislation and directives from his masters, at least two sealers discovered a loophole in the sanctions. The prohibitions imposed referred to 'Bass' Straits. The clever mariners claimed immunity from prosecution. They advised the colonial authorities that they were in the 'Banks' Straits rather than 'Bass' Straits as they were residents of Clark Island or Lungtalanana, as the Tasmanians called it. Therefore, the legislation did not apply to them.²⁷

Eventually, the constant tug of war and tension between Robinson and the sealers reached a boiling point. Later in 1831, Munro and another sealer, Mansell, sought an audience with the Lieutenant Governor in Hobart. By this time, they were sick and tired of the Conciliator's aggressive meddling in their affairs. They came armed with a strategy. The men arrived with a young child

---

[23] Other directives were given including taking details of names and descriptions of the so-called guilty parties so that warrants could be issued, and warnings given to sealers to quit the islands. Minutes of the Executive Council, 3 March, 1831, 85.

[24] Copy dispatch from Lieutenant Governor Arthur to the Secretary Sir George Murray, Hobart Town, 4 April, 1831, 78.

[25] Victoria 1, *Act XI*, 29 August, 1838.

[26] See Plomley, 440, fn. 60.

[27] Plomley confirmed the success of the sealers in avoiding sanctions in a *minor* footnote to *Friendly Mission* where he indicates that 'the sealers went about things with skill and cunning', 457, fn. 166.

and carried a Bible. At that meeting, Munro was able to convince Arthur that, instead of being the subject of legal sanction and treated as criminals, the sealers could assist with the delivery of other First Nations peoples in the region. But there was a caveat. They would only agree if they could keep most of the women. Munro achieved his aim by not only appealing to his own role as a respectable constable, but also through evangelical zeal. He pleaded that he read the Bible to his own children and First Nations partners who had been taught to read. Mansell claimed that he 'practised what Munro preached', by also reading the bible to their young charge.[28] Arthur was convinced and consented.

After finding Arthur was entirely receptive to their plea, Munro and Mansell returned to the Straits. They were full of confidence, aggressively confronting Robinson with the 'communication' from the Lieutenant Governor. George was then forced to deliver up the First Nations women, whom had been removed and handed to Munro "for protection", while allowing the others to keep most of the women with them. It was a black day for the Conciliator, He felt humiliated by his foes. Robinson, now apoplectic, wrote in his journal:

> the sealers since their return… appear to make-sport with the government and state to my people Mr Robinson has no more authority than they have.[29]

By 1832, by reason of the strategies adopted by the Straitsmen, the old assumption that colonial authorities could remove sealers from anywhere in the Fishery was obsolete. . Robinson and his associates had become increasingly frustrated. Matters worsened when the Conciliator found to his dismay that the military and some of his assistants were plotting against him. That was despite assurances in the colonial press that Robinson held uniform support from all colonial authorities. These deceits were referenced in Robinson's own journals: 'The government is not vesting me with full and sufficient power and authority to act'. Not only that but he added, with a sense of despair, his enforcer Clucas was 'always

---

[28] Plomley, 355.
[29] Ibid.

conniving' with the sealers:

> Discovered nothing of the sealers although it is pretty evident, they are on this island. In my absence nothing is done. Everything appears to go wrong.[30]

By then he had little military support from the Government. The sealers were getting away with "blue murder".[31]

The sealers resisted and played games with Robinson, telling him stories as part of their plan. They did this by utilising a "divide and conquer" mentality whereby the Conciliator was given one version of events and his enforcers another. With such a strategy, the mariners prevented Robinson and authorities from implementing sanctions that had the support of the colonial press, religious fraternity and most probably the elites in England and Sydney.. By 1837, the mariners, their partners and children had re-occupied many of the islands, such as Preservation, Gun Carriage, Clarke, Woody and Swan, or had sought other adventures of a maritime nature. Two year later Robinson had abandoned the First Nations people to their terrible fate on Flinders Island and was appointed the Protector of the Aborigines in the Port Phillip District.

Much of the success that the sealers enjoyed in frustrating men like Whyte, Skelton, Robinson and Lockyer was due to the strategies they adopted and to the failures by colonial authorities to bring these so-called "criminals" to justice. In that regard, the officials were unable to rely on their primary witnesses, First Nation Peoples, as they were not allowed to give evidence. Almost as important was the fact that there developed a resistance practice that the mariners' Aboriginal female partners used against men like Robinson. This practice arose when the First Nations people realised that the alternative to a life now mostly settled, was almost certain death from disease and illness on Flinders Island if they complied with the Conciliator's enticements. Although many of the relationships the sealers developed with the women over time were initially secured by kidnapping and abduction it is ironic that these same mariners facilitated the survival (at least in part)

---
[30] Plomley, 346.
[31] Ibid., 431.

Mariners on the Margins

of the Tasmanian First Nations people. Many but not all of these Straitsmen had complex relationships in which they were both perpetrators and partners.

Chapter 12: Perpetrators and Partners

The Survivor

Even by 1810, George Briggs had already established a strong relationship with Mannalargenna, the leader of the *Trawlwoolway* clan. So strong was that relationship that the First Nations headman had gifted Briggs his daughter, Woretemoeteryenner in that year. This would have secured a bond between whites and blacks and furthered the continuance of the relationship between sealers and the local nation in that region. Provided the mariner kept the First Nations women safe and well fed, it meant a secure passage for him and the Kelly gang when they were sailing in that Bass Strait islands region in early 1816. Briggs had been around those islands since he had been employed in the sealing trade since about 1801. He had learnt the language of the Trawlwoolway and had developed a reasonably good relationship with some (but certainly not all) of the local nations.

Photographs of Woretemoeteryenner when older, depict a rather thin, dark haired woman with piercing eyes and a pleasant, relaxed manner. She became accepted as "Mrs Briggs" by the colonists. This gave her a somewhat unique status, for being described in this manner was a 'distinction' apparently not afforded to any other Palawa woman who came to live in a common-law relationship with a sealer. She bore several children, including Dalrymple (Dolly), Eliza in 1817, Mary in 1818, and John in 1820. Another child was burnt at a sealers' camp, although the circumstances remain nebulous. According to Maggie Walter and Louise Daniels,[1] Dalrymple appears to be the first child born of a relationship between a white man and an Australian woman in

[1] Maggie Walter and Louise Daniels, "Personalising the History Wars: Woretemoeteryenner's Story" in *International Journal of Critical Indigenous Studies*, Vol.1, No.1, 2008, 35.

Van Diemen's Land.[2] At some point, a decision was made to give Dolly, then aged about six years old, over to the care of the Van Demonian surgeon Dr Mountgarrett. The doctor adopted her soon afterwards; Whether this decision was made by Briggs, his wife, or both of them is unknown. Dolly lived in Mountgarrett's household in Port Dalrymple for many years on the basis that her mother could come and visit her at any time, which she sometimes did.

Woretemoeteryenner remained with Briggs for about 10 years until 1820, but the relationship was not exclusive, as is made clear in Kelly's journal while he circumnavigated Tasmania. Briggs had two wives and five children on Cape Barren Island, an 'arrangement' that did not create any bad blood with her father because polygamy was a common tform of raltionship practised by several mariners living in the Straits and the First Nations tribes and clans.

When the Kelly crew came into contact with Mannalargenna and his people at Ringarooma Point, Briggs indicated to him that Woretemoeteryenner was safe. The leader responded that he knew as he saw "her smoke" communicating with him almost every day.

After 1820, the relationship between Briggs and his wife broke down irretrievably. For at that time, he allegedly traded her to John (James) Thomas for a guinea. Thomas, who was nicknamed "Long Tom" had been employed in two very prominent respectable colonial capacities, as a pilot from 1812, and later as a constable at Port Dalrymple. However, when he later decided to visit the islands in the Straits, he chose to settle on Preservation Island where Munro lived. In 1831, Robinson in his notes about the Straitsmen, described Thomas as having inhabited that island for two years with 'two Aboriginal women at present concealed'. According to other records, he partnered with several First Nations women over his life of about 86 years. When his new 'partner' Mrs Briggs came to reside on the island with her son John is not known. Indeed, little is known of her life between the time she was sold to Thomas and about 1825, so one can only speculate about her relationship

---

[2] This may or may not be true as relationships between white men and black women in Tasmania had most probably commenced well before the Briggs' relationship. No doubt children probably were born to mixed-race parents and survived the harsh conditions in Tasmania and the islands.

with that sealer during this period.

In late 1825, Woretemoeteryenner suddenly re-appeared in the colonial records. She had freed herself from a sedentary existence. As she was a capable mariner, she joined a sealing crew composed of sealers and First Nations women to venture to the French islands of St Paul and Amsterdam, a noted seal haven. This may have been prompted by the depletion in seal stocks around Bass Strait. Reaching King Georges Sound, the crew did not stay long before anchoring at St Pauls. Unfortunately, when they reached that volcanic outcrop, the seas were too treacherous to fish. So, the captain decided to make for Rodrigues Island, leaving Mrs Briggs, another female and one sealer stranded at St Pauls, promising to collect them once he replenished supplies. But this did not eventuate.

Around December 1825, Woretemoeteryenner and the other castaways took matters into their own hands. A rare visitor anchored at the outcrop and the stranded sealing party were accepted on board a vessel sailing to the town of St Louis on Mauritius. They languished there until early May 1827, when the colonial government became aware of the women's predicament and funded a return voyage to Sydney.[3] Eventually, Mrs Briggs, along with the one other surviving First Nation woman, were returned to Launceston. By then, the women had become close friends. Unfortunately, Briggs' companion died suddenly, leaving her grief-stricken.

Woretemoeteryenner did not remain on the mainland long, soon returning to the Straits. She next appeared in the official records in about 1831 as living with some Aboriginal women on Penguin Island under the control or safekeeping of a man called Turnbull, of whom we know next to nothing. Walyer probably was there at the same time. By then, Robinson was on his pied piper quest to entice or force all the women located with the sealers in the islands to follow him to the Flinders Island Aboriginal establishment, Wybalenna.[4] When Robinson's agent Parish arrived to do his

---

[3] Apparently, one woman and a child died while at Mauritius.
[4] In one version, the word means 'Black Man's Houses'.

bidding, the women were concealed. But the First Nations women may have avoided Parish but for the fact that he also used a female tracker, Tekartee.[5] Robinson's journal entries noted that the women went willingly with Parish, but we have no idea of knowing if this was really the case.[6] Given Walyer's temperament and hostility towards the white 'invaders', it was unlikely.

When Woretemoeteryenner reached Wybalenna, she was given an Anglicised name, Margaret. From that point, she was the subject of Robinson's attempts to 'conciliate and civilise' the remaining First Nations survivors. While there, she formed a relationship with an Aboriginal man called 'Phillip'. He died in 1839. By this stage, some of Mrs Briggs' children were living on the main island, and her daughter, Dalrymple, by much perseverance, made a successful application by petition to have her mother brought into her care. So, Woretemoeteryenner left the confines of the Establishment and came to live for the rest of her life in Perth with Dolly, her husband, an ex-convict, and her grandchildren in 1841. It is important to note that she was allegedly the only Aboriginal Tasmanian ever to leave Wybalenna without restriction, which may indicate just how "civilised" and trustworthy the authorities thought she had become. On 13 October 1847, when she was over 50 years old, she passed away.[7]

Like almost all of the First Nations people, Woretemoeteryenner herself never had the opportunity or means to tell about the relationships she had with Briggs, Thomas, Turnbull, the other sealers on the journey to Mauritius, nor Phillip. However, there is enough information available through the colonial records to understand that she was able to adapt to the Anglo colonial society, eventually living among the more respected colonial settlers despite her removal from Trawlwoolway country. The events in her life demonstrate a common theme where First Nations women

---
[5] Tekartee was born about 1809 and was taken by Parish to the Establishment in or about 1830 but died at Maria Island the next year. She was described as a 'fine tall straight woman' in *Bass Strait People 1790-1850, Aborigines, Sealers and others*. (Word Press Publications, 2010), No. 45, 5.
[6] Plomley. *Friendly Mission*, 294, 296-297.
[7] Walter, M., & Daniels, L. (2008). Personalising the History Wars: Woretemoeteryenner's Story. *International Journal of Critical Indigenous Studies*, 1(1), 41.

crossed the boundaries of both worlds while adapting to changing circumstances in her role as mother, partner and mariner. She was a survivor who was prepared to adopt white ways to prevent her early demise.

The Warrior

In contrast to Woretemoeteryenner's experience, and at the other end of the relationship spectrum, there is another more colourful history. The life and times of Tarenorerer, also known as 'Walyer' (or sometime 'Walloa'), a *Plairherehillerplue* clan woman. She was born around 1800 also in north-eastern Tasmania. From the late 1820s, she gained a fearsome reputation among the colonists. The settlers perceived her as a renegade leader of the surviving First Nations peoples. She was portrayed as an angry pariah who hated both colonisers and some Aboriginal clans. Over a few short years, she led her gang of First Nations warriors into wars against both white and black. The sealers found her a handful; a chameleon-like character who had a complex and divergent relationship with these men. Often armed with muskets and pistols, she would have terrified all who stood in her way. Recently, the Bandimaya painter, Julie Dowling, depicted her on Country displaying a fierce piercing gaze, dressed in a skin cloak and green dress and well-armed.

She came to live with the sealers early on in her adult life, but how she did is open to debate. Three possibilities arise. One was that she was either sold to sealers directly by her own nation. Another was that she had been abducted by another clan and traded in exchange for flour and dogs. A third was that she may have decided to join the sealers in Bass Strait after causing trouble with her clan. Apparently, four of her siblings joined a sealing collective sometime later,[8] so one can assume that their relationships with the sealers at that time was reasonably harmonious. This would no doubt have occurred by 1828, when Walyer is recorded as living with sealers, who educated her in European ways. They taught her English, how to handle the whaleboats and, of most relevance,

---

[8] See http://www.utas.edu.au/library/companion_to_tasmainan_history/ W/Walyer.htm, January, 2009, 2.

how to use firearms, a skill which was to haunt the good burghers of Van Diemen's Land shortly afterwards. For reasons unknown, Walyer abruptly left the sealing community in 1828 to return to the mainland. Once in familiar Country, she formed a new First Nations resistance alliance near Port Sorell based around the Plairhekenhillerplue (Emu Bay) nation. Her four sisters followed in her footsteps. After training her followers to use white man's weaponry, Walyer and her gang commenced a hostile and indiscriminately aggressive campaign to attack other First Nations and white settler properties and livestock, which lasted about two years. Her strategy was specifically designed to drive the "luta tawin" out.[9] During this short 'reign of terror' she also conducted a hostile campaign against the employees of the Van Diemen's Land Company, some of whom were known to have committed outrages against her people. Walyer would have been aware of this.

Although she eventually came back to live with the sealers, she was somewhat resistant to attempts to force her to work. Exasperated, the mariners quickly removed her to Penguin Island. This did not deter Walyer from further resistance. When she finally was enticed by Parish to accept his 'offer' to bring her to Swan Island, she endeavoured again to foment rebellion among the women.[10] Anecdotal evidence of her aggression, power and influence, probably conveyed by the more 'friendly' First Nations people , such as Woorady, Manalagaenna, or perhaps Truganina. reached the Conciliator. Robinson already had knowledge of her exploits and colourfully described her:

> From several aborigines, I have received information respecting an amazon named Tarerenore alias 'Walyer' who was at the head of an aboriginal banditti. This woman speaks English, and issues orders in a most determined manner. Several cattle belonging to the company have been speared, and several petty

---

[9] Luta Tawin is the name that some current Palawa historians use to describe 'white man'. See Vicki Matson-Green 'Part 11 Leaders among Pallawah Women' in *Tasmanian Historical Research Association*, P & P 41/2, June, 1994, 67.

[10] See Maryanne. Jebb and Anna. Haebich, "Across the Great Divide: Gender Relations on Australian Frontiers", in Kay Saunders and Raymond Evans (eds.) *Gender Relations in Australia: Domination and Negotiation* (Sydney, Harcourt Brace, 1994), 40.

> thefts have been committed, which I have traced to this woman. This Amazon is at war with several nations of aborigines, and many aborigines have been slain by her party. The Amazon is an athletic woman, middle-aged, and is a native of the East Coast. She has collected together the disaffected of several nations, and roams over a vastylent of country committing dire outrages.[11]

It is clear that 'the Amazon' was conducting an orchestrated campaign of violence. Her targets were not only some First Nations, but also white settlers, who now occupied much of the land where she had previously lived with her people. Walyer had significant power over the members of the newly formed Australian renegade band, and over the colonial settlers and authority figures, who feared her greatly. Her campaign continued until about 1830, when her followers had dwindled in numbers and the gang disbanded. At that stage, she returned to live with the sealers on Penguin Island. This may have been her only available option. She was accompanied by Trildoborrer, one of her siblings.[12] It is not clear whether she returned voluntarily or by force.[13] However, what is clear is that she had evaded capture or even worse by all her sworn enemies. This was a remarkable achievement given the hostility she had generated, the strategy mounted by Arthur to drive the First Nations people into confined spaces in the dystopian Black War and the superior forces lined up against her. Robinson's patience with her waned significantly in late 1830. She was causing alarm with her unpredictable behaviour. Walyer was trying to get the women to revolt against Robinson and his minions informing them that the colonial men were going to shoot them all. One of the sealers Turnbull had faced almost certain death at her hands but just managed to escape and had become aware that she had taught

---

[11] The meaning of the word 'vastylent' appears unknown, although the word 'vasty' means immense and therefore it is likely to mean something like 'an immense area'.

[12] Brian Plomley. *Weep in Silence, A History of the Flinders Island Aboriginal Settlement with the Flinders Island Journal of George Augustus Robinson 1835-1839* (Hobart: Blubber Head Press, 1987), 830.

[13] Vicki Maikutena Matson-Green, an Indigenous historian, asserts that she was removed by sealers to the Hunter Islands whereas Ian McFarlan says that she returned voluntarily. https://www.utas.edu.au/library/companion_to_tasmanian_history/W/Walyer.htm

her female companions how to load and fire a gun The Conciliator, alarmed by what he was told, sought through his lackey Parish to imprison her. But Walyer had been concealed by other sealers and continued living with the mariners, hunting seals and dragging mutton birds out of holes. However, by December 1830, Robinson was keen to end her reign of terror:

> By these men (sealers) she has been tutored in all sorts of mischief. She became so desperate – and possessing a great deal of cunning – she was not only dread by the whites, numbers of whom have been massacred by her, she was the terror to all the natives she came in contact with, a great many of whom this Amazon caused to be killed.[14]

In February 1831 Robinson made an entry in his diary whereby he traced nearly all the 'mischief perpetrated upon the different settlements' to her recruits.

She may have been in a relationship with the mariner known as 'Norfolk Island Jack' Williams, but we have no further detail of the nature of that relationship. At some time during 1831, she was allegedly 'given up' to the 'authorities' by some sealers, an event which delighted Robinson, who exuberantly wrote:

> A matter of considerable importance to the peace and tranquillity of those districts where she and her formidable coadjutors had made themselves so conspicuous in their wanton barbarous aggression.... A most fortunate thing that this woman is apprehended and stopped in her murderous career... The dire atrocities she would have occasioned would be the most dreadful that could possibly be conceived.[15]

Once in the hands of the Conciliator, she could have been charged with multiple offences. And even faced the death penalty if convicted. Ironically, despite the rhetoric of Arthur and Robinson about her alleged criminality, she never faced Western justice. Whether or not this was because of Robinson's influence is open to conjecture. But that did not matter as the Conciliator achieved his aim as she was effectively "incarcerated" in the settlement at Wybalenna. That is where she spent the last few months of her life,

---

[14] Plomley. *Weep in Silence*, 334.
[15] See http://www.adb.online.anu.edu.au/biogs/AS10455b.htm January, 2009.

finally succumbing to influenza in 1831, just like most of the First Nations people who ended their days there. This was a particularly miserable end for a woman of considerable power and influence within the Aboriginal Tasmanian community, a woman whose relationships with many other First Nations peoples was difficult.

Walyer has been the subject of debate among writers and historians, including those of Indigenous background. Some, like the black writer Vicki Maikutena Matson-Green, see Walyer as a resistance warrior leading the charge to rid their lands of white oppressors. Others see her as someone who should be categorised as a First Nations hero. The colonial authorities, including Robinson, tagged her as a criminal. The sealers had what appeared to be a mixed and ambivalent relationship with her. At one stage, according to Robinson, she was so hostile to the Straitsmen that she even wanted to kill a sealer and steal his whaleboat even when she became involved in trying to rescue other mariners who had been stranded on a reef. At other times, Walyer's relationships were clearly positive. But it is reasonably clear that she had fought alongside Australian men and against white settlers for a short but very active period. Eventually, she realised it was in her best interest to cohabit with the sealers in the Straits rather than succumb to the Conciliator's influences. Her power over other First Nations people was such that the conciliator was concerned she would deliberately assist the other women to 'mutiny'.[16] That could have jettisoned the Conciliator's campaign. At the very least, she was a leader of her nation and developed resistance practices with her comrades endeavouring to forestall the ultimate threats to her people and culture. Perhaps the controversial sealer and one time King of Iceland, Jorgen Jorgensen, was right for once when he wrote:

> It is not improbable that some future writer might have extolled Walloa (sic Walyer), the female native into a heroine, as the defender of her nation's woods against the aggressions of the British Red Queen (meaning Boudiccea) who, it is said, resisted the Roman Arms for nine years.

---

[16] Plomley, *Friendly Mission*, 296.

The lives of Walyer and Woretemoeteyenner and their relationships with sealers represent a typical diverse and complex cross-cultural dynamic that developed and changed over time. Their partly shared 'history' illustrates a broad range of the patterns that occurred in these troubled, ambivalent and divergent relationships. Both were subject to either a friendly or enforced exchange system that was common between blacks and whites. They were part of polygamous relationships which were also typical. Each acquired an education in the white man's ways when it came to speaking English and the use of boats and sealing equipment. The women participated in the sealing trade and found their way by force or otherwise at Wybalenna. They certainly would have been subject to exploitation and violence in one way or another from some of these men. Finally, and importantly, they adapted to the changing colonial environment they were faced with. However, there were differences. Mrs Briggs was a survivor, despite being subject to many challenges that confronted her. Walyer was a warrior confronting the colonisers with venom and hostility before succumbing to her incarceration at The Establishment. Collectively, they were, to a large extent, representative of the histories of other First Nation women in relationships or encounters with sealers during the relevant colonial timeframe.

It is not possible to categorise the divergent and complex relationships that existed and developed over time between black women and white mariners into a binary. Certainly, many of the First Nations people initially had been abducted by sealers or forced into arrangements against their will. For example, the naval surgeon Cunningham. wrote several letters about his visits to the southern Antipodes in the 1820s. In his 1827 volume, he devoted part of one letter to what had caused a stir in colonial circles:

> The men have reached that point by coasting along in boats and having seized and carried off native women.[17]

While such events were common, many of the forced relationships changed over time as the sealers grew older and became

---

[17] Cunningham, Vol. 2, fn. 206.

more reliant on their partners while the women asserted themselves to retain their families and culture. Then there were others who formed meaningful and strong long-standing partnerships with the men for personal reasons. One example was the marriage of the American mariner Chase to Marianne Letitia, the part-First Nations daughter of Lieutenant Governor David Collins.[18] Some arrangements were temporary sexual liaisons. These were ones where sealers sought out the women for sexual encounters, and then chose to either leave or exchange them with other mariners.

There were many liaisons that were polygamous. In such collectives, several women either voluntarily or by force were part of a large family with the First Nations women acting as concubines. Then several of these arrangements developed so that the nature of the partnership changed over time. All reliable records indicate that the relationships between the mariners and the women were complex and evolving. This chapter seeks to dispel the myths and stereotypes that have developed through the histories written since that time, including the notion that these relationships were all rigidly one-dimensional, whereby the women were *always* subject to some type of "slave trade", force or constant exploitation.

When the colonial mariners first encountered First Nations peoples there was little hostility between the races. By chance or good fortune, the two divergent collectives often entered into barter systems for their benefit. Unfortunately, in several cases, this changed to aggression and violence over time. These included incidences following misunderstandings between parties or conduct resulting in one-sided or mutual hostility. So far as can be ascertained from the historical material, only one or perhaps two of these violent confrontations could amount to what has been defined as a 'massacre'.[19] One of these encounters occurred in early 1806. Sealers operating from the sloop The George were surrounded by Kudingal men on the beach Twofold Bay. By then, the vessel had been wrecked with its crew stranded. The dispute

---
[18] Death Notice for Chase (aka 'Chace') *The Sydney Gazette,* 26 July 1826.
[19] Lyndall Ryan in her recent attempt to document all of the massacres of Indigenous people in Australia by whites defined 'massacre' as 'the indiscriminate killing of six or more undefended people'.

may have started because of previous attempts by sealers or others to obtain the services of females by force, but there is no certainty about this. It appears that, out of fear or frustration, the sealers fired their muskets at the First Nations men who gathered on the beach, killing several and wounding more. The Kudingal retreated. The incident was reported by the Governor to Earl Camden shortly afterwards:

> I am sorry to observe that a small private colonial vessel laden with sealskins, was stranded in Twofold Bay, near the south part of this coast.
>
> The natives in great numbers surrounded the few men belonging to the vessel, commencing their attack by setting the grass on the surrounding ground on fire, and throwing spears, which, according to report, rendered it necessary to fire on them, when some of the natives were killed.[20]

According to the report in the local press, the 11 sealers shot nine local men "in self-defence". Afterwards, in a ghoulish attempt to ward off reprisals, the mariners hanged the bodies in the trees around the bay. The bodies were collected by the natives the next morning.[21] The crew may have been saved from further attack or deprivation by the piratical crew of the Venus, which anchored in the bay rescuing the terrified mariners. Apart from this incident, it is not possible to find any event where sealers were responsible for massacring several Aboriginal people at one time. However, that is not to say that sealers and other mariners did not commit ad hoc murders and other violent acts perpetrated against First Nations peoples.

In the main, there was much less conflict between sealers and First Nations peoples along the coastlines of the Fishery than between settlers and employees of the Van Diemen's Land Company and those people. The latter repeatedly clashed either over the occupation by colonial settlers of Country and hunting regions or with ex-convict Company men. Sealers were not involved in disputes over land or Country. One of the most

---

[20] Governor Philip Gidley King to Earl Camden 15 March 1806. Also reported in *The Sydney Gazette*, 6 April, 1806.
[21] Ibid.

outrageous of these events occurred at Cape Grim in 1828 when over 30 Peerapper people lost their lives at the hands of these men. Following this massacre, several of the surviving Aboriginal women sought refuge and fled to the sealers' camp near Robbins Passage to seek protection. Robinson on a mission to investigate the circumstances of the massacre voyaged there an interviewed the women. Some were forthcoming and gave graphic accounts of the murders. Despite his scathing report identifying some of the perpetrators, and, as was often the case, not one faced justice.

Violent encounters between sealers and First Nations people occurred on a much more ad hoc and sporadic basis. Mostly, these confrontations were over the forced removal of women by the mariners. One particular example was a gang, most aggressive in their attempts to force women from their nations, when they voyaged to the South Australian coast from Kangaroo Island. This crew of five sealers landed at Cape Jervis, and then walked to Lake Alexandrina. There they waited until the Aboriginal men had gone off hunting and then set upon the women, forcing them into their boat before returning to Hog Bay on the island where they were put to use in their sealing enterprises. When the womens' menfolkfound out, they sought revenge. Attacking the mariners on a walk inland however, only resulted in one sealer being speared in the foot. Some of the women later escaped including one who swam 14 kilometers across the Backstairs Passage to the mainland. She survived. There were other cases where First Nations people undertook surprise attacks on mariners on Van Diemen's Land, often for reasons unknown. For example, in 1805, such men assaulted eight sealers and burnt 2,000 seal skins at Great Oyster Bay. Four sealers were killed by First Nations warriors at Cape Portland in 1824, while two more died at Eddystone Point in 1828.

Despite a level of hostility between white and First Nations peoples on first encounters and later, such as that existing on the southern coast of New South Wales,[22] there were harmonious

---

[22] According to Mike Donaldson, Les Bursill and Mary Jacobs in their *A History of Aboriginal Illawarra*, Vol. 2: *Colonisation* the arrival of whaling and sealing ships to work the South Coast from 1801 initiated much violence at Twofold, Batemans and Jervis Bays.

relationships between sealers and First Nations Tasmanians that existed in some regions well prior to the Black War. One example is that of Briggs and the northeastern clans referred to above. Another was the early arrangements between sealers and the Tyereelore people, where there were joint operations involving the women on the islands.[23] That harmony dissipated when it came to the forced removal of Aboriginal women. In addition, it may have been due to greater competition between the mariners and First Nations s peoples for increasingly scarce seal populations. There is no doubt that many sealers treated these people (women in particular) very poorly, but they were not the only such perpetrators. After all, it was not these mariners who wanted to acquire land by force or 'settlement' from the original owners. Most sealers inhabited islands or places where First Nations peoples had never lived, such as on the islands in Bass Strait.[24] As more settlers acquired land for farming and other purposes around the Antipodes, increasing hostility developed between those people and the original owners. Incursions by white settlers and employees of the Van Diemen's Land Company into Country that was occupied by, and had significant cultural and spiritual meaning for, the Tasmanians, also resulted in an escalation of violence. By 1830, the authorities were becoming concerned about the treatment of the First Nations people at the hands of settlers, employees of the Van Diemen's Land Company, escaped and ex-convicts and sealers. For example, Arthur, when writing a letter to the Colonial Secretary in 1830, expressed his concern (while carefully avoiding naming the Company men) in this way:

> That the lawless convicts… with the distant convict stock keepers in the interior and the sealers have acted… With great inhumanity to the Black Nations particularly in seizing their women and promoting in the minds of savages the strongest feelings of hatred and revenge.[25]

---

[23] See, for example, Patsy Cameron *Grease and Ochre; The Blending of two cultures at the Tasmanian Colonial Sea Frontier,* Thesis submitted to University of Tasmania, November, 2008, 79-111.

[24] Most, if not all, of the Australian women who lived with the sealers were natives of the mainlands of Van Diemen's Land or New Holland.

[25] Lieutenant Governor George Arthur to Sir George Murray, 18 September 1830,

The lack of European women in the southern Antipodes was an obvious reason why sexually deprived colonial mariners would seek to kidnap Aboriginal women. Over time another reason prevailed. The First Nations females across the southern Fishery were outstanding hunters and fishers. This was an added incentive to lusty but hungry men. What happened from about the middle of the second decade of the 19th century was that these mariners took opportunities to solve their basic desires and made the most of them.

Early raids seeking women often occurred in circumstances where the local inhabitants had never even seen a man of European descent. Often, wherever possible, the local people endeavoured to avoid such contact by running or hiding away.[26] At the time kidnappings took place many sealers themselves had been subject to various extremes of violence, whether in Britain or on the high seas. As they had experienced violent and lawless existences as maritime men, these men may have looked to impose themselves on people whom they would have perceived as coming from the only class lower than themselves.[27]

In so doing, they knew that their conduct and behaviour would never become subject to any criminal penalty. One of the earliest examples of the kidnapping and forced removal of a First Nations woman by either convicts or sealers occurred about 1807 near Wineglass Bay. The Oyster Bay female Wauba Debar was about 15 years old at the time. She managed to escape taking her captors' dogs with her. Recaptured a short time later, she became part of a sealing crew by force or otherwise. Prior to her demise in 1816, she and her two sealing companions were fishing off the east coast when their boat capsized. Despite suffering a broken arm, Wauba Debar saved both men from drowning, Such heroic efforts gained the respect of the white community in that region.

HRA resumed series III, Vol. IX, 166.
[26] This avoidance behaviour was typical of reactions by First Nations peoples to incursions by white adventurers and explorers in the early western history of first contact. It may indicate either a fear or reluctance to engage with the "visitors".
[27] See Kay Saunders and Raymond Evans (eds.), *Race Relations in Australia Domination and Negotiation* (Marrickville: Harcourt Brace Jovanovich, 1992), 21-22.

She was not unique. Essentially several colonial men forcibly removed women from their families Once secured, many were subject to rape and physical abuse. A few were then exchanged by men for money, commodities or free of charge. Several, such as James Thompson, an adventurer, Thomas Tucker, described a 'notorious' character by Robinson, who also was regarded by the Conciliator as a ringleader and a disabled sealer by the name of Charles Peterson were all active perpetrators.. Tucker also allegedly exchanged one of his female companions with John Beadon at Dog Island. Apart from Briggs' 'transfer' of his wife referred to previously, another sealer named John Morgan allegedly 'sold' his female concubine to a mariner called Williams. The mariner Thompson traded his companion for seal skins. Sealer John Smith handed over the First Nations woman the whites called by the demeaning name 'Boatswain' to the sealer Proctor. Sometimes First Nations women voluntarily chose a new partner such as Moretermorerluneher (Polly) who came to live with William Johnson, after her former companion Charles Petersen, drowned.[28]

Other sealers were abusive and violent early on in their independent careers. Jimmy Everett, who came to the colony on a whaler as a free man, was accused of deliberately "shooting" a First Nations woman on Woody Island, while the sealers Anderson and Gamble deposed to Robinson about several atrocities committed by mariners against these females. Such atrocities included what we now call false imprisonment and physical mutilation for perceived wrongdoing. One of the worst incidences, according to the Conciliator, was the slicing of ears and buttocks of a woman by a particularly cruel sealer. Much of the evidence of these nefarious and tragic events comes from the journals of Robinson, following his 'interviews' with the first Nations women Some intelligence was volunteered by the Straitsmen, but they had reason to keep it all a secret.

Although such exploitation was prevalent, there was a significant cohort of sealers who were not guilty of such abhorrent behaviour. As well, over time, some of the perpetrators of such

---

[28] Plomley and Henley, 48. "Polly" then became part of John Batman's household.

conduct developed divergent and far more positive relationships. But that was all forgotten in the perception that all of the sealers were abusers, exploiters and slave traders. In due course, what happened was that all other "perpetrators", originally identified by the colonial press as acting against First Nations interests on Van Diemen's Land, were forgotten in the desire of Western empires to distance themselves from the 'scourge' of slavery. That led to the development of the trope that sealers were slave traders of the worst kind.

Robinson in his role as devout Christian, was in the forefront of furthering this misleading trope. Part of the development of the anti-slavery movement in the colonies was being led by missionaries and the clergy. The polygamous relationships that many sealers enjoyed were, of course, counter to the prevailing, acceptable Christian doctrine that pervaded European cultures. When it became known by one means or another that First Nations women might have been transferred from one sealer to another, it was an easy step to tag the mariners as 'slave traders'.

The trade in slaves had been abolished throughout the Empire in 1807, although it had not become outlawed until much later. It was a serious topic of conversation in the drawing rooms and coffee houses of England, America and elsewhere. The urge to get rid of its scourge was gaining momentum everywhere. Humanists and evangelists in particular were concerned at the declining populations of First Nations peoples, particularly in Tasmania and Africa. Committees had been formed designed to investigate the fate of various native races. Quakers were often at the forefront of campaigns for the abolition of slavery. The tide against slavery was turning despite the enormous profits derived from it by capitalist traders up until the early 1800s.

By 1815, there had been murmurs in maritime circles about some perceived "slave trading" activity taking place in the Fishery. The first person who appears to have tagged the Straitsmen as 'slave traders' was the colonial master William Stewart:

> They have a custom of getting native women of Van Diemen's Land among them who they mostly obtain by force and keep

> them as slaves or Negroes, hunting and foraging for them...
> and by way of punishment half hang them... or flog them most unmercifully...
>
> Several of them have two to six women who they claim as their private property.[29]

Both Captain Sutherland, in his report to his masters in Sydney in 1819, and the editor of the *Hobart Town Gazette* in 1826[30] expressed similar sentiments. But the journalist appeared to be more concerned about white men cohabiting with "the dark daughters of the Papanas" than about slavery itself.

The perception that sealers might be slave traders received its greatest support during the 1830s when Robinson interviewed several First Nations women. His and others perception was that the sealers were treating their common law wives like African slaves in some sort of systematic collective trading economy. This was a debatable trope with little evidence to support it. Notwithstanding this fallacy, the press were keen not to let the truth get in the way of a rip-roaring yarn. Accounts of slave-trading drew the attention of many in the populace who were keen readers of such stories in the colonial press. Captain Sutherland, when reporting back to those who had funded his expedition to Kangaroo Island, described the sealers as having 'seized the natives', particularly their women and keeping them in a state of slavery...[31] Denigrating and marginalising the mariners as slave traders would have promoted the desire of removing them from the competition for scarce resources. This stereotyping of the mariners as slave traders continued later when Lockyer undertook his expedition to explore the southwestern tip of Western Australia in 1829. He was scathing in his assessment of the mariners' treatment of the local Nyungar women, leading to the arrest of a few sealers.

By the 1830s, evangelicals such as Robinson, along with Quaker missionaries James Backhouse and William Walker came to Van Diemen's Land and entered this discursive space.

---
[29] Letter from W. Stewart to the Colonial Secretary, Sydney, 28 September, 1815.
[30] *Hobart Town Gazette*, 26 August, 1826.
[31] This was despite the fact that the sealers had assisted him in collecting the carcasses of 1500 kangaroos and 4500 seal skins on board his vessel.

This culminated in the further marginalisation of the sealer as a depraved slave trader, exploiter, criminal and creature far worse than the plantation owners of the Americas, who were incapable of Christian redemption. Robinson was appalled by the fact that many sealers lived entirely different lives from mainstream colonial society, firstly by surviving in polygamous relationships, secondly by not practising the Christian faith, and finally by being participants with their partners in indecent revelry, including sexualized dancing, which was confronting to him.

Often, Robinson described the relationship between a sealer and his female partner as one of master and slave.[32] He was keen to point out that the sealers had raided both Van Diemen's Land and the mainland for women since about 1810, and that the first Nations women living with the men were 'no better than slaves' who were 'flogged, assaulted and cut and even kiln' [sic]. After interviewing Mary, a First Nations woman, he recorded that she:

> Informed me the sealers… carry on a complete system of slavery and they barter women in exchange for flour and potatoes…they took her away by force… [there are] fifty women in the Straits and plenty of children… this slave traffic is very common in the Straits and women so bartered and sold are subject to every hardship which their merciless tyrants can think of… Surely this is the African slave trade in miniature and the voice of reason and humanity loudly calls for its abolition.[33]

Despite this pejorative stance, even Robinson's decipherer Plomley, pointed out that the Conciliator's records were 'highly coloured and exaggerated'.[34] This was supported by the colonial secretary in 1832, who was concerned that reports about the sealers were prejudicial and 'may have been exaggerated'.[35] Some of Robinson's journal entries were so difficult to read they may not be interpreted with certainty.[36]

---

[32] See, for example, the entries at pp. 295 and 324 of Plomley's *Friendly Mission*.
[33] Ibid., 82.
[34] Ibid., 436.
[35] Colonial Secretary to Governor Darling, 21 February, 1832, quoted by Plomley at 683.
[36] Robinson kept very detailed journals, notes and commentary for the entire period of his journey through Van Diemen's Land and afterwards from about 1830 to 1835.

Robinson's unsavoury portrait of the sealer as slave trader was widely accepted, despite contrary facts. The conciliator's unfavourable image was copied slavishly by later colonial historians. In 1852, when the sealing industry had effectively run its course, John West, a Christian Minister, wrote a history of Tasmania in two volumes. In the best of colonial prose, he summarised all the negative stereotypes that had become associated with the sealers.[37] In 1884, the humanitarian James Bonwick, in an emotionally charged narrative, created a memorial to the "extinct" Tasmanian Aborigine, chastising settlers and sealers, while praising the French for their humanity. He portrayed Robinson in entirely romantic terms while describing the sealers as 'primitive Straitsmen' who oppressed the 'poor stolen gins' who were 'literally the slaves of the sealers'.[38] However, despite his negativity, West conceded that the mariners had some reasonably affectionate relationships with the women. He was humanitarian and intelligent enough to recognise that the mariners should have been compensated for the loss of their agricultural holdings after being expelled by Robinson. Further, he realised that they changed their "mode of life to more legitimate purposes" when they partnered with the First Nations women in undertaking agricultural pursuits. It is this latter realization which reflects more accurately the fact that the independent sealers, many of who had exploited, abused and held these women by force, changed and developed in their relationships over time.

Similarly, even though Robinson was anxious to portray the mariners as evil slave traders, there were entries that either presented or implied a completely different picture. He acknowledged that not all women were badly treated and that some men treated their partners with kindness. One such mariner was Munro. He appeared to fit the category of one who developed more positive relationships later in his life. He was known to have reasonably good partnerships

---

[37] John West, *History of Tasmania* (Launceston: Henry Dowling, 1852), 22, in which he records that the sealers were "convicts whose sentences had expired or such as had contrived to escape" who blended "the profession of the petty pirate and the fisherman".

[38] James Bonwick, *The Lost Tasmanian Race* (London: Sampson Low, Marston Searle and Rivington,1884), 191-195.

with the women who came to live with him on Preservation Island. The Conciliator wrote that 'some spoke approvingly of his household',[39] with the First Nations women being able to contribute significantly to the culture that was developing.

On other occasions, Robinson also noted that there were women who were reluctant to leave their partners and wanted to remain in the company on the islands.[40] One was Fanny, who expressed a strong desire to remain with her Kangaroo Island sealer, Baker.[41] Even more telling are the journal entries relating to Walyer, who had left her nation to live with the sealers, considering herself safer with them than being subject to the violence of other nations, white settlers and soldiers on Country. She only left the mariners' camp by being induced to go with Parish on a false promise thus falling into a well-set trap.[42]

A contrary more balanced opinion to Robinson and others was tenable at the time. When the French commander D'Urville anchored in one of the harbours of Kangaroo Island in 1826, in the L'Astrolabe, he "fell in with" an islander collective there and had a chance to observe the relationships first-hand:

> Aboriginal women found life with European men more pleasing than with men of their own race because European men treated them with much more respect.[43]

This opinion was corroborated by two of his more learned maritime crew, Qiouy and Gainard, when they encountered mariners at King Georges Sound. Here, they observed that the 'Englishmen' had some Australian women with them who were:

> …very useful to them in getting sustenance for them… or even with guns. They quickly become very skilled with the latter: once these unfortunate women have forgotten their state of freedom in which they are illtreated by their husbands anyway, they can only find pleasant the lives they live with the Europeans who treat them far better.[44]

---

[39] Plomley and Hemsley, 21.
[40] This is conceded also by Plomley, 18.
[41] Ibid., 82-83.
[42] Ibid., 296-297.
[43] D'Urville. Vol.1, 197-198.
[44] Ibid., 45 (from the Officers' Diaries).

Nothing from the Frenchmen about slavery! Indeed, in reflecting on the role that the women play in their lives, the sealers were happy to reveal to the French that the women were essential to them, not only in their operations but also in avoiding death by starvation.

This different perception of the sealer as operating within a cooperative partnership with Aboriginal women came about as the French had no axe to grind with these mariners; whereas the traders, Robinson and colonial editors did.

Also, to some extent, the "exchange" system and the use of force to kidnap women mirrored what had occurred with Aboriginal nations from time immemorial. Prior to the arrival of the sealers in places of first encounter, it was not uncommon for clans to either exchange women in a trading relationship to cement ties or abduct females from their enemies. In December 1831, while on a journey with Robinson, Woorady informed the Conciliator that the Melukerdees, occupiers of the Huon Valley region, were constantly abducting females belonging to the Mowernee and other tribes by force. Such tribes were so afraid of this aggressive nation that they willingly gave up their women to their enemies.

While acknowledging that these mariners used Indigenous women for sexual satisfaction, due to the almost total absence of white females,[45] it is also interesting to note that, by the early 1800s, sealers had observed the extraordinary ability and dexterity of these women as hunters and fishers. Many mariners would have realised the advantages of utilising First Nations women for that purpose alone. It is doubtful whether the mariners were capable swimmers; whereas it is clear from primary sources that the women were adept at it, across the entire expanse of the Fishery. There were many reports of mariners dying by drowning in the watery environs they occupied. One example was Robinson's record in December 1830, in which two Hunter Island sealers drowned when their temporary makeshift craft capsized as they tried to reach Clarke Island.

Early examples of the usefulness of First Nations partners to

---

[45] As far as I am aware, there were very few single white females living on any of the islands at this time

their white companions were evident as early as 1802 when Baudin in the Astrolabe reached King Island off the north coast of Van Diemen's Land. Anchoring in a bay, he encountered the sealer Cowper (and his gang). Baudin was informed that the mariners were there for the purposes of obtaining seal skins and elephant oil following orders from the Sydney trader Campbell.[46]

The French zoologist Peron journalled that Cowper lived with a First Nations woman, described as the sealer's 'wife and chief housekeeper'. Whether this meant that there was more than one female acting in the second capacity is uncertain, but the Frenchman did not express any adverse comments. Later, in 1816, at different times in his journey circumnavigating Tasmania, Briggs came into contact with two warring "chiefs" of the northern tribes. They were both well aware of the personal relationships he had formed with several First Nations women.

As far as First Nations leaders were concerned, there was nothing unusual in the sealer having more than one Australian woman as his companion and partner. Indeed, it was readily accepted in First Nations circles. In the 1820s and 1830s, around Kangaroo Island and Albany, there were many mariners, such as Everett, George Meredith Junior and Gamble, who had several Australian women as partners. These women were active as crew on the whaleboat voyages and hunters, providers, carers, and produced many lifestyle objects required by their companions.

When the Kelly crew meet with Tolobunganna in January 1816, it was the women who delivered kangaroos to the mariners in exchange for seals. Called upon by their leader to procure the mammals, the women, not the mariners, took the initiative and controlled the whole process. According to Kelly, the Palawa insisted the crew not 'come near them' until they had disposed of the seals slumbering on the rocks. They then undertook most of the work to prepare the seals for cooking. It was only then that the women requested a share of the catch, with which the sealers complied. The event, as recorded by Kelly, suggested the

---

[46] Daniel Cowper had originally been based at Kent Bay having journeyed there on the *Nautilus* in 1798.

women controlled the process. Sealers chose not to interfere with those traditional arrangements. Kelly's observations about these relationships highlighted that, sometimes, it was the women who were dominant participants in the procurement of seals and other prey.

Not only were women very successful seal hunters, they also had a significant degree of autonomy among Aboriginal communities. This allowed them freedom to conduct certain economic and cultural activities without the consent of their menfolk. They were able to undertake seal hunting expeditions using waddies and clubs on their own. This autonomy would have been observed by the sealers, which meant the women could and often did act independently of them particularly as the sealers grew older and developed trust in them.[47]

During both the early and final colonial sealing decades, the active participation of Aboriginal women across the Fishery in collective hybrid families was common. For example, prior to 1820, on the northeast coast of Van Diemen's Land, the First Nations people gathered in anticipation of the arrival of the sealers at the beginning of the "killing" season. The men then anchored in their whaleboats offshore. They would meet and greet the local people, who would demonstrate their appreciation by performing a dance. Then a meeting would determine which women were to assist them with the subsequent seal hunt. Several First Nations people would be in the employ of the sealers for short periods. Many returned to their nation, often carrying seal carcasses. Others, who may have been abducted from another nation, would be exchanged for dogs, flour, mutton birds, and sometimes for seals.[48]

Fast-forward to 1831 when Kelly, now part of the Hobart gentry, was invited to give evidence to the Aborigines Committee about the relationships between the First Nations women and their colonial husbands:

---

[47] Lynette Russell, "Dirty Domestics and Worse Cooks: Aboriginal Women's Agency and Domestic Frontiers, Southern Australia 1800-1850," in *Frontiers: A Journal of Women's Studies*, Vol. 28, No.12, 21.
[48] See Ryan, 3.

> The sealers in Bass Strait sometimes stole the native women from the main and at one time the native men would sell a native woman for 4 or 5 carcasses of seals. Some of the sealers had three or four black native women who they ill-treated… most of the sealers are an abandoned ferocious set…

But then came this observation:

> The women were not always unwilling to go and after a time preferred stopping on the islands in the Straits.[49]

Kelly's evidence was given when attitudes had well and truly shifted; sealers had become the object of scorn and ridicule in the eyes of the press and authorities. But his words illustrate that by then many of the First Nations women voluntarily wanted to remain in the company of their common law husbands.

Unfortunately, the voice of these women in the historical records is almost absent. But, by close examination of documents, the use of First Nations oral history, the assistance of archaeology and ethnography and the untidy notes of Robinson, we can discover some of these voices. The journals Robinson kept of sealers and First Nations women is the only major and complete historical work on this subject.[50] Nonetheless, it is quite clear that abductions of women across the expanse of the Australian southern Antipodes by mariners were common. But it was not possible for anyone to establish who these First Nation women were or where exactly they came from until Robinson's journals were published well after 1830. The Conciliator made extensive notes about the mariners and the origins of the partners they were living with. These records appear to demonstrate that, so far as Kangaroo Island was concerned, there were about 22 Van Demonian women living with the sealers there, but even that estimate is difficult to establish with any certainty.[51] From the 14 that Robinson identifies as being on the island, 11 or

---

[49] British Parliamentary Papers on the subject of the military operations lately carried on against the Aboriginal inhabitants of Van Diemen's Land. Colonial Department Downing Street, Howick, 23 September, 1831, 51.
[50] Plomley and Henley, 34-69.
[51] In that regard, Rebe Taylor admits there were possibly many more that were not accounted for, although Robinson only records 14 living on the island by 1831. There was at least one who was definitely not on the Conciliator's list. Taylor, 34.

12 came from Tasmania's north coast, while another two or three came from Bruny Island and were related to Truganini.[52]

Over on Bass Strait, Robinson accounted for 74 First Nations women living with sealers on the islands by 1831. Plomley and Henley identified about 62. Yet the difficulty of establishing accurately how many women were living with sealers, wherever they were located, is illustrated by Manning Clark, one of Australia's most respected historians. He estimated that there were upwards of 200 men and women inhabiting Kangaroo Island in 1826, only four or five years before Robinson concluded that there were only 14 women living there![53]

If Robinson is to be believed, then there were several serial offenders who were said to have abducted the women. From a quick analysis of the numbers, Plomley and Henley estimated that at least 35 of the Australian women were removed by force, another 16 were living with the sealers in a common-law arrangement, two were married to their partners, and the status of four others appears to be unknown. As far as Robinson was concerned, some perpetrators included the Constable of the Straits, Munro, who is alleged to have removed three of these women: Dromedeemmer, known as "Mary"; Drummernerlooner, also known as "Jumbo" or "Louisa"; and Mirnermannerme also known as "Maria Monamie", all from the mainland.[54] Briggs (Kelly's travelling companion) is alleged to have abducted Meetoneyernanner, also known as "Dumpe" and Woretermoeteyenner, also known as "Bung".[55] Black John Baker was a prolific offender, absconding with at least four: Ghoneyannenner, also known as "Peacock"; Lowhenunhe, also known as "Mary"; Maakekerledede, also known as "Sal"; and Murrerninghe, also known as "Kit".[56] From my review of Friendly

---

[52] The most famous of the First Nations women of the period, Trukaninni (or Truganini) was enthusiastic about the Conciliator's efforts to "save" her and the other Australians for a time and accompanied him on his journey northwards from Bruny Island.

[53] See Manning Clark, *History of Australia. The Beginning of an Australian Civilization 1824 to 1851,* Vol. 3 (Collingwood: Melbourne University Press,1973), 12.

[54] Plomley and Henley, 112 and 116.

[55] Ibid., 115-116 and 123.

[56] Ibid., 113 and 116.

Mission, it would appear that there may have been about another 20 sealers who engaged in the forceful removal of the Palawa from Tasmania.

Some of the women as participants in the sealing communities did not necessarily stay with their abductors. Several came, by one means or another, to survive in a more mobile fluid and temporal lifestyle almost unimpeded. In choosing voluntarily to make lifestyle changes they were proactive in seeking a better outcome for themselves and some agency. For example, Mirnermannerme, after being abducted by Munro, allegedly lived with David James Kelly of Hunter Island and became a mother to some children before settling with John Myetye at the same place. Later, she was found voyaging on a sealing vessel to Mauritius. Pierrapplener, also known as "Dinah", was probably living with James Kirby in 1824. Later, she spent time sailing between the Straits and Kangaroo Island with one of the most successful small-scale sealers, Everett, and his partner, the islander, Henry Whalley. Dinah came into contact with the crew of the *Nereus* before finding her way to King Georges Sound. She remained sealing there until Major Lockyer arranged for her to board the Ann destined for Sydney. However, Dinah jumped ship at Port Dalrymple. By October 1832, she was recorded living with the sealer Robert Rew, but W. J. Darling, who had become the Superintendent of Wybalenna, had her removed from the mariner. Despite Darling's best efforts, Rew had the last laugh when he successfully petitioned for Dinah's return to him. He had alleged that she had been with him since the death of John Myetye, some years before.

A not insignificant number of women who partnered with the sealers in the Fishery came from New Holland rather than Van Diemen's Land. John Anderson,[57] also known as "Abyssinia Jack", was an English sealer who arrived a free man on board the Archduke Charles on 16 February 1813. He chose to reside on at least three

---

[57] There were many sealers who styled themselves "John" or "Jack" Anderson. It would be naïve to assume that all of them were officially that name as many mariners for one reason or another would want to hide their true identity. Also, this is not the famous Black-Jack Anderson who is alleged to have terrified the sealing traders to the west of Bass Strait for many years.

different islands in the Straits. Partnering with Emue (also known as 'Emma'), they had 10 children, five of whom survived. Emue appeared to have originated from the Kaurna region near Rapid Bay, South Australia. She probably was abducted by the sealer George Meredith Junior, a notorious repeat offender, the son of the successful and respected whaler George Meredith Senior. His father employed him on sealing and whaling vessels in and around Bass Strait and Kangaroo Island. But Meredith Junior met his fate when he was killed by First Nations inhabitants of that region as "pay-back" for his abduction of some women following a raid he and others orchestrated from Kangaroo Island. The First Nations peoples who were the subject of violence across the colony had long memories and had acquired a certain notoriety among the colonisers for revenge.

Many of the First Nations women lived lives marred by abduction and deception. One was Kalloongoo. In about July 1836, while Emma was still living with Anderson, Robinson's military troops (led by Corporal Ramsay) arrived at the Bass Strait islands[58] on another mission to remove women from the sealers by force. Here, they located Abyssinia Jack and two other men, including Everett, who, apparently, willingly "gave up" their women. In that regard, Ramsay reported back to Robinson that there were two sealing vessels occupied by several New Holland women and some "half-castes".

In January 1837, Robinson met with Anderson on Woody Island. Here, he saw at least three women, including Emma, and Kalloongoo aged about 20 years, (also known as Sarah), who had a boy with her. Initially she was reluctant to accept overtures from Robinson's henchmen to leave the islands. It took until June 1837 for a Corporal Miller, in the employ of Robinson, anchoring at Woody Island, to convince Kalloongoo to voyage with him to the settlement at Flinders Island. Like most of the Conciliator's lackeys, he promised her repatriation back to the Kaurna lands.[59]

---

[58] Just to the north of Flinders Island.
[59] The Kaurna people are the traditional inhabitants of Adelaide and the plains regions near it.

To Sarah's dismay, this did not happen. She spent the next two years at the settlement before being transported by Robinson to Phillip Island in February 1839. During that time, Sarah came to live in his household where Robinson, for reasons unknown, changed her name to Charlotte. On being interrogated by Robinson, she informed him that she had been kidnapped from a point near Port Lincoln by the sealer James Allen and taken to Kangaroo Island. Here, she remained until being seized by the sealer Johnson. She was sold to a Bill Dutton, who subsequently abandoned her, taking a child of the relationship with him. Sarah alleged to Robinson that she suffered significant violence at the hands of the sealers when first apprehended. Those mariners, she said, were supported and encouraged by their associates; First Nations men.[60]

So, there is no doubt that significant violence was perpetrated by several men against several Aboriginal women, particularly from 1810 until the mid-1820s when there was less scrutiny of the sealers by colonial authority. This would have included forced sexual intercourse resulting in the births of several offspring. Perhaps this is best clarified when one considers that at least five of the women in Plomley and Henley's "census" were alleged to have either aborted or killed what were then described as 'half cast' children. There does not appear to be any direct evidence about why this occurred, but it may well have been a result of the extreme hatred the victims bore to the actions of violent men.

First Nations writers and historians have divergent opinions about the colonial history of these cross-cultural relationships. Jan West, a Palawa woman, descendant of the sealer Everett and his female partner, wrote 'that she felt confused about the history of her grandfather's alleged violent conduct'[61] as written by Robinson. She wanted to 'get back to the 1830s'. The Conciliator's perception of Everett may have been misguided. He alleged that the sealer was guilty of murdering a First Nations woman. In attempting to deal with her great-great-grandfather's conduct, West asked a question

---

[60] See Rob Amery, "Kaurna in Tasmania: A case of mistaken identity," in *Aboriginal History 1996*, Vol. 20, 37-42.
[61] Jan West. *Pride against Prejudice* (Canberra: Australian Institute of Aboriginal Studies, 1987).

that perhaps all historians should be asking: 'How do we know that is the truth?' Attempting to answer, she took aim at Robinson, whom she said could not be believed because he portrayed the sealer as being without progeny, which was clearly false. She went on to say: 'People say that he murdered her, but it doesn't occur to them that she may have died from some disease...'[62] It is open to conjecture whether Everett was guilty of a capital crime, in which case Ms West might be endeavouring to ignore this, or whether Robinson's hatred of this particular mariner may well extend so far as to falsifying or ignoring the historical record.

Other historians have also provided a different perspective. Some have also asserted that the relationships became much more complex where the Palawa did not perceive themselves to be slaves and participated in the Islander collectives with the men freely as wives and partners.[63] Certainly, as a consequence of the miserable failure of the colonisers to prevent the almost complete annihilation of the Tasmanian First Nations people following the Black War and the misguided attempt to force the surviving local peoples onto Flinders Island, the sealers and their Palawa common law wives had a mutual interest in surviving against all odds—which they did by engaging in cross-cultural dynamic partnerships.

By the Conciliator's time, many women had become active partners with the men in a hybrid economy and society that involved not only sealing but many other activities. By the 1830s in Bass Strait, many of the partnerships had led to fixed, stable, cultural and economically independent communities, where permanent habitable huts or buildings had been erected. There were gardens, where crops of various kinds were being grown, and animals such as dogs, horses, goats, pigs and sheep were kept by the families.

When Robinson undertook a tour of the islands in the Straits, he found several well-established islander collectives . On one such voyage, he met Munro on Preservation Island. He was at his most objective, in describing the sealer as having a 'good garden, rabbits,

---

[62] West, 99.
[63] Cameron, 122.

pigs', and as one who 'reads the Bible'. He observed three 'half-caste' children living with the sealer. Afterwards, he visited two other mariners, George Robinson and Charlie Peterson, now in their dotage, who had been living with their respective partners for many years. The older Robinson convinced the younger one to not remove his partner because of the importance she brought to his life on the island and the support that she provided him.

The hybrid partnerships may have been further cemented following the births of children. The progeny often bore the name of their sealer fathers. Even now, those surnames are still used. This demonstrated the sealers' acceptance that they were now a recognised family. Boultbee, when visiting Preservation Island, wrote in his journal that the sealers had children with the Palawa, whose 'dispositions are very prepossessing', with some being sent to Sydney for the purposes of being educated at the 'government school'.[64] F. N. Scott, a resident of King Island, described the women as spending their time hunting, while their partners managed their property and also arranged for their offspring to be educated.[65] Rosalie Here kept a journal of her voyage on the Carolyn where she recorded that she met 'one sweet little boy born to a fisherman and his mother, a native, who spoke English well and who had a little kangaroo skin which we never could prevail on him to take off.'[66] This demonstrated a level of stability in the relationships that flew in the face of the negative stereotype of the sealers. It also indicated that the partners in these relationships were considering a better future and outcome for their families than perhaps they had endured in the past.

One such sealer was William Dutton. By 1828, Dutton had built his own hut on Portland Bay, while growing vegetables in his own garden. Dutton seems to have been somewhere in Bass Strait when the sealer William Allen allegedly sold a First Nations woman, Renaninghe, to him. She came to live with the mariner as his sole

---

[64] Munro lived with at least three Australian women and was described by Boultbee as having a 'cool judgement and natural stability, evidently of Scotch extraction'.
[65] Starke, 201.
[66] Plomley and Hemsley, 23.

partner at the Bay. He fathered a child, Sophia, by this relationship and registered her birth at Launceston,[67] demonstrating his acknowledged responsibility for her. Also, John Scott (also known as Old Scott) had been living at Westernport with a First Nations woman for many years prior to 1826. That year, Captain Whyte in the Duke of York anchored there and observed that Scott and his partner had three children residing with them. When D'Urville anchored there in the same year, he found Scott was now the head of a sealing gang and their families settled on Phillip Island, living in 'triangular-shaped' huts.

After the French reached Port Jackson and instilled a fear of French invasion in the minds of the English authorities, a Captain Samuel Wright was immediately tasked to sail to Westernport with a military crew in the *Dragon* accompanied by a Captain Weatherall in the *Fly*. In the boats, were several convicts and a cohort of settlers. Wright was on a mission to establish a settlement outpost designed to thwart French incursion. When the boats anchored, Wright immediately sought a 'meeting' with Scott and his colleagues . He left no doubt that he wanted them to depart so that he would have no opposition to his plans. The mariners would have none of it. They and their wives made life as difficult as they could for the new arrivals. After two years, Whyte's dreams of establishing a colonial outpost had failed miserably, leaving the sealers to continue unimpeded by any authority. But, by 1827, Scott had finally left Victoria and was firmly established on Tasmania where he seems to have become a respectable member of the community.

It may well have been that Scott had distanced himself from his former maritime associates as he disparaged them in his dealings with colonial authorities.[68] However, despite the new sense of respectability that Scott enjoyed at King Island, it is interesting to

---

[67] G. A. Robinson's Journal Entry ML A7032, 1 June, 1837.
[68] *Hobart Town Gazette*, 25 March, 1826 in which the editor reports: 'John Scott, who has long been an inhabitant of the Straits, and has cohabited there with a black woman, by whom he has three children, declares that he has known three hundred pups to have perished on one bank, owing to the premature desertion of the mothers, driven away by this unseasonable disturbance of the sealers.'

note that he was living there with four First Nations women from Van Diemen's Land who made up his "family", thus maintaining a polygamous relationship that would have been frowned upon by all of the mainstream colonists.

Robinson himself also eventually made some positive observations of the children born from these relationships. In 1830, the Conciliator voyaged to Robbins Island. which is situated just off the far north-west coast of Tasmania.[105] It was home to the Parperloihener people prior to the arrival of the colonizers. He had a meeting with six Palawa, one male Australian and several sealers. Robinson also observed some 'half-caste' children and dogs who had lived for years with the sealers in several cabins covered in grass.[69] The next day, he met another four sealers, including a New Zealander who appeared to be the leader, and two more Australian women. The meeting was very friendly. Robinson observed that the men 'did not abduct the women'. The sealers were 'surprised' when he disclosed his purpose was to remove the women on government authority.[70] Given that these relationships (like many others) appeared to be settled, stable and productive, this would have caused significant anxiety in the minds of the Islanders. It may have also fostered the development of the strategy to resist the drive to remove the women. Their circumstances were reminders of the stability and cultural and economic interdependence of the partnerships wherever Robinson went.

Over the years, the Islander communities developed more sophisticated cultural practices that brought the various collectives in the divergent marine regions together. At some point, the women created a dance called by some (including Robinson) the 'Devil Dance'. They performed this not only for the Islanders but also visitors, such as Robinson. If anything, this reinforced the Conciliator's belief that the men were licentious exploiters of the women. This dance would have further justified Robinson in making every effort to remove the Palawa and "Christianise" them. He described the Islanders' practices as being 'obscene' and

---

[69] Plomley, 179.
[70] Ibid.,180.

'the scene of debauchery', which was 'unfit to mention', while also acknowledging that it was something unique to the Straits.[71] The dance survived Robinson.

Apart from the complex hybrid relationships that developed between the sealers and the Indigenous women, there were other relationships that the mariners enjoyed with the Aboriginal male inhabitants of the Fishery. Although it was the Indigenous women who were more dexterous at killing seals, the prominent leaders among the sealers employed both men and women when it came to the operation of their small-scale businesses, particularly in securing their services for extensive sealing ventures. This made good sense when one considers that their labour came at little cost, allowed the mariners to rely on the knowledge and experience of the local men, and provided a level of security for the sealing captain against aggression on the part of any local nation they may have encountered along the various coastlines. They could rely on the First Nations men as negotiators, liaisons and peacemakers at these times.

In 1833, John Jones, a commercial trader, voyaged to Kangaroo Island in the Henry. He visited Cape Jervis and successfully negotiated with the local Aboriginal community to secure the employ of five men for his sealing venture. Two remained with Jones for five months, sometimes sleeping on shore, and, when their journey concluded, he paid these men in kind with 'pistols, powder and shot'. As a consequence, Jones was never harassed or attacked by any First Nations people during this period.[72] Black-Jack'Anderson, Everett, and Dutton also engaged the services of such men and women on many occasions in their escapades across the Australian Bight, from Kangaroo Island to King Georges Sound.

In New Zealand, during the colonial sealing period, the employment of First Nations peoples as part of mobile sealing crews and the relationships that developed between Māori and mariners took some time to come to fruition. For several years after

---

[71] Plomley, *Friendly Mission*, 295.
[72] Taylor, 60.

Chapter 12: Perpetrators and Partners

first encounters, violence and hostility reigned. Partly because of this, the economic and personal arrangements had a similar nature and pattern to those occurring across the Tasman, but there were differences.

It was much more difficult for horny maritime men to simply abduct females without the fear of unrelenting revenge and reprisal. If a mariner wanted a Māori "wife", he needed to seek approval from her clan or tribe and become part of the clan or family by adopting their customs and culture. They would have needed the consent of the tribe's chief, because the only alternative was certain death. Some sealers were still able to secure a female partner by other means. Often, the relationships were as much about economic and trade opportunities as about sex.

The general modus operandi of the sealing crews employed by the Sydney traders in the Foveaux Straits required the gangs to live a much more mobile existence than their counterparts.[73] But, after a time, some mariners came to live permanently in the southern New Zealand region, seeking ways to establish a better overall relationship with the local peoples. It soon became clear that the local peoples were keen to learn about Western practices such as strategies and methodologies for hunting animals and fish. Just as important was the acquisition of various European chattels, particularly weapons. There was a mutual exchange of maritime skills. Often, such sealers were used by the Māori to seek trading relationships with mainstream merchants or to assist the tribe in their skirmishes with their enemies. Although violence continued to trouble the relationships between the Pakeha sealers and Māori from time to time, in general, the relationships became more harmonious.

One of these colonial mariners was James Caddell. He was a young man and the only survivor on the Sydney Cove, a sealing vessel, cruising near the Bay of Islands, when attacked by some Māori in 1807. His life was spared when he threw himself on an old chief's ka-ka-how,[74] just before he was to be knifed to death.

---

[73] Cumpston, 63 and 66.
[74] An outer blanket or garment.

He became part of the local Māori clan, and, forming a friendship with the chief's daughter, Tokitoki, eventually married her. Caddell learned significant fighting skills, had his faced tattooed and was soon able to speak the local language fluently. By 1822, Caddell had become a chief, earning respect due to his skill and abilities as a warrior and also because of his close ties with his wife's noble family.

Later that year, the sloop *Snapper*, captained by W. L. Edwardson, was on an expedition to procure a native plant, phormium, from Chalky Bay in the South Island. While there, he encountered Caddell and his partner. By then, the 30-year-old former sealer had lost his fluency in English but was able to convince the captain to provide him and his partner with a passage to Port Jackson. Once there, the couple became the talk of the town appearing in public in Māori dress, which drew in fascinated colonial onlookers.[75] Caddell became known as James Mowri. Within two months, the Caddells were on their way back to Ruapuke Island on the Mermaid. There, they assisted Captain John Kent to purchase flax before returning to Sydney to demonstrate their skills preparing this natural fibre. No doubt, Tokitoki had a significant role to play in this task and in educating Caddell about the Māori cultural and social traditions and mores. Later, the sealer passed on the knowledge that he had acquired to Thomas Shepherd in 1826.[76] His life as a warrior by then was a distant memory, even though he would have probably fought against other colonial mariners on the side of his newly adopted family.

Adopting Māori mores and entering a Māori family was sometimes a better option than dealing with hostile colonial competitors. Take, for example, Jacky Price, who during the 1820s formed an intimate relationship with Hinewhitia, an important Pahia woman. Unfortunately for Price, a rival mariner by the name of Robert Kent was also present. Price brought Kent's reputation into disrepute when he mischievously informed some Pahia people

---

[75] John Hall-Jones writing about James Caddell in *Dictionary of New Zealand Biography (1990) Te Ara Encyclopaedia of New Zealand*.

[76] After this date, nothing is known of the life of James Caddell, who simply disappears from all records.

that Robert was a 'slave' who had no authority. When Kent found this out, he was furious. Confronting the sealer and his family, Price would have been murdered if not for the intercession of Hinewitia, who managed to save Price through her influence among the local Ruapuke.[77]

A sealer who chose to adopt a completely independent life across the Tasman with his Māori partners was Thomas Chaseland who is mentioned earlier. As previously described, he was a physically powerful man who had a reputation for his strength and ability in the sealing and whaling industries. He had engendered fear in many, including the Māori, but he was not quite ready to strike out on his own. He started his sealing life in the south of New Zealand by joining a sealing gang living on the coastal fringes and 'progressed by having enduring monogamous relationships with two Māori women over his long life'. Firstly, realising the value of adopting the Māori way of life, he formed an intimate partnership with Puna, the daughter of a local Elder.

The sealer and Puna developed a formidable de facto arrangement whereby they worked his sealing and whaling businesses together. They were on the brig *Industry* when it foundered off Codfish Island. The only survivors of the wreck were the sealer, his partner, and a person named George Moss. Chaseland, who was a strong swimmer, seized hold of his partner and Moss separately before struggling to reach the shore. He then collapsed and would have drowned but for Puna's intercession. The Māori asserted that his partner was instrumental in navigating the harsh conditions faced at the time. After Puna died, Tommy, who also acquired the local name of Tame Titirene, then had further good fortune when he married Pakawhatu. They established a family and remained together until the whaler passed away in 1869.

---

[77] See Angela Wanhalla, *Matters of the Heart: A History of Interracial Marriage in New Zealand* (Auckland: Auckland University Press, 2013).

Caddell's seemingly successful marriage to the Māori princess Tokitoki, Price's loving saviour Hinewhitia and Chaseland's stable relationship with Puna and Pakawhatu were not always typical. Many kinds of relationships developed from the first white encounter with the Māori until the 1840s, when the sealing industry was in decline. Just as was the case in New Holland, these intimate arrangements varied from casual encounters to seasonal arrangements involving sex for money, colonial provisions, or weapons to long-term marriages, often based on local traditions.

While sealers and other mariners enjoyed some harmonious and friendly relationships with many of the Māori, there were violent confrontations as well. Apparently, Chaseland himself was instrumental in two such events. These occurred when he was a resident of a sealing station near Jackson's Bay on the west coast of New Zealand together with a gang, including two African Americans. In the 1820s, members of the Māori from a local village decided to visit the crew's camp by canoe at night apparently in an attempt to take the "white man's treasures". A skirmish took place in which at least one of the sealers was killed. Revenge was swift when Chaseland and his gang, now furious, pursued the Māori, killing some tribesmen before turning their attention on another village further south. At least 30 First Nations New Zealanders died during the resulting violent confrontation. According to local folklore, the sealer was prominent in the slaughter of the local inhabitants and was later rebuked by one of the Māori, who was only a child at the time this incident occurred but had a good memory.

Another example of hostility occurred in 1822, when the sealer John Stewart voyaged with his New Holland partner and their children from Kangaroo Island to the south part of New Zealand. Shortly after anchoring in the Foveaux Straits, they were captured by a First Nations tribe. Probably realising there was no alternative, they adopted the Māori way of life. Once he became a trusted "member", the sealer was employed as a pilot to assist the local tribe in vanquishing Americans. The Yankees had upset the local inhabitants with their overeager and aggressive pursuit of the leviathan and pinniped (similar to what had occurred in the Straits). It is not known exactly what happened to the woman and her children. In a separate incident, an American sealing party were set upon by the Māori. All the Americans were killed. Only one person, a South Australian First Nations woman living with the mariners managed to find her way to Sydney in April 1824 unharmed.

Despite such confrontations, recent archaeological evidence has established the likelihood of more harmonious arrangements between the mariners and Māori beyond the South Island. In 1825, apparently some mariners established a settlement at Sealers Bay on Codfish Island on the north-western side of Stewart Island (known as Whenua Hou by the local peoples). The settlement was likely occupied by men, who had absconded from various mainstream sealing ships, together with some Māori women and their collective offspring. One of those sealers was the former convict John Kelly, who had married a local Māori woman of influence called Kuikui. Like many sealers in that region, Kelly was very mobile, only remaining on the island for just over a season before moving to Ruapuke. He soon realised, like many sealers in Bass Strait, that the only way he was going to make a reasonable living was by diversifying his business model. He made a modest income by growing vegetables, catching mutton birds and crewing whaling vessels. Like many other Pakeha, he embraced polygamy. This was not just for sexual comfort but also to develop a stronger and more friendly relationship with previously hostile and aggressive First Nations inhabitants and to increase the prospects of achieving economic success.

Archaeologists who excavated the site where the Codfish Island settlement was established have uncovered physical remains that indicate that there was an intermingling of the two cultures, with European-style housing and cooking artefacts mixed with remnants of local foodstuffs.[78] Such evidence demonstrates a more sedentary and settled hybrid existence for these families.

---

[78] Ian Smith, "Māori Pakeha and Kiwi: Peoples Culture and sequence" in *New Zealand Archaeology* (Canberra: ANU Press, 2008), 367-380.

The various cross-cultural relationships and partnerships that developed across the Southern Fishery during the colonial period in Bass Strait, Kangaroo Island, Westernport, South Australia, New Zealand or King Georges Sound, were complex and hybrid, evolving over time. Although it may be possible to tag several of these relationships as involving a victim and perpetrator, particularly in respect of the Tasmanian women and their male mariners, over time, mutual economic and domestic partnerships developed. More to the point, Robinson portraying the sealers as responsible for the demise of the Tasmanian First Nations people is problematic to say the least. Rather, if the mariners had not changed their economic model and developed a resistance practice with their female partners, the colonial community might not have survived at all.

Chapter 13: Resistance, Survival and Cultural Change in the Straits

As the colonial Antipodean sealers grew older, the spoils of the hunt became scarcer. By 1830 or so the average number of seal skins known to have been sold or exchanged by the independent sealers had dwindled. No longer were mariners returning to the ports with thousands of skins and gallons of oil. For example, in November and December 1830, returns for the gang of the sealers Brown, Williams, Proctor, Drew, Tomlins, Tucker, Baily and Mansfield recorded that they only flensed 131 seals.

Examining other data demonstrated that the most successful seal catcher in the Straits was Dobson who managed only to take skins from 282 fur seals for two entire seasons! Robinson, on hearing of this poor outcome, made the comment that with such a paltry return they could not survive on sealing alone. How true that was! The mariners and their partners were compelled to develop and change their lifestyles and economies to make the hunt for seals a secondary occupation. In so doing, the First Nations women's role became much more prominent (and in some cases dominant) in the partnerships that still existed.

By the mid-1830s, the average age of a sealer was probably about 40 years. That would have been considered old in colonial times. The mariners were beset with age-related conditions and had to rely much more on their wives and children than ever before. The predominantly male driven culture shifted to a hybrid, cross cultural lifestyle and economy. This occurred not only in the Straits but also on Kangaroo Island and in the Recherche Archipelago.

In November 1830, the Conciliator visited the aged sealer George Robinson on Woody Island. He was surprised to find that mariner, blind in one eye, had been 'industrious', cultivating 'about two acres of land', with several crops growing including wheat, onions, potatoes and cabbage. The younger man was impressed at this Arcadian tract and described the scenery as 'quite romantic'. He found the disabled sealer had fowls, pigs and domesticated animals on his plot and that George had been active curing 'bacon', being the first person to do so in the Straits. The old mariner gifted G.A. Robinson some hen's eggs, 'two large pieces of crystal and some beads'. Unlike other mariners who would later make life difficult for the Conciliator, he had a 'civil' meeting with the aged sealer. No mention at all was made of the women who were living with George on the island, but the crystal and beads would have been sourced or made by them. It was the First Nations women keeping George alive and supporting his farming endeavours.

Even before that, Boultbee, on his sealing adventures, was also impressed by the children of the hybrid relationships. The adventurer had been part of a crew of a sealing boat known as the Sally. The vessel had anchored at Kents Bay near Cape Barren Island. Soon, two whaleboats with about twelve mariners, their female companions and some dogs approached. At first, there was some hostility, but Boultbee in general found the crews to be decent in their dealings, calling the sealers 'worthies'. He had interactions with their children noting:

> They are a clever sort of people and have a handsome countenance notwithstanding the ugly physiognomies of their mothers.... Some of them have been sent to Sydney for the purpose of being educated at the Government school.[1]

At the time, education in the colony was generally run by either Anglicans or missionaries. Earlier attempts at public schooling had failed. It is highly likely that the mariners had to pay for a Sydney education for their offspring, thus illustrating that some at least were producing good incomes from their now varied endeavours.

Meanwhile on Kangaroo Island, an alternative lifestyle and economy had been adopted by Henry Wallen, George 'Fireball' Bates and Nate Thomas. Thomas had arrived in the colony seeking a life of adventure in 1818. He had become a settler on that island

---
[1] Begg and Begg, 62.

Chapter 13: Resistance, Survival and Cultural Change in the Straits

when he disembarked from the brig Nereus, commanded by Thomas Swindells, on its way back to Port Jackson in about 1824. Once there, he quickly sought the affections of a female partner. *The South Australia Register* recorded that, by September 1844, he had a First Nations common law wife and three children in a settled existence. His offspring were described by Tolmer, a visiting Inspector of Police, as combining 'the intelligence of the white with the activity of the native'.

These snapshots of the more settled cross-cultural relationships that had developed along the southern Antipodean Fishery were not uncommon. They speak of a permanency that had been lacking previously. Such relationships had come about at a time when most of the original inhabitants of Van Diemen's Land were experiencing a steady depletion of their populations in a dystopian colonial universe. This had resulted from either violence, disease or illness, following the end of the Black War and the misguided attempts by Robinson and others to herd the Palawa into Wybalenna. The selection of the site for this notorious 'Blacks' Home' had been troubled. An Aboriginal committee had been formed by officials to consider a location to house the remaining few hundred Palawa in the islands of the Straits. Initial proposals included King, Bruny and Maria Islands and some of the Kent Group outcrops. The selection of such places, far removed from Country, was to be made officially, to "save" the First Nations people of Tasmania from extinction by promoting Western civilisation and Christian values to the survivors. But there were more sinister motives at play.

The committee comprised many Christian ministers along with the former sealer Kelly, and others who met over several days between 20 January and 3 February 1831. Their brief was to find 'the most eligible place for the immediate formation of an establishment to receive those natives already captured, and for the future reception of the *'whole of the aborigines'* [emphasis added]. After much consideration, a unanimous decision recommended Gun Carriage Island in the Furneaux Group as the place to establish a "Reserve". Swan Island was also considered. But, over time, the powers-that-be had a rethink. These islands was not found to be at all suitable. They resolved that The Lagoons on Flinders Island would be suitable.[2]

By 1832, prior to Wybalenna's completion, a young and enlightened William Darling, brother of the colonial Governor, had replaced the incompetent Seargeant Wright as superintendent to the newly formed settlement at the Lagoons. Darling had written letters to Arthur designed to reassure him that the Aboriginal establishment was meeting all expectations of the government. He added that there were only a few of the First Nations people still free elsewhere. He estimated (although he could not be positive) that by then there were about 10 or 12 women living in the Eastern Straits, another two on King Island, and an unknown number on Kangaroo Island still cohabiting with the sealers. Whether this was accurate is doubtful.

The remoteness of some islands and the strategies adopted by the mariners and their women to avoid capture creates added uncertainty. Describing the Lagoons residents as 'a happy good tempered and intelligent race of beings', Darling changed from having a liberal open demeanour to becoming less than happy with them after some months. Over time, he portrayed the women as being 'addicted to lechery', implying that the sealers had used tobacco to lure them, a practice which Darling hoped to stop. Emphasising the ill treatment that the women had experienced, he emphasised that he had met no Australian woman who wanted to return to or stay with the mariners.

However, from the same correspondence it is clear the women and the sealers resisted attempts by the superintendent and others to compel the women to leave their partners. The superintendent had observed, when anchored near one island, barking dogs alerted the sealers to his presence. With the support of one of the First Nations women, the sealers quietly stole away from there with their partners to avoid confrontation. Further, it is obvious from letters written by colonial authorities that the sealers were actively undermining attempts by Darling and others to entice the women

---

[2] The Lagoons were on the west coast of the island but proved less than satisfactory as the weather was adverse and drinking water was contaminated.

Chapter 13: Resistance, Survival and Cultural Change in the Straits

to this establishment.

Meanwhile the Islanders went about portraying it as a place where none of their basic needs and wants would be met, describing it as 'miserable'.[3] The site had proven to be a mistake. Several First Nations people removed by Robinson to that place died and eventually a more suitable location was found at Settlement Point, some 25 kilometres from the present-day town of Whitemark halfway up the western coast of Flinders Island. This became known as Wybalenna. Over several years, various buildings were constructed there to house, confine and "re-educate" and employ the First Nations inhabitants. Over a cleared tract of land convicts, Palawa and military personnel built a church, cottages, gardens, office, industrial premises, sheds, a tanner, a piggery and even a boat shed.

When you visit Wybalenna now, you are greeted by an open vast sloping vista dotted with trees, with some ruins. The only substantial structures remaining are the chapel and graveyard, the later ironically being mainly occupied by the upright plaques denoting local white deceased people. One stone edifice has been erected in honour of the First Nations people who died there during the colonial period. Windswept and lonely, it is a sad, silent, haunting place.

While Wybalenna was being established and occupied, Robinson was in the vanguard of those seeking to bring the "Aboriginal problem" of Van Diemen's Land to a close. But his original motive was by this time coloured by more selfish considerations. He was aware that he was going to be handsomely rewarded by the government for his efforts, having already received £400 in cash and a land grant. He then lobbied Arthur more strenuously for additional 'compensation' and was successful. Apart from that, he later managed to be appointed the establishment's superintendent, no doubt for an additional stipend. But he achieved this by boasting to anyone who would listen that he had cleared Van Diemen's Land of all of its original First Nations people.[4]

---

[3] W. J. Darling to Lieutenant Governor Arthur, 4 May, 1832.
[4] Robinson received £700 and a pension of £200 and land for his sons Charles

Matters were going from bad to worse on Flinders Island. The First Nations people living at the Establishment were dying from diseases contracted there. They had lost all hope. This was despite Robinson's mischievous promises to some that they could return eventually to Country. But they were not the only ones who were conscious of their plight. Despite the rhetoric promulgated by the Conciliator and his "assistants", they were unable to either remove or confine the Straitsmen and many of their female partners. The mariners were basically passing on intelligence to those First Nations people who were either refusing to go to Wybalenna or avoiding attempts to bring them in by relaying a terrifying portrait of what was happening to their mobs on Flinders. The fact was it was close to the dystopian reality confronting the original inhabitants already. The narrative conveyed by the mariners terrified the free Palawa who took every opportunity to resist. Most of the women on the islands were still living essentially mobile nomadic lives, using their canoes and other watercraft to criss-cross waterways and journey to the mainland. The lifestyles that they lived to some extent mirrored their previous existences, and it became difficult for the Conciliator to "round up" the "resisters".

The Straitsmen and their partners had adopted a resistance strategy. Faced with attempts by Robinson, Darling and their military and maritime associates to remove all their partners, the sealers rebelled. The mariner Rew petitioned Arthur to request he be given permission to retain his First Nations women on Hunter Island. Darling was, to some extent, supportive of this request. However, in the same correspondence, Darling condemned the sealers in unequivocal terms:

> a drunken, lying, lazy and lawless set, evil and smooth-tongued wherever their interest [was] concerned, who were employed but a small portion of the year in sealing and the remainder of the time they lead a lazy and indolent life...[5]

He also asserted the women who assisted the men by hunting for skins, curing mutton birds and plucking the feathers were in a

---

and George. See Cassandra Pybus, *Truganini*, 158.
[5] W. J. Darling to the Colonial Secretary, 7 December, 1832.

Chapter 13: Resistance, Survival and Cultural Change in the Straits

state of slavery. When the men were confronted by officials, they concealed their partners to prevent them being taken. In addition, some of them organised Christian marriages to prevent them being removed altogether.

The early optimism apparent in Darling's correspondence of 1832 to his masters, in which he expresses a strong belief that the 'natives' would be susceptible to Christianising and civilising, changed over time to one of despondency and even despair. It becomes clear that, apart from the problem with the sealers, there were other pressing issues to overcome. The First Nations people on Flinders were less than cooperative. Many women voted with their feet secretly returning to the sealers. By June of that year, and, as the winter chills were setting in, at least three Palawa had voluntarily left to live with the sealers Dobson, Drew and Kelly. Many others also 'found life there [at the Establishment] more irksome or less free than with their white husbands' and escaped.[6] Meanwhile, the death toll of First Nations people there continued to mount, and Darling (and others in power) were by then certain the these peoples would become 'extinct.'[7]

The tragedy that was unfolding on Flinders Island had begun to cause deep and long-lasting concerns for the colonial government and their English masters. By 1835, even Robinson knew the plan to confine the 'natives' had failed miserably. Defeated, he gave what can only be described as a "living" eulogy:

> Look back, my friends, you who have known them for a short time. Look back, you who have known them for a longer period and I will look back to the time when I knew them in their own native wilderness when we were first known to each other. Let us give full scope to our recollections and call to mind all the incidents and associations connected therewith, and then turn to those memories of our departed friends and weep in silence.[8]

Weep in silence he might do, but much of the tragedy on Flinders was not due to the sealers but to the Conciliator and his

---

[6] Plomley, 1008.
[7] See, for example, Darling's letter to Arthur, 24 June 1834.
[8] George Augustus Robinson. *Journal, 25 December, 1835*. Not that he necessarily would have publicly blamed himself for the tragedy.

champions in the government and church. Fortunately, for the mariners and the First Nations people, despite Robinson's best endeavours to remove all stakeholders from the islands, he was only temporarily successful. Only a few mariners gave up their Islander existences, and only some of their partners were lured permanently into the confines of the Settlement.

In the meantime, Robinson's good reputation and character was under attack elsewhere as well. He was subject to criticism as early as 1832. In that year, the Quakers James Backhouse and William Walker, on their evangelical and fact-finding tour of Australia, met with him. Initially, the missionaries perceived that he was a respected zealous Christian. They thought he was conducting an impressive operation to benefit the First Nations Tasmanians. The missionaries expressed their wholehearted approval of the Establishment. But nine months later, they had dramatically changed their opinion of him:

> George Augustus Robinson is a person who had either fallen from his steadfastness as a Christian, or that he is not the person that we once thought we had reason to believe him... This is not the man who possesses the requisite qualifications, either as regards his judgement or his principles, if we be not greatly deceived in our conclusions respecting him.[9]

This adverse opinion was repeated by others towards the close of that decade as Robinson was becoming a pariah and a liability for the government. Probably seeing the writing on the wall, in 1837, he abandoned the Tasmanian Aboriginal people and lobbied hard to be appointed to a position as Protector of Aborigines at the new Port Phillip establishment near present-day Melbourne. He was successful and quickly departed from Van Diemen's Land. At the time he arranged for Truganini and a few handpicked First Nations people to voyage with him, leaving the Settlement behind, without any real concern for the surviving seriously ill and depleted inhabitants.

After the Conciliator had left the Straits and been rewarded by the Lieutenant Governor for his efforts, many more First

---

[9] George Walker. *Journal 3.11.1832, B 709*, 171-2.

Nations women returned to the islands. The partnerships between these women and the sealers remained totally independent of the influence of colonial authority and religious zealots like Robinson. By then many inquiries were being instigated as an outcome of grave concerns for the adverse effects on First Nations populations all over the world. The Australian colony was not immune from this scrutiny. A paper prepared by the more liberal Governor Richard Bourke found its way into the *Quarterly Review* published by John Murray in 1838. It ironically acknowledged that the imposition of the English "colonising" system had been worse than the slave trade as far as the 'native' tribes were concerned. Bourke made no less than 20 suggestions that could be adopted to ameliorate the condition of the First Nations peoples before summarising these suggestions:

> In conclusion-the great principles of native treatment are thus-their exaltation, intermixture with ourselves, beneficial employment, religious conversion, instructions in our language, and thereby the progressive development of their minds and understanding.[10]

Bourke's honest but naïve and misguided attempt to provide an "integration plan" for the First Nations people was not going to assist those who were still resident at Wybalenna where the situation was worsening. The Select Committee in London was now fully aware that the plight of those residents was caused principally by Robinson's ill-conceived plans.[11] By December 1839, the French explorer D' Urville was back again in the Antipodes. He sailed the L'Astrolabe into Hobart Town on a hydrographic and scientific mission. This time he did not encounter any sealers at all. However, while in Van Diemen's Land, his officers made some observations noting that the Tasmanian First Nations people were on the point of being "exterminated".

The very next year, Robinson's self-serving report about his experiences on Flinders Island and Port Phillip was before the Aboriginal Protection Society for consideration. The Society

---

[10] Richard Bourke, 6 June 1837 in *Murray's Review*, 16 January, 1838.
[11] *Report from the Select Committee, British Parliamentary Papers*, February, 1837, 14.

discussed what could be done to assist 'native' populations to survive and prosper despite the conduct of generations of colonisers. In their third annual report, the Society was very conscious of the fact that the Wybalenna experiment had failed miserably, despite the conciliator's attempts to paint it differently. This was their candid assessment of the terrible outcomes imposed by Robinson on the First Nations people:

> Your committee cannot help regretting, while they apprehend the speedy extinction of the once simple inoffensive islanders of Van Diemen's Land, and connect that event with the process, so efficient for its accomplishment, pursued at Flinders Island, that from the first a system had been applied more suitable to the habits of a roving people, instead of the highly artificial one whose details have been referred to…

The report details a plethora of deaths that occurred at the settlement between December 1836 and June 1839. It ends by expressing the hope that the Governor, Sir John Franklin, would use his best endeavours to secure 'justice and mercy' for the 'poor remnant of a banished and ill-used race'.[12]

Apart from a remnant population at the Establishment, nearly all other First Nations people from Tasmania were living as islanders. Meanwhile, across at Kangaroo Island, many of the collective communities were thriving. The *Perth Gazette* noted that several First Nations women were still living in relationships with sealers. Many had been there for years and, after the United Kingdom settlers had arrived in 1836, had been absorbed into the general Islander community. The small-scale sealing industry at Kangaroo Island was probably at its peak, with huts and settlements dotted around the many bays located there. Nathaniel Thomas had formed a strong partnership with 'Fireball' Bates, a long-term resident in the Creek Bay area. He built a cottage and established a farm, which accommodated a herd of over 500 goats. Thomas and other sealers were often dependent on the industry of their female partners, who provided more than just companionship. These women also made clothing, provided food and introduced them to the world of

---

[12] *The Third Annual Report of the Aboriginal Protection Society* (London; P. White and Son Devonshire Square), 23 June, 1840.

natural medicines. Thomas was dependent upon Betty (sometimes referred to as 'Betsy'), who had been brought to the island in about 1819 by a man regarded by other sealers as the 'governor', namely Henry Wallen. Thomas and Betty resided on their farm and had two daughters before they moved to Penneshaw, where the sealer was appointed as a lightkeeper. As time progressed, he established the first public school in that town. W. H. Leigh, on his visit to Kangaroo Island in the late 1830s, made a few positive observations about the blending of cultures there.

Other sealers in the western region of the Fishery had adopted a more dynamic and nomadic approach to their trade. One was James Everett, who realised early on the abilities of First Nations people to successfully catch seal, and that is why he employed several of these men and women in his crews for that purpose. Other men who loved this mobile and free spirited existence included Thomas Foster, who partnered with an Indigenous woman with whom he fathered three children. Foster eventually voyaged to live in Otaheite and was employed as a maritime pilot there. Contrast this lifestyle with that of Robert 'Bob' Gamble. Originally operating out of Van Diemen's Land, by the middle to late 1830s, he was in charge of a mobile crew from his base at Bald Island, a short distance from King Georges Sound. He continued to rely primarily on sealing but only because of the abilities of his crews. His gang consisted of his common law female partners and some children.

Meanwhile, in the Bass Strait Islands, the lack of seals forced the mariners and partners to take steps to improve their chances of survival. Whether by design or otherwise, they commenced to establish small-scale hybrid industries, either by themselves or in small collectives. The Straitsmen had observed how successful the First Nations women were at capturing mutton birds, which was a livelihood that pre-dated the colonisers by millennia. The females were employed for that purpose, so that an independent community industry known as 'birding' began to develop. Robinson made special mention in his journal about the First Nations methodology employed in this trade when he wrote:

> The women have a stick about three feet long called a spit which they put into the hole. If there is a bird they tear up the ground with the stick and lay hold of him... the eggs are very good and about the size of a duck egg.

After the birds were killed, the women removed the feathers and drained the oil from their bodies. Most parts of the birds were then sold by the sealers when they came into Port Dalrymple and other well-settled places.[13] But birding was only one of several hunting and agricultural pursuits engaged in by the Islanders.

By 1841, John Lort Stokes, an American hydrographer, was exploring Bass Strait and some of the 334 islands around Tasmania on the Beagle. He had been sailing on that vessel previously with Charles Darwin. Originally employed as a surveyor, he had taken command of the vessel due to the demise of its captain. While on his journey, he encountered at least three separate families of Islanders in the Straits, their partners and progeny, and made some observations in his journal.[14]

Eventually, those observations found their way into his two-volume work published some years later.[15] As he had no axe to grind with any colonial party; his recordings can be regarded as reasonably accurate and objective. When Stokes arrived at New Year Island (just off the coast of King Island to the northwest of Van Diemen's Land), he wrote of the Straitsman living there having two wives who were 'natives of Tasmania'. Further, he noted the women were clothed in 'very comfortable greatcoats made of kangaroo skins', and 'seemed quite contented with their condition'. Their children 'appeared sharp and intelligent', mirroring what Boultbee had observed previously. When a large whale boat sailed by, he wondered how one man could operate it. The sealer who owned it later provided an answer telling Stokes that It was because 'his wives, the two native women, assisted him to work the boat'.

---
[13] Taylor, 24.
[14] He informed his readers that the sealers were divided into Eastern and Western-island communities.
[15] J. Lort Stokes. *Discoveries in Australia with An Account of The Coasts And Rivers Explored And Surveyed During The Voyage of H.M.S. Beagle, In The Years 1837-38-39-40-41-42-43*. By Command Of The Lords Commissioners of The Admiralty. (London: T. and W. Boone, 1846).

Apart from these observations, which are consistent with those expressed by others, the Yankee was informed that their 'principal occupation' was now seeking out the 'Sooty Petrel'.[16] This they told him was their main source of food. The mariners explained that the various components of the bird, including the feathers, were sold. At the same time, Stokes noticed water was readily available, and vegetables were being grown. The islanders informed him the latter were cultivated on many of the islands inhabited by other sealers. Stokes later sailed south to the now private Walker's Island off the north-west coast of Van Diemen's Land where he met 'the wives of some sealers'. The men were away procuring pinnipeds on King Island. Noting the similarity to the New Year islanders in that they wore animal skins, he observed that one woman spoke 'very good English' and took 'good care of her person', arranging flowers in her hair. He added that she 'dressed with some pretensions to elegance'. The women were accompanied by a 'pack of dogs' who assisted in bringing down wallabies. The First Nations females told him how significant this was to them as they could trade their skins for rewards.

Later, Stokes sailed across to Preservation Island. Here, he met Munro together with other Straitsmen and some of the wives. The hydrographer made several observations about the background to the relationships, economy, and hybrid culture, which by that stage was well and truly settled. The Islanders informed him that in the early days of their encounters (when the mariners were sealing at what was then known as St George's Rocks) 'a clan came down on the main opposite and made a signal for them to approach'. They went, taking with them the carcasses of two or three seals, for which the natives gifted as many women. The Yankee added in his journal that the women 'perhaps, were glad of the change, as the First Nations men of Tasmania often treat them shamefully'. This was similar to comments made previously by the French in the Recherche. He noted that arrangements were in place whereby the mariners often went sealing while their partners hunted wallabies. As an outcome, the communities were 'well supplied'

---

[16] The mutton birds.

with food. From his observations, it appeared that the Straitsmen treated their wives 'with anything but unkindness'. While there, he gathered together some demographic statistics, noting that there were 'twenty-five children' of the partnerships living either on Preservation Island or 'the islands in the neighbourhood'. Noticing the children's generally healthy dispositions, he described them as making 'excellent sailors' and 'formidable harpooners' whom he himself would have employed on the Beagle but for the fact that his surveying work was about to be completed. He was surprised to learn some read the bible and were literate.

In his journals, Stokes also described the cross-cultural involvement by male and female Islanders in the procurement of the mutton birds and the "birding" economy. That task involved a blending of two disparate cultures. The sooty petrels had been sought consistently by First Nations people for generations.

When the Islander culture developed in the 1820s, the First Nations people used their traditional digging sticks as a device to carry the birds. They also started wearing gloves and using tools supplied by the mariners, according to the historian Lyndall Ryan. Snakes were very prevalent down the bird holes, and the gloves would have given the women added protection. Once the prey was killed, the various components of each bird were removed from the carcass. The oil and fat could be sold for use as fuel, while the feathers filled many a bed cover. The flesh was salted then sold or stored for the winter season as a food source.[17]

As Stokes and others had discovered, by the late 1830s, sealing was not a viable industry for the Islander collectives. The poet, travel writer and novelist of the time, Louisa Anne Twamley,[18] observed in her travel writing:

> The men employed in sealing on these islands derive their chief sustenance from the Mutton Birds, which they take in various ways.[19]

---

[17] Ryan, *Patterns of Migration*, 12.
[18] She wrote under the name of her husband as 'Mrs Charles Meredith' and published a volume titled *Poems* (1835) together with two novels and a travel book called *Last Series, Bush Friends in Tasmania* (1892).
[19] Louise Anne Twamley (Mrs Charles Meredith). *Notes and Sketches of New*

Chapter 13: Resistance, Survival and Cultural Change in the Straits

Twamley (who may have derived intelligence from her husband, a former sealer) described one of the 'ways' that the men captured and caught the birds:

> A high pen of stakes wattled together on a low part of the coast, into which the poor Mutton Birds, who always run down to the water to take wing, are driven with dogs and shouting, and there as they cannot rise off the land, they can be killed at leisure.

Although this seems like a cruel and barbaric practice now, it meant economic survival for the families on the islands. They were able to sell the feathers for pillows, even though the smell of them was "disagreeable". The meat, which apparently tasted like red herring, was also traded.

Stokes had also observed that the sealers 'build a hedge a little above the beach' which could be up to half a mile long. This forced the birds into the centre where they fell into a large hole and were 'smothered'. Then the islanders pulled them out, plucked the feathers and pressed them into bags for sale at Port Dalrymple and elsewhere. In the towns they fetched threepence a pound for the family.[20] The price had decreased substantially over time, being originally one shilling a pound. The families voyaged to markets on the mainland twice a year where their produce was sold. The women were also responsible for the collection of mutton bird eggs. But, just like Twamley, Stokes found this to be a dangerous exercise, due to the number of poisonous snakes that lived in the burrows. He noted a cat had died recently from a snake bite.[21]

Stokes' and Twamley's objective observations of the islander families they encountered flies completely in the face of the fixed immutable historical colonial perception of sealers as barbaric, savage, brutal, piratical and slave trading troglodytes. Not only that, but it demonstrates that the island communities were now very well-established. It speaks of a developing culture in the islands while the tragedy at Wybalenna was unfolding. The fact was that,

---

South Wales During a residence in that colony from 1839 to 1844 (Sydney: Ure Smith, 1973), 33-34.
[20] He was amazed at just how many birds were taken at any one time, noting that generally they transport about 30 bags of feathers from 18,000 birds.
[21] Lort Stokes, Chapters 1.9 and 2.13.

for many, these islander relationships had changed from ones where sealers dominated by force or otherwise and asserted their own separate cultural practices to those where the partnerships became more settled, hybrid and diverse. Over time, the cultural practices which First Nations women had engaged in for centuries effectively "crossed" with those of their mariner partners. In some cases, they were not mutually exclusive, so they blended together and created something new for the Straits people. In other arrangements, the women and the men adopted each other's culture and methodologies. Finally, there were some practices where the women continued to utilise their traditional arrangements without any involvement from the mariners.. The Palawa for some considerable time had been free to pursue traditional cultural and economic activities within the partnerships that had been formed with the sealers.

Kay Merry, a historian from Flinders University, asserts that archaeological digs in the Straits and on Kangaroo Island have produced evidence of an "intermingling" of cultures. She goes so far as to say that this in itself facilitated the survival of the Tasmanian First Nations people.[22] The women were then principally involved in the procurement of the remnants of the seal populations that still inhabited the various islands in the Straits. An example of this was observed early by Kelly of their habit of mimicking the seals to lull them into a false sense of security would still have been practised without much assistance from the men. When it came to procuring marine mammals from more inaccessible places, it was a "team" effort, with the whole family involved in manning the whaleboats to seek out the remaining pinniped populations (as observed by Stokes above).

On Gun Carriage Island, Robinson had previously found a well-established Islander community, which he described as a 'delightful place'. There were several cottages, outbuilding and large gardens, where potatoes were grown and pigs confined. He also

---

[22] Kay Merry, 'The Cross-Cultural Relationships between the sealers and Aboriginal women at Bass Strait and Kangaroo Island in the early Nineteenth Century' in *Counterpoints 2003* (2000), 80-81.

observed that the women were in the business of procuring crystals and mutton birds utilising western technology.[23]

When Boultbee voyaged around Bass Strait (and later New Zealand), he "fell in with" a group of 10 sealers and joined the crew of a whaleboat named Sally around 13 August 1824. During voyages with this crew, he made some interesting observations about the relationships between the sealers and the women and the lifestyles led by the Islander communities. When anchoring at Cape Barren Island, he found the men and the women were dressed in jackets, coats and moccasins of kangaroo skins. He was particularly impressed with the industrious nature of the women when they were engaged in "birding" activities. Voyaging further to Preservation Island, he concluded that the constable of the Straits must have treated the women well because of what he had been told by the women. What appears to have developed was a new Islander community and culture where the women were able to hand down medicinal remedies while preserving their folklore.[24]

The children born to the sealer-First Nations partnerships also adopted the new economic and cultural practices of their parents. Educator and historian Bonwick was informed about these young people after he came to live in Hobart in 1841. One of the sealers was an Irishman named Brien. He had abducted a First Nations woman with whom he had a child called "Bill". Bill apparently spoke English very well and quickly became an able assistant to the sealer in his economic activities. The child was proficient as a sailor on the whaleboat, slaughtering seals, and could use firearms. When the mariner was absent, he also traded skins and melons for garments, spirits and tobacco with passing whalers, following the practices of his father.[25]

Meanwhile, to the west of the Straits on Kangaroo Island, a blending of cultures also occurred. The economy and lifestyles adopted by the mariners and their female partners meant that sealing was well supplemented by other activities. These included

---

[23] Plomley, 272-273.
[24] See Plomley and Hensley, 21.
[25] Bonwick, 289.

kangaroo and wallaby hunting while mutton birds were exploited for their feathers only. For example, in 1836, a mariner was reported to be grinding his harvested wheat between two flat stones in a manner utilised by First Nations women from the deep distant past. The wheat was then crushed and used in making damper. By 1844, there were reports of nooses made from canvas by the women, which they employed in the capture of wallabies, along with other technologies that they had acquired from their maritime husbands.[26] The Kangaroo islanders also changed their culinary habits, with sealers consuming a variety of foods which First Nations men and women had been eating for centuries. These included the procurement of termites, grubs, goanna and emu eggs, and possums, in addition to a variety of bush foods, including native currants and tea. The additional food sources complemented the meat and vegetables provided from the farms and gardens of the mariners. The sealer Nat Thomas was observed by a journalist in 1853 frying various insects and earth creatures. His partner and others living with sealers made moccasins stitched together from kangaroo tails, while fur coats were also being stitched and worn by the Islanders.

The development of unique islander cultures based on mutual cooperation and recognition (if not in some cases respect) came about as a direct result of the isolation of the communities from mainstream society, and the need to eke out a living in a dwindling maritime economy. One of the important ways that the islander communities and partnerships survived was by adapting the two cultures to new economic and agricultural methods that did not entirely rely on the sea. Over time, it was the women who also became the permanent residents on islands such as Hunter, Cape Barren, King, and Kangaroo, where they were drying and curing seal and kangaroo skins. At the same time, they were involved in catching wallabies and possums, utilising the prize dogs[27] that the mariners possessed. They dived for kelp and crayfish, constructed

---

[26] *South Australian Register*, 25 September, 1844.
[27] According to Reverend Knopwood in 1807, a good dog would cost £25 which was the equivalent of an average annual salary then. Others might cost you 1/3 of that and upwards.

huts, and made useful chattels or adornments such as baskets and necklaces. They also entertained the men and themselves by performing ceremonial dances.

But the women were also more proactive than that. In the new islander communities, the female partners took on leadership roles and fostered collective decision making. It is arguable that a predominantly matriarchal society was forming.[28] Notwithstanding the lack of focus by historians and others on the roles women played in the islander economies and cultures, the voice of First Nations is heard through other means. Two of those means are through oral story-telling and ceremonial dancing. Ida West (née Armstrong), an Aboriginal Elder and aunt who was descended from sealer James Everett, wrote in her memoirs about the life she lived on Flinders Island and the stories handed down by her older relatives. She recorded how her mixed islander family used to prepare for the mutton birding season, which was from November to April yearly. Men and women would leave Flinders Island and sail north to the islands of Babel and Chapple to procure the older birds. They then returned home to prepare the sheds, where racks had already been cleaned ready for the harvest.[29]

Further evidence of the new sub-culture was found in the dances. If there was business to be transacted between communities, and negotiations were completed, all the islanders would join in and celebrate a successful venture by conducting ceremonial dancing and feasting on the beaches close to where the collectives operated. These events were in keeping with traditions of the various Australian nations, including the Trouwunnan, whose cultural practices were identified by Ryan and Plomley.[30] The women continued to believe in the various spirits and devils that the First Nations people had from time immemorial come to associate with the islands. They incorporated those beliefs into the new Islander

---

[28] As asserted by Patsy Cameron, in 'Pallawah Women: Their Historic Contribution to Our Survival', Part 1, "A Matriarchal Heritage", in *Tasmanian Historical Research Association*, Vol. 41, No. 2, 1994, 66.
[29] Ida West. *Pride against Prejudice; Reminiscences of a Tasmanian Aborigine* (Canberra: Australian Institute of Aboriginal Studies, 1984), 59.
[30] See Plomley, *Friendly Mission,* 312 and 888.

culture. The Palawa also continued to cut cicatrices into their bodies as a reflection of their previous cultural beliefs.

The manifestations of this hybrid culture is now well recognised. Modern-day historians, both white and black, such as Patsy Cameron, Vicki Matson-Green, Jan West and Kay Merry have written extensively on the subject.[31] While such hybrid cultures developed, there was no abandonment of traditional Tasmanian First Nations practices, and the Islanders have continued to maintain their separate identity and culture.

When Truganini passed away in 1876, white Imperial discourse declared that the First Nations Tasmanians had become extinct. But that was far from the case. After 1840, the communities were organised enough to petition the colonial governor to seek licences and rights over the mutton bird rookeries that existed on the islands.[32] Since then, what is identified by the First Nations Tasmanians as the Palawa community has continued to live and prosper despite many difficulties.

In the 1850s and 1860s, Lucy Beeton, a First Nations woman who was the daughter of Thomas Beeton, a sealer and a Cape Portland woman, Bet Smith, established and taught at a school on the islands, as education was considered highly desirable in the community. During her time living on Gun Carraige Island, she was also very active in trading particularly in mutton birds. Like many of the other islander women, Lucy cared for her aging father and took control of his enterprise after his death.

Cultural practices such as mutton birding, the use of various ochres, ceremony, and the making of shell necklaces are all evident today within the tight knit First Nations families.[33] There have

---

[31] Patsy Cameron, 'Palawa Women: Their historical contribution to our survival' and Vicki Matson-Green, Part 2 'Leaders Among the Palawa Women' both in *Tasmanian Historical Research Association,* 41-42, June, 1994; Maria Moneypenny, 'Going out and coming in: Cooperation and collaboration between Aborigines and Europeans in early Tasmania', in *Tasmanian Historical Studies*; 5(1), 1995-1996, 64-75.

[32] See Christopher D. Berk, *Palawa Kani and the Value of Language in Aboriginal Tasmania* in the Online Wiley Library, 10 January, 2017.

[33] Vicki Matson-Green / Maykutenna and Tanya Harper; 'Palawa Women: Carrying the Burdens and finding the solutions'; in *Labour History,* No. 69 (Liverpool: Aboriginal Workers Liverpool University Press, November, 1995), 65-74.

also been very important attempts made to ensure the traditional languages of the First Nations Tasmanians are promoted, fostered and taught. This process has a name: Palawa kani, meaning 'Tassie Blackfella Talk'. Just like other First Nations peoples, the fostering and promotion of these languages is now commonly regarded as essential to their cultural survival. But the continuation of the hybrid culture would not have been possible without the political will and strength of strong female leaders, despite attempts made by others to marginalise them.

The blending and development of cultures also occurred across the Tasman as well. This occurred mainly after sealers were 'adopted' into Māori villages and nations. These mariners shared western methodologies with the First Nations peoples and took up those economic and cultural methods and systems that they encountered. In exchange, the men introduced the village peoples to firearms, dogs, navigational techniques and aids that were foreign to them. Cadell and Chaseland were two of many mariners who married local Māori women and gave their adopted villages not only objects but also their valuable experience and knowledge. This enabled the First Nations peoples to advance their economies and become more efficient at harpooning whales and slaughtering seals. The New Zealanders also adopted the sealers' common usage of dogs to "round up" and procure various game. Many Māori learned how to use the white man's firesticks and valued the technology highly, often acquiring the muskets in exchange for flax and fish. But, by the late 1830s, right across the southern Fishery, mariners living a marginal existence were no longer surviving on sealing as an industry. It was in substantial decline. Other industries predominated including mutton birding, flax, sandalwood and whaling. Marginal mariners cooperated with Māori men and women in developing substantial trading relationships that criss-crossed the southern Antipodes.

Chapter 14: Barely a Ripple—the End of Colonial Sealing

In July 1834, the editor of the *Launceston Advertiser* reported that sealers were scavenging from vessels that had foundered off the islands in the Straits. This was a strategy designed to supplement their income. They zeroed in on that source due to the ever-decreasing seal populations throughout the Fishery.[1] The propensity for the Straitsmen, in particular, to confiscate valuable cargoes from wrecks by opportunistic (or far more nefarious) means became the subject of speculation in the years afterwards. It reached its zenith in December 1839 when the 243-ton barque *Britomart* failed to reach Hobart on a voyage from Port Phillip. The editors of colonial newspapers wrote that the boat was carrying 30 passengers. No one could fathom what had happened. Of more relevance was its cargo. Some believed that £150,000 in gold coins was being transported destined for the opening of the first bank of Van Diemen's Land.

At the time, many vessels had been wrecked in the Straits in somewhat suspicious circumstances. Rumours were circulating that either pirates or some sealers were involved. Munro was still the appointed Constable of the Straits, living on Preservation Island. It was believed he had insider knowledge of the fate of the *Britomart* and human and commodity cargoes. On 6 January, 1840, he wrote to Port Officer Captain Moriarty, and his letter was delivered by a Mr Gill, master of the schooner *Sir John Franklin*. The letter gave James' carefully crafted version of events:

> Herewith I forward you per bearer (Mr Gill...) the register, journals, letters and newspapers of the barque Britomart, which were washed ashore upon Preservation Island about 22nd or 26th De-

[1] Editor, *Launceston Advertiser*, 24 July, 1834, on the sealers' success in purchasing cargo for 'small consideration', following the sinking of the *Prince Regent* in the Straits.

cember last. The vessel I suppose must have been wrecked upon Goose Island or some of the low islands in its neighbourhood. The papers letters and register have been partly dried, they are, however, a little mutilated but none have been opened. Enclosed in one package is a half sovereign and twenty shillings and eleven pence in silver, which were opened with their own weight and by the loose manner in which they were folded; they are directed to Mr. L. Williams, Union Bank, Hobart. There are several pieces of the wreck, with a few casks etc washing upon the shores of the islands hereabouts, but nothing of any consequence or value…

I have the honour to be, Sir, your most obedient and very humble servant.
James Munro

And then added:

P.S. Should anything else turn up in these quarters, I shall make it my duty to forward you further particulars, by the earliest conveyance. J.M.

The letter appeared in an article written by the editor of the *Colonial Times* a short time later.[2]

It is a cleverly constructed piece of subterfuge from Munro. The letter demonstrated his diplomatic and political skills. But what it omits to say is most relevant. There is nothing in his letter about the location of the barque. Nothing about any vast quantity of gold coin, or about the fate of the 30 passengers that were on board. Nothing about what or who could have caused the disappearance of the vessel.

Shortly after the wreck, there were anecdotal reports of some sealers visiting Launceston with large quantities of cash, which they spent on alcohol, tobacco and other chattels. A very drunk sealer had boasted about his knowledge of the wreck but wanted cash to reveal anything. These reports aroused suspicions of criminal activity and pirating but did not lead to any prosecutions.[3] Once again, the newspaper editors resorted to a 'call to arms', asking the authorities to act against the sealers. One newspaper man even questioned whether a most serious crime had been committed:

[2] Editor, *Colonial Times*, Hobart, 21 January, 1840.
[3] The editor of the *Hobart Town Courier and Van Diemen's Land Gazette* reached no conclusion but reported: 'If the people in the Straits are pirates, Munro's disinclination to reveal anything is natural enough', 6 March, 1840.

> There is a dereliction on the part of the government if immediate steps are not taken to unravel the mystery which surrounds the fate of thirty individuals on board the *Britomart*. It is a matter of no importance to know whether they were drowned or murdered?[4]

Whether foul play was involved was never established despite the rallying cries of the press men. A search of the area was undertaken by the crew of the government cutter Vansittart. Certainly, piracy was suspected, and the fingers of many in authority pointed directly at the remaining Straitsmen. All attempts at the time to locate the missing barque failed miserably. Because there was insufficient evidence of wrongdoing, no one was ever charged nor was there any official inquiry. Once again, the newspaper men's exhortations to the authorities failed. The remaining sealers were now firmly in their sights, with possible sanctions applied. The sealers could no longer run their own race. They made the obvious choice and remained silent. It took another 130 or more years before the wreck was found in the waters between Clarke and Preservations Islands.

The Britomart incident and suspicions of piracy represents a new low point for the Bass Strait sealers. Nearly all of the regions where mariners had sought to slaughter seals had been abandoned. It was only the islander communities in the Straits and on Kangaroo Island that remained active. It had become virtually impossible to make a living from sealing. The mariners also now had the additional burden of a renewed focus of colonial authorities and the editors of the Sydney and Hobart presses. The Conciliator had departed from his failed venture at Wybalenna and left the pursuit of the mariners in the hands of others. It became a major colonial unsolved mystery.

Towards the end of the third decade nothing was being done about the perceived "sealer problem". In January 1837, a Captain Hurburgh visited the sealers in the Straits. By then, a few mariners had re-occupied both Gun Carriage and Preservation Islands where Munro still resided. Munro himself continued to eke out an existence as a farmer where he stayed until his death in 1845, despite

---

[4] *Hobart Town Courier and Van Diemen's Land Gazette*, 6 March, 1840.

further events that could have destroyed his cosy existence. When asked by Robinson what he was seeking there, he replied that he only wanted contentment and that he had found it on Preservation Island.[5] This is not surprising. The island is surrounded on a calm day by the most picturesque aqua marine waters known as the Armstrong Channel. It has a sheltered harbour area for vessels. Many granite boulders are located there to be used as protection where necessary. On the southern end is a large pond, dug out by the survivors of the Sydney Cove. It was where Munro and his partners would have drawn water when needed. A boat would have sailed a relatively easy voyage from there to the mainland in good weather to seek out supplies. Many colonial vessels passed close by and would have anchored there, which would have enabled Munro and others to trade vegetables and seal skins for colonial supplies.

Other mariners were living in settlements on Clarke, Woody and Swan Islands. Some mainland Australian women were cohabiting with them, together with Maria Bengally, a woman of part-Indian descent. It seems these women had replaced many of the Tasmanians, who were mostly now either "secured" within the confines of Wybalenna or dead.

By the late 1830s, apart from the remnant sealers and their Islander families, there were new arrivals who commenced to operate small-scale business ventures in the Straits. They also realised that trying to survive on sealing alone would lead to starvation. These men realised they had to adapt by conducting divergent enterprises. One was David Howie, a Scotsman. Convicted of stealing and transported to Tasmania, he eventually established a home on King Island. There, he commenced operating as a sealer but expanded the industries in which he worked to make a living. He assessed that he could make a significant profit if he traded in kangaroo skins and guano. These commodities he collected and sold by the ton in Launceston. He allegedly made £50 per ton of the seabird droppings, which were used to make fertilizer, and one pound for

---

[5] Boultbee, in his *Journal of a Rambler,* described Munro as a man of 'cool judgement and natural ability'.

every kangaroo skin.[6] But, like Munro and other mariners, he found other more nefarious opportunities to make his fortune.

In August 1845, the 815-tonne emigrant barque *Cataraqui*, with hundreds of passengers on board, was shipwrecked near King Island in what became known as Australia's worst maritime disaster. This was close to where Howie and his sealing mates resided. Only nine people, including one passenger, Solomon Brown, survived. Somehow, they managed to swim ashore. Suffering from bitter cold, soaked to the skin and shivering with little or no protection, they were comforted by Howie and his gang. The sealers provided them with some basic necessities and created a windbreak. Eventually, quite by chance, the Midge anchored there and transported them to Melbourne. Anecdotally, Howie was also responsible for rescuing several other persons from shipwrecks off the coast of this island, but his role in the events leading to ships being wrecked is suspicious. He lived on King Island with his Tasmanian First Nations wife Mary Bogue and their son David Howie Bogue. Unfortunately, his wife and child were drowned in a boating accident off Stanley sometime later. The sealer then married a woman called Jane Wilson, who bore three daughters with him[7], and he lived for a further 10 years, having spent some time seeking his fortune in the Australian goldfields.

Howie was not alone. Nearly all the Islander communities shared a similar footprint. The families were composed of mainly older sealers with younger First Nations partners and their offspring. There were many reasons why the Islanders, including any remaining First Nations Australians and other sealers like Howie, Munro and Beeton continued to eke out a living from the islands. Apart from forming strong family ties in collective settled communities, they had established permanent farms and had adapted and varied their economies to suit. Many sealers had been living on the islands for more than 30 years and were well suited to the environmental conditions. They had survived against all odds to an advanced age, averaging 60 years. The life expectancy of any

---

[6] £50 per ton is apparently the equivalent of £4,000 per ton today.
[7] See Plomley and Henley, 47.

person born around 1800 was less than 40 years worldwide. In contrast, by 1950, the average age was 69 years in Australia.[8] Their longevity may well have been partly due to the maritime origins of many who learned to subsist in the navy and on merchant ships, developing a strong physique through years of back-breaking toil. It was also probably due to the care and support they received from their partners and suitable environmental conditions. For unlike many other maritime environments around Australia, many of the islands in Bass Strait were fertile, with good water supply, which enabled the Islander communities to grow vegetables that they consumed, while their own domesticated animals, such as goats and sheep, thrived.

Not only that, the efforts of Robinson and others to remove the sealers and their female partners from the Straits, were in the main unsuccessful. The sealers were, on the whole, very clever in either avoiding Robinson and his "troops", making representations to the authorities in such a way that curtailed his activities or pleading with authorities to permit them to continue residing on the islands with at least one partner. Furthermore, despite all the adverse rhetoric from Sydney Traders, Christian missionaries, authorities from Hobart and Sydney, and surveyors and commercial maritime men, no real serious attempt was ever made to bring the sealing community to account. In addition, the authorities, fortuitously for the Straitsmen, had appointed sealers to positions of power. Munro was not the only one. In 1846, David Howie was also appointed special constable to King Island, after he urged the authorities to do so ironically to prevent piracy and looting from shipwrecks that had foundered in that area. This was despite the fact that he had previously participated in such nefarious activities himself. Finally, David Kelly was appointed special constable on Gun Carriage Island, and then on Long Island in 1857. All these factors meant that the Straitsmen and their partners effectively had complete control of their island environments and were free to please themselves without any restraint whatsoever. It was like appointing the fox to

---

[8] See Max Roser *et al.*, *Life Expectancy Tables Our World in Data*, published 2013 and revised October, 2019, www.ourworlddata.org

the chicken coop, at least in the case of Munro and Howie, who lived lives bordering on the edge of illegality.

During the 1840s, communities were observed where the Islanders lived in huts on several of the islands of the Furneaux Group.[9] It has even been suggested that the First Nations population located within these collectives had actually grown in size, although it is hard to ascertain if that is correct.[10] Anecdotal evidence suggests that, by 1857, the population in the Islander communities of Bass Strait numbered about 90 people, most of whom were sealers, their partners and the children born of these unions.

While some mariners continued to reside in the Straits within the collective environment of the Islander community, others decided that, because of the depletion of the seal population, it was time to look for other maritime opportunities. Many of the sealers had seen "the writing on the wall". Several joined whaling or other maritime vessels, abandoning their abodes, but a core number remained.[11] By 1840, the seals had become very scarce in most of their previous habitats around the entire Fishery.[12] Some over-zealous exploitation by traders and sealers had resulted in the wholesale destruction of, most of the seal rookeries, in a very rapid timeframe. For example, by 1813, Macquarie Island had no elephant seals living around the north end of the island, as they had been "fished out" within three years, according to the chameleon-like former sealer Kelly. Dogs left there were now also destroying the resident bird populations.[13]

Some sealers were successful in developing interests in the

---

[9] James Backhouse, George Robinson, Lort Stokes and Robert Clark all wrote about these observations in the 1840s and 1850s.

[10] See Irynej Skira, 'I hope you will be my friend: Tasmanian Aborigines in the Furneaux Group in the nineteenth century, in *Aboriginal History,* 1997, Vol. 21, 31.

[11] Apparently, John Dobson, James Everett, Hugh Scott, John Taylor, John Thomas, Edward Tomlins and John Tucker had decided to leave the Straits and seek their fortunes elsewhere, according to the Colonial Secretary's Office [CSO 5/9/384].

[12] In 1839, Lt Charles Wilkes of the United States' exploring expedition 1838 to 1842 reported, following a visit to Macquarie Island, that it 'affords no inducement for a visit', 131-132.

[13] *The Sydney Gazette,* 15 April ,1815.

fledgling whaling industry. By 1840, harpooning whales was beginning to provide very profitable returns to the commercial traders who operated around the Fishery, particularly the Americans. Among the more notable of the colonial men who foresaw the death of the sealing industry was Chaseland. But there were others as well. James Kelly had turned his attention to the whaling industry before 1826, and by then was a founding member of the Derwent Whaling Club along with four others. Over 25 years, Kelly formed at least three whaling partnerships, initially being involved in bay whaling around the Derwent and Bruny Island, before also voyaging to New Zealand where he was moderately successful.

At the apex of his career, the former sealer owned several whaling stations and many vessels, having successfully become a trader rather than a master.[14] A third sealer, William Dutton, had realised, while carrying out sealing voyages around the south coast of Victoria, that he quickly needed to develop an interest as a whaler or go under. Unlike Kelly and Chaseland, he was mainly in the employ of others when he first diversified into that industry.

Around 1833, he was in charge of a mission to establish a whale fishery station in Portland Bay, and he returned many times during the "fishing" season to hunt the whales there. Later, he was commander of various vessels that plied their trade between Bass Strait, Victoria and New Zealand. Just like Chaseland, he enjoyed a stellar career chasing the leviathan. So successful was Dutton that he was considered 'the most expert whaler upon the coast', according to Tasmanian historian John S. Cumpston.[15]

Outside of the Islander community, there were still a few sealers operating from Kangaroo Island, Portland Bay, Macquarie Island, the southern coast of New Zealand and also King George's Sound. Most had also diversified into other activities including whaling, farming and agriculture. When the sealers explored the region around King Georges Sound early on, some settled on islands in

---
[14] See Bowden, especially 62-85.
[15] John Cumpston, *Australian Dictionary of Biography,* National Centre of Biography, Australian National University Vol. 1, (Collingwood: Melbourne University Press,1966).

the Doubtful Island Bay area and continued to live off seals and wild geese while trading their skins and oil at the township of Albany. Apart from Black-Jack Anderson, there were others, like the sealers John Williams and Robert Gamble, who lived their lives productively in a peaceful and less threatening manner in this environment. Williams owned the sailing vessel Fanny, built in Van Diemen's Land and known for its speed. He was reported to have earned up to £1,500 working the vessel. Gamble, a one-time "associate" of the pirate Anderson, lived on Bald Island and successfully hunted seals well into the 1840s. Both of these men and others living in southern Western Australia survived the downturn in the sealing industry by changing their operations substantially. Out of season, they were known to hunt wallabies and kangaroos from a variety of the locations along the coast. They traded the meat from these animals for biscuit, flour, and salted pork with French and American whalers.

The international visitors proliferated in that part of the Fishery, making a "killing" from that pursuit. Other sealers used their skills to act as pilots on foreign vessels, assisting them to navigate their way into locations where whales might be found. In exchange, they were apparently paid a stipend of £50 per day in the season. Still, others became so self-sufficient that they only required flour from the principal colonial settlements, as their farming and hunting operations provided for all their other needs.[16]

Even in 1836, when the mainstream settlers started to arrive, Kangaroo Island supported eight sealers with about 16 First Nations women. Most notable were Thomas and Bates, who were farming in Antechamber Bay. James Williams, an Irish convict, Henry Whaley and a young Englishman, were living at Pelican Lagoon. William Cooper and Peter Johnson were operating out of Nepean Bay. Black Jack's close friend, John Bathurst had survived the death of his partner and was also living there. The ages of these men ranged from Henry Whaley, who was about 20, to Peter Johnson, who was about 70. These men and their female companions had managed to diversify their economies and establish rural occupations. Whaley

---

[16] Clark, *The Perth Gazette and Western Australian Journal*, 8 October, 1842.

had also established a farm at Three Wells River. Here, he plied his trade maximising his four acres of wheat and a large kitchen garden, together with pigs and poultry. His house was built from timber and thatched. There were three First Nations women living with him and some other unknown sealer.

When W. H. Leigh came to the island during 1837, he observed that 'Governor Whallen's farmhouse' was 10 feet long by five, with bark-covered sides that resembled the letter "A". He noted that the 'Governor' was growing wheat and potatoes. In August 1844, Inspector Tolmer of the South Australian police, on a visit to the island, reported that Thomas had an 'excellent' farm at Antechamber Bay. He also had constructed a good house and dairy supporting a herd of about 300 goats and many chickens. In further fostering tropes of racial stereotyping, he asserted that Thomas had three 'interesting' children combining 'the intelligence of the white with the activity of the native'.[17]

Also living at Morrison Point was Jacobs, an old sealer who had been on the island for 17 years, and the aforementioned Bathurst. By that time, according to Tolmer, there were approximately 12 First Nations women residing on the island; they were mostly from Tasmania, but some were from the mainland. However, the islander community there was about to change. Once the South Australian government decided to establish a permanent settlement on the island in 1836, the sealing community gradually dissipated, or was absorbed into a farming community, with few exceptions.

The decline of the sealing industry had been brought about by traders, masters and sealers who were greedy and avaricious in their endeavour to procure as many seals as possible. So aggressive had mariners throughout the world been in their attempts to slaughter the pinnipeds for commercial gain that scientists in 2023 still argued that some of the seal species remain in danger as their numbers have been reduced significantly. A good example is the New Zealand fur seal, which used to inhabit the Recherche Archipelago in southern Western Australia in reasonable numbers, Unfortunately, by the middle of the 20th century, there were few reports of any being

---
[17] See Plomley and Henley, 15.

sighted there.[18] This sad state of affairs was repeated time and time again in environments where seal rookeries previously thrived. What was left of the industry was several independent mariners who continued to slaughter a few seals, if they could find them.

---

[18] See Oliver Berry *et al.*, "Population Recovery of the New Zealand Fur Seal in southern Australia: a molecular DNA analysis" in *Journal of Mammalogy*, Vol. 93, Issue 2, 30 April, 2012.

Chapter 15: Lessons from the Colonial Sealing Epoch

The American novelist Dan Brown wrote:

> History is always written by the winners. When two cultures clash the loser is obliterated, and the winner writes the history books—books which glorify their own cause and disparage the conquered foe.

There is no doubt that history is often written in this way. The fact remains that the so-called "facts" of history are often fraught with doubt. What is written can be interpreted in divergent ways even when facts are uncertain. And so it is the case with the mariners on the margins. To a large extent, their history has to be imagined or cobbled together primarily from examining and interpreting primary written sources, oral traditions and archaeological finds. In the case of the colonial sealing epoch, the primary sources have been essentially written by those controlling the colonial historical account; in effect, the "winners".

These sources may be the journals of observers such as Cunningham and Sutherland, the interviews conducted by G. A. Robinson, the various press entries made over the course of the relevant period, the official reports from "authorities" such as Lockyer, and the observations of commercial masters, such as Bishop, Hasselborough and the like. It also includes the notes and sketches of explorers like the Russian Bellingshausen and the French D'Urville and Baudin, apart from the written testimonies given to J. T. Bigge and various later commissions of inquiry and courts.

With probably only a few exceptions, the voices of the sealers and the First Nations stakeholders, both men and women, are absent. The exceptions include the journal entries of sealer adventurer

Boultbee and the intrepid James Kelly, as well as oral First Nations stories and digs undertaken across the Antipodes. There is also the oral intelligence the sealer John Nunn provided to W. B. Clarke in 1850 and testimony given by sealers in court proceedings against their former employers and to Bigge. These give us an opportunity to consider another version of the history of the mariners.

The Sydney and Hobart traders were also not very fond of keeping diaries or journals, particularly about locations which were meant to be kept a secret to seek commercial advantages. They were also reluctant to keep diaries or journals, with the exception of the returns they gained from each sealing voyage and advertisements seeking mariners to crew their vessels. In addition to that, the sanctions that had been imposed in London and elsewhere meant that they needed to be scrupulous in avoiding any information that could be used by the Company to try and sanction or bring proceedings against them. Such was the case, for example, with the mariners who operated out of the Chathams.

On the other hand, the more literate maritime masters, such as Bishop and Kelly, did provide an alternative narrative to that of the newspaper editors and traders, who had axes to grind with the mariners. Even where primary sources have the sealers and their masters as their focus, one has to be sceptical, as the newspaper articles, reports, letters and journal entries are often written with a particular audience in mind whom they wished to impress or attract.

Much of the mariners' history has been lost or forgotten during the attempts made by historians to focus their attention on the orthodox version of historical events in Australian history. How the colony succeeded mainly by riding on the "sheep's back", the growth of agriculture, and the discovery of gold in the 1850s. When sealers and masters are mentioned, it is as a footnote to other so-called more important matters and, so far as the independent sealers are concerned, their history is mainly written in pejorative terms. The fact of the matter is that traders, masters and sealers were living a marginal existence most of the time and, from time to time, their behaviour towards each other, and particularly to the First

Nations peoples of the Antipodes, could be called into question. There are also the oral and written testimonies of the First Nations people, drawing on stories and memories handed down through the generations. But, as First Nations writer Jan West points out, how do we know what really happened?

The 20th century American philosopher George Santayana warned: 'Those who do not remember the past are condemned to repeat it.'[1] So, remembering the past also means learning from it. The valuable lessons that can be learned arising out of the colonial sealing epoch are many. Firstly, if people choose to adopt a different lifestyle outside what is considered "normal", while also competing with mainstream commercial interests, this does not necessarily mean they are a threat to society and should be pilloried for so doing. Secondly, as foreshadowed in a previous chapter, the dominating forces operating within society often creates stereotypes of these unorthodox humans, fuelled by those who control the written history. They do this without any regard to the fact that people are divergent in their natures and often have both positive and negative traits, some of which may benefit society at large, as in the case of the sealers. Thirdly, the over-exploitation of natural resources, such as the pinnipeds, perpetrated by greedy humans, often has an adverse commercial outcome and a substantial deleterious effect on the natural environment. Fourthly, greed can come at the expense of other human beings, who in good faith operate under unscrupulous employers who exploit them without compunction and cause massive adverse consequences, such as in the case of the abandonment on a massive scale of sealers. Fifthly, sometimes well-meaning mainstream authority and religious figures have throughout history tried to "understand" and then adopt measures for the amelioration of First Nations peoples, only to find that such measures result in tragic consequences, as occurred in Tasmania. Sixthly, while men can act appallingly towards others, such as those perpetrating violence and abuse against the First Nations peoples, there is the possibility that these same oppressors can adapt to changing circumstances and work with the exploited

---

[1] *The Life of Reason,* (Cambridge: MIT Press, 2007).

to ameliorate their lives. Finally, faced with Armageddon, humans can adopt ingenious and flexible arrangements to diversify and change lifestyles, cultures and economies for the better.

Although the pursuit of seals by mariners in the early 19th century was relatively short-lived, it provided not only a staple for a languishing colony economy but also kick-started the ship building industry, while providing employment for several maritime men. Without it, the colony would have been in desperate straits. Some traders made profits, but many failed in their attempt at enterprise. Independent sealers eked out an existence and survived due to their ability to change and adapt in a depleted marine environment. They were only able to do this on the most part by reason of their partnerships with First Nations women. Unfortunately, there were severe (but not permanent) adverse consequences for the seal populations and, later, to some extent, to the First Nations peoples, particularly those in Tasmania. But, despite the mostly adverse effects of the sealing industry, seal rookeries have replenished, albeit still diminished in some parts of the Antipodes. Furthermore, the First Nations people have continued to occupy and prosper in the islands of the Straits and the Tasmanian mainland.

The colonial sealers are long gone from the maritime world. Their history, and that of the sealing industry, is almost completely unknown to most Australasians. This work has been an attempt to provide a fresh, more balanced account of the colonial sealing industry that deals with all stakeholders of the time. Some attention is given over to our pre-history and the role that First Nations people have played in it from time immemorial. Exploitation of all of those on the margins in the Fishery occurred on different levels leaving long term scars. Prior historical accounts have mostly focused on the negative attributes of the sealers while promoting the interests of the traders. Men and women in history are not all squeaky clean, nor are they the devil incarnate. This also applies to the independent mariners. From their history, the anecdotal and oral traditions of the First Nations people with whom they lived, and the orthodox written history of the masters and traders who employed them, we can learn valuable lessons.

Bibliography

Primary sources

Angas, G. F. *Savage Life and Scenes in Australia and New Zealand*. London: Smith Elder, 1847. Vol.1.

Appendix to Report from Select Committee on Aborigines (British Settlements) (London: House of Commons), 1837.

Arthur, Lt Governor George to Sir George Murray. 18 September 1830. *HRA Resumed Series III*. Vol. IX.

Arthur, Lieutenant Governor George to the Secretary Sir George Murray, Hobart Town, 4 April 1831. *HRA Series 1*. Vol. 16.

Asiatic Mirror in *Historical Records of New South Wales*, Vol. 4, 757-769.

Banks, Joseph. "Some remarks on the present state of the colony of Sidney [sic] in New South Wales & on the means most likely to render it a productive instead of an expensive settlement." 4 June 1806 (series 35.35). http://transcripts.sl.nsw.gov.au/page/some-remarks-present-state-colony-sidney-sic-new-south-wales-means-most-likely-render-it-0

Banks, Sir Joseph. *Endeavour Journal* (Sydney: Angus & Robertson, 1963).

Bass, George in Collins, David. *An Account of the English Colony in New South Wales*. Vol. 2 (London: T. Cadell Jun and W. Davies, 1798).

Begg, A., Charles and Begg, Neil C. *The World of John Boultbee including an account of sealing in Australia and New Zealand* (Christchurch: Whitcoulls Publishers, 1979). (The Journal Entries of John Boultbee, 1824 to 1825).

Bigge, John Thomas. *Report of the Commissioner of Inquiry into the State of the Colony of New South Wales,* 1822. https://babel.hathitrust.org/cgi/pt?id=umn.31951001565328b&seq=5

Bigge, John. "Examination of James Kelly", in *Historical Records of Australia*, Series III, Vol. 3. 3 May 1820.

Bourke, Richard. 6 June 1837 in *Murray's Review*, 16 January 1838.

Bradley, William. *A Journal of a Voyage to New South Wales* (Sydney: Public Library of New South Wales, 1802).

British Parliamentary Papers on the subject of the military operations lately carried on against the Aboriginal inhabitants of Van Diemen's Land. Howick: Colonial Department, 23 September 1831.

Collins, David. *Account of the English Colony of New South Wales,* Vol. 1 (London: T. Cadell Jun. and W. Davies, 1798) https://www.gutenberg.org/ebooks/12565

Collins, David. *An Account of the English Colony of New South Wales* Vol. 2. (London: T. Cadell Jun. and W. Davies, 1798) https://digital.library.sydney.edu.au/nodes/view/11248

Collins, David. Letter to Board of Trade, June 30, 1806; Banks Papers.

Convict Transportation Inquiry. *The Spectator*, republished in the *Nenagh Guardian*, County Tipperary, Ireland, 5 September 1838. https://www.nationalarchives.ie/wp-content/uploads/2019/03/Ireland-Australia-transportation_DB.pdf

Cook, James in J. C. Beaglehole (ed.). *The Journals of Captain James Cook on his Voyage of Discovery, Voyage of Resolution and Adventure 1772-1775.* (London: Cambridge University Press for the Hakluyt Society, 1961).

Cunningham, Peter. *Two Years in New South Wales.* Vol. 2 (London: Henry Colburn), 182.

Cox, William. *Journal.* August 1814.

Dafoe, Daniel. *Robinson Crus,oe* (Harmondsworth Middlesex: Penguin Books, 1719).

Darling W. J. to Lieutenant Governor Arthur, 4 May, 1832.

Darling W. J. to the Colonial Secretary, 7 December, 1832.

Delano, Amasa. *Narrative of Voyages and Travels in the Northern and Southern Hemispheres comprising three voyages round the World together with a voyage of survey and discovery in the Pacific Ocean and Oriental Islands* (Boston: E.G. House, 1817).

Delano, Amasa. Letter to His Excellency Governor King from the ship **Perseverance**, 4 August 1804 https://www.google.com.au/books/edition/Narrative_of_Voyages_and_Travels_in_the/34QqAQAAIAAJ?hl=en&gbpv=1&dq=letter+amasa+delano+to+governor+king&pg=PA463&printsec=frontcov.

Dickenson Mann, David. *The Present Picture of New South Wales.* (Portland Place, London: John Booth, 1811).

D'Urville, Jules Dumont, trs. by Helen Rosenman. *An Account in Two Volumes of Two Voyages to the South Seas* (Collingwood: Melbourne University Press,1987).

Editor. "Botany Bay". in *Edinburgh Review 32,* 1819, in Johnson, Judith and Anderson, Monica. *Australia Imagined: Views from the British Periodical Press 1800 to 1900* (Crawley: University of Western Australia Press, 2005).

Extract of a Letter from Mr Thompson from King's Island. *HRNSW 18*, January, 1803. Extracts of the Minutes of the Executive Council, 14 March, 1831.

Fanning, Edmund. *Voyages around the World* (London: O. Rich,1834).

Flinders, Matthew. *A Voyage to Terra Australis* (London: G & W Nicol, 1814), Vols.1 and 2. http://gutenberg.net.au/ebooks/e00049.html#chapter1-7

Government and General Order, 19 August 1806. J. Harris Naval Officer recorded in *Historical Records of New South Wales,* Vol. 6.

Governor Hunter to Under Secretary King. *Historical Records of New South Wales,* 22 March 1802 Volume 4.

Governor King to Lord Hobart. 9 May, 1803.

Governor Philip Gidley King to Earl Camden. 15 March, 1806.

Governor Phillip to Secretary Stephens. *HRNSW*, Volume 1 Part 2. Sydney, 18 November, 1791

Grant, James. *Voyage of Discovery to N.S.W. in the Lady Nelson in 1800-2* (London: Printed by C. Roworth Bell Yard for T. Egerton Military Library Whitehall, 1803). http://gutenberg.net.au/ebooks13/1300421h.html#ch-09

Haklyut, Richard. *The Principal Navigations, Voyages, Traffiques and Discoveries of the English Nation* (Harmondsworth Middlesex: Penguin Books, 1598-1600).

Harris J. Naval Officer. *Historical Records of New South Wales,* Vol. 6, 19 August 1806.

Harris, John to Le Corre. in *Sydney Gazette,* 27 November, 1803.

Captain John Hart, in T. F. Bride, *Letters from Victorian Pioneers being a series of*

papers on the early occupation of the colony, the Aborigines etc (Melbourne: Heinemann, 1969).
Heeres, J. E. (ed.), *Abel Janszoon Tasman's Journal* (Amsterdam: Frederick Muller & Co, 1898). http://gutenberg.net.au/ebooks06/0600571h.html
Historical Records of Australia. Resumed Series III, Volume IX, Tasmania, January to December 1830. Various Entries.
— Series 3, Volume 3, 461.
— Series 5, Volume 1, 315.
Historical Records of New South Wales, King and Bligh, 4 June, 1803.
— Vol. 5, 132.
— Vol. 5 (1803-1805), 1 March, 1804.
— Captain Wilson to Sir Joseph Banks Monument Yard, 27 June, 1806.
— Vol. 4, 439 and 729, 785.
— June, 1806.
— Captain Wilson to Sir Joseph Banks, Monument Yard, 27 June, 1806.
— The Board of Trade to the East India Company, 30 June 1806.
Hook, Charles. Letter to Gordon, 2 June, 1811.
Hunter, Governor John. Letter to Under Secretary King, 28 July, 1799, in *Historical Records of Australia*, Series 1, Vol. 2, 1797-1800.
Jorgensen, Jorge. *Observations on Pacific Trade and Sealing and Whaling in Australian Waters before 1805* (Wellington: Paremata Press, 1969).
—. *A Shred of Autobiography, Containing Various Anecdotes, Personal and Historical, Connected with these Colonies* (Adelaide: Sullivan's Cove, 1981).
Kelly, James, and Hobbs, James. *Van Diemen's Land in 1815 and 1824* (Hobart: Sullivan's Cove,1984).
King, Governor Phillip Gidley, Letter to Lord Henry Bathurst. 1 March, 1804.
— Letter to Colonel Willam Paterson, in *Historical Records of Australia*. 1.5.23, 1 June 1804.
— Report to Lord Henry Hobart, 14 August 1804.
— Letter to Under-Secretary Edward Cooke, 1 November 1805, in *Historical Records of New South Wales*, Vol. 5, 717.
— General Order, 30 March 1805.
King, Phillip Parker. *Narrative of a Survey of the Intertropical and Western Coasts of Australia performed between the years 1818 and 1822 in Two Volumes*. Vol. 2 (London: John Murray, 1827). https://books.google.com.au/books?id=RjdCAAAAIAAJ&dq=phillip%20parker%20king%20a%20survey%20google%20books%20volume%202&source=gbs_book_other_versions
Lang, John Dunmore. *Reminiscences of My Life and Times, auto biographical cuttings 1878* (Melbourne: Heinemann, 1972).
Leigh, W. H. *Travels & Adventures in South Australia, 1836-1838* (Sydney: Currawong Press,1982).
Lockyer, Major E. Journal in *Historical Records of Australia*. Series III, Vol. 6 https://purl.slwa.wa.gov.au/slwa_b1247610_49 slwa_b1247610_4
Melville, Henry. *Henry Melville's History of Van Diemen's Land* (Sydney: The Grahame Book Company Pty Ltd,1835).
Minutes of the Executive Council. 14 March, 1831.
— Military Operations against the Aborigines of Tasmania, in *Report from the Select Committee on Aborigines* (Shannon: Irish University Press, 20 February,1837).
Mortimer, George. *Observations and Remarks Made During a Voyage* (London: T.

Cadell, 1791).
New South Wales Trade, in *Historical Records of New South Wales*. Vol. 6, 27 June, 1806.
Nind, Scott. *Description of the Natives of King Georges Sound (Swan River Colony) and Adjoining Country*, in Green, Neville (ed.) **Nyungar – the People** (Perth: Creative Research, 1979).
Nunn, John. *Narrative of the wreck of the 'Favorite' on the island of Desolation detailing the adventures, sufferings, and privations of John Nunn; an historical account of the island, and its whale and seal fisheries* W. B. Clarke, M. D. (ed.) (London: W. E. Painter,1850). https://babel.hathitrust.org/cgi/pt?id=hvd.hwg1z3&view=1up&seq=9
Peron, M. F. *A Voyage of Discovery to the southern hemisphere performed by the order of Emperor Napoleon during the years 1801, 1802, 1803 and 1804*. Translated by Richard Phillips (London: Richard Phillips, 1809).
Plomley N. J. (Brian). *Friendly Mission* (Kingsgrove: Halstead Press Pty Ltd, 1966).
Report from the Select Committee, in British Parliamentary Papers. February, 1837.
Robinson, G. A. Letter to Lieutenant Governor George Arthur. Flinders Island, January, 1836.
Rogers, Captain Woodes. *Cruising Voyage around the World Begun August 1708 and finished October 14* (London: Cassell & Company, 1712), 171. https://books.google.com.au/books/about/A_Cruising_Voyage_Round_the_World.html?id=e1Gmdlw7fpgC
Smith, Sydney. Botany Bay, in *Edinburgh Review,* Vol. 32, 1819. 28-48, in Johnston, Judith and Anderson, Monica, *Australia Imagined: Views from the British Periodical Press 1800-1900* (Crawley, West Australia: University of Western Australia Press, 2005).
South Australian Register, 25 September, 1844.
Stewart, William. Letter to the Colonial Secretary, Sydney, 28 September, 1815, in *Historical Records of Australia,* Series I, Vol. 8.
Stokes, J. Lort. *Discoveries in Australia with An Account of The Coasts and Rivers Explored And Surveyed During The Voyage of H.M.S. Beagle, In The Years 1837-38-39-40-41-42-43. By Command Of The Lords Commissioners of The Admiralty* (London: T. and W. Boone, 1846).
Surgeon's Letter, in *Historical Records of New South Wales*, Vol. 5, 8 October, 1803.
— Vol. 6, 5 October, 1807.
Sutherland, Captain George. Appendix in Wakefield, Edwin Gibbon, *Plan of a Company to be established for the Purpose of founding a Colony of Southern Australia* (London: Ridgway and Sons, 1832).
Third Annual Report of the Aboriginal Protection Society (London: P. White and Son, 1840).
Thompson. Extract of a Letter from King's Island, in *Historical Records of New South Wales,* 18 January, 1803.
Thomson, John to Captain Shanck. Sydney, New South Wales, 8 September 1791, in *Historical Records of New South Wales*, Vol. 1.
Trade and Commerce, in *Historical Records of New South Wales*. Series X, Vol. 6, 4 June, 1803.
Twamley, Louise Anne (Mrs Charles Meredith). *Notes and Sketches of New South Wales During a residence in that colony from 1839 to 1844* (Sydney: Ure Smith, 1973).

Lieutenant Governor Arthur, George. *Letters to His Majesty's Secretary of State for the Colonies, on the subject of the Military Operations lately carried on against the Aboriginal Inhabitants of Van Diemen's Land* (London: Howick Press, 1831).

Vancouver, George. *Voyage of Discovery to the North Pacific Ocean and Round the World* (Piccadilly, London: John Stockdale, 1801). https://babel.hathitrust.org/cgi/pt?id=uc1.31175035620395&view=1up&seq=7

Wakefield, Edward Gibbon. *Plan of a Company to be established for the purpose of founding a colony in Southern Australia, purchasing land therein, and preparing the land so purchased for the Reception of Immigrants* (London: Piccadilly, Ridgway and Sons,1832).

Walker, George. *Journal*, 3 November, 1832, B 709.

Wilkes, Charles. *Narrative of the United States Exploring Expedition, 1838-42,* Vol. 2 (London: Wiley and Putnam, 1845). https://library.si.edu/digital-library/book/narrativeunited00wilk

Newspapers

Colonial Times, **Hobart**. Tuesday 21 January 1840.
—10 February 1826.
Hobart Town Courier and Van Diemen's Land Gazette. 6 March, 1840.
Launceston Advertiser, 24 July, 1834.
Nelson Examiner, 20 July, 1844 (G. Munro)
New York Evening Post, 18 April, 1826.
The Australian, 28 October, 1824.
— 9 March 1826 https://trove.nla.gov.au/newspaper/article/37072584?searchTerm=the%20australian%209%20March%201826
— 9 December, 1826.
— 20 March, 1827. https://trove.nla.gov.au/newspaper/article/37074870
— 4 June, 1828.
The Hobart Town Gazette, 28 March, 1818.
— 14 November, 1818.
— 25 March, 1826.
—10 June, 1826 p. 2 https://trove.nla.gov.au/newspaper/article/8791205
— 1 July, 1826, p. 4, 'King Island' **4**
— 26 August, 1826.
— 21 October, 1826.
The Inquirer. 25 August, 1841 and 15 September, 1841.
The Perth Gazette and Western Australian Journal. 3 October, 1835. p. 574.
   https://trove.nla.gov.au/newspaper/article/8791205
—13 August, 1836. http://trove.nla.gov.au/newspaper/article/640335
— 8 October, 1842, p.3. https://trove.nla.gov.au/newspaper/article/640335#
— 17 October, 1840.
The Sydney Gazette and New South Wales Advertiser. 15 May, 1803.
— 28 August, 1803.
— 3 December, 1803.
— 4 December, 1803.
— December, 1804, p. 4. https://trove.nla.gov.au/newspaper/article/640335#
— 1 January, 1804.

— 15 April, 1804.
— 22 July, 1804.
— 11 November, 1804.
— 27 January, 1805.
— 31 August, 1805.
— 5 September, 1805, Blaxcell, G. Acting Secretary.
— 3 November, 1805.
— 4 May, 1806, "Ship News", 4.
— 9 March, 1806.
— "Ship News", 4 May, 1806.
— 3 July, 1808.
— 6 January, 1809.
— 19 March, 1809.
— 16 April, 1809, "Ship News"
— 7 April, 1810, "Ship News"
—18 August, 1810.
— (after 5), January, 1811.
— 15 April, 1815.
— 2 March, 1816.
— 1 June, 1816.
— 19 June, 1819.
— 17 June, 1820.
— 17 March, 1821.
— 12 December, 1822.
— 1 July, 1824.
— 26 July ,1826. http://trove.nla.gov.au//ndp/del/printAriclejpg/2183009/3_1
— 26 July, 1826.
Death Notice for Samuel Chase. https://oa.anu.edu.au/obituary/chace-samuel-rodman-24931

Court Cases

Brady v Campbell [1811]. NSW SupC 5; [1811] NSWKR 5 (17 April ,1811).
Bryant v Hook [1812]. NSWSupC 2; [1812] NSWKR 2 (31 January, 1812).
Cullen v Owen Folger Smith. 2 July, 1811, Court of Civil Jurisdiction.
O'Burne v Campbell [1812]. NSWSupC 3; [1812] NSWKR 3 (4 February, 1812).
Tolman v Kelly. [1839] TAS Superior Cases 40 (8 November, 1839).
Wood v Campbell. [1812] NSWSupC 1; [1812] NSWKR 1 (20 January, 1812).

Legislation

The Abolition of the Slave Trade Act 1807 (UK) 47 George III Sess. 1 c 36.
The Slavery Abolition Act of 1833 (UK) 3 and 4 William IV.C.73.
Act 3 Vic No. XVI An Act to allow Aboriginal Natives of New South Wales to be received as competent witnesses in Criminal Cases, 8 October 1839.
http://www.edu.au/au/legis/nsw/num_act/
Act 3 Vic No. XI An Act to facilitate the Apprehension of Offenders escaping from the island of Van Diemen's Land from South Australia to the Colony of New

South Wales. 29 August, 1838
http://www.austlii.edu.au/au/legis/nsw/num_act/ viewed 24 June 2020
British Act of Parliament 42 **Geo** III, **C** 77.
Victoria 1 Act XI, 29 August, 1838.

Secondary Sources

Amery, Rob. "Kaurna in Tasmania: A case of mistaken identity", in *Aboriginal History 1996*, Vol. 20.

Anderson, Kay and Perrin, Colin. "The miserablest people in the world. Race Humanism and the Australian Aborigine", in *The Australian Journal of Anthropology 18*, No.1. 18-39.

Anderson, Ross. *Beneath the Colonial Gaze*, Thesis, University of Western Australia, 2016.

Attwood, Bain and Almond, John (eds.). *Power Knowledge and Aborigines* (Bundoora: La Trobe University Press, 1992).

Bach, John. *A Maritime History of Australia* (Sydney: Pan Books, 1976).

Bashford, Alison and Macintyre, Stuart (eds.). *The Cambridge History of Australia*, Vol. 1 (Cambridge: Cambridge University Press, 2013).

Bass Strait People to 1850 https://bassstraitto1850.wordpress.com/biographies-of-people-living-in-or-visiting-bass-strait-to-1850/

Battye, James Sykes. *Western Australia: A History from its discovery to the inauguration of the Commonwealth* (Oxford: Clarendon Press,1924).

Becke, Louis. "The Americans in the South Sea" (1901), in *The Tapu Of Banderah and Other Stories* http://gutenberg.net.au/ebooks/fr100233.txt

Berk Christopher D. *Palawa Kani and the Value of Language in Aboriginal Tasmania, in Online Wiley Library*, 10 January, 2017 https://onlinelibrary.wiley.com/doi/10.1002/ocea.5148

Berry, Oliver, *et al. Population Recovery of the New Zealand Fur Seal in Southern Australia: a molecular DNA analysis in Journal of Mammalogy,* Vol. 93, Issue 2, 30 April, 2012. https://academic.oup.com/jmammal/article/93/2/482/921676

Biscoe, John. "The Journal of John Biscoe", in George Murray (ed.) in *Antarctica Manual for the use of the expedition of 1901* (London: Royal Geographic Society, 1901).

Blacket, John. *The Early History of South Australia; A Romantic Experiment in Colonisation* (Adelaide: Vardon & Sons, 1907).

Bolster, W. Jeffrey. *Black Jacks: African American Seaman in the Age of Sail* (Cambridge: Harvard University Press, 1997).

Bolton, Geoffrey. *Spoils and Spoilers, Australians make their Environment 1788-1980* (St Leonards: Allen & Unwin,1981).

Bonner, Nigel. *The Natural History of Seals* (London: Christopher Helm,1989).

Bonwick, James. *The Lost Tasmanian Race* (London: Johnston Reprint Company Ltd, 1884).

— "The Writing of Colonial History" in *Home News*, 29 March 1895. reprinted (Wagga Wagga: *RMIHE* 1987).

— *The Last of the Tasmanians. On the Black War of Van Diemen's Land* (London: Sampson Low, Son and Matson, 1870).

Bowden, Keith Macrae. *Captain James Kelly of Hobart Town* (Collingwood: Melbourne University Press, 1964).

Boyce, James. *Van Diemen's Land* (Melbourne: Black Inc, 2008).

Brett, Andre. "Australia and the Secretive Exploitation of the Chatham Islands to 1842", in *Journal of Australian Studies* (Collingwood: Melbourne University Press, 1 January, 2017). https://ro.uow.edu.au/lhapapers/3555

Calder, James (ed.) *Van Diemen's Land in 1815* (Hobart: Sullivan's Cove, 1984).

Cameron, Patsy. "Palawa Women: Their historical contribution to our survival." and Matson-Green, Vicki. "Leaders Among the Palawa Women", in *Tasmanian Historical Research Association,* June, 1994, 41-42.

Cameron, Patsy, *Grease and Ochre; The Blending of two cultures at the Tasmanian Colonial Sea Frontier*, Thesis submitted to University of Tasmania, November, 2008.

Carey, Brycchan and Salih, Sarah. "Introduction", in Carey Brycchan, Ellis, Markman and Salih, Sarah, *Discourses on Slavery and Abolition: Britain and Its Colonies 1760-1838* (London: Palgrave MacMillan, 2004).

Castle, Tim. "Constructing Death. Newspaper Reports of executions in New South Wales 1826 to 1837", in *Journal of Australian Colonial History 9.* 2007.

Chapman, Valerie and Read, Peter (eds.). *Terrible Hard Biscuit: A Reader in Aboriginal History* (St Leonards: Allen & Unwin,1996).

Churchward, L. G. *Australia & America 1788-1972 An Alternative History* (Chippendale: Alternative Publishing Cooperative, 1979).

Clark, Manning. *History of Australia. The Beginning of an Australian Civilization 1824 to 1851,* Vol. 3 (Collingwood: Melbourne University Press, 1973).

Clarke, Phillip. "Early European Interaction with Aboriginal Hunter Gatherers on Kangaroo Island, South Australia", in *Aboriginal History 20* (1996).

Copeland, Gordon. "The Mysteries of Karta (alias Kangaroo Island) in Creation, Colonizers and Crusoes", in *Counterpoints*, July, 2002.

Coutts, P.J.F. "The Māori of Dusky Sound: a review of the historical sources", in *Journal of Polynesian Society*, Vol. 78, No. 2 (June, 1969).

Cumpston, John Stewart. *First Visitors to Bass Strait* (Canberra: Roebuck Society Publication, 1973).

— *Kangaroo Island 1800-1836* (Canberra: Roebuck Society Publication No.1 National Printers, 1970).

— *Macquarie Island* (Canberra: Department of External Affairs, 1968).

— *Australian Dictionary of Biography.* adb.anu.edu.au/biography/Dutton –william-2011.

— *Shipping Arrivals and Departures, Sydney 1788-1825* (Canberra: Roebuck Books, 1977).

Curthoys, Anne; "Indigenous Subjects" in Deryck and Ward, Stuart, *Australia's Empire Schreuder,* (Oxford: Oxford University Press, 2010) 48-102.

Debenham, Frank (ed.). *The Voyage of Captain Bellingshausen to the Antarctic Seas 1819 –1821* (London: The Haklyut Society, 2010).

Donaldson, Mike, Bursill, Luke and Jacobs, Mary. *A History of Aboriginal Illawarra, Vol. 2: Colonisation.* 2017. https://ro.uow.edu.au/cgi/viewcontent.cgi?article=4020&context=lhapapers

Dunderdale, George. *The Book of the Bush Containing Many Truthful Sketches of The Early Colonial Life Of Squatters, Whalers, Convicts, Diggers, And Others Who Left Their Native Land And Never Returned* (London: Law Lock and Co, 1898).

Duyker, Edward and Duyker, Maryse (eds). *Bruny D'Entrecasteaux Voyages to Australia and the Pacific 1791 to 1793* (Collingwood: Melbourne University Press, 2001).

Elliot, Henry Wood. *The Fur Seal Islands of Alaska.* (Washington: Creative Media

Partners, 2023) https://books.google.com/books/about/The_Seal_islands_of_Alaska.html?id=Iu8_AAAAYAAJ quoting Dampier

Evans, Raymond. "Creating an object of Real Terror. The Tabling of the First Bigge Report" in Crotty, Martin and Roberts, David (eds.) *Turning Points in Australian History* (Kensington: University of New South Wales Press, 2008).

Flannery, Tim (ed.) *John Nicole Mariner. Life and Adventures 1776-1801* (Melbourne: Text Publishing, 1979).

Florek, Dr Stan. *Tentative Chronology of Indigenous Canoes of Eastern Australia*, 26 June 2012. https://australian.museum/blog/science/tentative-chronology-of-indigenous-canoes-of-eastern-australia/

Gibbs, Martin. "Conflict and Commerce, American Whalers and the Western Australian Colonies 1826-1888", in *The Great Circle*, Vol. 22, No. 2 (2000), 3-22.

Gill, J.C.H. *Notes on the Sealing Industry of Early Australia* (St. Lucia: University of Queensland Press). Read to a meeting of the Society, 23 February 1967. https://espace.library.uq.edu.au/view/UQ:213028

Greenwood, Gordon. *Early American-Australian Relations from the arrival of the Spaniards in America to the close of 1830* (Collingwood: Melbourne University Press, 1944).

Griffiths, Tom (ed.) *The Life and Adventures of Edward Snell: Illustrated Diary of an Artist, Engineer and Adventurer in the Australian Colonies 1849-1859* (North Ryde: Angus and Robertson, 1988).

Haebich, Anna. *Broken Circles. Fragmenting Indigenous Families 1800-2000* (Fremantle, Fremantle Arts Centre Press, 2000).

Hainsworth, David Roger. *The Sydney Traders Simeon Lord and his Contemporaries* (North Melbourne: Cassell Australia Limited, 1971).

— *Builders and Adventurers* (North Melbourne: Cassell Australia Limited, 1968).

— "Iron men in wooden ships the Sydney sealers 1800-1825", in *Labour History* No. 13 (1967).

Hall-Jones, John, James Caddell. *Dictionary of New Zealand Biography [1990] Te Ara Encyclopaedia of New Zealand,* viewed at https://teara.govt.nz/en/biographies/1c1/caddell-james#:~:text=The%20story%20of%20James%20Caddell,in%20the%20sealer%20Sydney%20Cov

Hart, Captain John, in Bride, T. F. *Letters from Victorian Pioneers being a series of papers on the early occupation of the colony, the Aborigines etc* (Melbourne: Heinemann, 1969).

Hill, David. *The Great Race* (North Sydney: William Heinemann, 2012).

James, Thomas Horton. *Six months in South Australia* (Holborn near London: Joseph Cross, 1838).

Ihde, Erin; "Pirates of the Pacific: The Convict Seizure of the Wellington", in *Great Circle* 30, No.1.

Ingleton, Geoffrey C. *Matthew Flinders Navigator and Chartmaker* (Guilford : Genesis Publications Limited, 1986).

Jebb, Mary Anne and Haebich, Anne. "Across the Great Divide. Gender Relations on Australian Frontiers", in Saunders, Kay and Evan, Raymond (eds.) *Gender Relations in Australia. Domination and Negotiation* (Sydney: Harcourt Brace Jovanovich, 1992), 20-41.

Jetson, Tim. "Island of Contentment? Preservation Island", in Tasmanian Historical Research Association, *Annual Report*, 1995, 29-45.

Johnson, Anna. "The Little Empire of Wybalenna: Becoming Colonial Australia" in *Journal of Australian Studies* 20:81, 17-31. https://www.researchgate.net/publication/233121232_The_little_empire_of_Wybalenna_Becoming_colo-

nial in Australia
Johnson, Anna and Rolls, Mitchell (eds). *Reading Robinson Companion Essays to Friendly Mission* (Hobart: Quintus Press, 2008).
Johnson, Les. *Major Edmund Lockyer Forgotten Australian Pioneer* (Perth: Western Australian Museum, 2002).
Karskens, Grace. *The Colony. A History of Early Sydney* (Crows' Nest: Allen and Unwin, 2009).
Kirkwood, Roger and Goldsworthy, Simon. *Fur Seals and Sea Lions* (Clayton: CSIRO Publishing, 2013).
Kriwoken, Lorne K. and Williamson, John W. *Antarctica and Southern Ocean Connections* (Hobart, Tasmania: Polar Record 29, 1993). file:///C:/Users/David/Downloads/Hobart_Tasmania_Antarctic.pdf
Macquarie Dictionary. Revised Third Edition, 1977.
Mawer, Grenville Allen. *Ahab's Trade* (St Leonards: Allen and Unwin, 1999).
Maykutenner (aka Matson-Green, Vicki). "Tasmania 2", in *Contested Ground: Australian Aborigines under the British Crown* (St Leonards: Allen & Unwin,1995).
Maykutenner (aka Matson-Green, Vicki) and Harper, Tanya. "Palawa Women: Carrying the Burdens and finding the solutions", in *Labour History,* No. 69 (Liverpool, United Kingdom: Liverpool University Press, November 1995.
McKenna, Mark. *From the Edge. Australia's Lost Histories* (Collingwood: Melbourne University Press, 2016).
McMahon, Anne. "Tasmanian Women as Slaves", in *Tasmanian Historical Research Association* 23, June, 1976, 44-49.
McNab, Robert. *Old Whaling Days* (Wellington: Whitcombe and Tombs Ltd, 1913).
McNab, Robert. *Murihiku: a History of the South Island of New Zealand and the islands adjacent and lying to the south, from 1642 to 1835* (Wellington: Whitcombe and Tombs Ltd, 1909). http://nzetc.victoria.ac.nz/tm/scholarly/tei-McNMuri-t1-body-d1-d14.html
McNeill, J. R. (ed.). "Environmental History in the Pacific World", in *The Pacific World* Vol. 2 (Farnham: Ashgate Publishing Limited, 2001).
Merry, Kay; "The Cross-Cultural Relationships between sealers and the Tasmanian women in Bass Strait and Kangaroo Island in the early Nineteenth Century", 80-88, in *Counterpoints* 3, No.1 (2003).
Mollison, Bill and Everitt, Coral. *The Tasmanian Aborigines and their Descendants,* December 1978. http://www.cifhs.com/sarecords/Mollison%20and%20Everitt.html
Moneypenny, Maria. "Going out and coming in: Cooperation and Collaboration between Aborigines and Europeans in Early Tasmania", in *Tasmanian Historical Studies* 5, No.1, 1995-6, 64-71.
Moorhead, Alan. *The Fatal Impact* (Harmondsworth Middlesex: Penguin Books, 1966).
Murray, Keith. O. *First There came Ships* (Perth: Lamb Print, 2004).
Murray-Smith, Stephen. "Beyond the Pale. The Islander Community of Bass Strait in the Nineteenth Century", in *Tasmanian Historical Research Association* 20, No. 4, 1973, 167-197.
O'May, Harry. *Hobart River Craft and the sealers of Bass Strait* (Tasmania: Government Printer, 1973).
Parry, J. H. *Trade and Dominion. The European Overseas Empires in the Eighteenth Century* (London: Weidenfeld and Nicholson, 1971).
Pearson, Michael. "The Technology of Whaling in Australian Waters in the 19th Century" (Sandy Bay: Blubber Head Press, 1987) https://www/jstor.org.

stable/29543108

Plomley, N. J. Brian and Henley, Kirsten Anne. *The Sealers of Bass Strait and the Cape Barren Island Community* (Sandy Bay: Blubber Head Press, 1990).

Pretyman, E. R. "Some notes on the life and times of Captain James Kelly", in *Papers and Proceedings of the Royal Society of Tasmania* Vol.105,105-112. (Read to Members of the Royal Society 7.7.1970) https://eprints.utas.edu.au/13417/4/1971_Pretyman_Life_and_times_Captain_James_Kelly.pdf

Prickett, Nigel. "Trans-Tasman stories: Australian Aborigines in New Zealand sealing and shore whaling", in *Terra Australis* 29. (Auckland War Museum, Auckland: ANU Press, June 2008) http://press-files.anu.edu.au/downloads/press/p26551/pdf/ch22.pdf

Provost, J. Selkirk. "Joseph Murrell – Sealer" in *Descent Magazine*, 81.

Purdy, John. *Oriental Navigator* (London: Whittle and Laurie, 1816).

Pybus, Cassandra. *Black Founders: the Unknown Story of Australia's First Black Settlers* (Kensington: University of New South Wales Press Limited, 2006).

Pybus, Cassandra. Statement to the Legislative Council Select Committee on Aboriginal Lands, 10 April, 2000.

— *Truganini Journey through the Apocalypse* (St Leonards: Allen & Unwin, 2020).

Quartly, Marian, Janson, Susan and Grimshaw, Patricia. Documents on women in colonial Australia, in *Freedom Bound* 1 (St Leonards: Allen & Unwin, 1995).

Rae-Ellis, Vivienne. *Black Robinson Protector of Aborigines* (Collingwood: Melbourne University Press, 1988).

Rediker, Marcus. *Villains of All Nations Atlantic Pirates in the Golden Age* (London: Verso Press, 2004).

Reynolds, Henry. *The Other Side of the Frontier* (Kensington: University of New South Wales Press, 2006).

Richards, Rhys. *Sealing in the Southern Oceans 1788-1833* (Wellington: Paremata Press, 2010).

Ritchie, John. *Punishment and Profit, the Reports of Commissioner John Bigge on the Colonies of New South Wales and Van Diemen's Land 1822-1823 Their origins, nature and significance* (Melbourne: Heinemann, 1970).

Roberts, Mick. "Three Times Buried", in *Time Gents, Australian Pub Project*, 14 July, 2016, https://timegents.com/2016/07/14/three-times-buried

Robertson, Geoffrey. *Crimes against Humanity. The Struggle for Global Justice* (London: The Penguin Press, 1999).

Robson, Lloyd. *A History of Tasmania, Vol. 1, Van Diemen's Land from early times to 1855* (Melbourne: Oxford University Press, 1983).

Roe, Michael (ed.). *The Journal and Letters of Captain Charles Bishop on the Northwest Coast of America, in the Pacific and in New South Wales 1794-1799* (London: Cambridge University Press, 1967).

Roser, Max et al. Life Expectancy Tables *Our World in Data* published 2013 and revised October 2019 https://ourworldindata.org/life-expectancy

Russell, Lynette. "A New Holland Half Caste. Sealer and Whaler Tommy Chaseland", in *History Australia* Vol. 5, No. 1 (Melbourne: Monash University Press, 2008).

Russel, Lynette. "Dirty Domestics and Worse Cooks: Aboriginal women's Agency and Domestic Frontiers, Southern Australia 1800-1850" in *Frontiers: A Journal of Women's Studies,* Vol. 28, No.12.

Ryan, Lyndall. "The Struggle for Recognition: Part Aborigines in Bass Strait in the Nineteenth Century," in *Aboriginal History* 1, No.1, 1977, 27-52.

— *The Aboriginal Tasmanians* (St. Lucia: University of Queensland Press, 1981).

— *Tasmanian Aborigines A history since 1803* (St Leonards: Allen & Unwin, 2012).
Saunders, Kay and Evans, Raymond (eds.). *Race Relations in Australia Domination and Negotiation* (Marrickville: Harcourt Brace Jovanovich Group Australia Pty Ltd,1992).
Shortland, Edward. *The Southern Districts of New Zealand; A Journal with passing references to the Customs of the Aborigines* (London: Longman Brown and Green,1851).
Skira, Irynej. "I hope you will be my friend: Tasmanian Aborigines in the Furneaux Group in the nineteenth century – population and land tenure", in *Aboriginal History*, Vol. 21, 1997.
Smith, Coultman. *Tales of Old Tasmania* (Adelaide: Rigby Limited, 1978).
Smith, Ian, "Māori, Pakeha and Kiwi: Peoples, cultures and sequence in New Zealand archaeology", in G. Clark, F. Leach and S. O'Connor (eds.) *Islands of Inquiry: Colonisation, Seafaring and the Archaeology of Maritime Landscapes. Terra Australis* 29, (Canberra: ANU E Press, 1 June, 2008) http://press-files.anu.edu.au/downloads/press/p26551/pdf/ch23.pdf
Smith, Ian W. G. *The New Zealand sealing industry History archaeology and heritage* (Wellington: Department of Conservation, 2002).
Smith, Patsy Adam. *There was a Ship* (Melbourne: Penguin Books, 1995).
Stewart, Estelle May and Bowman, Jesse Chester. "History of Wages in the United States from Colonial Times to 1928", in *Bulletin of the United States Bureau of Labor Statistics* No. 499, October 1929 https://fraser.stlouisfed.org/files/docs/publications/bls/bls_0604_1934.pdf
Stora, Jan and Lougas, Lembi. "Human Exploitation and history of seals in the Baltic during the late Holocene", in Monks, Gregory (ed.) *The Exploitation and Cultural Importance of Sea Mammals* (Oxford: Oxbrow Books, 2005).
Stuart, Iain. "Sealing and Whaling Seascapes", in Lawrence, Susan and Staniforth, Mark (eds.). *The Archaeology of Whaling in Southern Australia and New Zealand* (Gundaroo: Brolga Press, 1998).
—. "Sea Rats, bandits and roistering buccaneers: What were the Bass Strait Sealers really like?", in *Journal of the Royal Australian Historical Society* Vol. 53, Part 1.
Sutton, Regina. *Mari Nawi Aboriginal Odysseys 1790 to 1850* (Sydney: State Library of New South Wales, 2010).
Taylor, Rebe. *Unearthed; The Aboriginal Tasmanians of Kangaroo Island* (Kent Town: Wakefield Press, 2002).
"The Palawa Voice", in *Companion to Tasmanian History* https://www.utas.edu.au/library/companion_to_tasmanian_history/P/Palawa%20Voice.htm
Trevarthan, Cora. *Trans-Tasman World. The Social and Cultural influence of the sealing industry in Australia, 1792 to 1842.* (Melbourne: Department of History, Melbourne University, October 2006).
Wace, Nigel and Lovett, Bessie. "Yankee Maritime Activities and the Early History of Australia", in *Research School of Pacific Studies* No. A/2 (Canberra: ANU,1973).
Walter, Maggie and Daniels, Louise. "Personalising the History Wars: Woretemoeteryenner's Story", in *International Journal of Critical Indigenous Studies* Vol.1, No.1, 2008.
Wanhalla, Angela. *Matters of the Heart: A History of Interracial Marriage in New Zealand* (Auckland: Auckland University Press, 2013). https://www.google.com.au/books/edition/Matters_of_the_Heart/TOdaAwAAQBAJ?hl=en&gbpv=1&pg=PT3&printsec=frontcover

Wentworth, William Charles. **William Cox**, *Journal July 1814-January 1815* (Sydney: State Library of New South Wales).
West, Ida. *Pride against Prejudice; Reminiscences of a Tasmanian Aborigine* (Canberra: Australian Institute of Aboriginal Studies, 1984).
West, John. *History of Tasmania* (Launceston: Henry Dowling, 1852).
Western Tasmania Aboriginal Cultural Landscape, Arthur River Rd, Arthur River, TAS, Australia Australian Government Department of Climate Change and Energy Australian Heritage Database, 13 February, 2013.

Fiction

Forrestal, Elain. *Black-Jack Anderson* (Melbourne: Penguin Books, 2008).
Hay, Sarah. *Skins* (St Leonards: Allen & Unwin, 2008).

www.ingramcontent.com/pod-product-compliance
Lightning Source LLC
Chambersburg PA
CBHW070855170426
43202CB00012B/2083